Pacific Northwest

Seattle, Portland, Victoria, Vancouver, and Other Area Destinations

ECONOGUIDE.COM | 2001–02

WITHDRAWN

Corey Sandler

CONTEMPORARY BOOKS

To wandering brother Neil

Contemporary Books

A Division of The **McGraw-Hill** Companies

Copyright © 2001 by Word Association, Inc. All rights reserved. Printed in the United States of America. Except as permitted under the United States Copyright Act of 1976, no part of this publication may be reproduced or distributed in any form or by any means, or stored in a database or retrieval system, without the prior written permission of the publisher.

1 2 3 4 5 6 7 8 9 0   LBM/LBM   0 9 8 7 6 5 4 3 2 1

International Standard Book Number: 0-8092-2632-4
International Standard Serial Number: 1532-6713

This book was set in Stone Serif by Word Association, Inc.
Printed and bound by Lake Book Manufacturing

Cover photograph copyright © Stuart McCall/Stone

Econoguide is a registered trademark of Word Association, Inc.

McGraw-Hill books are available at special quantity discounts to use as premiums and sales promotions, or for use in corporate training programs. For more information, please write to the Director of Special Sales, Professional Publishing, McGraw-Hill, Two Penn Plaza, New York, NY 10121-2298. Or contact your local bookstore.

This book is printed on acid-free paper.

Contents

Acknowledgments

As always, dozens of hard-working and creative people helped move my words from the keyboard to the book you hold in your hands.

Among the many to thank are editor Adam Miller of NTC/Contemporary Books. Also at Contemporary, Julia Anderson managed the production processes with professional courtesy and good nature.

I want to thank Val Forman, here at Word Association, for editing the manuscript with high skill and good humor.

As always, thanks to Janice Keefe for running the office and the author so well.

And, thanks to you for buying this book. We all hope you find it of value; please let us know how we can improve the book in future editions. (Enclose a stamped envelope if you'd like a reply; no phone calls, please.)

Corey Sandler
Econoguide Travel Books
P.O. Box 2779
Nantucket, MA 02584 USA

To send electronic mail, use the following address:
info@econoguide.com.

You can also consult our Web page at:
www.econoguide.com.

I hope you'll consider the other books in the *Econoguide* series, also by Corey Sandler. You can find them at bookstores, or ask your bookseller to order them.

Econoguide Canada
Econoguide Walt Disney World, Universal Orlando
Econoguide Disneyland Resort, Universal Studios Hollywood
Econoguide Las Vegas
Econoguide Washington, D.C., Williamsburg

Econoguide London
Econoguide Paris
Econoguide Cruises
Econoguide Miami (Spring of 2001)

And there's also:
 Golf U.S.A.

About the Author

Corey Sandler is a former newsman and editor for the Associated Press, Gannett Newspapers, Ziff-Davis Publishing, and IDG. He has written more than 150 books on travel, video games, and computers; his titles have been translated into French, Spanish, German, Italian, Portuguese, Bulgarian, Polish, Hebrew, and Chinese. Other recent bestsellers include *Fix Your Own PC, Sixth Edition* from IDG Books and *Secrets of the Savvy Consumer* and *Buy More Pay Less* from Prentice Hall Press.

When he's not traveling, he hides out with his wife and two children on Nantucket island, thirty miles off the coast of Massachusetts.

Part I
Introduction to the Pacific Northwest

Chapter 1
A Different Place

Oregon and Washington are famous in some circles for an unofficial local motto: "Thanks for coming. Now go away."

It's not meant to be unfriendly, for you'll find some of the most accommodating and happy people in the Pacific Northwest. It's just that the residents are pretty well satisfied with what they've got—a corner of the United States with some of the most spectacular scenery, lush forests and farms, and wonderful extremes of volcanoes, glaciers, desert plains, and roaring river rapids. The Pacific Northwest is very different from the rest of the country, thank you very much.

That doesn't mean you can't come and visit for a while and marvel at the wonders of western Oregon and Washington. In the pages that follow, you'll find more than enough reasons to make the trip.

In the 2001–02 edition of *Econoguide Pacific Northwest*, our traveler's portrait also crosses the border to include Canada's British Columbia and a bit of Alberta, places so vast and diverse they could qualify as a wondrous, thriving country of their own.

About This Book

How do you cover a place such as the Pacific Northwest within the covers of a book of a mere 300 or so pages?

For that matter, how could you give Oregon, Washington, and British Columbia justice in a book of 600 pages, or 1,200 pages?

First, we're economical with what we include. *Econoguide Pacific Northwest* does not attempt to describe everything in Oregon, Washington, and British Columbia. Instead, we concentrate on just the best; this book offers an eclectic selection of the best and most interesting.

If you're looking for an encyclopedia, bring a truck to the bookstore and pick up one of the heavyweights that promise to tell you about every roadside attraction, every little museum, and every town, no matter how insignificant. Then leave the encyclopedia at home and travel with us.

At the heart of the idea behind *Econoguide* travel books is this goal: to show how to get the most out of your time and money in travel.

We've gone back and updated every detail of the book for the 2001–02 edition, adding wondrous new places to see almost everywhere we visited.

Note to Readers

In the opening chapters of the book, you'll learn some valuable tips on how to get the best prices on airline tickets, car rentals, and hotel rooms.

Look to your left, look to your right. One of you three people on vacation is paying the regular price for airfare, hotels, meals, and shopping. One is paying a premium price for a less-than-first-rate package. And one is paying a deeply discounted special rate for the best of everything.

Which one would you rather be?

At the back of the book, we're happy to present a special section of discount coupons for *Econoguide* readers.

All of the offers represent real savings. Be sure to read the coupons carefully, though, because of exclusions during holiday periods and other fine print. The author and publisher of this book do not endorse any of the businesses whose coupons appear here, and the presence of a coupon in this section does not in any way affect the author's opinions expressed in this book. But we do love a bargain when we find one.

We've made every attempt to include up-to-the-minute information in this book, but things always change. Be sure to call ahead to confirm operating hours and prices at attractions, and be especially careful to check during holiday periods.

And, here's a minor but important note to Internet users. Throughout this book you'll find references to web pages. We've taken care to present them in a form that makes them easy to enter on your computer; note that when an address completes a sentence you'll find a typeset period at the end. For example, the web address for *Econoguide* travel books is www.econoguide.com.

Every web address in this book (and most every one in use on the Internet) ends with a domain type (.com, .org, .edu, and such) with a page address (.htm, .html, .idx, and the like), with a country code (.ca, .uk, .fr, and so on), or with a locator symbol such as /.

In any case, when you enter an Internet address you find in this book, do not include a trailing period.

Chapter 2
Being There: *Econoguide* Travel Tips

I love to travel but I hate to waste time and money. It all but kills me to know that I spent $200 more than I should have for an airline ticket, or that the next guy over has a nicer hotel room at a better price. Put another way, my goal is take more vacations or spend more time in wondrous places than most people, and have a better time while I'm at it.

Let's get something straight here, though: this is not a guide for the cheapskate, a $10-a-night tour of dreadful dives and uninspiring but free sights.

I'm perfectly willing to spend money for value received. And here, in *Econoguide Pacific Northwest*, our joint goal will be to find the very best for our time and money.

Air Travel

The way I figure it, one major airline is pretty much like another. Sure, one company may offer a larger bag of peanuts while the other promises its flight attendants have more accommodating smiles. Me, I'm much more interested in other things:

1. safety,
2. the most convenient schedule, and
3. the lowest price.

Sometimes I'm willing to trade price for convenience; I'll never risk my neck for a few dollars.

But that doesn't mean I don't try my hardest to get the very best price on airline tickets. I watch the newspapers for seasonal sales and price wars, clip coupons from the usual and not-so-usual sources, consult the burgeoning world of Internet travel agencies, and happily play one airline against the other.

Alice in Airlineland

There are three golden rules to saving hundreds of dollars on travel: be flexible, be flexible, and be flexible.

• Be flexible about when you choose to travel. Travel, if you can, during the off-season or low-season when airfares, hotel rooms, and attractions offer substantial discounts.

3

• Be flexible about the day of the week you travel. You can often save hundreds of dollars by changing your departure date one or two days. Ask your travel agent or airline reservationist for current fare rules and restrictions.

The lightest air travel days are generally midweek, Saturday afternoons, and Sunday mornings. The busiest days are Sunday evenings, Monday mornings, and Friday.

In general, you will receive the lowest possible fare if you include a Saturday in your trip, buying what is known as an excursion fare. Airlines use this as a way to exclude business travelers from the cheapest fares, assuming they will want to be home by Friday night.

• Be flexible on the hour of your departure. There is generally lower demand—and therefore lower prices—for flights that leave in the middle of the day or very late at night.

• Be flexible on the route you will take, or your willingness to put up with a change of plane or stopover. Once again, you are putting the law of supply and demand in your favor. A direct flight from Boston to Seattle for a family of four may cost hundreds of dollars more than a flight from Boston that includes a change of planes in Chicago (a United Airlines hub) or Minneapolis (a Northwest hub).

• Don't overlook the possibility of flying out of a different airport, either. For example, metropolitan New Yorkers can find domestic flights from La Guardia, Newark, or White Plains. Suburbanites of Boston might want to consider flights from Worcester or Providence as possibly cheaper alternatives to Logan Airport. In the Los Angeles area, there are planes going in and out of LAX, Orange County, Burbank, and Palm Springs to name a few airports. Look for airports where there is competition, rather than places where one airline all but owns the terminal.

Look for airports that are served by low-cost carriers. For example, I was quoted fares from $398 to $535 to fly from Boston to Seattle on several major airlines. I then checked flights from nearby Providence, which is served by several discount carriers including Southwest Airlines. There I found fares as low as $208 on some of the same airlines, forced to match Southwest. For a family of four, that's $800 to $1,300 in savings, enough to pay for a chauffeured limousine to the airport and a down payment on a new car of your own.

• Plan way ahead of time and purchase the most deeply discounted advance tickets, which are usually noncancelable. Most carriers limit the number of discount tickets on any particular flight; although there may be plenty of seats left on the day you want to travel, they may be offered at higher rates.

In a significant change in recent years, most airlines have modified "nonrefundable" fares to become "noncancelable." What this means is that if you are forced to cancel or change your trip, your tickets retain their value and can be applied against another trip, usually for a fee of about $75 per ticket.

• Conversely, you can take a big chance and wait for the last possible moment, keeping in contact with charter tour operators and accepting a bargain price on a "leftover" seat and hotel reservation. You may also find that some airlines will reduce the prices on leftover seats within a few weeks of departure date; don't be afraid to check regularly with the airline, or ask your travel agent to do it for you. In fact, some travel agencies have automated computer programs that keep a constant electronic eagle eye on available seats and fares.

• Take advantage of special discount programs such as senior citizens' clubs, military discounts, or offerings from organizations to which you may belong. If you are in the over-60 category, you may not even have to belong to a group such as AARP; simply ask the airline reservationist if there is a discount available. You may have to prove your age when you pick up your ticket.

• The day of the week on which you buy your tickets may also make a price difference. Airlines often test out higher fares over the relatively quiet weekends. They're looking to see if their competitors will match their higher rates; if the other carriers don't bite, the fares often float back down by Monday morning. Shop during the week.

Other Money-Saving Strategies

Airlines are forever weeping and gnashing their teeth about huge losses due to cutthroat competition. And then they regularly turn around and drop their prices radically with major sales. I don't waste time worrying about the bottom line of the airlines; it's my own wallet I want to keep full. Therefore, the savvy traveler keeps an eye out for airline fare wars all the time. Read the ads in newspapers and keep an ear open for news broadcasts that often cover the outbreak of price drops. If you have a good relationship with a travel agent, you can ask to be notified of any fare sales.

The most common times for airfare wars are in the weeks leading up to the quietest seasons for carriers, including the period from mid-May to mid-June (except the Memorial Day weekend), between Labor Day and Thanksgiving, and again in the winter with the exception of Christmas, New Year's, and President's Day holiday periods.

Study the fine print on discount coupons distributed directly by the airlines or through third parties such as supermarkets, catalog companies, and direct marketers. In my experience, these coupons are often less valuable than they seem. Read the fine print carefully, and be sure to ask the reservationist if the price quoted with the coupon is higher than another fare for which you qualify.

Consider buying from discounters, known in the industry as consolidators or, less flatteringly, as "bucket shops." Look for ads in the classified sections of many Sunday newspaper travel sections. These companies buy the airlines' slow-to-sell tickets in volume and resell them to consumers at rock-bottom prices.

Look for ticket broker and bucket shop ads online and in the classified ads in *USA Today*, the "Mart" section of the *Wall Street Journal*, the back pages of *The Village Voice,* or in specialty magazines aimed at frequent flyers.

Some travel agencies can also offer you consolidator tickets. Just be sure to weigh the savings on the ticket price against any restrictions attached to the tickets: they may not be changeable, and they usually do not accrue frequent flyer mileage, for example.

Don't be afraid to ask for a refund on previously purchased tickets if fares go down for the period of your travel. The airline may refund the difference, or you may be able to reticket your itinerary at the new fare, paying a $75 penalty for cashing in the old tickets. Be persistent: if the difference in fare is significant, it may be worth making a visit to the airport to meet with a supervisor at the ticket counter.

Beating the Airlines at Their Own Game

In my opinion, the airlines deserve all the headaches we travelers can give them because of the illogical and costly pricing schemes they throw at us—deals such as a fare of $350 to fly ninety miles between two cities where they hold a monopoly, and $198 bargain fares to travel 3,000 miles across the nation. Or round-trip fares of $300 if you leave on a Thursday and return on a Monday, and $1,200 if you leave on a Monday and return on the next Thursday.

But a creative traveler can find ways to work around most of these roadblocks. Nothing I'm going to suggest here is against the law; some of the tips, though, are against the rules of some airlines. Here are a couple of strategies.

Nested Tickets. This scheme generally works in either of two situations—where regular fares are more than twice as high as excursion fares that include a Saturday night stay over, or in situations where you plan to fly between two locations twice in less than a year.

Let's say you want to fly from Boston to Portland. Buy two sets of tickets in your name. The first is from Boston to Portland and back. This set has the return date for when you want to come back from your second trip. The other set of tickets is from Portland to Boston and back to Portland; this time making the first leg of the ticket for the date you want to come back from the first trip, and the second leg of the trip the date you want to depart for the second trip.

If this sounds complicated, that's because it is. It will be up to you to keep your tickets straight when you travel. Some airlines have threatened to crack down on such practices by searching their computer databases for multiple reservations. That doesn't mean you can't buy such tickets. Check with a travel agent for advice.

One solution: buy one set of tickets on one airline and the other set on another carrier.

Split Tickets. Fare wars sometimes result in super-cheap fares through a connecting city. For example, an airline seeking to boost traffic through a hub in Cincinnati might set up a situation in which it is less expensive to get from New York to Seattle by buying a round-trip ticket from New York to Cincinnati, and then a separate round-trip ticket from Cincinnati to Seattle.

Be sure to book a schedule that allows enough time between flights; if you miss your connection you could end up losing time and money.

Standing Up for Standing By

One of the little-known secrets of air travel on most airlines and most types of tickets is the fact that travelers who have valid tickets are allowed to stand by for flights other than the ones for which they have reservations; if there are empty seats on the flight, standby ticketholders are permitted to board.

Here's what I do know: if I cannot get the exact flight I want for a trip, I make the closest acceptable reservations available and then show up early at the airport and head for the check-in counter for the flight I really want to take. Unless you are seeking to travel during an impossibly overbooked holiday period or arrive on a bad weather day when flights have been canceled, your chances of successfully standing by for a flight are usually pretty good.

Overbooking

Overbooking is a polite industry term that refers to the legal practice of selling more than an airline can deliver. It all stems, alas, from the unfortunate habit of many travelers who neglect to cancel flight reservations that will not be used. Airlines study the patterns on various flights and city pairs and apply a formula that allows them to sell more tickets than there are seats, in the expectation that a certain percentage will not show up at the airport.

But what happens if all passengers holding reservations show up? Obviously, the result will be more travelers than seats, and some will have to be left behind.

The involuntary bump list will begin with the names of passengers who are late to check in. Airlines must ask for volunteers before bumping any passengers who have followed the rules on check-in.

Now, assuming that no one is willing to give up their seat just for the fun of it, the airline will offer some sort of compensation—either a free ticket or cash, or both. It is up to the passenger and the airline to negotiate an acceptable deal. The U.S. Department of Transportation's consumer protection regulations set some minimum levels of compensation for passengers who are bumped from a flight as a result of overbooking.

It is not considered "bumping" if a flight is canceled because of weather, equipment problems, or the lack of a flight crew. You are also not eligible for compensation if the airline substitutes a smaller aircraft for operational or safety reasons, or if the flight involves an aircraft with sixty seats or less.

How to Get Bumped

Why in the world would you want to be bumped? Well, perhaps you'd like to look at missing your plane as an opportunity to earn a little money for your time instead of as an annoyance. Is a two-hour delay worth $100 an hour? How about $800 for a family of four to wait a few hours on the way home—that should pay for a week's hotel on your next trip.

If you're not in a rush to get to the Pacific Northwest—or to get home—you might want to volunteer to be bumped. I wouldn't recommend this on the busiest travel days of the year, or if you are booked on the last flight of the day, unless you are also looking forward to a free night in an airport motel.

My very best haul: on a flight home from London, my family of four received a free night's stay in a luxury hotel, $1,000 each in tickets, and an upgrade on our flight home the next day.

Bad Weather, Bad Planes, Strikes, and Other Headaches

You don't want pilots to fly into weather they consider unsafe, of course. You also wouldn't want them to take up a plane with a mechanical problem. No matter how you feel about unions, you probably don't want to cross a picket line to board a plane piloted by strikebreakers. And so, you should accept an airline's cancellation of a flight for any of these legitimate reasons.

Here's the bad news, though: if a flight is canceled for an "act of God" or a labor dispute, the airline is not required to do anything for you except refund your money. In practice, carriers will usually make a good effort to find another way to get you to your destination more or less on time. This could mean rebooking on another flight on the same airline, or on a different carrier. It could mean a delay of a day or more in the worst situations, such as a major snowstorm.

Here is a summary of your rather limited rights as an air passenger:

• An airline is required to compensate you above the cost of your ticket only if you are bumped from an oversold flight against your will.

• If you volunteer to be bumped, you can negotiate for the best deal with the ticket agent or a supervisor; for your inconvenience, you can generally expect to be offered a free round-trip ticket on the airline.

• If your scheduled flight is unable to deliver you directly to the destination on your ticket, and alternate transportation such as a bus or limousine is provided, the airline is required to pay you twice the amount of your one-way fare if your arrival will be more than two hours later than the original ticket promised.

• If you purchased your ticket with a credit card, the airline must credit your account within seven days of receiving an application for a refund.

All that said, in many cases you will be able to convince an agent or a supervisor to go beyond the letter of the law. I've found that the best strategy is to politely but firmly stand your ground. Ask the ticket clerk for another flight, for a free night in a hotel and a flight in the morning, or for any other reasonable accommodation. Don't take no for an answer, but remain polite and ask for a supervisor if necessary. Sooner or later, they'll do something to get you out of the way.

And then there are labor problems such as those that faced American Airlines and USAirways in recent years. Your best defense against a strike is to anticipate it before it happens; keep your ears open for labor problems when you make a reservation. Then keep in touch with your travel agent or the airline itself in the days leading up to any strike deadline. It is often easier to make alternate plans or seek a refund in the days immediately before a strike; wait until the last minute and you're going to be joining a very long line of upset people.

In the face of a strike, a major airline will attempt to reroute you on another airline if possible; if you buy your own ticket on another carrier you are unlikely to be reimbursed. If your flight is canceled, you will certainly be able to claim a full refund of your fare or obtain a voucher in its value without paying any penalties.

Airline Safety

There are no guarantees in life, but in general flying on an airplane is considerably safer than driving to the airport. All of the major air carriers have very good safety records; some are better than others. I pay attention to news reports about Federal Aviation Administration inspections and rulings, and then make adjustments. And although I love to squeeze George Washington until he yelps, I avoid start-up and super cut-rate airlines because I have my doubts about how much money they can afford to devote to maintenance.

Among major airlines, the fatal accident rate during the last twenty-five years stands somewhere between .3 and .74 incidents per 1 million flights. Not included in these listings are small commuter airlines (except those that are affiliated with major carriers).

The very low numbers, experts say, make them poor predictors of future incidents. Instead, you should pay more attention to reports of FAA or National Transportation Safety Board rulings on maintenance and training problems.

About Travel Agencies

Here's my advice about travel agents, in a nutshell: get a good one, or go it alone. Good travel agents are those who remember who they work for: you. Of course, there is a built-in conflict of interest here, because the agent is in most cases paid by someone else.

Agents receive a commission on airline tickets, hotel reservations, car rentals, and many other services they sell you. The more they sell (or the higher the price), the more they earn.

I would recommend you start the planning for any trip by calling the airlines and a few hotels and finding the best package you can put together for yourself. Then call your travel agent and ask them to do better.

If your agent contributes knowledge or experience, comes up with dollar-saving alternatives to your own package, or offers some other kind of convenience, then go ahead and book through the agency. If, as I often find, you know a lot more about your destination and are willing to spend a lot more time to save money than will the agent, do it yourself.

A number of large agencies offer rebates on part of their commissions to travelers. Some of these companies cater only to frequent flyers who will bring in a lot of business; other rebate agencies offer only limited services to clients.

You can find discount travel agencies through many major credit card companies (Citibank and American Express among them) or through associations and clubs. Some warehouse shopping clubs have rebate travel agencies.

And if you establish a regular relationship with your travel agency and bring them enough business to make them glad to hear from you, don't be afraid to ask them for a discount equal to a few percentage points.

One other important new tool for travelers is the Internet. Here you'll find computerized travel agencies that offer airline, hotel, car, cruise, and package reservations. You won't receive personalized assistance, but you will be able to make as many price checks and itinerary routings as you'd like without apology. Several of the services feature special deals, including companion fares and rebates you won't find offered elsewhere.

Some of the best Internet agencies include:

Atevo	💻 www.atevo.com/
Microsoft Expedia	💻 www.expedia.com
The Trip	💻 www.thetrip.com
Travelocity	💻 www.travelocity.com

You can also book directly with a number of major airlines, sometimes taking advantage of special Internet prices, or bonus frequent flyer mileage. Among the airlines that offer online booking are:

American Airlines	💻 www.aa.com
Continental Airlines	💻 www.continental.com
Delta Airlines	💻 www.delta.com
Northwest Airlines	💻 www.nwa.com
Southwest	💻 www.southwest.com
United Airlines	💻 www.united.com
US Airways	💻 www.usairways.com

Tour Packages and Charter Flights

Tour packages and flights sold by tour operators or travel agents may look similar, but the consumer may end up with significantly different rights.

It all depends whether the flight is a scheduled or nonscheduled flight. A scheduled flight is one that is listed in the *Official Airline Guide* and available to the general public through a travel agent or from the airline. This doesn't mean that a scheduled flight will necessarily be on a major carrier or that you will be flying on a 747 jumbo jet; it could just as easily be the propeller-driven pride of Hayseed Airlines. In any case, though, a scheduled flight does have to meet stringent federal government certification requirements.

A nonscheduled flight is also known as a charter flight. The term is sometimes also applied to a complete package that includes a nonscheduled flight, hotel accommodations, ground transportation, and other elements. Charter flights are generally a creation of a tour operator who will purchase all the seats on a specific flight to a specific destination or who will rent an airplane and crew from an air carrier.

Charter flights and charter tours are regulated by the federal government, but your rights as a consumer are much more limited than those afforded to scheduled flight customers.

You wouldn't buy a hamburger without knowing the price and specifications (two all-beef patties on a sesame seed bun, etc.). Why, then, would you spend hundreds or even thousands of dollars on a tour and not understand the contract that underlies the transaction?

When you purchase a charter flight or a tour package, you should review and sign a contract that spells out your rights. This contract is sometimes referred to as the "Operator Participant Contract" or the "Terms and Conditions." Look for this contract in the booklet or brochure that describes the packages; ask for it if one is not offered. Remember that the contract is designed mostly to benefit the tour operator, and each contract may be different from others you may have agreed to in the past. The basic rule here is: if you don't understand it, don't sign it.

How to Book a Package or Charter Flight

If possible, use a travel agent—preferably one you know and trust from prior experience. In general, the tour operator pays the travel agent's commission. Some tour packages, however, are available only from the operator who organized the tour; in certain cases, you may be able to negotiate a better price by dealing directly with the operator, although you are giving up one layer of protection for your rights.

Pay for your ticket with a credit card; this is a cardinal rule for almost any situation in which you are prepaying for a service or product.

Realize that charter airlines don't have large fleets of planes available to substitute in the event of a mechanical problem or an extensive weather delay. They may not be able to arrange for a substitute plane from another carrier.

If you are still willing to try a charter after all of these warnings, make one more check of the bottom line before you sign the contract. First of all, is the air travel significantly less expensive than the lowest nonrefundable fare from a scheduled carrier? (Remember that you are, in effect, buying a nonrefundable fare with most charter flight contracts.)

Have you included taxes, service charges, baggage transfer fees, or other charges the tour operator may put into the contract? Are the savings significantly more than the 10 percent the charter operator may (typically) boost the price without your permission? Do any savings come at a cost of time? Put a value on your time.

Finally, don't buy a complete package until you have compared it to the a la carte cost of such a trip. Call the hotels offered by the tour operator, or similar ones in the same area, and ask them a simple question: "What is your best price for a room?" Be sure to mention any discount programs that are applicable, including AAA or other organizations. Do the same for car rental agencies, and place a call to any attractions you plan to visit to get current prices.

Negotiating for a Room

Notice the title of this section: I didn't call it "buying" a room. The fact of the matter is that hotel rooms, like almost everything else, are subject to negotiation and change.

Here is how to pay the highest possible price for a hotel room: walk up to the front desk without a reservation and say, "I'd like a room." Unless the "No Vacancy" sign is lit, you may have to pay the "rack rate," which is the published maximum nightly charge.

Here are a few ways to pay the lowest possible price:

1. Before you head for your vacation, spend an hour on the phone and call directly to a half dozen hotels that seem to be in the price range you'd like to spend. (I recommend membership in AAA and use of their annual tour books as starting points for your research. If you are of a certain age, join AARP. And

there are also good bargains to be had by using the Internet, either directly to web booking pages run by major chains, including Choice (Quality, Comfort, Choice, Sleep Inn and others), Hilton, Radisson, and Holiday Inn. You can also obtain reduced rates, and more easily comparison shop, through gateways such as Expedia. And finally, there are several hotel discount companies that offer specific deals in major cities and resort areas. Some of these companies offer discount coupons in this book.

2. When you get a reservations clerk on the phone, start by asking for the room rate. Then ask them for their best rate. Does that sound like an unnecessary second request?

[True story: I called a major hotel chain and asked for the rates for a night at a Chicago location. "That will be $149 per night," I was told. "Ouch," I said. "Oh, would you like to spend less?" the reservationist said. I admitted that I would, and she punched a few keys on her keyboard. "They have a special promotion going on. How about $109 per night?" she asked.

Not bad for a city hotel, I reasoned, but still I hadn't asked the big question. "What is your best rate?" I asked. "Oh, our best rate? That would be $79," said the agent.

But, wait: "I'm a member of AAA, by the way." Another pause. "That's fine, Mr. Sandler. The nightly room rate will be $71.10. Have a nice day."]

When you feel you've negotiated the best deal you can obtain over the phone, make a reservation at the hotel of your choice. Be sure to go over the dates and prices one more time, and obtain the name of the person you spoke with and a confirmation number if available.

3. When you show up at your hotel on the first night, stop and look at the marquee outside; see if the hotel is advertising a discount rate. Here's where you need to be bold. Walk up to the desk as if you did not have a reservation, and ask the clerk: "What is your best room rate for tonight?" If the rate they quote you is less than the rate in your reservation, you are now properly armed to ask for a reduction in your room rate.

Similarly, if the room rate advertised out front drops during your stay, don't be shy about asking that your charges be reduced. Just be sure to ask for the reduction before you spend another night at the old rate, and obtain the name of the clerk who promises a change. If the hotel tries a lame excuse such as, "That's only for new check-ins," you can offer to check out and then check back in again. That will usually work; you can always check out and go to the hotel across the road that will usually match the rates of its competitor.

4. Are you planning to stay a full week? Ask for a weekly rate. If the room clerk says there is no such rate, ask to speak to the manager: the manager may be willing to shave a few dollars per day off the rate for a long-term stay.

Renting a Car

All the major car rental agencies, and a selection of smaller ones, have offices throughout the Pacific Northwest. Most of the companies operate from the major airports, but a few also have pickup and drop-off sites in big cities and at some large hotels.

In general, you'll get the best deals on car rentals by booking in advance. Rental companies, like airlines and hotels, usually have a limited number of deep-discount rates that they use to lure customers and once those are gone, you may end up paying a higher rate than the guy next to you at the counter for the same class of car.

However, as you fly across the country, read the airline's magazine in the seatback pocket. There are often special car rental rates advertised for destinations served by the airline. It may be worthwhile to take the ad with you to the rental counter and ask for a better rate than the one you have reserved.

If you fly into a large city, be aware that the least expensive car rental agencies usually do not have stations at the airport itself. You will have to wait for a shuttle bus to take you from the terminal to their lot, and you must return the car to the outlying area at the end of your trip. This may add about twenty to thirty minutes to your arrival and departure schedule.

Pay attention, too, when the rental agent explains the fuel policy. The most common plan says you must return the car with a full tank; if the agency must refill the tank, you will be billed a service charge plus what is usually a very high per-gallon rate. Other optional plans include one where the rental agency sells you a full tank when you first drive away and takes no note of how much gas remains when you return the car. Unless you somehow manage to return the car with the engine running on fumes, you are in effect making a gift to the agency with every gallon you bring back. I prefer the first option, making a point to refill the tank on the way to the airport on getaway day.

Car rental companies will try—with varying levels of pressure—to convince you to purchase special insurance coverage. They'll tell you it's "only" $7 or $9 per day. What a deal! That works out to about $2,500 or $3,000 per year for a set of rental wheels. The coverage is intended primarily to protect the rental company, not you.

Check with your insurance agent before you travel to determine how well your personal automobile policy will cover a rental car and its contents. I recommend you use a credit card that offers rental car insurance; such insurance usually covers the deductible below your personal policy. The extra auto insurance by itself is usually worth an upgrade to a "gold card" or similar card.

The only sticky area comes for those visitors who have a driver's license but no car, and therefore no insurance. Again, consult your credit card company.

Although it is theoretically possible to rent a car without a credit card, you will find it to be a rather inconvenient process. If they cannot hold your credit card account hostage, most agencies will require a large cash deposit—perhaps as much as several thousand dollars—before they will give you the keys.

And finally, check with the rental company about its policies on taking the car out of the state. Some companies will charge you extra if you are planning to take the car across a state line.

Finally, if you expect to cross the border to Canada, be sure the rental company allows this. You may find it very expensive or impossible to obtain a one-way rental that begins in Washington or Oregon and ends in Canada, or the other way around.

Crossing the Border

U.S. citizens or permanent residents of the United States can enter Canada without a passport or visa.

Most crossings, especially by private car, are routine. A customs agent will ask your place of birth and purpose of entry; they may enter your vehicle's driver's license into a computer database to verify some of your answers.

You may be pressed a bit harder if you are entering by bus or train or in a rented vehicle. And it has been my experience that some arrivals by airline can be much more formalized than arrival by car.

In any case, you should carry with you some evidence of citizenship, such as a passport if you have one, a birth or baptismal certificate, voter registration card, or a certificate of citizenship or naturalization. Combine these with a driver's license or other form of identification that has a photo.

Permanent residents of the United States who are not citizens should carry a resident alien card with them into Canada.

Single parents traveling with children must provide proof of citizenship for the child as well as a letter of consent from the absent parent.

If you are not a U.S. citizen or permanent resident, you must have a valid passport; check with the Canadian consulate before travel to see if additional papers are required for entry to Canada or re-entry to your home country.

Personal Possessions

Clothing and goods for personal use by visitors during their stay in Canada are admitted free of duty.

You may bring a limited amount of tobacco and alcohol products for personal use without paying duty; the drinking age is nineteen in British Columbia and eighteen in Alberta.

If you are entering with valuable items such as jewelry, cameras, tape recorders, computers, or sporting equipment, you should consider whether to register them with the customs service in your home country before you depart or carry proof of purchase to prove they were bought outside Canada.

Gifts other than tobacco and alcoholic beverages brought into or mailed to Canada by non-residents are allowed free entry if the value of gifts for any one recipient from any one donor does not exceed $60. Gifts valued at more than $60 are subject to regular duty and taxes on the excess value.

Revolvers, pistols, and automatic firearms are prohibited entry into Canada; all hunting rifles and shotguns must be declared.

For more information on customs and immigration regulations, contact Revenue Canada, Customs and Excise at ☎ (800) 461-9999 or ☎ (204) 983-3500 (outside Canada) or 🖳 www.ccra-adrc.gc.ca, or Immigration Canada at ☎ (716) 858-9590 or 🖳 www.canada-congenbuffalo.org.

Canada On Sale

Let's get one of the most important things about Canada out of the way right up front: in recent years, the international exchange rate for Canadian dollars has made for tremendous savings for visitors from the United States and some other nations that have strong economies.

In late 2000, the U.S. dollar was worth about $1.51 in Canadian currency; going the other way, a Canadian dollar was worth about 66 cents in U.S. funds. A hotel room or a piece of clothing priced at $151 Canadian cost American visitors about $100.

At the same time, a British pound was worth $2.22 in Canadian currency. A hotel room priced at $151 Canadian would cost about £68.

You can obtain the latest exchange rates from many major newspapers, including the *Wall Street Journal* and from online sources. One of many currency conversion programs available on the web is offered by Yahoo, at 💻 http://quote.yahoo.com.

All this doesn't mean that everything is 34 percent off for Americans in Canada. Items that are imported into Canada from elsewhere in the world are likely to be marked up to reflect the exchange rate. But products of Canada— including food, hotel rooms, and tickets to museums and attractions—are usually a great bargain.

Whenever you convert from one country's currency to another, a percentage of the exchange is pocketed by the bank or company that is making the swap. You'll get the best deal by going directly to a bank, and the worst deal by spending money with a merchant who keeps some of the difference as gain and then takes your money to a bank that will reduce the value of your transaction by extracting its own profit on the deal.

The best way to make your purchases in Canada is with a credit card, which converts currency at the most favorable inter-bank rate. Almost every store, restaurant, and attraction will accept Visa, MasterCard, or American Express cards; the receipt you sign will be denominated in Canadian dollars but converted to American dollars on the statement you receive at home.

A second option is to use an ATM card from your home bank to obtain Canadian cash from a teller machine. Again, you should receive a good rate on the currency exchange, although your bank may apply a service charge for use of the card in a foreign country.

You can also obtain travelers checks denominated in Canadian dollars before you travel. The exchange rate is usually good, but you may have to pay a service charge for the travelers checks, and you may end up with some leftover checks at the end of your trip that will have to be converted to U.S. dollars— with a cost for that service.

You'll receive the least bang for your bucks by using American currency or travelers checks at stores.

Finally, there is no guarantee the disparity in exchange rates between the United States and Canada will continue, although the American economy has been outperforming that of Canada, on a relative basis, for many years.

Taxes in Canada

A goods and services tax of 7 percent is added to the price of most purchases in Canada. Visitors can obtain an instant rebate of the GST for goods taken out of the country and for accommodations, up to $500 Canadian, at participating duty-free shops at airports and border crossings. Or visitors can file for a refund from Revenue Canada by submitting receipts and proper paperwork; the visitor must leave the country within sixty days of purchase, and the application must be filed within a year of expenditures.

On top of the GST, provinces apply sales tax of 7 percent, and a 10 percent tax on liquor. There is also a 10 percent accommodation tax on hotel rooms.

Visitors can also apply for refunds of sales taxes in Manitoba (PST) or Québec (TVQ).

For information on GST rebates from within Canada, call ☎ (800) 668-4748. From outside of the country, call ☎ (902) 432-5608.

Legalities and Finances

Speed limits across Canada are posted in kilometers per hour. (To convert to miles per hour, multiply by .62.) A typical speed limit on a multi-lane highway is 90 or 100 kmh, or 55 or 63 mph.

Gasoline is sold by the litre. One litre is about 1.05 U.S. quarts; therefore, four litres is about 20 percent larger than a gallon.

The emergency telephone number for police, fire, and ambulance is 911 in much of Canada; where that number is not in use, just dial 0 and advise the operator that you are reporting an emergency.

Canadian postage stamps must be used on all mail posted in Canada, to points within the country or to foreign destinations.

The nation's currency is based on the Canadian dollar, made up of 100 cents. Coins include five-cent, ten-cent, twenty-five cent, one-dollar, and two-dollar pieces. The gold-colored dollar coin has a picture of a common loon bird on one side, and from that it draws its nickname: the loonie. In 1996, a two-tone, two-dollar coin was introduced with a picture of a polar bear; it's nickname: the twonie.

Nearly all major credit cards are accepted across Canada; in fact, they may be more acceptable than at many locations in the United States. You can use credit cards to pay parking meters in some places, for most admission tickets, and nearly all purchases.

Part II
Oregon

Chapter 3
Introduction to Oregon

In the middle of the nineteenth century, Oregon was the promised land, the impossibly green land that drew tens of thousands of Americans on an almost indescribably arduous, sometimes perilous six-month trek westward.

They came in search of fertile farmland, whispers of gold, and dreams of commerce to developing markets to the south in California and north in Canada and Alaska.

Today, Oregon is a natural magnet, one of the most spectacular and diverse states of the modern union. In some ways, it is little changed from the way it appeared to the first pioneers:

• The **Oregon coast** is a rugged, windswept stretch of stark beauty and amazing marine life on the beach and offshore that stretches the length of the state from California to Washington.

• **Mount Hood** and the **Columbia River Gorge** represent amazing highs and lows of nature in Oregon, both within an hour of metropolitan Portland.

• The **Willamette Valley** was the Promised Land for many of the pioneers on the Oregon Trail; today it is one of the richest fruit, nut, and flower gardens of the nation.

• **Portland** is a thoroughly modern big city, an inland port where the mighty Columbia meets the Willamette River. The City of Roses is the commercial and cultural hub of the state.

• **Central Oregon** includes some of the best recreational opportunities in the state, including the massive Mount Bachelor.

• **Southern Oregon** is home to gems as lyrical and different as Crater Lake and the renowned Oregon Shakespeare Festival in Ashland.

About Oregon

Oregon is the tenth largest state in the union, covering 98,386 square miles. The highest elevation point is Mount Hood at 11,235 feet, and the lowest is at sea level along the coast.

Across that huge expanse of land, though, the population is just a bit more than 3 million, with half of the people living in the Portland area.

OREGON

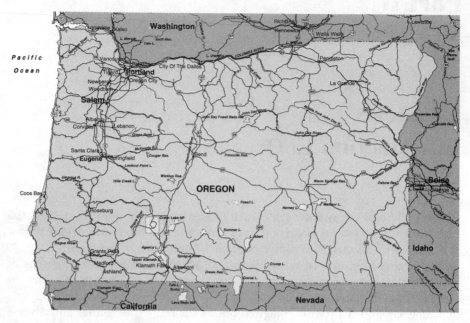

There are more than 6,000 lakes and 112,000 miles of rivers and streams. Nearly half of Oregon's total area is forested, totaling nearly 30 million acres. Included are 13 national forests and 200 state parks. Two national monuments, the John Day Fossil Beds and the Oregon Caves, are found in Oregon, as is the Newberry Crater, one of two national volcanic monuments in the country. The deepest lake in the United States, at 1,932 feet, is located at Crater Lake National Park. And, there are thirteen downhill ski areas in three mountain ranges.

Most of Oregon is in the Pacific time zone, three hours behind Eastern time. The most eastern community in Oregon is Ontario, located in the Mountain time zone.

The state has more than 7,000 bridges, 53 of them covered. And there are seventeen ghost towns.

The apparel companies of Nike, Norm Thompson, Avia, Adidas, Jantzen, Pendleton, and Columbia Sportswear are all based in Oregon. And shopper's be wise: there is no sales tax.

History of Oregon

The first residents of the Pacific West were believed to be emigrants from Mongolia who crossed Siberia and Alaska about 13,000 years ago.

There were about eighty Native American tribes in Oregon before the establishment of pioneer settlements. Today there are nine Native American Confederations in Oregon: the Siletz Tribes, the Grand Ronde Tribe, the Confederated Tribes of Warm Springs, the Umatilla Tribes, the Coos Tribe, the

Coquille Tribe, the Klamath Tribe, the Burns Paiute Tribe, and the Cow Creek Band of the Umpqua. Many contemporary place names are derived from Indian tribal names such as Multnomah, Willamette, Siuslaw, and Clackamas.

It was the eighteenth century before European explorers, principally Spanish and British, entered the area in search of the "great river of the West." American John Gray, who in 1792 sailed up a river into interior Oregon, named the waterway for his ship, the Columbia Rediviva.

The discovery of the Columbia River lead President Thomas Jefferson to send Meriwether Lewis and William Clark on a great expedition from the East Coast to the West to explore and find out if there was a northwest passage across the continent. Their journey, from 1804 to 1807, found a rich land, but no passage. However, Lewis and Clark's explorations and that of Captain Gray helped the newborn United States lay claim to the region.

The first European settlers were trappers and fur traders, lead by the Hudson's Bay Company, a British concern that had extensive operations in Canada. That company built the original capital of what was to become the Oregon Territory in Oregon City, at the north end of the Willamette Valley. Oregon City was the first incorporated city west of the Rockies.

In the 1840s came the first major influx of settlers, from the East Coast overland and by sea after a long and difficult passage around the tip of South America.

Before the arrival of the pioneers, currency for trade was the beaver pelt. In the 1850s, the "Beaver" coin eventually became the official exchange currency for the west; the coins were made from melting down the wheels of covered wagons. To this day, one of the nicknames of Oregon is the Beaver State.

The Oregon Trail

In the 1840s, thousands of people sold off most of their possessions, left their homes, and set out on a slow walk or oxen-drawn wagon ride across open prairies, desert, and rugged mountain ranges to head for Oregon, California, and other points west.

Some 53,000 emigrants came by wagon over the 2,000-mile **Oregon Trail** from Missouri to western Oregon in the 1840s and 1850s. Most of the pioneers settled in the fertile Willamette Valley.

One of the spurs to immigration was the Land Donation Law, a government program that gave 320 acres to white male pioneers and 640 acres to married white couples.

The trail stretched about 2,000 miles from Independence, Missouri, to the Columbia River region of Oregon. It cut through the northeastern corner of Kansas, and then through the lower portions of Nebraska, Wyoming, and Idaho before traversing northern Oregon.

Including occasional stops at forts and trading posts for reprovisioning and repairs, the journey ordinarily took about four to six months.

Great wagon trains of settlers filled the trail in the 1840s, joined by gold rushers heading for California later that decade.

The final leg of the Oregon Trail stretched 547 miles across Oregon itself. Emigrants crossed the Snake River and entered into Oregon through what is

Bridgework. There are fifty-three covered bridges still standing in Oregon, most of them in the Willamette Valley. Built to keep ice from forming on the wooden roadways over rivers and streams, at one time more than 450 of the spans existed in Oregon. Today's oldest covered bridge, built in 1914, is at Upper Drift Creek.

today the town of Nyssa. Climbing over Keeney Pass, then crossing the Malheur River at Vale, travelers entered a dry alkali desert, up the Burnt River Canyon and through the pass below Flagstaff Hill. Two last challenges, the Blue Mountains and the desolate Columbia Plateau stood before the Willamette Valley and the end of the trail.

Along much of the trail, Native Americans helped guide the settlers and traded with them; there were also teams of traveling salesmen who worked their way eastward along the trail to sell supplies.

In the early years of the migration, when the wagons reached The Dalles they were loaded onto rafts for a somewhat treacherous journey down the Columbia River. In 1846 the Barlow Toll Road was opened, offering an overland route through dense forest.

The Oregon Trail was used longer than any of the other overland routes to the west; when it was finally replaced by railroads, the trail was still used for cattle drives eastward.

Today, near Baker City, the Oregon Trail Interpretive Center preserves sections of undisturbed ruts and a wagon encampment, and it displays life-sized dioramas. The center includes 23,000 acres of land.

The official end of the Oregon Trail was Oregon City, the only incorporated town west of the Mississippi River at the time.

Oregon City, which served as the first capital of Oregon, is strategically located at the falls of the Willamette River, about fifteen miles south of Portland. It is also known for the first newspaper west of the Missouri River, the first paper mill in the west, the nation's first long-distance electric power transmission, and the first coinage mint.

The region became the Oregon Territory in 1848 and a non-slaveholding state in 1859 in the contentious period before the outbreak of the U.S. Civil War.

When relatively small deposits of gold were found along the coast and in the high country in 1861 and 1862, there were new settlements established there. Settlers in these areas, though, provoked wars with the Indians that lasted many years. The Rogue River, Modoc, Paiute, Bannock, and Nez Perce Indian wars cost many lives, and in the end resulted in the Native Americans surrendering their land. The natives were also severely impacted by diseases brought by the settlers, including smallpox and diphtheria.

Oregon's isolation was greatly lessened in the 1870s with the coming of the railroads, first south to San Francisco and soon afterward a transcontinental link. This allowed the import of supplies and export of products overland. The stripping of the eastern forests accelerated the logging industry in Oregon.

In 1905 millions of visitors came to the celebrations at the Lewis and Clark Exposition, and many stayed in search of their own fortune. The shipyards and timber industry grew during the first World War, strengthening Portland's position as the economic center of the state.

The state's infrastructure was enhanced in the Depression Era of the 1930s by New Deal programs such as the Works Projects Administration and the Civilian Conservation Corps. Built during that time was the Timberline Lodge on Mount Hood, which was and is a centerpiece of the tourism industry. Hydroelectric dams and

Bicycle crossing. Oregon sets aside one percent of all highway taxes to preserve and construct bicycle paths. Particularly well served with bike paths is the flat Willamette Valley.

roads added at that time helped broaden settlement of the state, and irrigation water from the Columbia River aided agricultural development. The Bonneville Dam provided a plentiful source of power, which helped the creation of aluminum plants during World War II.

Today lumber is the state's largest source of revenue, followed by agriculture and tourism.

Oregon produces about one-fifth of the country's softwood lumber. In agriculture, Oregon is the nation's leading producer of Christmas trees, grass seed, peppermint, blackberries, and filberts.

Oregon Weather

OK, let's deal with the wet stuff right up front. It rains in Oregon, especially from late November through March in the western half of the state.

Central Oregon, on the other hand, receives even less annual rainfall than very dry Los Angeles.

Western Oregon is mostly moderate in temperature, ranging from the mid-30s to the 50s in the winter, and usually reaching summertime highs of no more than 85 degrees in Portland and a bit higher in Medford. A typical winter month brings about six inches of rain; you can count on some liquid sunshine nearly every day. Portland averages thirty-eight inches of rain a year, about the same as Baltimore and a few inches less than New York City.

On the coast in southwest Oregon around Brookings, the complex weather pattern known as the Brookings Effect creates warmer weather in a "banana belt" on the coast.

Central Oregon is wedged between the nearby Cascade Mountain Range and the high desert. In winter, lows drop to the mid-20s and only a few feet of snowfall is recorded at the base of the mountain range. In the summer, temperatures rise to the mid-80s, accompanied by strong winds in the Columbia Gorge.

On the east side of the Cascades, though, winter storms dump abundant snow, a boon to skiers and snowmobilers and a challenge to drivers. This side of the state has the greatest variation in temperatures, dropping to the teens through the winter and soaring to the mid-90s in the summer.

Far eastern Oregon is a high desert surrounded by a few mountain ranges, and it receives relatively little rainfall or snow. Highs in the winter average in the 30s and 40s, reaching the 80s and 90s in the summer.

Oregon residents are champions of the "layered" look, mixing rain jackets

Rarity. Oregon is the world's sole source of myrtlewood, a soft wood used for crafts and artwork. A cousin tree can be found in the Middle East.

and sweaters and lighter wear throughout the year; a trusty umbrella is also a worthwhile companion in the winter.

The Promised Land Lives On

The pioneers on the Oregon Trail had it right. In many ways, Oregon was the promised land, a place of milk and honey. Or at least a place of pears, shiitake, and salmon. Oregon has some of the most fruitful agricultural areas in the country.

Apples grown along the Columbia Gorge in Hood River and Southwest Oregon include Granny Smith, Gravenstein, Red Rome Beauty, and Golden Delicious.

Bosc, Red Blushed Comice, Nelis, and Seckel pears contribute to Oregon's ranking as the nation's third largest producer of pears.

Oregon ranks number one in berries, with crops of raspberries, blackberries, huckleberries, blueberries, strawberries, gooseberries, and cranberries.

Bing cherries, named for a Chinese gardener who cultivated a large experimental fruit tree estate outside of Portland, can be found throughout western Oregon in the early summer. Maraschino cherries also got their start in Oregon when a special preserving process was developed at Oregon State University in Corvallis. After Royal Anne cherries are cured and colored, they are pitted and canned with a special process. The cherries derive their distinctive flavor from the maraschino plant, a native of Italy, and are correctly pronounced "mar-a-skeen-o."

Oregon ranks first in the nation in production of peppermint. And the state harvests 98 percent of the nation's and 3.5 percent of the world's filberts, known in Oregon as hazelnuts.

Oregon's grape harvest, "the crush," takes place in early fall. Grape varieties include Pinot Noir, Pinot Gris, Chardonnay, Riesling, and Gewurtztraminer. From its beginning in the mid-1960s, the wine-making industry now includes more than 100 wineries.

Rare trumpet-shaped chanterelle mushrooms grow in foggy forests. Also found are shiitake, enoki, lobster, oyster, and gourmet morel mushrooms.

Falls City hosts a Mushroom Festival each year in celebration of local mushroom gathering. The United States Forest Service issues thousands of permits for the rare matsutake on the eastern slope of the Cascade Range.

Among the stars of the seafood market in Oregon is the Dungeness crab, typically weighing in at about three pounds. Other favorites include Chinook salmon and other varieties of salmon, sturgeon, halibut, oysters, scallops, and shrimp.

Chapter 4
Portland

The Native Americans named the campsite between Willamette Falls and Fort Vancouver "The Clearing." More modern nicknames include the "City of Roses," and the "City of Bridges."

In between, the city we now know as Portland was almost named Boston.

In 1843, William Overton, described as a drifter from Tennessee, and Asa Lovejoy, a lawyer from Massachusetts, beached their canoe on a bank of the Willamette River, about seventy-five miles from the Pacific Ocean where the Columbia River meets the Willamette.

According to legend, Overton saw great potential for the heavily timbered land at the base of the mountains, but he lacked the 25 cents needed to file a land claim. And so he struck a deal with the lawyer Lovejoy: in return for a quarter, Overton shared a claim to the 640-acre site known as "The Clearing."

Overton didn't stick around too long, bored with clearing trees and building roads. He sold his half of the claim to another easterner, Francis Pettygrove. The new partners, Lovejoy and Pettygrove, could not agree on a name for their new town. Lovejoy wanted to name the site after his hometown of Boston, while Pettygrove favored his origins of Portland, Maine.

The partners flipped a coin, now honored as the "Portland Penny." Pettygrove—and Portland—won the honor on two tosses out of three.

The natural deepwater port, protected from the sea, seemed to be an obvious location for a prosperous trading economy. But before Portland could become a respected city, it had its walk on the wild and shady side. In the late 1800s the North End of Portland was a center of the "shanghai" trade, when unscrupulous captains would pay bar owners and hotel operators to deliver them kidnapped crews.

One infamous scoundrel was Joseph "Bunco" Kelly, who was said to have sold a group of men embalming fluid instead of alcohol; many never awoke from their binge. In another case, Kelly was said to have delivered a carved wooden Indian from a storefront heavily wrapped in blankets; when the captain discovered the ruse the next morning, the statue was thrown overboard. It was recovered nearly sixty years later by a harbor dredge.

PORTLAND

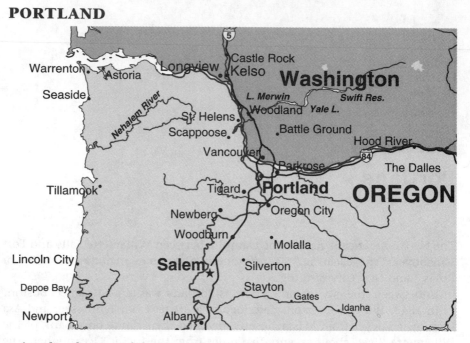

Another denizen of the North End was Sweet Mary. To evade taxes and city laws, she operated her bordello on a barge that cruised up and down the Willamette River.

Eventually, though, the success of the lumber trade and the provisioning business for the California Gold Rush, and later the Klondike fields, allowed the establishment of a more reputable economy.

Another legendary character in early Portland was lumber baron Simon Benson. Walking through his mill, Benson noted the smell of alcohol on his workers' breath. The mill workers told Benson they drank beer in the middle of the day because there was no fresh drinking water to be found downtown. Or at least, that was their story.

Benson commissioned twenty elegant drinking fountains for Portland; they still function today, now known as the Benson Bubblers.

Today's Portland

Plain and simple: Portland is one of the prettiest urban settings anywhere, home to more than 508,000 residents in the city and 1.8 million in the metropolitan area.

In one place you'll find an attractive waterfront, a bustling harbor, and a compact but fulfilling downtown. There's an extensive system of 37,000 acres of parks; one of them, Mount Tabor, includes an extinct volcano. Forest Park, at 5,000 acres, is the largest forested municipal park in the United States. Washington Park is home to the world famous Rose Test Gardens.

Tom McCall Waterfront Park opens the river to strollers, with walks, outdoor cafes, and marinas. The one-and-a-half-mile linear park borders Naito Parkway and the Willamette River, between the Hawthorne and Steel bridges in downtown Portland. You'll enjoy the place even more to know that city planners ripped out an interstate that once bordered the Willamette River and replaced it with the lovely park.

The park includes **Salmon Street Springs**, a fountain that has changing water patterns. At the north end of the park is the **Japanese-American Historical Plaza**, a sculpture garden that has a grove of cherry trees dedicated to Japanese-Americans held in detention camps in Oregon during World War II.

For information on the park and special events, call ☎ (503) 823-2223, ext. 5118, or consult 🖳 www.parks.ci.portland.or.us.

Outside the city you'll find the spectacular Columbia Gorge and Multnomah Falls; the Oregon coast is seventy miles west. Snowcapped Mount Hood, about sixty-five miles away, is visible in the distance from many points in the city. You can use Portland as a base to tour and ski Mount Hood or visit valley wineries or Bonneville Dam.

The city's mass transit system is one of the most advanced in the country, including buses and the MAX, an urban light rail line, as well as a downtown transit mall and Fareless Square, a 300-block free-ride zone in downtown.

Downtown Portland

Portland's city blocks are smaller than those of many major cities, lorded over by some handsome steel and glass skyscrapers as well as older Gothic-style structures, Victorian mansions, and the largest collection of cast-iron buildings west of the Mississippi.

Limits on growth have kept the surrounding countryside within a twenty-minute drive of the city's core. Restrictions on building height maintain views of the Cascade Mountain Range. And one percent of all major construction budgets is required to be dedicated to public art.

The City of Portland is divided east and west by the Willamette River, and north and south by Burnside Street.

Streets are marked east and west away from the river. Broadway stands in for Seventh Avenue and Park Avenue for Eighth Avenue.

Forest Park, just two minutes from downtown, offers more than 50 miles of interconnecting trails, more than 100 species of birds, including the Red Crossbill and Stellar Jay, and dozens of species of small animals.

On warm days, many residents and workers take to a seat in "Portland's living room," officially

The pride of Springfield. Cartoonist Matt Groening, creator of "The Simpsons," graduated from Portland's Lincoln High School in 1972, something he seems to have never gotten over. Many of the characters and locations in the popular television show have their roots in Portland. The Simpson family lives on Evergreen Terrace, at Groening's old address. Sideshow Bob Terwilliger is named after Terwilliger Boulevard; other street names were used for characters, including Ned Flanders, Reverend Lovejoy, and Mayor Quimby. And Springfield, Oregon, is just down the pike from Portland, although Groening credits the name of the Simpsons' hometown to the fictional home of a long-departed television icon, "Father Knows Best."

known as **Pioneer Courthouse Square**. The outdoor plaza in the heart of downtown includes places to sit and watch the world go by, an amphitheater for concerts, and a twenty-five-foot-tall weather machine sculpture that spews mist. At noon, with great drama, the machine issues a weather forecast. The square is located at 701 Southwest Sixth Avenue.

Portland's **Chinatown** begins at Northwest Fourth Avenue and Burnside Street, extending for several blocks from its elaborate ceremonial gate. The streets are lined with shops and restaurants, beneath ornate Oriental lamp poles and cherry trees. In 2000 the Portland Classical Chinese Garden opened, a collaboration with Suzhou, a sister city in mainland China.

The **Nob Hill** district was given its name in the late 1800s by a transplant from California who opened a grocery store in one of the more affluent neighborhoods of Portland. The elegant Victorian and Georgian mansions of the area, especially those on Northwest Twenty-First and Twenty-Third avenues between Burnside and Thurman, are somewhat evocative of the San Francisco originals. Today, many of the homes have been reborn as shops, pubs, and galleries.

In southeast Portland, **Antique Row** in Sellwood lures buyers to more than twenty shops. The **Skidmore District** is renowned for its beautiful cast-iron buildings, decorative fountains, and lively public squares. From March through Christmas, the Portland Saturday Market sets up shop each weekend.

Getting Around

Portland International Airport is about ten miles from downtown Portland. A taxi into town costs about $25 to $30; an airport express bus serves major hotels, and a slower Tri-Met bus runs from the airport to the downtown transit mall on Fifth Avenue. For information about the airport, call ☎ (800) 547-8411, or consult 🖳 www.portlandairportpdx.com.

Amtrak services downtown with a station at 800 Northwest Sixth Avenue, near Union Station. For information, call ☎ (800) 872-7245.

Within the city, mass transit includes the Tri-Met bus system and the **MAX Light Rail (Metropolitan Area Express)**.

Transport in Portland has a long and storied history; the first trolleys were horse and mule drawn, operating on First Avenue in 1872; the first electrified streetcar service began in 1890. In 1893 the East Side Railway Company offered the first electric railroad passenger service in the United States, carrying passengers and freight between Oregon City and Portland.

After World War I streetcars began to lose ground to the automobile. The last city streetcars were retired in 1950. Trolley buses ceased operating in 1958, replaced by gasoline powered buses.

But the idea was reborn in more modern times, and in 1986 the MAX Light Rail commenced operation to Gresham, renewing rail passenger service in Portland. In 1991 replicas of the Council Crest cars were added on some lines. And in 1998 Westside light rail service was introduced on tracks between Portland and Hillsboro.

You will need to pay your fare before boarding the train. Some MAX stations have inbound and outbound platforms, so be sure to check the directions.

All rides are free in Fareless Square, the downtown Portland area bounded by the Willamette River, Northwest Irving, and I-405.

In the fall of 2001, MAX is due to open a line to Portland International Airport. The six-mile extension will add four stations: Parkrose/Sumner, Cascade Station East and West, and at the terminal located adjacent to the south baggage claim area. The trip is expected to take about thirty-seven minutes from downtown Pioneer Square to the airport.

There are three fare zones. Fares are based on the number of zones you travel through. For example, if you begin in Zone 1 and travel to Zone 3, you need an All-Zone fare. If you begin in Zone 2 and travel to Zone 3, you need a 2-Zone fare.

Fares on MAX and buses are the same and transfers are free. In 2000, a two-zone ticket sold for $1.20, and an all-zone for $1.45. Reduced price fares were offered for youths and senior citizens. You can also purchase a 10-ticket book for approximately a 10 percent discount.

For information about MAX, call ☎ (503) 238-7433 7:30 A.M. to 5 P.M., or consult 🖳 www.tri-met.org/. For information about the Tri-Met bus system, call ☎ (503) 238-7433.

Attractions in Portland

Cultural activities begin with the Oregon Symphony and a healthy theater and musical district. On the more casual level are the ubiquitous coffee shops and more brewhouses than any other American city, many with jazz and blues performances. The world's largest bookstore, Powell's City of Books, anchors downtown. Many of the area sidewalks are adorned with literary quotes.

Among leading attractions is the Oregon Museum of Science and Industry (OMSI), the nation's fifth largest science museum. The Portland Art Museum houses one of the most comprehensive collections of Asian, Native American, and European art in the Pacific Northwest.

Portland's eastside is home to The Grotto, a place of inspiration and peace for visitors of every faith. The outdoor cathedral encompasses sixty-two acres of wooded beauty, gardens, fountains, and towering firs. One of the site's main draws is Our Lady's Grotto, a shrine carved into the face of a 110-foot cliff, and a white marble replica of Michelangelo's *Pieta*.

The origin of Portland's nickname as "The City of Roses" comes from the International Rose Test Garden; established in 1917 and boasting more than 519 varieties of blooms. Nearby in Washington Park is the Japanese Garden, which some call the most authentic of its type outside of Japan, with a tea house, five different gardens, and views of Portland and Mount Hood. Also nearby is the Oregon Zoo, home to more than 600 animals of some 200 species.

Museums in Portland

Founded in 1892, the **Portland Art Museum**'s treasures span thirty-five centuries of international art, one of the most comprehensive collections on the West Coast.

Monet, Renoir, Picasso, and Rodin share space with Native American and

Asian artwork. The permanent collection includes more than 32,000 works of art. The Vivian and Gordon Gilkey Center for Graphic Arts includes more than 22,000 works of art on paper, including prints, drawings, and photographs.

The Northwest Film Center at the museum presents films five nights a week; the center is also sponsor of the annual Portland International Film Festival.

The Butler Collection includes more than 1,800 Native American art pieces dating from the eighteenth century. One of the more unusual is a nine-foot-long Kwakiutl Potlatch dish representing a supernatural being named Tsonoqua; according to legend, she is a forest cannibal who bestows gifts upon those who meet her. Presumably the gifts do not include an invitation to dinner.

The museum, located at 1219 Southwest Park Avenue, is open Tuesday through Saturday 10 A.M. to 5 P.M., and Sunday noon to 5 P.M. The museum is also open the first Thursday of each month until 8 P.M. Admission: adult, ❸; senior, ❸; student (19 and older), ❷; child (5–18), ❷. For information, call ☎ (503) 226-2811. You can also consult 💻 www.pam.org.

One of the treasures of the **Oregon History Center** is a penny, although its historic worth may be much more. The penny on display is the piece used in the coin toss that decided Portland's name.

A large collection of photos and other documents are on display and available to researchers.

The center, at 1200 Southwest Park Avenue in Portland, is open year-round. From Tuesday to Saturday, the museum is open from 10 A.M. to 5 P.M.; on Thursday, until 8 P.M.; on Sunday, noon to 5 P.M. It is closed on Monday, except in summer months. For information, call ☎ (503) 306-5198 or consult 💻 www.ohs.org. Admission: adult, ❷; student, ❷; child (6–12), ❶.

Washington Park

Past downtown lie the West Hills, including the sprawling Washington Park. Within the park you'll find three of Portland's emeralds: the Oregon Zoo, the International Rose Test Garden, and the Japanese Garden.

For more than a century, the **Oregon Zoo** has been one of the premier attractions of the Pacific Northwest. The zoo's sixty-four acres are home to animals from all over the world, including elephants from Asia, penguins from Peru, and arctic polar bears.

The zoo opened in 1887 and was originally based on the private menagerie of Richard Knight, a local pharmacist. It moved from Washington Park to its present location in 1959.

The zoo is located at 4001 Southwest Canyon Road, just five minutes west of downtown Portland on Highway 26. Tri-Met Light Rail Service (MAX) stops 200 feet from the zoo entrance. For rail information, call ☎ (503) 238-7433; for zoo information, call ☎ (503) 226-1561 or consult 🖳 www.oregonzoo.org.

The zoo is open daily year-round, from 9 A.M. to 4 P.M. Admission: adult, ❸; senior (65+), ❷; child (3–11), ❷.

At the zoo, the Lilah Callen Holden Elephant Museum explores the long relationship between elephants and people. For information, call ☎ (503) 226-1561.

The **Washington Park and Zoo Railway** offers scenic excursions aboard diesel or steam-powered trains through the forests of Washington Park. At the Washington Park terminal there are lovely views of downtown Portland, Mount Hood, and Mount Saint Helens, and access to the International Rose Test Garden and the Japanese Garden.

All three of the trains were built to scale, five-sixths the size of the old narrow-gauge railways. It is the last railroad in the United States that has continually offered U.S. mail service. Letters deposited on the zoo railway receive a special hand-cancellation.

Mini-park. In a world of superlatives, Mill Ends Park claims the unusual title of the world's smallest park. The twenty-four inches of real estate at the corner of Southwest Naito Parkway and Taylor Street was made locally famous by a columnist for *The Oregonian*, Dick Fagan, who objected to an ugly pothole beneath his office window. He took it on himself to plant the hole with flowers, and write about the supposed goings-on in the "park," including the adventures of a leprechaun named Patrick O'Toole.

The four-mile round trip takes thirty-five minutes. The train runs weekends only from mid-April through the end of May 30, and then daily from Memorial Day through early October. It also operates evenings for ZooLights in the month of December.

Train rides: adult, ❶; senior (65+), ❶; child (3–11), ❶; child (2 and younger), free. Train riders must first pay zoo admission.

The zoo railway began with the move of the zoo in 1959. When plans for the small-gauge line were unveiled, train fans from around the region pitched in. School children sold "stock" at $1 per share and a children's book was sold to help pay for the zoo line.

The rolling stock includes the Zooliner, a diesel-powered streamliner replica of a classic General Motors Aerotrain. The Oregon Steam Locomotive is a replica of an 1800s streamer, patterned after the Virginia & Truckee Railroad's "Reno."

The **International Rose Test Garden**, the largest of three public rose gardens in Portland, is the oldest test garden in the United States, dating from 1917. The 4.5-acre garden, maintained by the Portland parks system, includes more than 8,000 roses from 550 varieties, with local favorites including Savoy Hotel, Livin' Easy, New Zealand, Climbing Ophelia, and Sweet Juliet.

From the terraced garden above the city, there's a terrific view of downtown Portland, Mount Hood, and Mount Saint Helens.

The garden, located at 400 Southwest Kingston Avenue, is open daily from 7 A.M. to 9 P.M. Open year-round, the best months for blooms are May through September. Admission is free, but donations are accepted.

For information, call ☎ (503) 823-3636 or consult 🖳 www.portlandparks.org.

Nearby, the **Japanese Garden** is as close as you can get to Japan without a passport. You can stroll through five meticulously landscaped gardens and take a break at the teahouse. Located at 611 Southwest Kingston Avenue, the garden is open year-round. Hours from October 1 to March 31 are 10 A.M.–4 P.M.; from April 1 to October 1, 10 A.M.–7 P.M. Admission: adult, ❸; senior, ❷; student, ❷; and child (5 and younger), free. For information, call ☎ (503) 223-4070 or ☎ (503) 223-1321.

The **World Forestry Center Museum** in Washington Park is an exploration of wood culture from around the world and the Pacific Northwest. The museum can trace its history back to the Lewis and Clark Centennial American Pacific Exposition and Oriental Fair that was held in Portland in 1905. One of the most popular exhibits at the fair was the Forestry Building; a giant log cabin. The cabin was a Portland landmark until it was destroyed by fire in 1964. After the fire, the Western Forestry Center was created as an educational institution with support from the timber museum and other sources. The center is based around its museum in Washington Park. In 1978, donated land added the Magness Memorial Tree Farm as a demonstration forest; in 1986, a global focus was added.

The host of the museum is a 60-foot-tall talking tree that will explain the story of the forest and its trees. Gallery exhibits include Forests of Stone: the Burnett Collection of Petrified Wood. Other exhibits include a recreated Pygmy settlement in a central African rain forest and an old-growth forest of the Pacific Northwest.

The museum is located at 4033 Southwest Canyon Road in Portland. For information, call ☎ (503) 228-1367 or consult 🖳 www.worldforest.org. The center is open 10 A.M. to 5 P.M., Memorial Day through Labor Day; and from 10 A.M. to 5 P.M. the rest of the year. Admission: adult, ❷; student, ❷; and senior, ❷.

In 1928, a committee of tree lovers in logging land recommended the creation of a municipal arboretum to preserve trees. The resulting 175-acre **Hoyt Arboretum** is home to some 850 species and trees, with 10 miles of hiking and strolling trails.

The site was once the Multnomah County Poor Farm. The original area had been a dense stand of Douglas Fir, which was gradually reduced to make room for different varieties of planted specimens. Hoyt Arboretum now has one of the largest collections of distinct species of gymnosperms (conifers) of any arboretum in the United States.

Among treasures is a Dawn Redwood, a species that became locally extinct eons ago. The Dawn Redwood was reintroduced from China, bearing its first cones when it was only four years old; the first cones produced in the Western Hemisphere in 50 million years.

The arboretum is in the Washington Park area at 4000 Fairview Boulevard. For information, call ☎ (503) 823-3654 or consult 🖳 www.parks. ci.portland.or.us. The grounds are open from 6 A.M. to 10 P.M. daily; the visitor center is open from 9 A.M. to 4 P.M. Free guided tours are offered Saturday and Sunday at 2 P.M. from April through October. Admission: free.

At the south end of the arboretum is the **Vietnam Veterans Living Memorial**, a black granite monument that spirals up a hill. The names of those killed or reported missing in action are inscribed on solemn markers.

Portland's Children's Museum is one of the oldest in the country, dating back to 1949. The initial collection of stuffed animals dates from 1895 to 1906.

Today the museum offers hands-on activities including a grocery store for kids, a bubble wall, and a clay shop. As this book goes to press, the museum is located at 3037 Southwest Second Avenue in Portland. But plans call for a move to a new home in mid-2001, the former site of the Oregon Museum of Science and Industry in Washington Park, across from the Oregon Zoo.

The museum may be closed from March through June of 2001 to allow for the move.

Our founder. Portlandia, a 36-foot, hammered-copper statue, reaches down to passersby from above the entrance to the Portland Building on Southwest Fifth Avenue between Main and Madison streets.

The statue is modeled after Lady Commerce, who appears on Portland's city seal. Too large to pass through the city's streets, Portlandia arrived in 1984 on a barge up the Willamette River.

For information, call ☎ (503) 823-2227 or consult 🖳 www.pdxchildrens museum.org. When operating, the museum is open year-round from 9 A.M. to 5 P.M., Tuesday through Sunday. Admission: ❷ per person (ages 1 and up).

Southeast Portland

One of the largest science museums in the nation, the **Oregon Museum of Science and Industry** includes hundreds of hands-on demonstrations of science and technology in six exhibit halls, plus a five-story domed Omnimax theater, the largest public planetarium in the Pacific Northwest; the museum also has its own submarine.

The museum's motion simulator ride carries as many as fifteen passengers; the capsule can move in six directions, making horizontal pitches, longitudinal rolls, and vertical lifts. The cabin employs a high-definition, rear-projection screen and surround-sound.

The ride can be reprogrammed with new adventures. One recent featured presentation was *Virtual Time Machine,* a whirlwind tour through major events in the Earth's history, which includes the birth of the planet and early life, the destruction of the dinosaurs, ancient Egypt, the voyage of Christopher Columbus, a World War I air battle, and man's first walk on the moon.

Docked alongside the museum is the U.S. Navy's last non-nuclear submarine, the USS *Blueback;* the vessel served thirty-one years in the Pacific Ocean. The sub was featured in the movie *The Hunt for Red October.* The 219-foot-long submarine squeezed a complement of eight officers and seventy-seven crew members aboard. Its maximum operating depth was 712 feet.

The Murdock Sky Theater features a state-of-the-art Digistar II star projector with many advanced features, which include video, computer-generated images, and other multimedia elements. The facility is the only major public planetarium in Oregon and Washington.

The museum is located at 1945 Southeast Water Avenue. For information, call ☎ (503) 797-6674 or consult 📖 www.omsi.edu.

The museum is open daily from Memorial Day to Labor Day, plus spring break, from 9:30 A.M. to 7 P.M. In the winter, from Labor Day to Memorial Day, the museum is open daily except Monday, with hours from 9:30 A.M. to 5:30 P.M.

General Admission: adult, ❸; youth (4–13), ❷. Omnimax Theater admission: adult, ❸; youth (4–13), ❷; senior, ❷. Motion simulator, Murdock Planetarium, laser matinee shows, submarine: ❷ each attraction. Laser evening show tickets are ❸. From 2 P.M. until closing on Thursday, general admission tickets for the planetarium, the submarine, and the Omnimax Theater (all three) is ❹.

You can also purchase a full museum package, which includes general admission, one Omnimax movie, one planetarium show or laser matinee show, and one submarine tour. Tickets: adult, ❹; youth, ❹.

Tours of the submarine are offered daily from 10 A.M. to 5 P.M.

The Grotto, officially known as the **National Sanctuary of Our Sorrowful Mother,** is a 62-acre Catholic sanctuary and botanical garden of the Friars of the Order of Servants of Mary.

The Grotto is one of the most popular attractions of Portland, drawing more than 175,000 guests of all faiths each year. Highlights include a marble replica of Michelangelo's *Pieta* carved into the base of a 110-foot cliff. An elevator travels to the top of the bluff to offer a panorama of the Columbia River Valley, the Cascade Mountain Range, and Mount Saint Helens. There is a Festival of Lights from November 30 until January 1.

The sanctuary is located at Northeast Eighty-Fifth Avenue and Northeast Sandy Boulevard in Portland. For information, call ☎ (503) 254-7371 or consult 📖 www.thegrotto.org. The Grotto is open daily. Admission is free; donations are welcomed. Garden tour: ❶.

Sunday Mass is conducted outdoors, weather permitting, at 10 A.M., and at noon from May to October. A weekday mass is celebrated at noon, and Saturday at 8 A.M.

Other Museums and Attractions in Portland

Pittock Mansion, the 1914 mansion of Henry Pittock, founder of Portland's daily newspaper, *The Oregonian*, is maintained with period furnishings and fine art. The National Historic Register property is on a lush 46-acre estate with views of the mountains, rivers, and the city of Portland.

The mansion is located at 3229 Northwest Pittock Drive. in Portland. For information, call ☎ (503) 823-3623. Open year-round, noon to 4 P.M. Admission: adult, ❷; senior (65+), ❷; and child (6–18), ❶.

For those of us old enough to remember, it's comforting to know that someone out there has collected a full set of Burma Shave signs that once studded the sides of American highways. Other treasures include a set of the dancing California Raisins made famous by Portland artist Will Vinton, and classic television commercials.

The **American Advertising Museum** is located at 5035 Southeast Twenty-Fourth Avenue in Portland. For information, call ☎ (503) 226-0000. The collection is open on Saturday from noon to 5 P.M. and by appointment at other times. Admission: adult, ❷; child (4–12) and senior, ❶; child (4 and younger), free.

The **Oregon Maritime Center & Museum** maintains a priceless collection of ship models, photos, and artifacts from the rich maritime history of the Portland region. Outside, docked on the Willamette River, is the steamer *Portland,* a working stream-powered tugboat that visitors can explore from stem to stern. The ship was used in the movie *Maverick,* starring Jodie Foster and Mel Gibson.

The museum is located at 113 Southwest Naito Parkway in Portland. For information, call ☎ (503) 224-7724. The center is open Friday through Sunday, 11 A.M.–4 P.M. Admission: adult, ❷; senior, ❶; youth (8–16), ❶; child (younger than 8), free.

Begun in 1950 by the Portland Chapter of the American Rhododendron Society as a test garden, over the years the **Crystal Springs Rhododendron Garden** has developed into a showplace for "rhodys" of all types, with some 1,500 varieties of rhododendrons and azaleas on display. All the plants in the seven-acre garden, which has a spring-fed lake, have been donated. In recent years, trees and shrubs that offer beautiful fall color were added for year-round beauty.

The garden is on Southeast Twenty-Eighth Avenue, north of Woodstock, in Portland. For information, call ☎ (503) 771-8386 or consult 🖳 www.parks.ci.portland.or.us. Admission: adult, $3, Thursday through Sunday from February through Labor Day; free every day remainder of the year.

Founded in 1974, the **Portland Saturday Market** is the largest open-air crafts market in the United States, drawing about 750,000 visitors each year. Never mind the name, the market is open every Saturday and Sunday from March through Christmas Eve. The market is also open for three or four weekdays just prior to Christmas for its annual Festival of the Last Minute.

You'll find more than 250 craft booths, as well as an international food court and live entertainment.

On Saturday, the market is open from 10 A.M. to 5 P.M.; on Sunday, hours are 11 A.M. to 4:30 P.M. Operations go on rain or shine; the market has only closed twice in its history, once for a blizzard and once for a volcanic eruption.

The rules of the market demand that everything is handcrafted by the vendors and sold by the person who made it. More than half of the craftspeople derive a majority of their income from sales at the market.

The market is located in the Old Town District, at 108 West Burnside Street, Portland. Admission: free. For information, call ☎ (503) 222-6072 or consult 🖳 www.saturdaymarket.org.

It says a lot about the soul of a city that one of its leading attractions is a bookstore. This is, though, no ordinary bookstore: **Powell's City of Books,** with more than a million volumes, is the nation's largest bookstore.

You'll be issued a map to find your way around the block-square store; it's located at 1005 West Burnside Street. The store is open daily from 9 A.M. to 11 P.M. For information, call ☎ (503) 228-4651 or consult 🖳 www.powells.com.

Portland's Cultural History

Few places in the Northwest are so full of cultural memories from very different eras as is **McMenamins Crystal Ballroom**. The Crystal Ballroom was built in 1914 and immediately became the heart of the cultural scene of the time. Much later, in the 1960s, the Crystal was one of the most important stops on the rock 'n roll tour, hosting some of the most important names of that time.

The ballroom has one of the only remaining "floating" dance floors; the surface is attached to 800 wooden rockers below the surface.

The tango was against the law in Portland in 1913, enforced by the official dance hall inspector, who was in charge of preventing immoral activity, including saloons, bowling alleys, vaudeville houses, and movie theaters. Despite the atmosphere, in January 1914 impresario Montrose Ringler opened Cotillion Hall, later renamed the Crystal Ballroom.

The ballroom was decorated with intricate wood and plasterwork, lit from above by suspended glass chandeliers. Within, the room featured pastoral murals, floor-to-ceiling windows, and palm fronds.

The rockers beneath the floor could be adjusted by a ratcheted gear to match various dance styles. It is one of the few such suspended floors still in existence.

In the early '60s, soul and R&B stars including James Brown, Ike & Tina Turner, B. B. King, Etta James, and others held the stage. In its rock heyday in 1967 and 1968, the Crystal played host to groups that include the Grateful Dead, Buffalo Springfield, Quicksilver Messenger Service, Jefferson Airplane, and many others.

The Crystal Ballroom had been closed and neglected for nearly three decades before it was restored by brothers Brian and Mike McMenamin, head of the pub and brewery chain that bears their name.

The Crystal Ballroom now offers shows and special events. Ringlers Pub on the first floor features pub fare and beer.

The ballroom is located at 1332 West Burnside Street in Portland. For information, call ☎ (503) 225-0047 or consult 💻 www.mcmenamins.com. Information on shows is available at ☎ (503) 225-5555, ext. 8811.

And then there is the king of pop culture, at least in some peoples' eyes. The **24-Hour Church of Elvis** is a semi-serious shrine to The King, complete with weddings, confessions, marriage counseling, and photo opportunities with "The King," or at least a reasonable equivalent. The performance art museum is located at 720 Southwest Ankeny Street. For information and an appointment to visit, call ☎ (503) 226-3671 or consult a Web page at 💻 www.churchofelvis.com.

Portland Rose Festival

There are a whole bunch of roses, but that's hardly all there is to be seen at the month-long **Portland Rose Festival.**

Under the umbrella of roses, you'll also find the Portland Art Show, visiting military vessels, car races, the Grand Floral Parade, the nation's largest children's parade, dragon boat races, the downtown Starlight Parade, a hot-air balloon festival, and an air show.

The **Portland Arts Festival** began in 1998 in the heart of the city's cultural district, the South Park Blocks at Portland State University. The free event features the works of 125 outstanding artists from Oregon and across the United States, competing for cash prizes. Tents display works including paintings, photography, sculpture, and jewelry; most pieces are for sale, and the artists are there to discuss their works.

Live entertainment is presented with local and touring bands. You can also sample fine food and local beer and wine at the Culinary Arts Courtyard.

The festivals take place all across the Greater Portland Area and surrounding communities. For information, call ☎ (503) 227-2681 or consult 🖳 www. rosefestival.org.

An unusual, international competition are the **Portland-Kaohsiung Sister City Dragon Boat Races,** held in mid-June on the Willamette River at Tom McCall Waterfront Park. Kaohsiung is a port city on the island nation of Taiwan.

Each spring the dragon boats are blessed and "awakened" when the fierce eyes of the dragon are painted; the dragons are asked to protect the city and provide prosperity and safety.

The **Rose Festival Air Show,** held at Hillsboro Airport in late June, is considered one of the top aviation events in the nation. Aircraft from biplanes to fighter jets, and just about every unusual permutation in between, perform for huge crowds.

There are stunt shows, military fly-bys, and specialty acts such as Robosaurus, a forty-two-foot tall, fire-breathing dinosaur robot that picks up and crushes small planes and cars.

Ticket prices range from about $8 to $18, with reduced prices on tickets purchased in advance. For information, call ☎ (503) 821-4396 from late April until the show date; prior to April, call ☎ (503) 227-2681.

Portland Theater, Culture, and Sports

The four theaters of the **Portland Center For the Performing Arts** entertain more than a million visitors each year with shows from ballet to Broadway.

The Center includes the **Portland Civic Auditorium** on Southwest Third Street between Market and Clay streets; the **Arlene Schnitzer Concert Hall** on Southwest Broadway at Main Street; and the **New Theatre Building**, also at Southwest Broadway at Main Street, which contains the **Newmark Theatre** and the **Dolores Winningstad Theatre.**

The ticket office is located in the lobby of the New Theatre Building, and is open Monday to Saturday from 10 A.M.–6 P.M., and two hours prior to showtime. The Civic Auditorium box office is open on days of performances only. The center is located at 1111 Southwest Broadway. For information, call ☎ (503) 248-4335 or consult 🖳 www.pcpa.com.

Free tours are offered Wednesday at 11 A.M., Saturday every half hour from 11 A.M. to 1 P.M., and on the first Thursday of every month at 6 P.M. Tours leave from the lobby of the New Theatre Building at Southwest Broadway and Main. Call to confirm availability.

The **Portland Civic Auditorium** is home to touring Broadway shows, ballets, and grand operas. Resident companies include the Portland Opera, Oregon Ballet Theatre, Oregon Children's Theatre, and Portland Community Concerts.

The **Arlene Schnitzer Concert Hall** is home to the world's largest electronic organ, originally built for Carnegie Hall. Resident companies include the Oregon Symphony, the Portland Arts and Lecture Series, the Portland Youth Philharmonic, and the Institute for Science, Engineering and Public Policy. The impressive Italian rococo revival building is on the National Historic Register.

The "Schnitz" was built in the 1920s as the Rapp Paramount Theater, a vaudeville palace. The Oregon Symphony, founded in 1896, is the oldest symphony in the West.

The New Theatre Building, a 1987 addition, includes state-of-the-art technical facilities. The Newmark Theatre was designed for drama productions; resident companies include Portland Center Stage and The Musical Theatre Company. The Dolores Winningstad Theatre was patterned after a Shakespearean courtyard stage; resident companies include Tygres Heart Shakespeare Company and Tears of Joy Puppet Theatre.

Other Theater Companies

Artists Repertory Theatre. 1516 Southwest Alder Street. ☎ (503) 241-9807. 🖳 www.artistsrep.org. September through June.

Echo Theatre. 1515 Southeast Thirty-Seventh Avenue. ☎ (503) 231-1232. Home of Do Jump! Movement Theatre, a school for acrobatics and trapeze, and stages for local and touring artists. October through May.

The Miracle Theatre Group (Teatro Milagro). 425 Southeast Sixth Street. ☎ (503) 236-7253. 🖳 www.milagro.org. The Northwest's largest Hispanic theater company with presentations in Portland and touring companies throughout the region.

The Northwest Childrens Theater. 1819 Northwest Everett Street. ☎ (503) 222-2190. October through May.

Oregon Children's Theatre Company. ☎ (503) 228-9571. 🖳 www.octc.org. Performances at Civic Auditorium and Portland Community College's Sylvania Campus in December, January, and April.

Portland Center Stage. 1111 Southwest Broadway. ☎ (503) 248-6309. September through April at Newmark Theatre of the Portland Center for the Performing Arts. Performances from September through April.

Stark Raving Theatre. The Asylum: 4319 Southeast Hawthorne Boulevard. ☎ (503) 232-7072. The Sanctuary: 3430 Southeast Belmont Street. ☎ (503) 232-7072. Modern works and classics.

Tygres Heart Shakespeare Company. 2119 North Kerby Avenue. ☎ (503) 288-8400. All Shakespeare. October through May at the Winningstad Theatre at the Portland Center for the Performing Arts.

The Musical Theatre Company. 1436 Southwest Montgomery Street. ☎

(503) 224-8730. From Gilbert and Sullivan to Brecht and Weil, at the Eastside Performance Center at Southeast Fourteenth Avenue and Stark.

Portland Opera Presents the KeyBank Best of Broadway. ☎ (503) 241-1802. Touring Broadway year-round at Civic Auditorium.

Tears of Joy Puppet Theatre. 1111 Southwest Broadway. ☎ (360) 695-3050. Winningstad Theatre at the Portland Center for the Performing Arts.

Dance Companies

Do Jump! 1515 Southeast Thirty-Seventh Avenue. ☎ (503) 231-1232. Dancers, acrobats, and trapeze artists.

Dreams Well Studio. 2857 Southeast Stark Street. ☎ (503) 231-0176.

Oregon Ballet Theatre. 1120 Southwest Tenth Avenue. ☎ (503) 227-0977, ext. 131. 🖳 www.obt.org. Productions at the Portland Center for the Performing Arts from September through May and regional and national tours.

Northwest Afrikan American Ballet. ☎ (503) 287-8852. Original choreography inspired by traditional dances from the Senegal, Gambia, Mali, and Guinea regions of West Africa.

Musical Performances

Oregon Symphony Association. 711 Southwest Alder Street, Suite 200. ☎ (503) 228-4294. Classical to pop, from September through mid-June.

Portland Opera. 1515 Southwest Morrison Street. ☎ (503) 241-1407. 🖳 www.portland opera.org. Performances at the Civic Auditorium from September through June.

Portland Youth Philharmonic. 1119 Southwest Park Avenue. ☎ (503) 223-5939. 🖳 www.portlandyouthphil.org. The oldest ensemble of its kind in the United States, dating back to 1924. Performances are held at the Arlene Schnitzer Concert Hall from November through May.

The more than 260 student musicians, ranging in age from 8 to 22, are selected in open auditions each season. The Philharmonic offers fall, winter, and spring concerts; the Concert-at-Christmas features the Conservatory Orchestra, Young String Ensemble, and Alumni Orchestra.

Portland Baroque Orchestra. 425 Southwest Twentieth Avenue. ☎ (503) 222-6000. 🖳 www.pbo.org. Baroque and classical music dating back to the 1600s, presented from October through April at Trinity Cathedral and Marylhurst College.

The Culture Bus

Who says buses lack culture? Certainly not the passengers on ART, the Cultural Bus. Officially known as bus #63, the vehicle links a dozen major Portland attractions, all for a very refined fare of about $1.20.

The bus, painted as a moving mural by local artist Henk Pender, takes riders to the International Rose Test Garden, the Japanese Garden, Lloyd Center shopping mall and ice rink, Metro Washington Park Zoo, Oregon Convention Center, Oregon History Center, Oregon Museum of Science and Industry (OMSI), Portland Art Museum, Portland Center for the Performing Arts, Portland Oregon Visitors Association's downtown visitor information center, Rose Quarter: Memorial Coliseum and Rose Garden arena, and Tom McCall Waterfront Park.

The bus operates daily, departing from Fourth Avenue and Main in downtown Portland. In addition to single fares, a full-day pass can also be purchased from the driver for ❷ and is good on all bus lines as well as the MAX light rail line. For a complete schedule, call Tri-Met at ☎ (503) 238-7433 or visit the Portland Oregon Visitors Association's visitor information center.

First Thursday

Once a month, on the first Thursday, art galleries in downtown Portland put on a special party, with openings for new exhibitions, receptions with artists, and special entertainment.

The heart of the gallery district is in the Old Town and Pearl districts, both within easy walking distance of the core downtown area. There is also a free First Thursday shuttle bus, which runs every half hour from 7:15 to 9:15 P.M., between downtown locations.

Sightseeing and Dinner Cruises

The Portland *Spirit,* and her smaller sister ships *Willamette Star* and the *Crystal Dolphin* offer lunch, brunch, and dinner cruises, plus Saturday moonlight dance cruises on the Willamette River and Columbia River.

The ships operate year-round. Dinner cruises: adult, about $55; senior and child, about $50. Two-hour lunch cruises: adult, about $30; senior, about $23; and child about $21. Midday cruises are also available without a meal: adult, ❹; senior, ❹; and child, ❸.

For information, call ☎ (800) 224-3901 or ☎ (503) 224-3900, or consult 🖳 www.portlandspirit.com.

The Sternwheelers *Columbia Gorge, Marine Park,* and *Rose* offer sightseeing and dinner cruises on the Columbia and Willamette Rivers.

For information on the *Columbia Gorge* and *Marine Park,* call ☎ (503) 223-3928. For information on the *Rose,* call ☎ (503) 286-7673.

Willamette Jetboats depart from the submarine dock at the Oregon Museum of Science and Industry and travel upriver past waterfront to Willamette Falls; the return trip views Portland's skyline from the water. The boats operate May through October. For information, call ☎ (503) 231-1532.

Sports and Recreation

The local kings of the hill are the Portland Trail Blazers, a powerhouse in the National Basketball Association.

Portland Trail Blazers. The National Basketball Association season runs from mid-October through June; the Blazers play to mostly sellout crowds at the Rose Garden arena. ☎ (503) 234-9291. 🖳 www.nba.com/blazers/.

The Winter Hawks. The Western Hockey League team plays from October through March at the Memorial Coliseum or the Rose Garden arena. ☎ (503) 238-6366. 🖳 www.winterhawks.com.

Tri City Rattlers. The Class A baseball team of the Northwest League plays thirty-eight home games in Pasco, Washington, from June through September. ☎ (503) 553-5400. 📖 www.pgepark.com.

Portland Pythons. The indoor professional soccer team plays at the Rose Garden arena from August through November. ☎ (503) 684-5425, ext. 14.

Portland Meadows. Horse racing from October through April. In the summer, the Meadows is used for concerts and outdoor events. ☎ (503) 285-9144. 📖 www.portlandmeadows.com.

Multnomah Greyhound Park. Greyhound dog racing from May through September. Fairview. ☎ (503) 667-7700. 📖 www.ez2winmgp.com.

Portland International Raceway. Auto racing, including the Championship Auto Racing Teams (CART) World Series event during the Portland Rose Festival in June. ☎ (503) 823-7223. 📖 www.teleport.com/~autorace/pir/.

The Bridges of Multnomah County

Portland is a city of bridges, with seventeen significant crossings that include the world's oldest working lift bridge (Hawthorne) and other notable structures.

Here are some of the more notable bridges, listed as you would find them heading inland on the Willamette River.

The **Saint Johns Bridge**, opened in 1931, is Portland's only suspension bridge; at the time of its opening, Saint Johns was the longest rope-strand suspension bridge in the world. The bridge is named for the community at its east end, which was named in honor of settler James Johns, who began a rowboat ferry system near the current bridge in 1852.

The **Fremont Bridge**, the most recent span of the Willamette River, opened in 1973; its 1,255-foot main span is the longest of any in Oregon. The bridge is named after explorer and army officer John Charles Fremont, who blazed the Oregon Trail in 1842 and later a route to California from The Dalles. Fremont ran for president in 1856 as a Republican anti-slavery candidate.

The **Broadway Bridge**, opened in 1913, is the longest drawbridge in Portland, a bascule design that uses a weight to counterbalance the lifting portion like a giant seesaw.

The **Steel Bridge**, opened in 1912, is an unusual design with separate decks for trains and automobiles; the lower deck can move independently of the upper. Today, the rail deck of the Steel Bridge is crossed by Portland's MAX light rail system.

The **Hawthorne Bridge** dates back to 1910, one of three bridges in the Portland area built by the inventor of the vertical-lift drawbridge, John Alexander Low Waddell; today it is the world's oldest working vertical-lift bridge.

The **Marquam Bridge** is the busiest crossing in Portland. It closed the final gap in the interstate highway system from California to Washington in 1966.

The Fountains of Portland

Portland is also a city of fountains, from antique civic monuments to modern art.

Among the most famous are the **Benson Bubblers**, commissioned in 1912 by lumber baron Simon Benson. Benson donated twenty bronze fountains to the city, and the government later installed forty more. The teetotaling Benson once claimed that saloon sales dropped by 40 percent after the bubblers were installed.

David P. Thompson, former governor of the Idaho territory, ambassador to Turkey, and Portland's mayor from 1879–1882, gave the bronze **Elk Fountain** to the city in 1900 to commemorate the animals that grazed in the wilderness around Portland. The sculpture, on Southwest Main Street between Southwest Third and Fourth avenues, sits on a granite base and reservoir, which was originally designed as a watering trough for horses. The sculpture was done by Roland Hinton Perry, whose spectacular Fountain of Neptune stands at the front of the Library of Congress in Washington, D.C.

For the 1888 dedication of the **Skidmore Fountain** on Southwest First Avenue and Ankeny Street at Ankeny Plaza, brewer Henry Weinhard offered to pump beer from his brewery into the fountain's pipes. City fathers declined the offer. The fountain's upper bowl is supported by four female figures; the bottom pool still has brass rings that held copper cups for drinking. Four lower troughs, filled by spillover from the bottom pool, were designed for dogs and horses. The fountain, the oldest piece of public art in Portland, is inscribed "Good Citizens are the Riches of a City."

Rebecca at the Well recounts the biblical legend of Abraham's search for a bride for Isaac; Rebecca's gracious act of drawing water for the camels of Abraham's servant identified her as the bride-to-be. The bronze and sandstone fountain was designed in 1926 and stands on South Park between Southwest Salmon and Main streets.

More recent watery works of art include the **Ira Keller Memorial Fountain**, facing the Portland Civic Auditorium on Southwest Fourth Avenue between Market and Clay streets. The top level is made up of brooks that run through a tree-shaded plaza, overflowing to create a waterfall. There's a bench behind the waterfall.

The **Lovejoy Fountain** at the Portland Center Building on Southwest Hall Street evokes the rivers of the High Sierras, spouting water from a concrete mountaintop to a canyon and wading pool below. The fountain is named for Asa Lovejoy, cofounder of the city of Portland.

Salmon Street Springs in Tom McCall Waterfront Park at the end of Salmon Street has 185 jets programmed to change with the city's mood. At full capacity, the fountain recycles 4,924 gallons of water per minute. The fountain is most popular on hot summer days when it becomes an outdoor cooler.

Portland Breweries

If you can't find a good glass of beer in Portland, you probably don't like beer.

The area claims the mantle of "Microbrew Capital of the World." By some estimations, Portland has more breweries and brew pubs per capita—about forty-three in 2000—than any other city in the United States.

In late July, the **Oregon Brewers Festival**, the largest event of its kind in North America, draws tens of thousands of connoisseurs to Tom McCall Waterfront Park to sample some seventy beers produced by local and visiting brewers. For information, call ☎ (503) 778-5917.

Admission to the festival is free; there is a small charge for a souvenir mug, and an additional fee for beer tokens, which are required for sampling brews. Local restaurants offer samples of their fare at booths, and musical entertainment is featured throughout the weekend.

For more methodical planning, you can obtain a copy of *Microbreweries in Oregon,* a brochure and map sold by the Oregon Brewers Guild. For information, call ☎ (503) 295-1862. You can also consult 🖳 www.oregonbeer.org/~beer.

Oregon's mild climate, similar to that of Europe's growing regions, is ideal for producing plentiful crops of hops; the state produces 19 percent of the nation's hops. In the Willamette Valley alone, more than fourteen different hop varieties are grown. The Cascade Hop, developed by Oregon State University, is ranked among the finest in the world.

Regional Craft Breweries

BridgePort Brewing Company. 1313 Northwest Marshall Street. ☎ (503) 241-7179. 🖳 www.firkin.com. Brewery tours are offered daily at 2 P.M. and 5 P.M. The Brew Pub is open daily from 11:30 A.M. to 11 P.M. and until midnight on Friday and Saturday; on Sunday, the pub is open from 1 P.M. to 10 P.M.

Production now reaches 25,000 barrels in a century-old rope warehouse in Portland's historic Pearl District; what looks like ivy climbing the outside of the building is actually hops.

BridgePort produces a variety of British-style ales, including "firkin" India Pale Ale (IPA) and Porter, as well as Extra Special Bitter (ESB) and Black Strap Stout. The brewery's flagship beer is Blue Heron Amber Ale, named in honor of Portland's official city bird, the Great Blue Heron.

The brewery is also famous for its pizza, which includes an unusual but no-longer secret ingredient: wort, a byproduct of beer production that gives the dough an unusual, nutty flavor.

BridgePort recently opened a second pub, the **BridgePort Ale House,** located at 3632 Southeast Hawthorne Boulevard on Portland's eastside. For information, call ☎ (503) 233-6540.

Full Sail Brewing Company. 506 Columbia Street, Hood River. ☎ (541) 386-2281 or ☎ (888) 254-2337. 🖳 www.fullsailbrewing.com.

The Brewery and Tasting Room are open from May to September, daily from noon to 8 P.M.; for the remainder of the year, hours are Thursday to Sunday from noon to 8 P.M. Tours are available every hour upon request.

Full Sail offers twelve distinctive lagers and ales including the award-winning Full Sail Amber Ale.

The company also operates a satellite brewery adjacent to the McCormick & Schmick's Harborside Pilsner Room, located in the RiverPlace Marina complex. For information, call ☎ (503) 222-5343.

Portland Brewing Company. 2730 Northwest Thirty-First Avenue. ☎ (503) 228-5269. 🖳 www.portlandbrew.com. Tours are offered on Saturday from 1 P.M. to 5 P.M.

The brewery is located in the Guilds Lake Industrial District in Northwest Portland, with a brew pub built around 140-barrel copper brewing vessels, imported from the Sixenbrau Brewery, whose legacy dates back to the sixteenth century in Nordlingern, Bavaria. Favorite beers include Portland Ale, MacTarnahan's Amber Ale, Oregon Honey Beer, Wheat Berry Brew, Haystack Black Porter, and Zigzag River Lager.

In 1852, German immigrant Henry Saxer established the first brewery in the Pacific Northwest in Portland. Saxer Brewing Company, re-established in 1992, merged with Portland Brewing in 2000.

Widmer Brothers Brewing Company. 929 North Russell Street. ☎ (503) 281-2437. 🖳 www.widmer.com.

Brewery tours are offered Friday at 3 P.M. and Saturday at 1 P.M. and 2 P.M.

The **Widmer Gasthaus Brew Pub** at the brewery is open daily from 11 A.M. to 10 P.M. and until 1 A.M. on Friday and Saturday.

Widmer Brothers Brewing Company is the top-selling craft brew producer in the Pacific Northwest and one of the largest in the nation. Specialties include America's Original Hefeweizen, Widberry, Blackbier, Amberbier, Vienna, Czech Pilsner, and Altbier. Seasonal offerings include Winternacht, Doppelbock, and Oktoberfest.

The **Widmer Brewing Company at the B. Moloch/Heathman Bakery and Pub** is in downtown Portland across the street from the Portland Center for the Performing Arts, serving as a pilot plant for new recipes and brewing techniques and offering a pub menu.

Another Widmer Brewing Company location is at the Center Court Café near the Rose Garden arena. The pub includes Widmer Cascades, a waterfall over glass covered with a special polymer film that changes from light to dark amber, creating the illusion of a huge wall of beer.

Hair of the Dog Brewing Company. 4509 Southeast Twenty-Third Avenue. ☎ (503) 232-6585. 🖳 www.hairofthedog.com.

Brewery tours by appointment only. The brewery is open weekdays from 9 A.M. to 5 P.M.

A micro-microbrewery that produces the Adam (a hearty Old-World ale), and the Golden Rose (a Belgium Tripel-style ale) in small batches in an old Campbell's Soup kettle. The brewery, in Southeast Portland's warehouse district, conditions its beer, the beer refermenting in the bottle and improving with age like wine. Its award-winning beers have such a high alcohol content, and are targeted for such a unique market, that the company must use a wine distributor to sell its products.

Lucky Labrador Brewing Company. 915 Southeast Hawthorne Boulevard. ☎ (503) 236-3555. 🖳 www.LuckyLab.com.

The brew pub is open daily from 11 A.M. to midnight, and Sunday from noon to 10 P.M.

The brewery and pub is located in an historic warehouse not far from Portland's lively Hawthorne Boulevard. Some of Lucky Lab's most popular brews include the Black Lab Stout, Hawthorne's Best Bitter, and König's Kölsch (a lighter, German-style brew).

McMenamins Pubs and Breweries. 2126 Southwest Halsey Street, Troutdale. ☎ (800) 669-8610. 🖳 www.mcmenamins.com.

Brewery tours weekdays 11 A.M., 1:30 P.M., and 5:30 P.M.; Saturday 10 A.M., 12:30 P.M., 3 P.M. The pub is open daily from 11 A.M. to 1 A.M.

The brew pub empire of brothers Mike and Brian McMenamin extends to some thirty brew pubs in the Portland metropolitan area, and another dozen elsewhere in the state and in Washington.

McMenamins Edgefield, twenty minutes east of Portland, sprawls across twenty-five acres; the property was once the site of the Multnomah County Poor Farm. The McMenamins converted the site into a resort with more than 100 guest rooms, a 150-seat movie theater, a fine-dining restaurant, a pub, a brewery, a winery, and herb gardens.

Also under the McMenamins banner are three movie theater/pubs: the Mission Theatre & Pub in Northwest Portland, the Bagdad Theatre & Pub in the Hawthorne District, and the Power Station Theater at McMenamins Edgefield. (Except for the 6 P.M. showing at the Power Station and matinee showings at the Bagdad, minors are not allowed in the theater/pubs.)

In 1997 the company reopened the historic Crystal Ballroom, now dubbed as **McMenamins Crystal Ballroom.** The structure, built in 1914, had been closed and neglected for nearly three decades.

Crystal Ballroom and Brewery tours are offered by appointment only. (See the discussion of the Crystal Ballroom earlier in this chapter.) For information, call ☎ (503) 225-0047, ext. 8811 or consult 🖳 www.mcmenamins.com.

The Old Market Pub & Brewery. 6959 Southwest Multnomah Boulevard. ☎ (503) 244-0450.

Brewery tours by appointment only. The Brew Pub is open Monday to Thursday 11 A.M. to midnight, Friday and Saturday until 1 A.M., and Sunday until 11 P.M.

The brewery is located in a renovated old-time produce market in the Multnomah Village area, about five miles from downtown Portland. Specialties include the very hoppy Backward Bitter, Mr. Toad's Wild Red, Mighty Mike's Manpower Stout, Great White Wheat, and Pinochle Pale. The signature offering is Gastropod Golden, a dry-hopped brew that is full of flavorful Münich malt.

Philadelphia's Steaks & Hoagies. 6410 Southeast Milwaukie Avenue. (503) 239-8544.

Brewery tours available on request. The restaurant is open daily from 9 A.M. to 11 P.M. weekends; 9 A.M. to 10 P.M. weekdays.

A tiny microbrewery in the Westmoreland Business District of Southeast Portland, one of the smallest licensed breweries in America. Specialties include Double Hopped Eagle Ale, Spectrum Amber, South Street Porter (offering a faint taste of chocolate), and Betsy Ross Light. The pub specializes in Philly cheesesteaks.

Rock Bottom Brewery. 10 Southwest Morrison Street. ☎ (503) 796-2739.

Brewery tours on request. The Brew Pub is open daily from 11 A.M. to 1 A.M., and until midnight on Sunday.

Specialties include Cryin' Coyote Western Ale, White Pelican Pale Ale, Big Horn Nut Brown Ale, and Black Seal Stout. Upstairs is a billiard parlor.

Chapter 5
Oregon's Scenic Highs and Lows

Columbia River Gorge and Mount Hood

One of the wonders of the world, sought after by scores of explorers, the **Columbia River Gorge** lies about an hour east of Portland.

The gorge, the only sea level passage through the Cascade Mountain Range, was explored in 1792 by Captain Robert Gray. The Lewis and Clark Expedition, sent by President Thomas Jefferson to explore the northwest and find a passage to the Pacific, went through the gorge in 1804 and 1805.

The river races westward from the desert through the mountains to the Pacific Ocean. Its path was carved by glaciers, Ice Age floodwaters, and volcanic lava flows. Today, the Columbia River forms a natural border between Oregon and Washington. Snowmelt from the Cascades nourishes numerous high waterfalls along the meandering Historic Columbia River Highway, known as the scenic highway. Dozens of hiking trails run throughout the gorge, ranging from sea level to heights of 5,000 feet.

The narrow gorge forms a natural wind tunnel, which attracts thrill-seeking windsurfers, especially in the summer when races are scheduled.

The **Columbia River Gorge National Scenic Area** is home to **Multnomah Falls**. At 620 feet, it is the fourth highest in the United States. **Beacon Rock**, an 800-foot volcanic core on the north side of the Columbia River, is the largest formation of its kind in the United States.

Native American tribes have hunted and fished the river for thousands of years, and the local tribes still have exclusive fishing rights on many sections.

The eastern entrance to the gorge is **The Dalles**, which was an important stop on the Oregon Trail, and before then a transfer point for French Canadian fur trappers sending their harvests to Fort Vancouver. The French named the rocky outcropping on the Columbia River rapids Les Dalles, or "the flagstones." Today's pronunciation is "The Dalls," as in pals.

With the development of the Oregon Trail and expansion in the west, The Dalles served as a terminal for steamboats on the river and stagecoaches heading into the interior. Later on the railroad came through the same corridor.

The **Fort Dalles Museum** occupies the site of the original Surgeon's Quarters

Key to Prices
❶ $3 and under
❷ $3 to $6
❸ $6 to $10
❹ $10 to $15
When prices are listed as a range, this indicates various combination options are available. Most attractions offer reduced-price tickets for children and many have family rates that include two adults and two or three children.

at Fort Dalles, established in 1857. The museum includes pioneer memorabilia and a collection of horse-drawn vehicles. The **Anderson Farmhouse National Landmark** is located nearby at Fifteenth and Garrison streets. Open daily from March to October from 9:30 A.M. to 5 P.M.; for the remainder of the year, it is open weekends from 10 A.M. to 4 P.M. and Monday, Thursday, and Friday from 1 to 4 P.M. For information, call ☎ (541) 296-4547.

You can explore the gorge's history at the **Columbia Gorge Discovery Center & Wasco County Historical Museum** at The Dalles. Exhibits reach back 40 million years when fiery volcanoes, massive landslides, and raging floods created the gorge. You'll learn how plants and animals colonized the gorge and surrounding rain forests and arid deserts, about ten thousand years of Native American life, and the triumphs and tragedies of the early explorers and pioneers.

The museum, located at 5000 Discovery Drive in The Dalles, is open every day from 10 A.M. to 6 P.M.; closed Christmas, Thanksgiving, and New Year's. Admission: adult, ❸; senior (62+), ❷; child (6–16), ❷; child (5 and younger), free. For information, call ☎ (541) 296-8600 or consult 💻 www.gorgediscovery.org.

For information on the region, call The Dalles Area Chamber of Commerce at ☎ (800) 255-3385, or consult 💻 www.thedalleschamber.com.

Scenic Drive: Columbia River Highway

Portland to The Dalles

Eighty-two miles one-way. Allow at least three to five hours to explore, plus ninety minutes for a return by interstate highway. The waterfalls are most abundant in the spring; driving conditions can be difficult in the winter.

Depart from **Portland** east on I-84 toward **Troutdale**. Depart the interstate at Exit 17, heading south to the Historic Columbia River Highway. The road climbs to Springdale and Corbett, offering spectacular views of Mount Hood.

Crown Point marks the western entry to the Gorge. At Crown Point State Park, **Vista House** has drawn visitors since 1916. The art nouveau observatory looks down on Beacon Rock across the gorge on the Washington side.

To the east and ahead of you, the Columbia River extends to the horizon. The road follows a delicately engineered path that has memorable switchbacks and curves. Further along, the road enters into a mossy rain forest and drops another 600 feet in a series of switchbacks. Within five miles, you'll come to four waterfalls: **Latourell**, **Shepperd's Dell**, **Bridal Veil**, and **Wahkeena**. (There's a parking area and a footpath close to each of the falls.)

Finally, there's **Multnomah Falls**, the most spectacular of all the cataracts. The water drops 620 feet in two tiers. You can hike from the Multnomah Falls Lodge to the Simon Benson Bridge, which crosses the lower cascade.

The road heads north to the shoreline near the **Bonneville Dam.** The struc-

Vista House perches on a bluff above the Columbia River Gorge
Photo by Steve Terrill, courtesy Oregon Tourism Division

ture, completed in 1937, was the first major dam on the Columbia River. It backs up the river some fifteen miles to the east; its hydroelectric plant produces more than a million kilowatts of power per day.

You can cross over the top of the two powerhouse dams. In Washington at the Bradford Island Visitor Center salmon and steelhead trout climb a fish ladder around the dam. Further on is the Visitor Orientation Center where you can take a self-guided tour of the hydroelectric plant and the interior of the dam.

The visitor centers are open daily from 9 A.M. to 5 P.M. from May to October. Admission: free. For information, call ☎ (541) 374-8820.

Back on the Columbia River Highway on the Oregon side of the river, it's on to Dodson, rejoining Interstate 84 for the stretch to Hood River and on to Mosier. Depart the highway at Exit 76 and head for Mosier.

A center of the fruit farm industry, **Mosier** was bypassed when the Interstate was built in the 1950s and remains happily frozen in time. Past the town is the **Rowena Plateau**, home of the **Tom McCall Preserve**, a 230-acre refuge for native plants and animals. At the Mayer State Park, the **Rowena Crest Overlook** is an eastern bookmark to Crown Point; its view includes the Rowena Loops, where the road descends to the town of Rowena.

The scenic highway ends at **The Dalles**, the eastern entry to the gorge, at the **Columbia Gorge Discovery Center** near Crate's Point.

You can make the return trip to Portland on Interstate 84 westbound.

For more information on the Historic Columbia River Highway, call the Columbia River Gorge National Scenic Center in Wacoma Center at ☎ (541) 386-2333, or The Dalles Area Chamber of Commerce at ☎ (800) 255-3385.

Mount Hood

Southeast of Portland, the awe-inspiring cone of Mount Hood, towering to 11,235 feet, is the remains of the north wall and rim of a long-extinct volcano.

Mount Hood is about sixty-seven miles from Portland, an easy drive on Route 26. Be sure to check road conditions in the winter.

Mount Hood and Trillium Lake
Photo by Bob Pool, courtesy Oregon Tourism Division

Although Mount Hood no longer spews ash and spits fire, there are still active steam vents high on the mountain. And volcanic activity in the area is hardly a thing of the past; nearby Mount St. Helens in Washington erupted in 1980.

The mountain was named for an English admiral of the West Indies. Pacific Northwest Native Americans called the mountain "Wy'east," believing it to be a spirit in and of itself; the legend spoke of jealous love for Mount St. Helens as the cause of volcanic eruptions.

Mount Hood today is home to five ski resorts, including the only year-round skiing in America with summer training off the summit, a place that is too cold and windswept for most winter use. (*See Chapter 10 for more details.*) Many of the ski runs are used for mountain bike trails and races during the summer.

Cross-country ski trails and off-road hikes follow the historic Barlow Trail, named after Oregon pioneer Sam Barlow, winding between Government Camp and Trillium Lake. The trail passes areas where pioneers camped and obtained supplies; there are still rope burns on trees, evidence of the efforts of the pioneers who had to lower the wagons down the steep slopes of the mountain.

The **Timberline Lodge**, at 6,000 feet, was built by the Civilian Conservation Corps during the recovery from the Depression. In keeping with its surroundings, most everything about the lodge is on a monumental scale. It was constructed out of huge fir and pine trees from nearby woods; other details include a 1,100-pound front door and a 750-pound brass and bronze weather vane.

The lodge was used for some exterior scenes for the movie *The Shining*.

Open year-round, the Timberline Lodge offers rooms and a restaurant. It is located off U.S. Highway 26 (the drive across the mountain to the Barlow Pass is part of the National Scenic Byway system).

Chapter 6
Oregon's Pacific Coast

The Plains Indians told the legend of "The River with No Shore," apparently without ever having seen the Pacific Ocean. When Sacajawea, Lewis and Clark's Shoshone guide, saw the Pacific Ocean for the first time, she vowed to tell the tribe their legend was true.

A Clatsop Indian legend says the rough coast of Oregon was created when Talapus, or Coyote, the trickster god, stood at the top of Neahkahnie Mountain on the north Oregon Coast and tossed chunks of molten rock into the water below. In an area of active volcanoes, again this legend would seem to have some basis in fact.

In 1913 Governor George Oswald declared Oregon's beaches public property; today, nearly 400 miles of coastline is open to public access.

Terrain varies from huge monoliths standing off the coast to sand dunes of forty miles in length and more than 550 feet tall and wide-open stretches of sand with sparse wind-shaped spruce and fir trees.

The **Oregon Dunes National Recreation Area**, between Florence and Coos Bay on the central coast, covers 32,000 acres.

There are ten active lighthouses on the Oregon coast, including Cape Blanco Lighthouse, which was installed in 1870 on the southern coastline.

The **Pacific Coast National Scenic Byway**, Highway 101, runs 400 miles from the California border near Brookings to the mouth of the Columbia River at Astoria on the Washington border. For much of its length, the road is within sight of the Pacific, passing by beaches, parks, lighthouses, and the quaint towns of the coast.

South Down the Coast from Astoria

Astoria has proudly maintained its roots of Scandinavian-tinged culture and a collection of Victorian homes of the 1880s. The town took its name from entrepreneur John Jacob Astor; at the end of the nineteenth century, the burgeoning seaport rivaled San Francisco down the coast.

One of Astoria's most famous Victorians is the **Flavell House**, at Eighth and Duane streets. Clatsop County's first millionaire, Captain George Flavell, commis-

OREGON'S PACIFIC COAST

sioned this early example of Italianate architecture in 1884.

Today, the home is a museum operated by the Clatsop County Historical Society. It is open daily. For information about hours and admission, call ☎ (503) 325-2203.

The town was used as backdrop for several motion pictures including *Free Willy* and *Kindergarten Cop*.

The 125-foot **Astoria Column** on Coxcomb Hill is decorated with murals telling the story of the settlement of the Northwest. Built in 1926, its exterior murals and figures were restored in recent years. At the top of 166 steps in a spiral staircase there's a panoramic view of the Columbia River, Youngs Bay, and lower Washington state.

The walkway along the Astoria waterfront is a great place to watch natural life including sea lions and birds, and human enterprise including ocean-going freighters and fishing vessels. Just off shore, harbor pilots make their rendezvous with the big ships to guide them past the treacherous Columbia Bar.

The **Columbia River Maritime Museum** explores the nautical heritage of the Columbia River and the northwest coast. Located at 1792 Marine Drive, the museum is open daily year-round from 9:30 A.M. to 5 P.M. Admission: adult, senior, and student, ❷; child (6–12), ❶. For information, call ☎ (503) 325-2323.

Across Youngs Bay to the west, the small fishing port of **Warrenton** sits directly on the Pacific. The mouth of the Columbia River at the Pacific Ocean is one of the most dangerous spots for ships in the United States; there are more than 200 recorded shipwrecks in the area, including some that are visible from shore.

Ten miles west of Astoria, **Fort Stevens** was constructed during the Civil War to protect the entrance of the Columbia River from fears that the war could spread to the western states; although it was manned during the war, the lucky soldiers there saw no action.

The fort, though, was maintained by the Army through the end of World War II, and has the distinction of being the only military installation in the continental United States to be fired on since the War of 1812. (At the time of the attack on Pearl Harbor in Hawaii, the island chain was a territory and not a state.)

On the night of June 21, 1942, a Japanese submarine eluded mines in the harbor by following fishing boats; it then approached and fired seventeen shells at the fort. The attack caused no damage, and gunners at the fort were unable to return fire because the sub was out of range.

Today, visitors can explore the abandoned gun batteries and the commander's station. The park at the site is the largest campground in the Oregon State Parks system. For information on the park, call ☎ (503) 861-1671.

On October 25, 1906, the 2,000-ton cargo ship Peter Iredale ran aground in dense fog and high winds. Her rusted iron frame is still visible from the beach at Warrenton and Fort Stevens.

South from Warrenton, the **Fort Clatsop National Memorial** is a replica of the Lewis and Clark expedition's winter campsite of 1805–1806. The thirty-three members of Lewis and Clark's expedition moved into their stockade fort, named in honor of the local Clatsop Indians, on Christmas Eve in 1805.

The original fort did not survive the wet climate of the area, but it was rebuilt in 1955 based on Clark's sketches. Now operated by the National Park Service, park rangers dressed in buckskin demonstrate some of the skills of the time, including carving dugout canoes, firing flintlock rifles, and preparing smoked meat. The park is open from mid-June to Labor Day daily from 8 A.M. to 6 P.M., and for the remainder of the year from 8 A.M. to 5 P.M. An entrance fee of ❷ is collected in spring and summer. For information on the park, call ☎ (503) 861-2471 or consult 🖳 www.nps.gov/focl/.

Seaside, once billed as "The End of the Lewis and Clark Trail," is today one of the most popular beach communities in Oregon. Seaside's history as a resort dates back to 1873, when railroad baron Ben Holladay built the Seaside House.

Broadway leads from the town to the beach, where a statue of Lewis and Clark peer out at the Pacific.

Seaside was the site of a saltmaking camp established by the Lewis and Clark expedition in the winter of 1805–1806. While the explorers camped at Fort Clatsop fifteen miles north, a group of men worked on the beach to prepare salt necessary to preserve food for the trip back east.

In modern times, the area has been developed with all of the trappings of an oceanfront tourist destination, including a boardwalk (known as the "Prom," or Promenade, it is more of a cement sidewalk than a boardwalk), all manner of gift shops, sticky summer food of all varieties, video arcades, and other come-ons. You can rent a bicycle or an oversized surrey.

The **Seaside Museum** includes artifacts of Clatsop Indians and the early tourist industry. Located at 570 Necanicum Street, it is open daily from 10 A.M. to 4 P.M. Admission: adult, senior, junior (13–20), ❶; child (12 and younger,

Key to Prices
❶ $3 and under
❷ $3 to $6
❸ $6 to $10
❹ $10 to $15
   When prices are listed as a range, this indicates various combination options are available. Most attractions offer reduced-price tickets for children and many have family rates that include two adults and two or three children.

with adult), free. For information, call ☎ (503) 738-7065).

For more information on Seaside, call the local tourism bureau at ☎ (888) 306-2326, or consult 📖 www.seasideor.com.

Continuing south from Seaside you'll come to **Cannon Beach**, a magnet for photographers and artists who come to see natural phenomenon such as **Haystack Rock** and **The Needles**. Haystack Rock is one of the world's largest monoliths at 235 feet high.

The galleries of Cannon Beach offer works by local artists, and there's an active art and music festival and theater schedule in the summer.

Highway 101 follows the coastline through Rockaway Beach and the port at Garibaldi at the head of Tillamook Bay. **Garibaldi** is a hard-working fishing port, home to fleets that bring in salmon, halibut, crab, and shrimp.

Tillamook stands at the end of the bay, best known as one of the nation's leading cheesemaking areas; the smell of cheddar—and cows—is in the air. The industry was born in the 1890s when an English immigrant brought his cheddar cheese skills to the small local dairies.

Today, the **Tillamook County Creamery Association**, just north of town, is the world's largest dairy, pumping out something like 40 million pounds of cheese annually. Nearly a million visitors come each year for a free self-guided tour and samples of cheese and ice cream. The dairy is located at 4175 North U.S. 101; for information, call ☎ (800) 547-7290 or ☎ (503) 815-1300.

The smaller **Blue Heron French Cheese Company**, south of Tillamook, makes Brie, Camembert, and other soft cheeses. Samples and cheese and wine are offered for a small fee; there's a petting zoo to entertain kids. For information, call ☎ (800) 275-0639 or ☎ (503) 842-8281.

The **Tillamook County Pioneer Museum** includes collections on Native Americans, logging, guns, military, rocks, and minerals of the area. Located at 2106 Second Street, it is open weekdays from 8 A.M. to 5 P.M., and Sunday from noon to 5 P.M. For information, call ☎ (503) 842-4553.

Three miles south of Tillamook is a preserved dinosaur, a World War II blimp base at the **Tillamook Naval Air Station**; the station was one of ten bases built as home to airships that patrolled the north Pacific in search of enemy submarines and warships. The **Tillamook Naval Air Museum** is home to two dirigibles, plus a collection of wartime military aircraft.

The museum, which occupies just a portion of the seven-acre wooden hangar, is located off Highway 101. It is open daily from 9 A.M. to dark from May to September, and from 9 A.M. to 5 P.M. the remainder of the year. Admission: adult, ❸; senior, ❸; and child, ❷. For information, call ☎ (503) 842-1130.

Continuing south from Tillamook, Highway 101 runs inland for about twenty-five miles, rejoining the coast at Neskowin. If you're determined to stay in sight of the sea, you can instead follow the Three Capes Loop, a smaller road that heads west from Tillamook to the coast; the road passes a few less-visited sights, including a lighthouse at Cape Meares, the Three Arch Rocks National Wildlife Refuge at Oceanside, and Cape Kiwanda State Park outside Pacific City.

Lincoln City's claim to fame is the Spin Sock, a variation of the windsock, invented here. It's sold in kite shops all along the coast. The city is bordered on the north by Roads End at the foot of Cascade Head. To the east is Devils Lake, a 680-acre freshwater lake at the base of the Coast Range foothills. The south boundary is Siletz Bay, the outlet for the Siletz River into the sea. And on the west are more than seven miles of Pacific beaches.

You can learn much about the story of the area from the late 1800s at the **North Lincoln County Historical Museum**, located in a restored community fire hall. Located at 4907 Southwest Highway 101, the museum is open Tuesday to Saturday from noon to 4 P.M. Admission: free. For information, call ☎ (541) 996-6614.

> **Whale watching.** Gray whales take tours along the Oregon coast each winter, usually from about December through April, although it is not unusual to see a pod off shore at any time of the year. Experts say as many as 23,000 of the creatures pass by in a typical season. You can spot the huge mammals from shore along the coast, or head out in their midst on whale-watching tours.
>
> For information on the best viewing times and places, call the Oregon Parks service's whale-watch center at ☎ (541) 563-2002.

For information about the area, call the Lincoln City Visitor and Convention Bureau at ☎ (800) 452-2151, or consult 🖳 www.oregoncoast.org.

Depoe Bay is only fifty feet wide at its mouth to the Pacific Ocean, encompassing only six acres. From what may be the world's smallest navigable harbor, you can take a whale-watch, sightseeing, or fishing boat.

Below Depoe Bay, the road climbs to Cape Foulweather, given its name by Captain Cook. The waters here, and at Devil's Punch Bowl State Park, are dramatic in their ferocity.

Newport is a busy fishing and resort town on Yaquina Bay. It is home to the Oregon Coast Aquarium, the Mark O. Hatfield Science Center, and the Newport Performing Arts Center. For information on Newport, call ☎ (800) 262-7844.

The **Yaquina Head Lighthouse**, at Yaquina Head State Park, dates to 1873.

Yachats (pronounced Yaw'hots) is about halfway between Washington and California. Just south, Highway 101 climbs to Cape Perpetua, the highest point on the Oregon coast. Nearby is the picture-perfect Heceta Head Lighthouse and Sea Lion Caves, with an elevator down to the world's largest sea cave. The caves are the only mainland shelter for Steller sea lions and the cavern is also home to a variety of sea birds, including the guillemot, a rare pigeon.

Some of the least crowded beaches in the state are found in the North Bend and Coos Bay area.

Nearby **Bandon**, a small southern coast community, calls itself the "Storm Watching Capital of the World" and offers weekly club meetings from January to April to talk about the weather and shipping.

The **Bandon Cheese Factory** produces cheddar; a tasting room and store is open to the public. Bandon is also one of the world's largest producers of cranberries, with 100 local growers producing more than 180,000 barrels a year. In September, therefore, Bandon becomes the "Cranberry Capital of Oregon."

Scenic Drive: Pacific Coast Scenic Byway
Astoria to Harbor and the California Border

One-way 358 miles. Allow at least ten to twelve hours. Mileage is shown in distance from Astoria.

Depart from **Astoria**, near the mouth of the Columbia River at the top of Oregon. Head south on U.S. Route 101, which follows the coast for nearly the entire length of the state.

Just outside Astoria is **Fort Clatsop National Memorial**, a reproduction of the 1805 winter campsite of Lewis and Clark; below Clatsop is **Seaside**, where the expedition harvested salt before heading back east. Today, Seaside (twenty-nine miles from Astoria) is a bustling beach resort.

The road passes through the artist colony of **Cannon Beach** before heading inland to **Tillamook**, the cheesemaking capital of Oregon and home of the blimp hangars at the Tillamook Naval Air Museum (sixty-eight miles). Another hour or so down the coast is **Lincoln City**, an art colony and kite lover's dream (106 miles).

The tiny harbor of **Depoe Bay** (150 miles) is a big draw, and a great stepping-off place for whale-watching, sightseeing, or fishing boats. The rugged sea coast from here to Newport, Waldport, Yachats, and Florence (185 miles) features scenic must-sees, including the Yaquina Head Lighthouse, Cape Perpetua, the Heceta Head Lighthouse, and Sea Lion Caves.

Near **Florence**, the rocky coast changes over to nearly fifty miles of gently rolling dunes stretching nearly all the way to **North Bend** (239 miles). That town and neighboring Coos Bay are the largest settlements on the coast.

Below Coos Bay is **Bandon** (260 miles), a self-proclaimed storm-watching, cheesemaking, and cranberry-gathering mecca.

The last stretch of the drive south runs through the busy fishing village of **Port Orford** (285 miles). The last two towns in Oregon are **Brookings** and **Harbor** (358 miles), part of the "banana belt" of Oregon, a sunny and warm gateway to the California border.

For information on the region, call the Oregon Coast Visitor Association at (800) 767-2064.

Chapter 7
The Willamette Valley

The sunny fields on the western slopes of the Cascade Mountains along the Willamette River are known by some as the "Breadbasket of the West." The valley produces bumper crops of fruit, corn, hops, wheat, nuts, and much more.

The region is also one of the nation's major suppliers of grass seed, grass sod, Christmas trees, and flower bulbs. In the summer, many farmers open roadside stands to sell homemade honeys, jams, vegetables, fruits (especially berries), and pickled delicacies.

There are also some thirty-five wineries paralleling Interstate 5 in the valley.

Salem

Salem, the capital of Oregon, is the third-largest city in the state, with a population of more than 120,000.

Located in the center of the Willamette Valley, forty-seven miles south of Portland and sixty-four miles north of Eugene, the state capital is within one of the most fertile and agriculturally productive regions of the world and one of the largest food processing centers in the country.

The Indian name for the locality was Chemeketa, believed to mean "meeting or resting place." Chemeketa may also have been the name of one of the bands of Calapooya Indians in the area.

In 1841 the Jason Lee Mission was moved from the Willamette River to a new site upstream on Mill Creek. In 1842, the missionaries established the Oregon Institute; when the mission was dissolved in 1844 a townsite was laid out on the institute lands. The exact origin of the name Salem, the anglicized form of the Hebrew word Shalom, meaning peace, is unclear; it may have been given by one of the trustees of the institute who came from Salem, Massachusetts.

Designation of Salem as state capital was controversial. The provisional government moved the capital to Salem from Oregon City in 1851; when legislators arrived they found a small town of only a few dozen residents. Four years later, the lawmakers moved the capital to Corvallis, only to find that even less satisfying. They came back to Salem the same year and have stayed since. Not that every citizen was happy about it; the capitol was torched in 1856.

55

State Capitol Mall, Salem
Photo by Bob Pool, courtesy Oregon Tourism Division

Today the capitol is one of the most enticing features of the town. Built to replace a structure that fell to another fire in 1935, the architecture and interior decorations are a mix of the bold heroic art of the Depression years and the prevailing art deco and Bauhaus styles of the time. The interior of the rotunda is decorated with four massive murals telling the story of Oregon; atop the dome is a gilded statue of the Oregon Pioneer. The Oregon legislature meets only in odd-numbered years.

The capitol building is open daily from 7:30 A.M. to 5:30 P.M., on Saturday from 9 A.M. to 4 P.M., and Sunday from noon to 4 P.M. Free tours are offered daily from mid-June to Labor Day. A limited number of tours of the tower with views of the city and the statue atop the dome are offered from Memorial Day to Labor Day. For a schedule, call ☎ (503) 986-1388.

Attractions in Salem

Another treasure of Salem is **Bush House,** a Victorian home built by Asahel Bush II from 1877–78 and occupied by his family for the next seventy-five years. Much of the Bush family's possessions are preserved as they were.

Bush came to Oregon in 1850 from Westfield, Massachusetts. A lawyer by training, he established the *Oregon Statesman* in Oregon City to serve as the voice of the Democratic party in the Oregon territory. He moved the paper and himself to Salem in 1853. He later moved on to banking, establishing the Ladd and Bush Bank; the newspaper and bank both still operate in Salem.

The home, built in Victorian Italianate style, sat in the midst of a sizable estate that included a large barn, a greenhouse, and open ground for pasturing cattle.

All twelve rooms open to the public are filled with choice furnishings, many brought to Oregon from Springfield, Massachusetts. Each of the ten fireplaces is cut from imported Italian marble. Many of the wallpapers in the home were imported from France and shipped around Cape Horn from the East Coast. An early gaslight system, Tirrill's Gas Machine, lit the residence.

The barn, rebuilt after a fire in 1963, serves as a community art center and the greenhouse has undergone extensive restoration. The open pastures are now a municipal park.

Bush House is located at 600 Mission Street Southeast. The entrance is on High Street, just south of Mission Street.

From May to September the house is open for tours daily except Monday from noon to 5 P.M. For the remainder of the year, the house is open daily except Monday from 2 P.M. to 5 P.M. Admission: adult, ❷; senior and student, ❶; child (6–12), ❶. For information, call ☎ (503) 363-4714.

Bush's Pasture Park is the setting for the annual **Salem Art Fair & Festival**, held in mid-July. The three-day fair draws more than 100,000 people to see art, crafts, and performing arts. For information, call ☎ (503) 581-2228.

Another heritage structure in Salem is **Deepwood Estate**, an ornate, multi-gabled Queen Anne-style home from 1894. Architectural details include Povey stained and beveled glass windows, eastern golden oak woodwork, and original 1894 electric light fixtures. English-style gardens were added in 1930. The six-acre Deepwood Estate includes gazebos, the original carriage house, outdoor wedding gardens, and a nature trail.

Deepwood Estate is located at 1116 Mission Street Southeast. The grounds are open from dawn to dusk daily; admission is free. House tours are offered from May through September daily, except Saturday from noon to 5 P.M., and for the remainder of the year daily, except Sunday and Monday. Admission: adult, ❷; student and senior, ❷; child, ❶. For information, call ☎ (503) 363-1825.

The **Jensen Arctic Museum** at Western Oregon University in Monmouth, about twenty minutes west of Salem, is the only museum on the west coast dedicated to the arctic culture. The museum's collections include art, tools, apparel, and information about indigenous arctic people. The museum was founded in 1985 by adventurer Paul H. Jensen.

The museum, on the university campus at 590 West Church Street in Monmouth, is open from 10 A.M. to 4 P.M. Wednesday through Saturday and at other times by appointment. Admission: donations accepted. For information, call ☎ (503) 838-8468.

A. C. Gilbert's Discovery Village is a hands-on museum for children and families, a fun-filled exploration of arts and sciences. Gilbert was one of the great geniuses of the world of toys, responsible for the invention of Erector Sets, American Flyer model trains, and Gilbert chemistry sets. A physician by training, he was also an Olympic gold medal winner in pole vaulting in 1909.

The museum is spread across five heritage houses and an outdoor discovery center. Adventures include a cave for exploration, a fossil dig, a bubble room, and much more. The outdoor area includes a gigantic Erector set tower and other tributes to Gilbert and to children of all ages.

Located at 116 Marion Street Northeast on Salem's Downtown Riverfront between the Center Street and Marion Street bridges, the museum is open Monday to Saturday from 10 A.M. to 5 P.M., and Sunday from noon to 3 P.M.

Admission: adult and child (3 and older), ❷; senior, ❷; child (2 and younger), free. For information, (503) 371-3631, or consult 🖳 www.acgilbert.org.

The **Mission Mill Museum** is a restored woolen mill from the Methodist mission days, with exhibits on the factory and religious activities. Located at 1313 Mill Street Southeast, the museum is open daily except Sunday from 10 A.M. to 5 P.M. ☎ (503) 585-7012. The woolen mill museum includes a working turbine and loom, Methodist mission houses, shops, and a cafe. Hours: Tuesday to Saturday, 10 A.M.–4:30 P.M. Admission: adult, ❸; senior, ❷; child (6–13) ❷.

For more information about Salem, call the Salem Convention & Visitors Association at ☎ (800) 874-7012, or consult 🖳 www.scva.org.

Eugene

At the south end of the Willamette Valley, **Eugene** is Oregon's second largest city, home to more than 130,000 people. Many of the residents seem happily planted in the counter-culture, a holdover from the '60s when Eugene was one of the capitals of the hippie nation. Part of the reason may be that Eugene is very much a university town, home to the University of Oregon, Northwest Christian College, Lane Community College, and Eugene Bible College.

In any case, it seems appropriate that this hip city is called by its first name.

The Willamette River runs through the heart of the city; the McKenzie River joins the Willamette north of town. Skinner Butte marks the north and Spencer Butte, a 310-acre city park, the south.

The first known residents of the Willamette Valley were the Kalapuya Indians; archeological evidence indicates they occupied the area for several centuries. The Kalapuya burned the grasses of the valley to clear brush and provide a habitat for the game and vegetation they depended on for food.

When the first white settlers arrived, the valley was mostly an open grassy prairie.The first cabin was built in 1846 by Eugene Franklin Skinner. The simple structure served as a general trading post and was authorized as a post office in 1850; along the way, Skinner's first name was attached to the community.

The first town site, laid out in 1852, proved to be less than ideal. After heavy winter rains, the area was nicknamed "Skinner's Mud Hole." A revised town plat on higher ground was made in 1853.

The town grew rapidly, based around flour, woolen, and saw mills built along the banks of the Willamette River. Eugene City was incorporated in 1862; the name was changed to the City of Eugene two years later. The city became a stagecoach stop in 1865 when the Territorial Road arrived, and in 1871, the Oregon-California Railway (now Southern Pacific) was completed to Eugene.

Eugene has a temperate climate, with an average temperature of 53 degrees Fahrenheit. The city receives forty-three inches of rain on average per year, mostly between September and June.

Attractions in Eugene

Eugene has many miles of biking, walking, and jogging paths along the Willamette River and in parks throughout the city. Canoes and kayaks can be rented for boating on the Willamette River. Fern Ridge Lake, just outside Eugene, is a favorite for picnicking, camping, swimming, water skiing, sailing, and fishing for trout, crappie, bass, and catfish. If you prefer more extreme sports, there's whitewater rafting on the McKenzie River, which has Class II and Class III rapids.

Eugene's **University of Oregon** campus (generally referred to as the U of O) includes the Museum of Art, with an excellent collection of Asian art, as well as African art, Russian icon paintings, and sculptures by Rodin. The U of O Museum of Natural History focuses on Oregon's ancient people and animals, as well as changing exhibits on other cultures.

Key to Prices
- ❶　$3 and under
- ❷　$3 to $6
- ❸　$6 to $10
- ❹　$10 to $15

When prices are listed as a range, this indicates various combination options are available. Most attractions offer reduced-price tickets for children and many have family rates that include two adults and two or three children.

The **Hult Center for the Performing Arts** offers ballet, symphonies, and opera. The renowned Oregon Bach Festival in late June and early July showcases more than forty concerts at the University's Beall Concert Hall and the Hult Center, featuring the music of Bach, Brahms, Mozart, and other works by classical and modern-day composers.

The center offers free tours every Thursday and Saturday. For information on the festival, call ☎ (541) 346-5666 or ☎ (541) 682-5000.

The **Oregon Country Fair**, held in late July just after the Bach Festival, is an outdoor musical festival and renaissance crafts fair, with more than a little bit of the '60s mixed in. The three-day party, held over a weekend, includes all manner of hippie regalia from tie-dye clothes to beads, candles, incense, and health food. Celebrants of another festive time gone by dress as minstrels, maids in waiting, and all manner of over-the-top royalty. Live acts include theater, music, juggling, and just plain strangeness.

The fair is held near Veneta, about fourteen miles west of Eugene on Highway 126. Tickets must be purchased in advance, and parking is limited; there are shuttle buses running from outlying lots.

For information on the festival, call ☎ (541) 343-4298.

The **Lane County Historical Museum** in Eugene has a collection of artifacts of the Oregon Trail and historic vehicles of the area. Located at 740 West Thirteenth Avenue, the museum is open Wednesday to Friday from 10 A.M. to 4 P.M., and Saturday from noon to 4 P.M. Admission: adult, senior, child, ❶. For information, call ☎ (541) 682-4242.

The **Mount Pisgah Arboretum** has seven miles of trails that wend their way through two hundred acres of diverse ecological habitats. Located at 38901 Frank Parrish Road, the arboretum is open year-round from dawn to dusk. Admission: donations accepted. For information, call ☎ (541) 747-3817.

The **University of Oregon Museum of Art** has a collection of Asian and Pacific Northwest Art, as well as changing special exhibitions. Located at 1430 Johnson Lane on the college campus, the museum is open Wednesday to Sunday from noon to 5 P.M. Admission: free. For information, call ☎ (541) 346-3027.

Also on campus is the **University of Oregon Museum of Natural History**, specializing in Oregon natural history with anthropological, archaeological, and natural science exhibits. Located at 1680 East Fifteenth Avenue, the museum is open Wednesday to Sunday from noon to 5 P.M. Admission: donation requested. For information, call (541) 346-3024.

The **Willamette Science and Technology Center**, known as WISTEC, is a hands-on science museum. Located at 2300 Leo Harris Parkway, next to Autzen Stadium, it is open Wednesday to Sunday from noon to 6 P.M. Admission: adult, ❷; senior and child, ❶. For information, call ☎ (541) 484-9027.

Built in 1888, the **Shelton-McMurphey-Johnson House** is a well-preserved Queen Anne revival-style home. Located at 303 Willamette Street, tours are offered Sunday and Tuesday from 1 to 4 P.M. Admission: adult, ❷; child (12 and younger), ❶. For information, call ☎ (541) 484-0808.

At the south end of the Eugene airport, the **Oregon Air & Space Museum** features aircraft, aviation artifacts, and models. Located at 90377 Boeing Drive, the museum is open Wednesday through Sunday from noon to 4 P.M. Admission: adult, ❷; child, ❶; senior, ❷. For information, call ☎ (541) 461-1101.

Chapter 8
Bend, Sisters, Mount Bachelor, and John Day

When the pioneers on the Oregon Trail came to a particular crook in the Deschutes River, they knew they were at an important cutoff point to other trails. They called the place "Farewell Bend."

Today, **Bend** is considered the hub of central Oregon, bordered on the north by the Warm Springs Reservation and by Smith Rock, a world-famous rock-climbing destination. Several ghost towns also lie to the north.

To the west is the Cascade Mountain Range with seven major mountains, including Mount Bachelor, and hundreds of summits lined up from north to south. To the east is the High Desert and Harney Basin, and to the south are lava caves and lakes formed by extinct volcanoes.

Bend

The **Museum at Warm Springs** preserves the history and traditions of the Confederated Tribes of the Warm Springs Reservation. Resembling a traditional Deschutes River encampment among the cottonwoods, artifacts are set among a Tule Mat Lodge and Plank House.

The **High Desert Museum** in Bend tells the natural history of the region through dioramas and other exhibits; outdoor nature trails lead to the habitats of porcupines, otters, and several species of birds. There's also a working sawmill from the late 1890s. The museum, at 59800 South Highway 97, is open daily from 9 A.M. to 5 P.M. For information and admission fees, call ☎ (541) 382-4754.

South of Bend are lava fields and ice caves that were created during the explosive volcanic era in Oregon about 6,000 years ago. You can drive to the top of a cinder cone for a view of 400 other cinder cones in the area. Also in the area are half-mile-long lava tubes, which are open for a walk-through.

Newberry National Volcanic Monument, about eleven miles south of Bend, is a collapsed volcano containing two lakes, obsidian flows, waterfalls, and hiking trails. The Newberry volcano has erupted uncounted times during

CENTRAL OREGON

the past 500,000 years or so. Paulina Peak, reaching to 7,985 feet, is actually only a piece of a once much-higher volcano that collapsed in an eruption.

Paulina Lake and East Lake fill the five-mile-wide crater. Once a single body of water, there are now two lakes separated by a lava flow. Paulina Lake drains over a 100-foot-high waterfall.

Near the Lava Lands Visitor Center is Lava Butte, which looks exactly like you would expect a volcanic cone to appear, rising 500 feet from the moonscape all around. A road leads to an observation deck at the top.

Two eerie remnants of the once-active area are the Lava Cast Forest, a lava forest created when molten rock passed through trees; the trees were consumed by the lava, but their shapes are preserved as 6,000-year-old natural stone castings. Also in the monument is Lava River Cave, a tube created when the surface solidified while lava continued to flow beneath; you can walk through the dry, nearly tubular cave. Bring a flashlight or rent a lamp from the visitor center for your expedition.

The monument is located about eleven miles south of Bend off U.S. Highway 97. For information, call the Lava Lands Visitor Center at ☎ (541) 593-2421.

The **Deschutes County Historical Center** includes among its treasures some of the pieces left behind by the bypassers on the Oregon Trail and artifacts from the early pioneers, loggers, and farmers. The museum overflows through the rooms of the old Reid School, built in 1914. Located at 129 NW Idaho Street, the museum is open Tuesday to Saturday from 10 A.M. to 4:30 P.M.

Sisters

The town of **Sisters**, within sight of the Three Sisters Mountains, and on the edge of a National Forest, has been a favorite of travelers since the 1800s. Much of the architecture is frozen in the late nineteenth century.

Nearby to Sisters are several llama ranches; more than 6,000 llamas in Deschutes County are bred for their hair and as pack animals.

Scenic Drive: McKenzie Pass–Santiam Pass

Sisters to McKenzie River, Santiam, Hoodoo Ski Area, and Back to Sisters

Round-trip eighty-two miles. Allow three to five hours. Note that McKenzie Pass is closed in winter months; the best time to drive this loop is from July to October. Be sure to check on road conditions any time of the year.

The loop from Sisters takes you along two high-mountain passes in the Cascades, over ancient jagged flows, and through two nearly untouched national forests.

Depart from the little town of **Sisters**, on the east side of the Cascades; fill your car's tank with gasoline to be on the safe side. You'll drive out of town on Oregon Route 242, ascending into the Deschutes National Forest. Ahead of you are the spectacular Three Sisters peaks.

West of Sisters, the road follows a wagon route of the 1860s, emerging from the forest at Windy Point and into a sixty-five-square-mile lava bed. Lording over the scene is Mount Washington to the north.

A bit further down the road, you'll enter **McKenzie Pass** at 5,325 feet. You can take a break to visit the Dee Wright Observatory with views of six Cascade peaks. The Lava River Trail makes a half-mile loop through the moonscape.

It's downhill from here, into the **Willamette National Forest**; side roads lead into hiking and picnic areas, including Scott Lake, where the waters reflect the surrounding peaks.

About nine miles from McKenzie Pass, you'll enter Deadhorse Grade; the road drops nearly 1,200 feet in less than four miles in a series of switchbacks and hairpin turns. Below the drop, the Proxy Falls Trailhead leads to a short hike to the hidden falls.

Oregon Route 242 ends about a mile and a half past the McKenzie Bridge Ranger Station, meeting up with Oregon Route 126, which runs from Eugene to Sisters. The road heads north along the McKenzie River to **Clear Lake**, the source of the river.

North of Clear Lake, the road joins with U.S. Route 20 and Oregon Route 22, turning east toward Sisters.

Just short of 4,817-foot Santiam Pass is **Hoodoo Ski Area**, open from December to March. After the snow clears, the road to Hoodoo continues to Big Lake, a recreation area with great views of Mount Washington, now to the south.

After the pass, the road descends through a warm-weather recreational area that includes Suttle Lake and Camp Sherman. On the left side of the road is the 6,436-foot cone of Black Butte.

For more information on the areas on this drive, call the Central Oregon Visitors Association at ☎ (800) 800-8334, the Convention and Visitors Association (Eugene) at ☎ (541) 484-5307, or the McKenzie Ranger District at ☎ (541) 822-3381.

Scenic Drive: Mount Bachelor and Cascade Lakes

Bend to Mount Bachelor, the Cascade lakes, Wickiup Reservoir, and Back to Bend

Round-trip 170 miles. Allow five to seven hours. Note that the road beyond Mount Bachelor is closed in winter months; the best time to drive this loop is from June to October. Be sure to check on road conditions any time of the year.

Follow signs from **Bend** toward Mount Bachelor and the Cascade Lakes on Century Drive, which becomes Oregon Route 372. In the distance is the snow cone of Mount Bachelor.

The road climbs into the **Deschutes National Forest**, a vast recreational area. You'll arrive at the base of Mount Bachelor about sixty miles from Bend.

The road is closed for much of the winter beyond this point. Skiers can head off to the mountain from fall through June of most years. In the summer, you can take a ski lift to the 9,065-foot peak of Mount Bachelor for a view of volcanic peaks and lava beds that stretch from California to Washington.

Past Mount Bachelor you'll enter into the region of the **Cascade Lakes**, including Todd Lake at the base of Bachelor and Broken Top.

The road climbs and descends through the lake region, past popular destinations that include Devils Lake, Elk Lake, and Lava Lake. Nearby, Little Lava Lake is the headwaters of the Deschutes River.

Past **Crane Prairie** you can head east off the highway onto Forest Service Road 42, which goes past Wickiup Reservoir and Twin lakes to meet up with U.S. Route 97 near Sunriver; from there you can head north to return to Bend.

Or, you can continue south on Oregon Route 46 to meet up with Oregon Route 58 near Crescent and Odell lakes; Route 58 continues southeastward to connect to U.S. Route 97 near Walker Mountain. From there it is about a sixty-five-mile trip north to return to Bend.

For more information on this region, call the Central Oregon Visitors Association at ☎ (800) 800-8334, or call the Bend Visitor and Convention Bureau at ☎ (800) 905-2363. You can also visit the Central Oregon Welcome Center on U.S. Route 97 in Bend before heading out on the trip.

John Day

John Day is one famous man, his name attached to two towns (**John Day** and **Dayville**), a river (the John Day River, the John Day River Middle Fork, and the John Day River North Fork), several national monuments (the John Day Fossil Beds National Monument with several locations and the North Fork John Day Wilderness), and the John Day Dam on the Columbia River southeast of Goldendale, Washington.

It's all the more interesting for the fact that John Day never visited the region, his fame extending into the west because of a somewhat embarrassing encounter.

John Day was a member of the Astor expedition of 1811. Out on a fur trapping trip on the Columbia River, he and a companion were ambushed by Cayuse Indians near the mouth of the Mau Hau River. Stripped naked and abandoned, the two men managed to make their way back to the base at Astoria where they were celebrated as heroes; the river was renamed for Day.

The John Day River runs nearly 300 miles from northeast Oregon's Blue Mountains west and north to the Columbia. The town of John Day and Dayville down the river grew during a gold rush on Canyon Creek in the 1860s.

Key to Prices
- ❶ $3 and under
- ❷ $3 to $6
- ❸ $6 to $10
- ❹ $10 to $15

When prices are listed as a range, this indicates various combination options are available. Most attractions offer reduced-price tickets for children and many have family rates that include two adults and two or three children.

Nearly $20 million in gold was taken from the area at its peak; thousands of prospectors came to the area, including many Chinese workers who had been employed building the transcontinental railroad. Many of the Chinese stayed on to work some of the stakes that were abandoned by whites who had moved on to more-promising areas.

One of the community leaders of the time was "Doc" Ing Hay, who operated an herbal pharmacy and store for the Chinese; many of the white miners also came to him for medical attention.

Today, the **Kam Wah Chung Museum** occupies the tiny building where Hay ran his store. Exhibits tell of the pharmacy, frontier history, and mining. The bunkroom's beams are blackened from opium smoke.

The museum, located in the city park of John Day, is open Monday to Thursday 9 A.M. to noon and 1 to 5 P.M., and weekends from 1 to 5 P.M. Admission: adult, ❶; senior, ❶; youth (13–18), ❶; and child (12–under), ❶. For information, call ☎ (541) 575-0028.

West of John Day and Dayville are the **John Day Fossil Beds National Monument**, with three sites: Sheep Rock, Painted Hills, and Clarno. All together, the 14,000 acres in preserve are one of the largest depositories of fossils in North America.

Thousands of teeth and bones as well as impressions of plant and marine fossils of as much as 50 million years in age have been found in the rocks. Most are still embedded in the clay; more than 100 animal species have been found.

Headquarters for the national monument is in John Day, at 431 Patterson Bridge Road. For information, call ☎ (541) 987-2333.

The Sheep Rock unit is about ten miles northwest of John Day, off Route 19. On display at the **Cant Ranch House Visitors Center** are fossils that include traces of a saber-toothed tiger. Paleontologists work in a laboratory at the center. The Cant Ranch House preserves a farm residence from the start of the twentieth century.

The Cant Ranch House Visitors Center is open daily from 9 A.M. to 5 P.M. For information, call ☎ (541) 987-2333.

The Painted Hills unit of the national monument, northwest of Mitchell off Route 26, is set amongst the various-colored ash beds from ancient volcanic eruptions. Trails lead out from the small monument headquarters to the hills and a wildlife preserve. For information, call ☎ (541) 462-3961.

The most isolated of the three sections of the national monument is the Clarno unit, at the base of a canyon dug by the upper John Day River. The monument is north of Route 218 between Fossil and Antelope. The fossil bed here is as much as 40 million years old, a preserved ancient forest.

Chapter 9
Southwest Oregon: Ashland, Oregon Caves, and Crater Lake

Southwest Oregon includes some of the wildest and most unusual landscapes of the Pacific Northwest, including the impossibly blue and improbably round Crater Lake within the collapsed volcanic cone of Mount Mazama.

Ashland: Natural and Literary Gems

The often-wild Rogue River flows out of Crater Lake to the Pacific Ocean, carving a spectacular gorge through the mountains.

Located about twelve miles south of Medford and fifteen miles north of the California border on Interstate 5, Ashland might have receded completely into history were it not for a local obsession with the 400-year-old works of an English playwright.

The **Oregon Shakespeare Festival** traces its roots back to the Chautauqua movement, a national effort born in the late nineteenth century in upstate New York to bring culture and entertainment to rural areas of the country.

Established in 1935, the Oregon Shakespeare Festival has the oldest existing full-scale Elizabethan stage in the Western Hemisphere. The festival presents an eight-month season of about twelve plays in three theaters. It claims the highest attendance of any non-profit theater in the United States.

Ashland's first Chautauqua building was erected in 1893, and over the ensuing years, families from all over Southern Oregon and Northern California came to see luminaries such as John Phillip Sousa and William Jennings Bryan. In 1917 a round, dome structure was erected for the meetings.

By the early 1920s, though, the Chautauqua movement went into decline and Ashland's annual meeting was ended. The dome was torn down in 1933, but the cement walls were left standing.

In 1935 Angus L. Bowmer, a young teacher from Southern Oregon Normal School (now Southern Oregon University), saw a resemblance between the Chautauqua walls and sketches of Shakespeare's Globe Theatre. The Oregon Shakespearean Festival was officially born on July 2, 1935, with a production of *Twelfth Night*. At the time, reserved seats cost $1; general admission was 50 cents for adults and 25 cents for children.

Ashland Shakespeare Festival
Photo courtesy Oregon Tourism Division

In 1992 the Allen Pavilion of the Elizabethan Theatre was completed, encircling the seating area and providing improved acoustics, sight lines and technical capabilities. Vomitoria (entryways for the actors from under the seating area to the stage) were added, adding to staging options.

Today the theater remains open to the sky, still within the ivy-covered walls of the old Chautauqua dome.

For ticket information on the Oregon Shakespeare Festival, call ☎ (541) 482-4331. The season runs from late May to October, with tickets for the summer season the most difficult to obtain; prices range from about $20 to $40.

There are also nine other theatre groups, featuring a wide variety of performances, including musicals, comedy and experimental theatre. Musical performances include opera, bluegrass, folk, and chamber music.

Ashland, built on the banks of Bear Creek, also has the Bear Creek Bike and Nature Trail. There is river rafting and jet boat rides on the Rogue and Klamath Rivers, and many pristine mountain lakes for anglers in search of steelhead, salmon, and trout.

Mount Ashland is a popular ski resort fifteen miles from downtown Ashland, with twenty-three ski runs and eighty miles of cross country trails.

For information on Ashland and nearby attractions, contact the Chamber of Commerce at ☎ (541) 482-3486. You can also contact the Southern Oregon Reservation Center at ☎ (800) 547-8052 or ☎ (541) 488-1011 for accommodations, attractions, and festival tickets.

Jacksonville

The Gold Rush town of **Jacksonville** in the foothills of the Siskyou Mountains west of Medford is frozen in time in the mid-nineteenth century, with more than ninety original brick and wooden buildings that date back to the

1850s. It is one of just a handful of American towns listed on the National Register of Historic Places.

One of the reasons for the preservation of Jacksonville is the work of pioneer photographer Peter Britt; many of his century-old photos have been used to restore homes to their original state.

Britt, a native of Switzerland, lived in Jacksonville. He was an accomplished photographer and horticulturist, taking the first photos of Crater Lake. These photographs later aided in the decision to designate it as a National Park.

His photographic work can be seen at the **Jacksonville Museum**, an 1883 Italianate building that formerly served as a courthouse. The museum is located at 206 North Fifth Street.

In addition to a display of Britt's photos, the Jacksonville Museum has exhibits on mining, the history of the Oregon and California Railroad in the Rogue Valley, and the Chinese influence in the region.

The **Children's Museum** nearby is housed in the 1910 Jacksonville County Jail; exhibits include old-fashioned toys, a pioneer jail, and a collection celebrating another Jacksonville native, Vance Colvig, the original voice for many Walt Disney characters, including Goofy, Grumpy (in *Snow White and the Seven Dwarfs*), and Pluto. He was also the first Bozo the Clown.

Admission to the Children's Museum and the Jacksonville Museum: adult, student, and senior **❶**. For information, call the Jacksonville Museum at ☎ (541) 773-6536.

Britt's elaborate and extensive gardens are continued at the **Peter Britt Gardens** at First and Pine Street.

Britt is also celebrated each summer at the **Britt Music Festival**, held from the last week of June through the first week of September at the Britt Pavilion just south of the gardens.

The series of about forty concerts includes jazz, popular, classical, bluegrass, and country music, as well as dance, musical theater, and Broadway musicals. Recent years have also included exotic cultural performances such as Japanese taiko dojo drums.

For information on the festival or to purchase tickets, call the Britt Festival at ☎ (800) 882-7488 or ☎ (541) 773-6077.

A visit to the **Beekman House**, circa 1876, brings history alive as actors dressed in costumes of the period portray the Beekman family in a living history exhibit. The Beekman Bank, established in 1863, is also open to visitors and has many of the original furnishings, including a collection of Wells Fargo memorabilia. The house is located at 470 East California Street and is open from Memorial Day through Labor Day daily from 1 to 5 P.M. Admission: adult, **❶**. For information, call ☎ (541) 773-6536.

The Applegate Trail

An alternative to the difficult trail through the Columbia River Gorge, which involved portaging around rapids and some difficult climbs, was a southern route that was established in 1846. Known as the **Applegate Trail**, it cut on the diagonal southwest from Idaho through the desert of northern Nevada and

California before crossing north into the lower portion of Oregon and the south end of the Willamette Valley.

The otherwise unremarkable town of Applegate southwest of Jacksonville was near the end of the trail. North of Applegate and Grants Pass, the little town of Wolf Creek was a stagecoach stop; author Jack London spent the night there in 1911.

Oregon Caves National Monument

You can catch a glimpse of the world beneath our feet at **Oregon Caves National Monument**, a three-mile stretch of subterranean chambers in the Rogue River National Forest in the southwestern corner of the state, just above the California border.

To get to the monument, drive south on Route 199 from Grants Pass and then turn east on Route 46 at the small town of Cave Junction.

The formation was discovered in 1874 when a hunter followed his dog into an opening in the side of a mountain; at first believed to be a whole series of caves, later exploration determined that there was, instead, one huge cavern. Scientists trace its origins back to a shallow sea of more than 200 million years ago. Shells of marine animals accumulated at the bottom of the sea; volcanic eruptions heated the sediment, turning it into marble. Seismic movement and a fast-moving underground stream carved out the chambers of the cave.

Guided tours of the cave and the River Styx that runs its length, are offered year-round. The ninety-minute expeditions pass about half a mile into the cool and sometimes wet cave. Admission: adult, ❸; child, ❷. For information on the tours, call ☎ (541) 592-3400.

Outside the cave is the **Oregon Caves Chateau**, a 1934 cedar structure listed on the National Register of Historic Places; the main dining room sits astride the River Styx as it exits the cave. Rooms and meals are available from late May to mid-October. For information and reservations, call ☎ (541) 592-3400.

Crater Lake

More than 7,000 years ago, Mount Mazama erupted violently. A series of explosions swept forests away, incinerating nearby wood to charcoal, and depositing ash over thousands of acres in southern and central Oregon.

The eruption also resulted in the creation of a huge caldera encircled by steep walls of the collapsed volcano. Though the floor of the caldera was carpeted with large deposits of ash and huge chunks of the mountain, the resulting **Crater Lake** is 1,932 feet deep, the deepest lake in the United States.

The deep blue water in the lake is sustained by snowfall and by thermal springs that discharge hot water from below. Annual snowfall in a season that reaches from October to March is about fifty feet.

Snow surrounds Crater Lake for much of the year, but the lake itself almost never freezes over completely because of the heat stored in the deep body of water from the summer sun.

Today Crater Lake is Oregon's only national park.

A pair of roadways leading to the rim of the crater are open from June through September, weather permitting. Among hiking paths is the Cleetwood Cove Trail, which leads from the rim 1,000 feet down to the lake's edge.

Swimming is not permitted in Crater Lake, but a boat tour is offered to Wizard Island in the middle of the caldera.

The Story of Crater Lake

Before the arrival of the white man, shamans forbade most Indians to view the lake; Indians said nothing about the existence of Crater Lake to trappers and pioneers who were in the area for fifty years before finding it.

Crater Lake
Photo by Larry Geddis, courtesy Oregon Tourism Division

Then, in 1853, prospectors searching for the lost Cabin Gold Mine found Crater Lake. In 1886, a U.S. Geological Survey party, using a weight suspended from piano wire, determined the lake to be 1,996 feet, remarkably close to more scientific modern sonar measurements of 1,932 feet.

The lake apparently contained no fish; settlers introduced a crop in 1888 and continued to stock the lake until the 1940s. Today, rainbow trout and kokanee salmon survive.

Activities in the park include hiking and cross-country skiing, snowshoeing, camping, and boat tours of Crater Lake. Boats depart from Cleetwood Cove several times each day from late June through mid-September. The tours, just less than two hours, visit Wizard Lake and travel near named formations, including the Phantom Ship. Passengers can get off at Wizard Island and explore, catching a later boat back to the dock.

And there's the imposing timber-and-stone **Crater Lake Lodge**, first built in 1909; it was completely reconstructed in 1989 in its original style. There are just seventy rooms in the lodge; the Watchman Restaurant offers an incredible view of the lake and rim of the volcano. For information and reservations, call ☎ (541) 830-8700.

Crater Lake National Park was established in 1902 and today encompasses 183,224 acres. The entrance fee to the park is ❹ per vehicle.

The park is open year-round; however, winter services are limited due to heavy snow. The restored Crater Lake Lodge, run by the National Park Service, is open May through October.

The northern entry to the park, off State Route 138, is closed in the winter. A year-round entrance is to the south, off Route 62. Be sure to call and check on road conditions in the winter.

For information on the park, call ☎ (541) 594-2211 or consult the Internet at 🖳 www. crater-lake.com. For lodge reservations, call ☎ (541) 830-8700.

Klamath

The **Klamath Basin National Wildlife Refuge,** near the California border, is the largest migratory area for the bald eagle in the continental United States. More than one million ducks and geese make the Upper Klamath Lake in the basin their home. Vast expanses of marsh, forest, and grassland make the region a mecca for bird watchers.

Once home to the Modoc and Klamath tribes, the Klamath Basin now includes several museums devoted to the lifestyles of the Native Americans. The Favell Museum of Western Art and Indian Artifacts has works from renowned Western artists and claims the largest collection of arrowheads in the western United States.

In **Klamath Falls,** a pair of small museums tell the story of the area.

The **Baldwin Hotel Museum,** set in a 1906 brick structure, explores the early history of the area's settlement. A number of early businesses, including a creamery, photo studio, and shop are reproduced. Located at 31 Main Street, the museum is open from June to September from 10 A.M. to 4 P.M. For information and admission rates, call ☎ (541) 883-4208.

The Klamath County Museum concentrates on the anthropology, history, geology, and wildlife of the Klamath Basin. An important display tells the unhappy story of the Modoc Indian War, which lasted from 1863 to 1890, a violent dispute between Modoc Indians and settlers and Army troops in the area. At 1451 Main Street, the museum is open daily from 9 A.M. to 5 P.M. except Sunday. Admission: adult, senior, and student, ❶. For information, call ☎ (541) 883-4209.

Scenic Drive: Amongst the Volcanos
Diamond Lake Junction to Crater Lake and Klamath Falls

One-way 140 miles. Allow at least five to seven hours. The north entrance to Crater Lake and the rim drive close in winter, from November through May.

You can make a round-trip back to Diamond Lake Junction by heading north on U.S. 97 from Klamath Falls, a sixty-two-mile trip.

Depart from **Diamond Lake Junction**, about halfway between Bend and Klamath Falls on U.S. Route 97. Pick up Oregon Route 138 eastbound to the north entrance of **Crater Lake National Park**.

Within Crater Lake, the road climbs through the moonscape landscape left behind by the massive eruption of Mount Mazama about 7,700 years ago. A thirty-three-mile-long drive around the rim affords an extraordinary view of the six-mile-wide caldera, which holds the deepest lake in the United States.

You can access the lake itself by foot on the Cleetwood Trail.

The **Rim Village Visitors Center** is open year-round; here you can obtain maps and current advisories on weather and conditions. Overnight accommodations are available at Crater Lake Lodge within the park.

When you exit the park at the year-round south entrance, pick up Oregon Route 62. From here, the Crater Lake Highway follows Annie Creek to **Fort Klamath;** open in summer only, the museum explores the unhappy story of native Modocs, driven from their lands in 1864 by white settlers and forced onto a reservation with the rival Klamath tribe. About 300 of the Indians left their reservation to hide out in the barren and forbidding lava beds south of Tule Lake where they were hunted by the U.S. Army in the Modoc War. In 1873, the surviving Modoc were captured and moved to another reservation in Oklahoma; their leaders were hung.

At Fort Klamath, head west on Weed Road to Sevenmile Road west, and then turn onto WestSide Road through the Winema National Forest.

This section of the road passes near **Upper Klamath Lake**, Oregon's largest freshwater lake, covering 133 square miles of a basin created by an earthquake fault. The lake is the seasonal home to more than 400 species of birds, including bald eagles, sandhill cranes, and pelicans.

The road meets up with Oregon Route 140 at Rocky Point, and heads south from there to **Klamath Falls** and U.S. Route 97.

For more information on the region, contact the Klamath County Department of Tourism at (800) 445-6728 or (541) 884-0666.

Chapter 10
Skiing in Oregon

The high-most high of skiing in Oregon is Mount Hood, and that's a pretty impressive credential.

How big is Oregon's Mount Hood? It is the single largest ski mountain in America, with a circumference at the base of about forty miles. It starts at a not-insignificant 3,600 feet and grows to a knee-wobbling headwall at 11,235 feet. And it is the home of no less than five ski resorts: Mount Hood Meadows, Timberline, Mount Hood SkiBowl, Cooper Spur, and Summit Ski Area.

Mount Hood itself is an awesome snow cone of a mountain, completely bare at the top. From Timberline, over the left shoulder you can see the exploded volcano of Mount St. Helens across the border in Washington state.

The mountain is also America's only year-round ski hill. Timberline is a bodacious ski area, worthy of a visit in the season when most of us turn our thoughts to skiing. But then, it's also a bodacious ski area in June. And July. Not to mention August and September.

The upper reaches—the Zig Zag Glacier, Palmer Glacier, and White River Glacier—are generally too darned cold in the winter, but deliver good-to-excellent conditions in the summer. Timberline's upper chairlift, the Palmer quad, is open only in the summer.

★★★★ Timberline Mountain Ski Area

In the winter, Timberline is mostly an intermediate world with some lovely above-the-treeline bowls below the Magic Mile Chair, open glades off the Blossom Chair, or cruising on the Main Run Victoria.

In the summer, the glaciers of the Palmer snowfields are strictly for experts and advanced skiers, with some serious steeps and some challenging weather conditions. But, hey, it's August. The quad chair to the snowfields runs all year except for a two-week break for maintenance in the fall.

Key to Ratings
★★★★ **North America's Best Ski Resorts.** Top 50 resorts in the United States and Canada.
★★★ **Best Regional Ski Resorts**
★★ **Best Local Areas**
★ **Small Ski Areas**

Several companies run summer ski camps at Mount Hood. For information about one of the camps, contact Mount Hood Summer Ski Camp at ☎ (503) 337-2230.

Another reason to visit Timberline is the fabulous Timberline Lodge, near the wintertime top and the summertime base.

The Timberline Lodge, at the 6,000-foot level, was constructed of massive hand-hewn beams by master craftsmen during the Depression as a WPA project, and dedicated by President Franklin Roosevelt in September 1937. It was declared a National Historic Landmark forty years later. Today, there are sixty rooms available for rent for about $100 to $160 per night.

You can also find places to stay in Government Camp and further down the mountain.

Timberline and Timberline Lodge's movie credits include *Bend in the River* with James Stewart and Arthur Kennedy, *All the Young Men* with Alan Ladd and Sidney Poitier, the remake of *Lost Horizon* with Peter Finch, and Stanley Kubrick's *The Shining*.

Timberline Lodge, OR 97028. Information: ☎ (503) 622-7979. 🖳 www.timber linelodge.com. Ski conditions: ☎ (503) 222-2211. Central lodging: ☎ (800) 547-1406. Typical season: 12 months a year.

Peak: 8,540. Base: 4,950 base. Vertical: 3,590.

Trails: 32. Skiable acres: 2,500. Average natural snowfall: 400 inches. Snowmaking: 0%. Longest Trail: 3 miles. Trail rating: 20% Novice, 60% Intermediate, 20% Expert.

Lifts: 6 (2 high-speed quads, 1 triple, 3 doubles).

Recent prices: adult weekend, $34; child, $19; senior $19

★★ Anthony Lakes Mountain Resort

Haines, OR 97833. Information: ☎ (541) 856-3277. 🖳 www.anthonylakes.com. Ski conditions: ☎ (541) 856-3277. Typical season: Late November to early April.

Peak: 8,000. Base: 7,100. Vertical: 900.

Trails: 23. Skiable acres: 360. Average natural snowfall: 120 inches. Snowmaking: 0%. Longest trail: 1.5 miles. Trail rating: 20% Novice, 38% Intermediate, 42% Expert. Features: 13 km cross-country trails.

Lifts: 2 (1 double, 1 surface tow).

Recent prices: adult all-day, $25; child, $12; student, $19; senior, $19

★ Cooper Spur Ski Area

11000 Cloud Cap Road, Mount Hood, Parkdale, OR 97041. Information: ☎ (541) 352-7803. Ski conditions: ☎ (541) 352-7803. Central lodging: ☎ (541) 352-6629. Typical season: End of November to mid-March.

Peak: 4,500. Base: 4,100. Vertical: 400.

Trails: 8. Skiable acres: 150. Average natural snowfall: 120 inches. Snowmaking: 0%. Longest trail: 1,500 ft. Trail rating: 40% Novice, 40% Intermediate, 20% Expert. Features: 100 km cross-country trails.

Lifts: 2 (2 surface).

Recent prices: adult all-day, $12; junior, $8

★★ Hoodoo Ski Area

Box 20, Highway 20, Sisters, OR 97759. Information: ☎ (541) 822-3799. ▤ www.hoodoo.com. Ski conditions: ☎ (541) 822-3337. Typical season: Thanksgiving to mid-April; closed Wednesday. Limited night skiing.

Peak: 5,711. Base: 4,668. Vertical: 1,035.

Trails: 31. Skiable acres: 806. Average natural snowfall: 270 inches. Snowmaking: 0%. Longest trail: 1 mile. Trail rating: 30% Novice, 30% Intermediate, 40% Expert. Features: 16 km cross-country trails.

Lifts: 5 (1 quad, 1 triple, 3 doubles).

Recent prices: adult weekday, $26; adult weekend, $29; junior/senior weekday, $19.50; junior/senior weekend, $22

★★ Mount Ashland Ski Area

1745 Highway 66, Ashland, OR 97520. Information: ☎ (541) 482-2897. ▤ www.mtashland.com. Ski conditions: ☎ (541) 482-2754. Typical season: Thanksgiving to mid-April.

Peak: 7,500. Base: 6,350. Vertical: 1,150.

Trails: 23. Skiable acres: 110. Average natural snowfall: 110 inches. Snowmaking: 0%. Longest trail: 1 mile. Trail rating: 15% Novice, 35% Intermediate, 50% Expert.

Lifts: 4 (2 triples, 2 doubles).

Recent prices: adult weekend, $27; junior/senior, $22

★★★ Mount Bachelor

P.O. Box 1031, Bend, OR 97709. Information: ☎ (800) 829-2442. ▤ www.mt bachelor.com. Ski conditions: ☎ (541) 382-7888. Central lodging: ☎ (800) 987-9968. Typical season: Mid-November to July.

Peak: 9,065. Base: 6,300. Vertical: 3,365.

Trails: 70. Skiable acres: 3,686. Average natural snowfall: 350 inches. Snowmaking: 0%. Longest trail: 1.5 miles. Trail rating: 15% Novice, 40% Intermediate, 45% Expert. Features: 56 km cross-country trails.

Lifts: 13 (7 high-speed quads, 3 triples, 1 double, 2 surface).

Recent prices: adult all-day, $43; child (7–12), $22; child (13–18), $32; senior (65+), $32

★★★ Mount Hood Meadows Ski Resort

P.O. Box 470, Mount Hood, OR 97041. Information: ☎ (503) 287-5438. ▤ www.skihood.com. Ski conditions: ☎ (503) 227-7669. Central lodging: ☎ (800) 754-4663. Typical season: Mid-November to early April.

Peak: 7,300. Base: 4,523. Vertical: 2,777.

Trails: 86. Skiable acres: 2,150. Average natural snowfall: 450 inches. Snowmaking: 0%. Longest trail: 3 miles. Trail rating: 15% Novice, 50% Intermediate, 35% Expert. Features: 15 km cross-country trails. Snowcat skiing adds 1,020 vertical feet.

Lifts: 12 (4 high-speed quads, 6 doubles, 2 surface).

Recent prices: adult all-day, $39; junior, $21; senior, $25; child, $6

★★ Mount Hood SkiBowl

8700 East Highway 26, Government Camp, OR 97028. Information: ☎ (503) 272-3206. 🖳 www.skibowl.citysearch.com. Ski conditions: ☎ (503) 222-2695. Typical season: Mid-November to mid-April.

Peak: 5,506. Base: 3,600. Vertical: 1,500.

Trails: 65. Skiable acres: 960. Average natural snowfall: 300 inches. Snowmaking: 0%. Longest trail: 3 miles. Trail rating: 20% Novice, 40% Intermediate, 40% Expert.

Lifts: 9 (4 doubles, 5 surface).

Recent prices: adult weekend, $28; junior weekend, $18; senior weekend, $15

★★ Willamette Pass

P.O. Box 5509, Eugene, OR 97405. Information: ☎ (541) 484-5030. 🖳 www.willamettepass.com. Ski conditions: ☎ (541) 345-7669. Typical season: End of November to mid-April.

Peak: 6,683. Base: 5,120. Vertical: 1,563.

Trails: 29. Skiable acres: 550. Average natural snowfall: 300 inches. Snowmaking: 0%. Longest trail: 2.25 miles. Trail rating: 20% Novice, 45% Intermediate, 35% Expert. Features: 20 km cross-country trails.

Lifts: 5 (4 triples, 1 double).

Recent prices: adult all-day, $29; youth, $16; senior, $14.50

Chapter 11
Oregon Events and Festivals

Be sure to call to confirm dates and times; some phone numbers may only operate near the date of the event.

Portland Area

February

Portland International Film Festival. Northwest Film Center. ☎ (503) 221-1156. www.nw film.org. More than 100 films from 30 countries, shown at downtown theaters. Mid.

March

N.W. Barbershop Ballad Contest. Forest Grove. ☎ (503) 357-3006. Early.
    Saint Josef's Day. Canby. ☎ (503) 651-3190. Late.

April

Oregon Zoo—Rabbit Romp. Portland. ☎ (503) 226-1561. Early.
    Spring Beerfest. Portland, Multnomah Greyhound Park. ☎ (503) 246-4503. A celebration of beers from more than thirty microbreweries, plus food, music, and dancing.
    Oregon Zoo—Packy's Birthday Party. Portland. ☎ (503) 226-1561. Mid.

May

Cinco de Mayo Festival. Portland, Tom McCall Waterfront Park. ☎ (503) 222-9807. 🖥 www.cincodemayo.org. Food, entertainment, dancing, arts-and-crafts booths, and a Mexican village, honoring Portland's sister city relationship with Guadalajara, Mexico. Early.
    The Japanese Garden's Children's Day Celebration. Portland. ☎ (503) 223-1321. Early.
    Master Gardeners Spring Show & Sale. Canby. ☎ (503) 777-9131. Early.
    Oregon Zoo—National Pet Week Celebration. Portland. ☎ (503) 226-1561. Early.
    Pioneer Living & Trail Days. Oregon City. ☎ (503) 657-9336. May or June.
    Canby Junior Festival of Jazz. Canby. ☎ (503) 266-5151. Mid.
    Draft Horse Plowing Exhibition. Washington County. ☎ (503) 645-5353. Mid.
    Indian Art Northwest. South Park area in downtown Portland. ☎ (503) 224-8650. 🖥 www.northwestindian.com. Hundreds of Native American artisans offer wares. Mid.
    Spring Fling. Molalla. ☎ (503) 829-6941. Mid.
    The Zoo's for You Day. Portland. ☎ (503) 226-1561. Mid. For people with disabilities.

Summer

Canby's Saturday Growers' Market. Canby. ☎ (503) 266-4600. Summer.
    Slice of Summer Concerts. Canby. ☎ (503) 266-2086 Summer Sundays.

June

Portland Rose Festival. Portland. ☎ (503) 227-2681. 🖳 www.rosefestival.org. Month-long celebration that includes a rose show, the Portland Art Show, visiting military vessels, car races, the Grand Floral Parade, the nation's largest children's parade, dragon boat races, the downtown Starlight Parade, a hot-air balloon festival, and an air show.
    Milk Carton Boat Races. Portland. ☎ (503) 227-2681. Early.
    Rose Festival Starlight Parade. Portland. ☎ (503) 227-2681. Early.
    Elmer's Pancake & Steak House Jazz Band Festival. Portland. ☎ (503) 227-2681. Mid.
    Japanese Garden: Ikebana Rose Show. Portland. ☎ (503) 223-1321. Mid.
    Milwaukie Festival Daze. Milwaukie. ☎ (503) 513-6416. Mid.
    Rhythm & Zoo Outdoor Concerts. Portland. ☎ (503) 226-1561. Mid.
    Rose Festival Dragon Boat Races. Portland. ☎ (503) 227-2681. Mid.
    Strawberry Festival. Wilsonville. ☎ (503) 682-0339. Mid.
    Lake Oswego Festival of the Arts. Lake Oswego. ☎ (503) 636-1060. Late.
    Portland Arts Festival. Portland. ☎ (503) 227-2681. Late.
    Rose Festival Airshow. Portland. ☎ (503) 227-2681. Late.
    The Rotary Rose Festival Ducky Derby. Portland. ☎ (503) 227-2681. Late.
    Tigard Festival of Balloons. Tigard. ☎ (503) 590-1828. Late.

July

Waterfront Blues Festival. Portland, Tom McCall Waterfront Park. ☎ (503) 282-0555 or ☎ (503) 973-3378. 🖳 www.waterfrontbluesfest.com. One of the largest blues festivals in the United States, offering live performances on two stages. Early.
    Chamber Music Northwest. Portland, Reed College and Catlin Gabel School. ☎ (503) 223-3202. 🖳 www.cmnw.org. Five-week series of concerts.
    Day in the Park 4th of July Celebration & Skyshow. Estacada. ☎ (503) 630-3483.
    General Canby Days. Canby. ☎ (503) 266-7545. July 4.
    Molalla Buckaroo Giant Street Parade. Molalla. ☎ (503) 829-6914. Early.
    Oregon Zoo—Roar Faire. Portland. ☎ (503) 226-1561. Early.
    The Japanese Garden's Tanbata Star Festival. Portland. ☎ (503) 223-1321. Early.
    Division/Clinton Street Fair & Showcase. Portland. ☎ (503) 774-2832. Mid.
    The Taste of Beaverton. Beaverton. ☎ (503) 644-0123. Mid.
    Oregon Brewers Festival. Portland, Tom McCall Waterfront Park; ☎ (503) 778-5917. 🖳 www.oregonbrewfest.com. The largest gathering of independent breweries in North America, with food, music, and special events. Late.
    Washington County Fair and Rodeo. Hillsboro. ☎ (503) 648-1416. Late.

August

The Chautauqua Festival. Gladstone. ☎ (503) 656-5225. Early.
    The Bite . . . A Taste of Portland. Portland, Tom McCall Waterfront Park. ☎ (503) 248-0600. Food by local chefs, regional wines, and music to benefit the Special Olympics.
    The Japanese Garden's Paper Arts Festival. Portland. ☎ (503) 223-1321. Mid.
    Tualatin Crawfish Festival. Tualatin. ☎ (503) 692-0780. Mid.
    Clackamas County Fair & Rodeo. Canby. ☎ (503) 266-1136. Late.
    Homowo Festival of African Arts. Portland. ☎ (503) 288-3025. Late.
    Big Wagon Days. Oregon City. ☎ (503) 657-9336. Late.
    Swan Island Indoor Dahlia Show. Canby. ☎ (503) 266-7711. Late.

September

Beavercreek Bust. Beavercreek. ☎ (503) 632-3494. Early.
    OMSI Reptile & Amphibian Show. Portland. ☎ (503) 797-4588. Early.
    Oregon Zoo—Senior Safari Day. Portland. ☎ (503) 226-1561. Late.
    Philip Foster Farm Cider & Harvest Festival. Eagle Creek. ☎ (503) 637-6324. Late.
    Saint Josef's Annual Grape Stomp. Canby. ☎ (503) 651-3190. Late.

Portland Creative Conference. Portland Center for the Performing Arts. ☎ (503) 234-1641. 🖳 www.cre8con.org. An exploration of the creative process, featuring film, television, advertising, and new media industries. Past speakers include Spike Lee, Gary Larson (creator of *The Far Side*), and Portland native Matt Groening (creator of "The Simpsons").

North by Northwest Music Festival. (512) 467-7979. 🖳 www.nxnw.com. Folk to funk, acoustic to alternative, rap to reggae, plus workshops on the business of music.

Celtic Music Fest. Champoeg Park Amphitheater, Camby. ☎ (503) 274-0019. Celtic food, crafts, music, and beer. The event, about thirty miles south of Portland, benefits organizations that provide support to battered and abused women and children. Early.

Mount Angel Oktoberfest. Village of Mount Angel. ☎ (503) 845-9440. Oregon's largest Oktoberfest, about thirty-five minutes southeast of Portland. Mid.

Horst Mager Oktoberfest. Oaks Amusement Park, Portland. ☎ (503) 232-3000. German bands, beer garden, food, and arts and crafts displays. Mid.

October

Abernethy's Birthday Celebration. Oregon City. ☎ (503) 657-9336. Early.
   Apple Festival. Molalla. ☎ (503) 829-6941. Early.
   The Great Annual Onion Festival. Sherwood. ☎ (503) 625-6751. Early.
   Chili Cookoff & Harvest Festival. Canby. ☎ (503) 266-6831. Mid.

November

A Pioneer Harvest. Oregon City. ☎ (503) 657-9336. Late.
   Holiday Lighting Ceremony. Canby. ☎ (503) 266-4600. Late.

December

Winter Ale Festival. Portland, Pioneer Courthouse Square. ☎ (503) 274-0019. Seasonal brews, holiday music, food, and crafts booths. Early.
   A Pioneer Holiday. Oregon City. ☎ (503) 657-9336.
   Festival of Lights at the Grotto. Portland, The Grotto. ☎ (503) 254-7371. 🖳 www.thegrotto.org. A month-long display of nearly 150,000 lights, the largest choral festival in the Pacific Northwest, and entertainment for children.
   Zoolights Festival. Portland, The Oregon Zoo. ☎ (503) 226-1561. 🖳 www.oregonzoo.org. Light displays, train rides, music, and other celebrations at the zoo.
   Wild Arts Festival. Portland. ☎ (503) 292-6855. Late.
   Holiday Concert. Lake Oswego. ☎ (503) 636-9673. Early.
   Japanese Garden's Geijutsu Sai Artist's Festival. Portland. ☎ (503) 223-1321. Early.
   Oldtown Christmas Celebration. Sherwood. ☎ (503) 625-6873 or ☎ (503) 625-5692. Early.

Oregon Coast

January

Annual Artistry in Wood Show. Lincoln City. ☎ (800) 452-2151. Early.
   Barbershop Quartet Cabaret. Seaside. ☎ (888) 306-2326. Mid.
   Chocolate & Coffee Lovers Festival. Seaside. ☎ (888) 306-2326. Late.

February

Annual Whale of a Wine Festival. Gold Beach. ☎ (541) 247-2113. Early.
   Nehalem 100 Year Ice Cream Social. Nehalem. ☎ (503) 368-5100. Early.
   Antique Week–Lincoln Days. Lincoln City. ☎ (800) 452-2151. Mid.
   Charleston Merchants' Annual Crab Feed. Charleston. ☎ (800) 824-8486. Mid.
   Warrenton Centennial Crab Feed. Warrenton. ☎ (503) 861-3426. Mid.
   Newport Seafood & Wine Festival. Newport. ☎ (541) 265-8801. Late.
   Oregon Dixieland Jubilee. Seaside. ☎ (888) 306-2326. Late.

March

Crafts Unlimited Country Easter Craft Sale. North Bend. Early.
  Oregon Dune Mushers' Annual Mail Run. North Bend to Florence. ☎ (541) 269-1269. Early.
  North Bend Annual Jazz Festival. ☎ (541) 756-4613. Mid.
  Sea-Side Chowder Cook-Off. Seaside. ☎ (888) 306-2326, Mid.
  Southcoast Dixieland Clambake Jazz Festival. Coos Bay/North Bend. ☎ (800) 824-8486. Mid.
  Great Oregon Spring Beach Cleanup. Oregon Coast. ☎ (800) 452-2051. Late.
  Spring Whale Watch Week. Lincoln City. ☎ (800) 452-2151. Late.
  Whale Watch Week–Cape Perpetua. Yachats. ☎ (541) 563-2002. Late.
  Whale Watching Oregon Coast. ☎ (503) 325-6311. Late March to early April.

April

Annual Easter Pet Parade and Egg Hunt. Gleneden Beach. ☎ (800) 452-2151. Early.
  Clam Chowder Festival Flower & Art Show. Gold Beach. ☎ (800) 525-2334. Early.
  Community Days. Lincoln City. ☎ (541) 994-3070. Early.
  Easter Egg Hunt–Bonnet Contest. Manzanita. ☎ (503) 368-5100. Early.
  Easter Egg Hunt. Cloverdale. ☎ (503) 392-4900. Early.
  Lion's Follies. Seaside. ☎ (503) 738-3311. Early.
  Rhodie Walk at the Connie Hansen Garden. Lincoln City. ☎ (800) 452-2151. Mid.
  Classic Wooden Boat Show. Depoe Bay. ☎ (541) 765-2889. Late.
  Crab & Seafood Festival. Hammond, Astoria, Warrenton. ☎ (503) 325-6311. Late.
  Puffin Kite Festival. Cannon Beach. ☎ (503) 436-2623. Late.
  Rhododendron Truss Show. North Bend. ☎ (541) 396-2718. Late.

May

Clam Chowder Festival Flower & Art Show. Gold Beach. ☎ (800) 525-2334. Early.
  Mother's Day Rhododendron Sunday at Shore Acres. Charleston. ☎ (800) 824-8486. Early.
  Oregon Coast Aquarium Spring Garden Show. Newport. ☎ (541) 867-3474. Early.
  Spring Kite Festival. Lincoln City. ☎ (800) 452-2151. Early.
  Annual Touch a Truck. Lincoln City. ☎ (800) 452-2151. Mid.
  Astoria Yacht Club Opening Day Festivities. Astoria. ☎ (503) 325-6612. Mid.
  Historic Walking Tour of Downtown Coos Bay. Coos Bay. ☎ (800) 824-8486. Mid.
  Kite Festival. Rockaway Beach. ☎ (503) 355-8108. Mid.
  Rhododendron Festival. Florence. ☎ (541) 997-3128. Mid.
  Annual Fleet of Flowers. Depoe Bay. ☎ (800) 452-2151. Late.
  Azalea Festival. Brookings. ☎ (800) 535-9469. Late.
  Seafood & Wine Festival. Bandon. ☎ (541) 347-4438. Late.

Summer

Fort Clatsop Living History. Astoria. ☎ (503) 861-2471,
  Sawdust Theatre. Coquille. ☎ (541) 396-3414.

June

Gay '90s Celebration. Coquille. ☎ (541) 396-3414. Early.
  Oregon Coast Aquarium Day of the Ocean. Newport. ☎ (541) 867-3474. Early.
  Sandcastle Day Festival. Cannon Beach. ☎ (503) 436-2623. Early.
  Jubilee. Cloverdale. ☎ (503) 392-3445. Late.
  Radio Controlled Model Airplane Show. Coos Bay. ☎ (541) 267-0871. Mid.
  Scandinavian Festival. Astoria. ☎ (503) 325-3099. Mid.
  Wheeler Crab Fest. Wheeler. ☎ (503) 368-5100. Mid.
  World Whale Day–Cape Perpetua. Yachats. ☎ (541) 563-2002. Mid.
  Father's Day Rose Sunday at Shore Acres. Charleston. ☎ (800) 824-8486. Late.

Tillamook County Rodeo. Tillamook. ☎ (503) 842-7525. Late.
Tillamook Dairy Festival & Parade. Tillamook. ☎ (503) 842-7525. Late.

July

4th of July Auction. Rockaway Beach. ☎ (503) 355-8108.
   4th of July Celebration & Fireworks. Coos Bay. ☎ (800) 824-8486.
   4th of July Celebration. Astoria. ☎ (503) 325-2323.
   4th of July Celebration. Florence. ☎ (541) 997-3128.
   4th of July Community Parade. Gleneden Beach. ☎ (800) 452-2151.
   4th of July Fireworks Display. Lincoln City. ☎ (800) 452-2151.
   4th of July Picnic Parade & Fireworks. Seaside. ☎ (888) 306-2326.
   Food Fun Fireworks! North Bend. ☎ (800) 953-4800. July 3.
   Lah de Dah 4th of July Parade & Fireworks Display. Yachats. ☎ (541) 547-3530.
   Old-Fashioned 4th of July Celebration. Bandon. ☎ (541) 347-9616.
   Pacific City Fireworks. Pacific City. ☎ (503) 965-7600.
   Pancake Breakfast and 4th of July Parade. Manzanita. ☎ (503) 368-7229.
   Parade and Old-Fashioned Festival. Seaside. ☎ (503) 738-7065. July 4.
   Rockaway Beach Annual 4th of July Parade & Fireworks. Rockaway Beach. ☎
(503) 355-2291.
   The Mill Casino 3rd of July Festivities. North Bend. ☎ (800) 953-4800.
   Dory Festival & Parade. Pacific City. ☎ (503) 965-7600. Mid.
   North Bend Heritage Jubilee. Northbend. ☎ (541) 756-4613. Mid.
   Oregon Coast Music Festival. Coos Bay. ☎ (541) 267-0938 or ☎ (800) 676-7563. Mid.
   Yachats Annual Smelt Fry. Yachats. ☎ (541) 547-3530. Mid.
   Yachats Music Festival. Yachats. ☎ (541) 547-3530. Mid.
   Ernest Bloch Music Festival. Newport. ☎ (541) 265-2787. Late.
   Garibaldi Days Festival. Garibaldi. ☎ (503) 322-0301. Late.
   Lincoln County Fair. Newport. ☎ (541) 265-6237. Late.

August

Tea & Scones. Astoria. ☎ (503) 325-2203.
   Clatsop County Fair. Astoria. ☎ (503) 325-4600. Early.
   Nehalem Arts Festival. Nehalem. ☎ (503) 368-5100. Early.
   Oregon Coast Aquarium Rhythms by the Bay Music Festival. Newport. ☎ (541)
867-3474. Early.
   Salmon BBQ. Charleston. ☎ (800) 824-8486. Early.
   Steamboat Meet. Wheeler. ☎ (503) 368-5100. Early.
   Tillamook County Fair. Tillamook. ☎ (503) 842-2272. Early.
   Astoria Regatta Festival. Astoria. ☎ (503) 325-3984. Mid.
   Coos County Fair & Rodeo. Myrtle Point. ☎ (541) 572-2002. Mid.
   Historic Homes Tour. Astoria. ☎ (503) 325-2203. Mid.
   Sand Blast Rod Run. Charleston. ☎ (541) 756-4768. Mid.
   Sandcastle Building Contest. Lincoln City. ☎ (800) 452-2151. Mid.
   Tillamook County Fair. Tillamook. ☎ (503) 842-2272. Mid.
   Blackberry Arts Festival. Coos Bay. ☎ (541) 269-0215. Late.
   Charleston Seafood Festival. Charleston. ☎ (541) 888-8083. Late.
   Nestucca Valley Artisans Festival. Pacific City. ☎ (503) 398-5945. Late.

September

Annual Jazz Festival. Lincoln City. ☎ (800) 452-2151. Early.
   Bandon Cranberry Festival. Bandon. ☎ (541) 347-9619. Early.
   Bite of Seaside. Seaside. ☎ (503) 738-8863. Early.
   Bull Bash—Bull Riding Competition. North Bend. ☎ (800) 953-4800. Early.
   Hillbilly Daze. Cloverdale. ☎ (503) 392-3456. Early.
   Lewis & Clark Kite Festival. Seaside. ☎ (888) 306-2326. Early.
   Salmon/Berry Fest. Wheeler. ☎ (503) 368-5100. Early.

Seaside Art Festival Quatat Marine Park. Seaside. ☎ (800) 394-3303. Early.
Shorebird Festival. Charleston. ☎ (541) 267-7202. Early.
Southern Oregon Dahlia Society Show. North Bend. ☎ (541) 267-0740. Early.
Autumn Festival. Rockaway Beach. ☎ (503) 355-8108. Mid.
Chowder Brews & Blues. Florence. ☎ (541) 997-3128. Late.
Cruz the Coos—Rolling Car Cruise. Coos Bay. ☎ (541) 269-0215. Mid.
Depoe Bay Salmon Bake. Depoe Bay. ☎ (800) 452-2151. Mid.
Southern Oregon Dahlia Society Show. North Bend. ☎ (541) 756-4613. Mid.

October

Fall International Kite Festival. Lincoln City. ☎ (800) 452-2151. Early.
   Hathaway Jones Tall Tales Festival. Gold Beach. ☎ (541) 247-6113. Mid.
   Boo Boogie Bash. North Bend. ☎ (800) 953-4800. Late.
   Halloween Dance & Family Activities. Yachats. ☎ (541) 547-3530. Late.
   Oregon Coast Aquarium Creatures of the Night Halloween Party. Newport. ☎
(541) 867-3474. Late.

November

Beach Lights Kickoff and Devils Lake Regatta. Lincoln City. ☎ (800) 452-2151. Late.
   Christmas Parade Lighting Ceremony & Caroling. Seaside. ☎ (888) 306-2326. Late.
   Holiday Lights & Open House at Shore Acres. Charleston. ☎ (541) 269-0215. Late
November to early January.
   Yachats Winter Celebrations. Yachats. ☎ (541) 547-3530. Late November to late
December.

December

Nutcracker Ballet. Astoria. ☎ (503) 325-3911. Early.
   Oregon Coast Aquarium Sea of Lights Holiday Festival. Newport. ☎ (541) 867-
3474. Early.
   Sail with Santa Holiday Cruise. Newport. ☎ (541) 867-3474. Early.
   Sea of Lights Holiday Party. Newport. ☎ (541) 867-3474. Early.
   Sounds of Christmas. Coos Bay. ☎ (541) 267-3823. Early.
   The Mill Casino Christmas Tree Lighting & Carolers. North Bend. ☎ (800) 953-
4800. Early.
   Winter Garden Party. Lincoln City. ☎ (800) 452-2151. Early.
   Zonta Christmas Arts and Crafts Festival. North Bend. ☎ (541) 888-8752. Mid.
   Nature's Coastal Holiday Light Festival. Brookings. ☎ (800) 525-9273. Mid.
   Plum Pudding. Astoria. ☎ (503) 325-2203. Mid-December to late January.
   New Year's Eve Celebration. North Bend. ☎ (541) 756-8800. Late.
   Whale Watch Week Yachats. ☎ (541) 563-3211. Late December to early January.
   Winter Whale Watch Week. Lincoln City. ☎ (800) 452-2151. Late.

Central Oregon

February

Eagle Watch. Culver. ☎ (541) 546-2873. Late.
   Lincoln's Pow Wow. Warm Springs. ☎ (541) 553-2461. Mid.

April

Easter Eggstravaganza. Redmond. ☎ (541) 923-5208 or ☎ (800) 574-1325. Early.
   The High Desert Museum–Family Science Festival. Bend. ☎ (541) 382-4754. Mid.

May

Treasures of Oregon. Moro. ☎ (541) 565-3232. Early.
   Collage of Culture. Madras. ☎ (541) 475-2350. Mid.

June

Oregon High School Rodeo. Bend. ☎ (541) 447-6575. Mid.
  Sisters Rodeo. Sisters. ☎ (541) 549-6691. Mid.
  Crooked River Rodeo. Prineville. ☎ (541) 447-4479. Late.
  Pi-Ume-She Treaty Days. Warm Springs. ☎ (541) 553-2461. Late.
  Rockhounds Association Pow Wow. Prineville. ☎ (541) 548-7477. Late.

July

4th of July Parade. Redmond. ☎ (541) 923-5191.
  Old-Fashioned 4th of July Celebration. Prineville. ☎ (541) 447-6307.
  Sparklers 4th of July Celebration. Madras. ☎ (541) 475-3106.
  Bend Summer Festival. Bend. ☎ (541) 385-6570. Early.
  Crooked River Ranch 4th of July Celebration. Crooked River Ranch. ☎ (541) 923-2679.
  Culver Great American Day. Culver. ☎ (541) 546-8641. Early.
  Jefferson County Fair & Rodeo. Madras. ☎ (541) 475-4460. Late.

August

Antique Summerfest. Redmond. ☎ (541) 504-3378. Mid.
  Dixieland Jazz Festival. Crescent Lake. ☎ (541) 433-2793. Mid.
  High Desert Celtic Celebration. Prineville. ☎ (541) 447-3561. Mid.
  Sunriver Music Festival. Sunriver. ☎ (541) 593-1084. Mid.

September

Lake Billy Chinook Day Celebration. Culver. ☎ (541) 546-2873. Mid.
  The High Desert Museum Artifact Day. Bend. ☎ (541) 382-4754. Mid.
  The High Desert Museum Cider Season Celebration. Bend. ☎ (541) 382-4754. Late.
  Railroad Days. Redmond. ☎ (541) 923-5208. Late.

October

Fossil Antique Show. Fossil. ☎ (541) 763-2355. Early.
  Sisters Harvest Faire. Sisters. ☎ (541) 549-0251. Early.

November

Starfest Light Tour. Redmond. ☎ (541) 923-2453. November and December.
  Antique Winterfest. Redmond. ☎ (541) 504-3378. Mid.
  Christmas Open House. Redmond. ☎ (541) 923-5208. Late.
  Starlight Christmas Parade. Redmond. ☎ (541) 923-5191. Late.
  The High Desert Museum Holiday Festival. Bend. ☎ (541) 382-4754. Late.

Mount Hood Area

April

The Dalles Dam Open House. The Dalles. ☎ (541) 296-9778. Late.
  Northwest Cherry Festival. The Dalles. ☎ (800) 255-3385. Late.

May

Mount Hood Railroad Train Robbery. Hood River. ☎ (800) 872-4661. Mid.
  Song Bird Celebration. Welches. ☎ (503) 622-4011. Late.

June

Hood River Hunter/Jumper Horse Show. Hood River Valley. ☎ (541) 387-6474. Mid.
  Mount Hood Railroad Train Robbery. Hood River. ☎ (800) 872-4661. Mid.
  Big River Band Festival. Arlington. ☎ (541) 454-2846. Late.
  Sternwheeler Days. Cascade Locks. ☎ (541) 374-8619. Late.

July

Cherry Harvest in Hood River. Hood River Valley. ☎ (541) 386-2000. Early to mid-July.
  Mount Hood Community 4th of July Celebration. Welches. ☎ (503) 622-3017. Early.
  Sandy Mountain Festival. Sandy. ☎ (503) 668-4006. Early.
  Fort Dalles Rodeo. The Dalles. ☎ (800) 255-3385. Mid.
  Gorge Games. Hood River. ☎ (541) 386-7774. Mid.
  Mount Hood Railroad Train Robbery. Hood River. ☎ (800) 872-4661. Mid.
  Oregon Old-Time Fiddlers. Welches. ☎ (503) 622-4011. Mid.
  Hood River County Fair. Hood River. ☎ (541) 354-2865. Late.

August

Mount Hood Railroad Train Robbery. Hood River. ☎ (800) 872-4661. Mid.
  Wasco County Fair. Tygh Valley. ☎ (800) 255-3385. Mid.
  Gravenstein Apple Days. Hood River Valley. ☎ (541) 386-2000. Late.
  Huckleberry Festival. Welches. ☎ (503) 622-4011. Late.

September

Mount Hood Railroad Train Robbery. Hood River. ☎ (800) 872-4661. Mid.
  Salmon Splash. Cascade Locks. ☎ (541) 374-8619. Mid.
  Mount Hood Railroad Native American Celebration. Hood River. ☎ (800) 872-4661. Late.

October

Salmon/Mushroom Festival. Welches. ☎ (503) 622-4011. Early.
  Mount Hood Railroad Halloween Spook Train. Hood River. ☎ (800) 872-4661. Late.

November

Pioneer Harvest Feast. Welches. ☎ (503) 622-4011. Early.
  Mount Hood Public Lands Clean-Up. Welches. ☎ (503) 622-4011. Mid.
  The Resort at the Mountain's Wine & Art Festival. Welches. ☎ (503) 622-3101. Late.
  Starlight Parade. The Dalles. ☎ (800) 255-3385. Late.

December

Community Tree Trimming. Hood River. ☎ (800) 386-1859. Early.
  Mount Hood Railroad Christmas Tree Train. Hood River. ☎ (800) 872-4661. Early.
  Christmas Along the Barlow Trail. Welches. ☎ (503) 622-4011. Mid.

Willamette Valley

January

Springfield Puppet Festival. Springfield. ☎ (541) 726-3766. January and February.

February

Ski Area Hoodoo Winter Carnival. Hoodoo. ☎ (541) 822-3799. Mid.
  Oregon Wine & Food Festival. Salem. ☎ (503) 362-3443. Mid.

March

Hoodoo Roundup. Hoodoo Ski Area. ☎ (541) 822-3799. Mid.
  Vintage Release Festival. Turner. ☎ (503) 588-9463. Mid.
  Scottish Heritage Festival. Salem. ☎ (541) 753-4341. Late.
  Woodburn Tulip Festival. Woodburn. ☎ (503) 982-8221. Late March to April.

May

Iris Festival Art Show. Keizer. ☎ (503) 390-3010.

Carriage Me Back. Brownville. ☎ (541) 466-3084. Early.
Founders Day at Champoeg State Heritage Area. St. Paul. ☎ (503) 678-1251. Early.
Sheep to Shawl Festivities. Salem. ☎ (503) 585-7012. Early.
Linn County Lamb & Wool Fair. Scio. ☎ (503) 394-3389. Mid.
Memorial Weekend Tour de Vine. Salem. ☎ (503) 986-0001. Late.
Prefontaine Classic. Eugene. ☎ (541) 484-5307. Late.
Salem Rodeo. Salem. ☎ (503) 581-4325. Late.
Tastevin Tour (Polk County Wineries). Salem. ☎ (503) 581-4325. Late.

June

Function in Junction Cruise-In. Junction City. ☎ (541) 689-7334. Early.
Lebanon Strawberry Festival. Lebanon. ☎ (541) 258-7164. Early.
Springfield Museum Garden Tour. Springfield. ☎ (541) 726-3677. Early.
Pioneer Picnic. Brownville. ☎ (541) 466-3380. Mid.
Oregon Bach Festival. Eugene. ☎ (800) 457-5445. Late June to mid-July.
World Beat Festival. Salem. ☎ (503) 581-2004. Late.

July

Old-Fashioned 4th of July & Fireworks. Harrisburg. ☎ (541) 995-8645.
Red, White & Blues Riverfront Festival. Corvallis. ☎ (541) 754-6624. July 4.
Stayton's Old-Fashioned 4th. Stayton. ☎ (503) 769-3464.
Willamina's Old-Fashioned 4th of July. Willamina. ☎ (503) 876-5777.
Art & the Vineyard. Eugene. ☎ (541) 484-5307. Early.
Fireworks Over Detroit Lake. Detroit. ☎ (503) 854-3696. Early.
Marion County Fair. Salem. ☎ (503) 585-9998. Early.
Oregon Country Fair. Veneta. ☎ (541) 343-4298. Early.
Philomath Frolic & Rodeo. Philomath. ☎ (541) 929-2611. Early.
Sportsman's Holiday & Sweet Home Rodeo. Sweet Home. ☎ (541) 367-6186. Early.
Turkey Rama. McMinnville. ☎ (503) 472-6196. Early.
Western Days Old-Fashioned 4th of July. Independence & Monmouth. ☎ (503) 838-4268. Early.
World Championship Timber Carnival. Albany. ☎ (541) 928-2391. Early.
da Vinci Days. Corvallis. ☎ (541) 757-6363. Mid.
Hubbard Hop Festival. Hubbard. ☎ (503) 982-8221. Mid.
Salem Art Fair & Festival. Salem. ☎ (503) 581-2228. Mid.
Tour da Vinci. Eugene. ☎ (800) 547-5445. Mid.
Art in the Park. Dallas.☎ (503) 606-9104. Late.
Bite of Salem. Salem. ☎ (503) 364-3123. Late July to early August.
Dallas Summerfest. Dallas. ☎ (503) 623-2564. Late.
Great Balloon Excape. Albany. ☎ (800) 526-2256. Late July to early August.
Linn County Fair. Albany. ☎ (800) 858-2005 or ☎ (541) 926-4314. Late.
McKenzie River Lions Leaburg Festival. Leaburg. ☎ (541) 896-3330. Late.
Newberg Old-Fashioned Festival. Newberg. ☎ (503) 538-9455. Late.
Oregon Bach Festival. Eugene. ☎ (800) 547-5445. Late.
Santiam Canyon Stampede/Rodeo. Sublimity. ☎ (503) 769-2799. Late.
Santiam Summerfest. Stayton. ☎ (503) 769-3464. Late.

August

Mexican Fiesta. Woodburn. ☎ (503) 982-8221. Early.
Polk County Fair. Rickreall. ☎ (503) 623-3048. Early.
Tour de Lane. Eugene. ☎ (800) 547-5445. Early.
Yamhill County Fair. McMinnville. ☎ (503) 434-7524. Early.
Aurora Colony Days. Aurora. ☎ (503) 678-2288. Mid.
Junction City Scandinavian Festival. Junction City. ☎ (541) 998-9372. Mid.
Oregon Jamboree. Sweet Home. ☎ (541) 367-8800. Mid.

Bull-O-Rama. Philomath. ☎ (541) 929-2611. Late.
Elephant Garlic Festival. North Plains. ☎ (800) 661-1799. Late.
Oregon State Fair. Salem. ☎ (503) 581-4325. Late.

September

Kermesse Mexican Independence Day Fiesta. Independence. ☎ (503) 838-4268. Early.
   Original Coburg Antique Fair. Coburg. ☎ (541) 688-1181. Early.
   Shrewsbury Renaissance Faire. Philomath. ☎ (541) 929-4897. Early.
   Silver Falls Musical Festival at Silver Falls State Park. Sublimity. ☎ (503) 873-3495. Early.
   Sublimity Harvest Festival. Sublimity. ☎ (503) 769-3579. Early.
   Walterville Community Fair. Walterville. ☎ (541) 747-9563. Early.
   Eugene Celebration. Eugene. ☎ (541) 484-5307. Mid.
   Mount Angel Oktoberfest. Mount Angel. ☎ (503) 845-9440. Mid.
   Oregon Grape Stomp Championship & Harvest Festival. Turner. ☎ (503) 588-9463. Mid.
   Scandinavian Fall Fair. Rickreall. ☎ (503) 391-7827. Mid.
   Corvallis Fall Festival. Corvallis. ☎ (541) 752-9655. Late.
   Indian Summer Folklife Festival. St. Paul. ☎ (503) 678-1251. Late.

October

Brocard's Antique Cider Press. Sweet Home. ☎ (541) 367-4840.
   Walker Family History. Albany. ☎ (541) 926-4680. Late.

November

Fire Department Turkey Carnival. Newberg. ☎ (503) 537-1230. Early.
   Christmas Storybook Land. Albany. ☎ (800) 526-2256. Late November to mid-December.

December

Night Time Magic. Albany. ☎ (800) 526-2256.
   Christmas in Sweet Home. Sweet Home. ☎ (541) 367-6186. Early.
   Christmas Parlour Tour. Albany. ☎ (800) 526-2256. Early.
   Festival of Lights Holiday Parade. Salem. ☎ (503) 581-4325. Early.
   Holiday Craft Bazaar & Downtown Celebration. Stayton. ☎ (503) 769-3464. Early.
   Lebanon Christmas Tree Lighting. Lebanon. ☎ (541) 258-7164. Early.
   Parade of Light. Junction City. ☎ (541) 998-9372. Early.
   Salem Greens Show. Salem. ☎ (503) 581-4325. Early.
   Willamette Christmas Greens Show. Salem. ☎ (503) 581-4325. Early.
   Willamina Christmas Lights Parade. Willamina. ☎ (503) 876-5777. Early.
   Winter Lights Festival. Wilsonville. ☎ (503) 638-6933. Early.
   Hoodoo New Year's Party. Hoodoo Ski Area. ☎ (541) 822-3337. December 31.

Southern Oregon
January

Invitational Sled Dog Races. Chemult. ☎ (541) 365-7001. Late.
   Bavarian Night Mount Ashland Ski Area. Ashland. ☎ (541) 482-2897. Late.

February

Bald Eagle Conference. Klamath Falls. ☎ (800) 445-6728. Mid.
   Oregon Shakespeare Festival. Ashland. ☎ (541) 482-4331. February to October.
   Sherm Anderson Memorial Cross Country Ski Race. Klamath Falls. ☎ (541) 883-3261. Mid.

March

Taste of Ashland. Ashland. ☎ (541) 488-8430. Late.

April

Pear Blossom Parade and Run. Medford. ☎ (541) 772-6293. Early.
    Wildflower Show. Glide. ☎ (541) 496-3616. Late.
    Western Art Show at the Favell Museum. Klamath Falls. ☎ (541) 882-9996. Late.
    Hoodoo Spring Fling. Hoodoo Ski Area. ☎ (541) 822-3337.

May

Oakland Historic Day. Oakland. ☎ (541) 459-4531. Early.
    Wildlife Safari Mother's Day Special. Winston. ☎ (800) 355-4848. Early.
    Boatnik Festival. Grants Pass. ☎ (800) 547-5927. Late.
    Bonanza Cemetery Memorial Day BBQ. Bonanza. ☎ (541) 545-6980. Late.

June

Umpqua Discovery Days. Roseburg. ☎ (800) 444-9584. Early.
    Antique Tractor Show & Pioneer Fair. Grants Pass. ☎ (800) 547-5927. Mid.
    Britt Festivals. Jacksonville. ☎ (800) 882-7488. Mid-June to early July.
    Illinois River Celebration & Parade. Cave Junction. ☎ (541) 592-6139. Mid.
    Living History Day at Collier State Park. Chiloquin. ☎ (541) 783-2471. Mid.
    Oregon Shakespeare Festival—Feast of Will. Ashland. ☎ (541) 482-4331. Mid.
    Umpqua Valley Round-Up. Roseburg. ☎ (541) 672-9731. Mid.
    Wildlife Safari Father's Day Special. Winston. ☎ (800) 355-4848. Mid.
    Umpqua Valley Summer Arts Festival. Roseburg. ☎ (541) 672-9731. Late.

July

4th of July Auto Races & Fireworks Spectacular. Roseburg. ☎ (541) 672-9731.
    4th of July Celebration at Veterans Park. Klamath Falls. ☎ (541) 884-3306.
    4th of July Fireworks & Celebration. Merrill. ☎ (541) 798-5808.
    Ashland's Old-Fashioned 4th of July Celebration. Ashland. ☎ (541) 482-3486.
    Firecracker Regatta. Klamath Falls.☎ (541) 883-3339. Early.
    Graffiti Week. Roseburg. ☎ (541) 672-1071. Early.
    Riddle Sawdust Jubilee. Riddle. ☎ (541) 874-2334. Early.
    Chiloquin Western Days. Chiloquin. ☎ (541) 783-2471. Mid.
    Living History Days & Country Faire. Fort Klamath. ☎ (541) 882-2340. Mid.
    Summer Fun Day & Car Cruise. Gilchrist. ☎ (541) 433-2523. Mid.
    Chiloquin Rodeo & Barbecue. Chiloquin. ☎ (541) 783-2471. Late.
    Jackson County Fair. Central Point. ☎ (541) 776-7237. Late.
    Klamath Tribes Restoration Celebration. Chiloquin. ☎ (541) 783-2471. Late.
    Pioneer Cup Canoe & Kayak Races & BBQ. Odell Lake. ☎ (541) 433-2540. Late.
    Calhoun Ridge Winery and Blues Festival. Roseburg. ☎ (800) 444-9584.

August

Douglas County Fair. Roseburg. ☎ (541) 672-9731. Early to Mid.
    Klamath County Fair & Jefferson Stampede Rodeo. Klamath Falls. ☎ (541) 883-3796. Early.
    Celtic Highland Games. Myrtle Creek. ☎ (541) 673-7463. Mid.
    Josephine County Fair. Grants Pass. ☎ (541) 476-3215. Mid.
    Rogue Valley Balloon Rally. Medford. ☎ (541) 779-7250. Mid.
    Wild Blackberry Festival. Cave Junction. ☎ (541) 592-3326. Mid.
    Canyonville Pioneer Days. Canyonville. ☎ (541) 839-4391. Late.
    Jedediah Smith Mountain Man Rendezvous. Grants Pass. ☎ (541) 476-2040. Late.

September

Antique Equipment Show & Threshing Bee. Hildebrand. ☎ (541) 545-6510. Early.
   Lion's Club Parade & Labor Day Festival. Cave Junction. ☎ (541) 592-4135. Early.
   Logger's Breakfast at Collier State Park. Chiloquin. ☎ (541) 783-2471. Early.
   Jackson County Oktoberfest. Jackson County. ☎ (541) 776-7237. Early.
   Wine, Art & Music Festival. Roseburg. ☎ (800) 444-9584. Early.
   Winston/Dillard Melon Festival. Winston. ☎ (541) 679-6739. Early.
   Myrtle Creek Bluegrass & Arts Festival, Civil War Encampment. Myrtle Creek.
☎ (541) 673-9759. Mid.
   Oktoberfest Microbrew Festival. Roseburg. ☎ (541) 672-9731. Late.

October

Harvest Fair & Wine Festival. Central Point. ☎ (541) 776-7237. Early.
   Medford Jazz Festival. Medford. ☎ (541) 770-6972. Early.

November

Festival of Light. Ashland.☎ (541) 482-348. Late November to late December.
   Victorian Christmas. Jacksonville. ☎ (541) 899-8118. Late November to late December.
   Wildlife Safari Thanksgiving Special. Winston. ☎ (800) 355-4848. Late.

December

Umpqua Valley Festival of Lights. Roseburg. ☎ (541) 672-3469.
   Candlelight Tour of Homes. Ashland. ☎ (541) 482-3486. Early.
   Illinois Valley Christmas Parade. Cave Junction.☎ (541) 592-3326. Early.
   Seasonal Tree Lighting. Bonanza. ☎ (541) 545-6513. Early.
   Snowflake Festival & Parade. Klamath Falls. ☎ (541) 883-5368. Early.
   Wildlife Safari's Wildlights. Winston. ☎ (800) 355-4848. Mid- to late December.
   Family New Year's Eve Ski Celebration at Mount Ashland. Ashland. ☎ (541) 482-
2897. Late.

Eastern Oregon

January

Hells Canyon Winterfest. Halfway. ☎ (800) 523-1235. Early.

February

Basque Dance. Ontario. ☎ (541) 889-8012. Late.
   Broadway Blast Downhill. Anthony Lakes. ☎ (800) 523-1235. Late.

March

Anthony Lakes Snow Blast. Anthony Lakes Mountain Resort. ☎ (541) 856-3277. Mid.
   Saint Patrick's Day Parade & Festival. Vale. ☎ (541) 473-3800. Mid.
   Wee Bit O'Ireland. Heppner. ☎ (541) 676-5536. Mid.

April

Anthony Lake Snow Rodeo. Anthony Lake Mountain Resort. ☎ (800) 523-1235. Early.
   Community Egg Hunt—Boardman City Park. Boardman. ☎ (541) 481-3014. Early.
   Easter Egg Hunt. Christmas Valley. ☎ (541) 576-2015. Early.
   Easter Egg Hunt. Vale. ☎ (541) 473-3800. Early.
   Migratory Bird Festival. Burns. ☎ (541) 573-2636. Early.
   Blue Mountain Old-Time Fiddlers Show. Irrigon. ☎ (541) 922-4399. Late.

May

   Spring Pow Wow. La Grande. ☎ (541) 962-3741. Early.
   Big Loop Rodeo. Jordan Valley. ☎ (541) 586-2607. Mid.

Summer

Great Joseph Bank Robbery Re-Enactment. Joseph. ☎ (541) 426-4622.

June

Eastern Oregon Livestock Show, PRCA Rodeo, Pari-Mutuel Racing. Union. ☎ (541) 963-4646. Early.

 Hog Wild Days. Island City. ☎ (541) 898-2235. Early.
 Music in the Parks. Boardman. ☎ (541) 481-3014. Early to late June.
 Old-Time Fiddlers Contest. Enterprise. ☎ (541) 426-4622. Early.
 '62 Days Celebration. Canyon City. ☎ (541) 575-0329. Mid.
 Cinnebar Family Days. Mount Vernon. ☎ (541) 426-4622. Mid.
 Enterprise Summer Fest. Enterprise. ☎ (541) 426-3773. Mid.
 Music in the Parks. Irrigon. ☎ (541) 922-3386. Mid- to late June.
 Obsidian Days. Hines. ☎ (541) 573-2251. Mid.
 Old-Time Fiddlers Jamboree. Burns. ☎ (541) 573-2863. Mid.
 The Basque Festival. Hines. ☎ (541) 573-6657. Late.
 Nyssa Nite Rodeo. Nyssa. ☎ (541) 372-3405. Late.

July

4th of July Celebration & Fireworks Display. Prairie City. ☎ (541) 820-3739.
 4th of July Celebration. Boardman. ☎ (541) 481-3014.
 4th of July Parade & Celebration. Christmas Valley. ☎ (541) 576-3008.
 4th of July Rodeo. Vale. ☎ (541) 473-3800.
 Dayville 4th of July Celebration. Dayville. ☎ (541) 987-2375.
 Festival of Free Flight. Lakeview. ☎ (541) 947-6040. Early.
 Firecracker Cash Bash & Trophy Race. Lakeview. ☎ (541) 947-3293. Early.
 Fireworks Display. Ontario. ☎ (888) 889-8012.
 Fort Rock Museum 4th of July Celebration. Fort Rock. ☎ (541) 576-2282.
 Grant County 4th of July Celebration. Prairie City. ☎ (541) 820-3605.
 Haines Stampede & Rodeo. Haines. ☎ (800) 523-1235. Early.
 La Grande 4th of July Celebration. La Grande. ☎ (541) 963-3161.
 Old-Fashioned 4th of July Celebration. Haines. ☎ (800) 523-1235.
 Old-Fashioned 4th of July. Wallowa. ☎ (541) 426-4622.
 Rock & Roll Reunion and Flea Market. Burns/Hines. ☎ (541) 573-2636. Early to mid.
 Tam Ka Liks Celebration/Nez Perce Pow Wow & Friendship Feast. Wallowa. ☎ (800) 585-4121. Mid.
 Thunderegg Days & Festival. Nyssa. ☎ (541) 372-3091. Early to mid.
 Wallowa Lake Fireworks. Joseph. ☎ (800) 585-4121.
 Catherine Creek Rodeo Buck-Turn-and-Burn Bull Rama. Union. ☎ (541) 562-5055. Mid.
 Grasshopper Festival. Monument. ☎ (541) 934-2399. Mid.
 Grassroots Festival. Union. ☎ (541) 562-5288. Mid.
 High Desert Marine Walleye Derby. Boardman. ☎ (541) 567-8419. Mid.
 Japan Nite Obon Festivities. Ontario. ☎ (541) 889-8012. Mid.
 Miners Jubilee. Baker City. ☎ (800) 523-1235. Mid.
 Music in the Parks. Boardman. ☎ (541) 481-3014. Early to mid-July.
 Music in the Parks. Irrigon. ☎ (541) 922-3386. Mid- to late July.
 Scottish Heritage Festival. Athena. ☎ (541) 566-3880. Mid.
 Chief Joseph Days Rodeo & Encampment. Joseph. ☎ (541) 426-4622. Late.
 Irrigon Watermelon Festival. Irrigon. ☎ (541) 922-3197. Late.
 Mosquito Festival. Paisley. ☎ (541) 943-3157. Late.
 Pioneer Heritage Festival. Baker City. ☎ (800) 523-1235. Late.

August

Blast From the Past Classic Car Show. Prairie City. ☎ (541) 820-3739. Early.
  Elgin Stampede PRCA Rodeo. Elgin. ☎ (541) 437-4007. Early.
  Grant County Fair. John Day. ☎ (541) 575-1900. Early to mid-August.
  Malheur County Fair. Ontario. ☎ (541) 889-8012. Early.
  Spanish Sweet Onion Festival. Ontario. ☎ (541) 889-8012. Early.
  Union County Fair. La Grande. ☎ (541) 963-2384. Early.
  Wallowa County Fair. Enterprise. ☎ (541) 426-4622. Early.
  Dufur Threshing Bee. Dufur. ☎ (541) 467-2349. Mid.
  Durkee Steak Feed. Durkee. ☎ (800) 523-1235. Mid.
  North American Jew's Harp Festival. Richland. ☎ (541) 894-2345. Late.
  Oregon Trail Days Old-Time Fiddle Contest. La Grande. ☎ (800) 848-9969. Late.
  Oregon Trail Days. La Grande. ☎ (800) 848-9969. Late.
  Oregon Trail Pro Rodeo & Morrow County Rodeo. Heppner. ☎ (541) 676-9474. Late.
  Summer Lake Blues Festival. Summer Lake. ☎ (541) 943-3216. Late.
  Wallowa County Historic Barn Tour. Enterprise. ☎ (541) 426-4622. Late.

September

Hells Canyon Mule Days. Enterprise. ☎ (541) 426-4622. Early.
  Lake County Fair & Round-Up. Lakeview. ☎ (541) 947-2925. Early.
  Celebrate La Grande. La Grande. ☎ (541) 963-3104. Mid.
  Circle Your Wagons All Horse Parade. Vale. ☎ (541) 473-3800. Mid.
  Fort Rock Valley Homestead Days. Fort Rock. ☎ (541) 576-2617. Mid.
  Harney County Fair, Rodeo & Race Meet. Burns. ☎ (541) 573-2636. Mid.
  Pendleton Round-Up. Pendleton. ☎ (541) 276-2553. Mid.
  Wallowa Valley Arts Festival. Joseph. ☎ (800) 585-4121. Mid.
  Lake Alpenfest. Wallowa. ☎ (800) 585-4121. Late.

October

October Faire. Ontario. ☎ (541) 889-8810. Early.

November

Grape & Grain Festival and Art Auction. John Day. ☎ (541) 575-0547. Late.
  Holiday Open House and Historic Homes & Buildings Tour. Prairie City. ☎ (541) 820-3739. Late.

December

Caroling, Santa & Tree Lighting Ceremony. Boardman. ☎ (541) 481-3014. Early.
  Children's Christmas Parade. Christmas Valley. ☎ (541) 576-2166. Early.
  Christmas Tree Lighting & Caroling Party. Vale. ☎ (541) 473-3800. Early.
  Festival of Trees. Ontario. ☎ (541) 889-8693. Early.
  Historic Baker City Christmas Parlor Tour. Baker City. ☎ (800) 523-1235. Early.
  Oregon Trail Holiday Open House. Baker City. ☎ (800) 523-1235. Early.
  Winter Wonderland Parade. Ontario. ☎ (888) 889-8012. Early.
  Children's Christmas Party. Christmas Valley. ☎ (541) 576-2015. Mid.
  Timber Trucker's Light Parade. John Day. ☎ (541) 575-0710. Mid.
  Holiday Fare. Ontario. ☎ (541) 889-8012.

Chapter 12
Oregon Tourism Organizations

The Oregon Tourism Commission offers current information on attractions and regions. For information, call ☎ (800) 547-7842 or ☎ (503) 986-0000.

Central Oregon Coast Association. P.O. Box 2094. Newport, OR 97365. ☎ (800) 767-2064 or ☎ (541) 265-2064.

Central Oregon Visitors Association. 63085 North Highway 97, #104. Bend, OR 97701. ☎ (800) 800-8334 or ☎ (541) 382-8334.

Clackamas County Tourism Development Council. P.O. Box 182, 621 High Street, Oregon City, OR 97068. ☎ (800) 647-3843 or ☎ (503) 655-5511.

Columbia River Gorge Visitors Association. 404 West Second Street, The Dalles, OR 97058. ☎ (800) 984-6743.

Eastern Oregon Visitors Association/Oregon Trail Marketing Coalition. P.O. Box 1087, Baker City, OR 97814. ☎ (800) 332-1843 or ☎ (541) 523-9200.

Eugene/Convention & Visitors Association of Lane County. P.O. Box 10286, 115 West Eighth, Suite 190, Eugene, OR 97440. ☎ (800) 547-5445 or ☎ (541) 484-5307.

North Central Oregon Tourism Promotion Committee. 404 West Second Street, The Dalles, OR 97058. ☎ (800) 255-3385 or ☎ (541) 296-2231.

Northwest Oregon Tourism Alliance. 26 Southwest Salmon, Box S5, Portland, OR 97204. ☎ (800) 962-3700 or ☎ (503)222-2223.

Oregon's Outback Visitor Association. 724 Main Street, Suite 200, Klamath Falls, OR 97601. ☎ (800) 598-6877

Southern Oregon Visitors Association. 548 Business Park Drive, Medford, OR 97504. ☎ (800) 448-4856 or ☎ (541) 779-4691.

Washington County Visitors Association. 5075 Southwest Griffith Drive, #120, Beaverton, OR 97005. ☎ (800) 537-3149 or ☎ (503) 644-5555.

Willamette Valley Visitors Association. P.O. Box 965, 300 Second Avenue Southwest, Albany, OR 97321. ☎ (800) 526-2256 or ☎ (541) 928-0911.

Other Information Sources in Oregon

American Youth Hostels. ☎ (503) 236-3380

Oregon Bed and Breakfast Directory. ☎ (800) 841-5448 or ☎ (541) 476-2700.

Oregon Bed and Breakfast Guild. ☎ (800) 944-6196 or ☎ (541) 201-0511.

Bureau of Land Management. ☎ (503) 952-6002

Crater Lake National Park. Tours, hours of operation. ☎ (541) 594-2211.

Oregon Arts Commission. Gallery and Oregon artist information. ☎ (503) 986-0088

Oregon Department of Fish and Wildlife. Hunting, fishing licenses, and information. ☎ (800) 275-3474 or ☎ (503) 229-5403.

Oregon Department of Transportation. ☎ (503) 986-3200.

Oregon Fair Association. ☎ (503) 370-7019.
Oregon Outdoors Association. Outdoor adventure travel and guide service. ☎ (800) 747-9552.
Oregon Lodging Association. Directory of accommodations statewide. ☎ (503) 255-5135.
Oregon Marine Board. Boating facilities. ☎ (503) 378-8587.
Oregon Ski Industry Association. ☎ (503) 768-4299.
Oregon State Capitol. Tours. ☎ (503) 986-1388.
Oregon State Parks. Campsite reservations, maps, brochures. ☎ (800) 551-6949.
Portland International Airport. ☎ (503) 460-4234.
U.S. Fish & Wildlife. ☎ (503) 231-6828.
U.S. Forest Service. Recreation information, maps, brochures. ☎ (503) 872-2750.

Oregon Tourism Associations

Central Oregon Coast Association. Box 2094, Newport, OR 97365. ☎ (541) 265-2064 or ☎ (800) 767-2064. 🖳 www.coca@newportnet.com.
Central Oregon Visitors Association. 63085 North Highway 97, #104, Bend, OR 97701. ☎ (541) 382-8334 or ☎ (800) 800-8334. 🖳 www.empnet.com/cova.
Clackamas County Tourism Development Council. Box 182, 621 High Street, West Linn, OR 97068. ☎ (503) 655-5511 or ☎ (800) 647-3843. 🖳 www.clackamas-ore gon.com.
Columbia River Gorge Visitors Association. 404 West Second Street, The Dalles, OR 97058. ☎ (800) 984-6743.
Eastern Oregon Visitors Association/Oregon Trail Marketing Coalition. Box 1087, Baker City, OR 97814. ☎ (541) 523-9200 or ☎ (800) 332-1843. 🖳 www.eova.org.
Eugene/Convention & Visitors Association of Lane County. Box 10286, 115 West Eighth, Suite 190, Eugene, OR 97440. ☎ (541) 484-5307 or ☎ (800) 547-5445.
North Central Oregon Tourism Promotion Committee. 404 West Second Street, The Dalles, OR 97058. ☎ (541) 296-2231 or ☎ (800) 255-3385.
Northwest Oregon Tourism Alliance. 26 Southwest Salmon, Box S5, Portland, OR 97204. ☎ (503) 222-2223 or ☎ (800) 962-3700.
Oregon Tourism Commission. 775 Summer Street, Northeast, Salem, OR 97310. ☎ (800) 547-7842.
Oregon's Outback. 724 Main Street, Suite 200, Klamath Falls, OR 97601. ☎ (800) 598-6877.
Southern Oregon Visitors Association. 548 Business Park Drive, Medford, OR 97504. ☎ (541) 779-4691 or ☎ (800) 448-4856. 🖳 www.sova.org.
Washington County Visitors Association. 5075 Southwest Griffith Drive, #120, Beaverton, OR 97005. ☎ (503) 644-5555 or ☎ (800) 537-3149.
Willamette Valley Visitors Association. Box 965, 300 Second Avenue Southwest, Albany, OR 97321. ☎ (800) 526-2256 or ☎ (541) 928-0911.

Visitor Bureaus

Albany. Albany Visitors Association. Box 965, 300 Second Avenue Southwest, Albany, OR 97321. ☎ (541) 928-0911 or ☎ (800) 526-2256. 🖳 www.albanyvisitors.com.
Ashland. Ashland Chamber of Commerce. Box 1360, 110 East Main, Ashland, OR 97520. ☎ (541) 482-3486.
Astoria. Astoria/Warrenton Area Chamber of Commerce. Box 176, 111 West Marine Drive, Astoria, OR 97103. ☎ (503) 325-6311 or ☎ (800) 875-6807.
Baker City. Baker County Visitors & Convention Bureau. 490 Campbell Street, Baker City, OR 97814. ☎ (541) 523-3356 or ☎ (800) 523-1235.
Bandon. Bandon Chamber of Commerce. Box 1515, 300 Southeast Second Street, Bandon, OR 97411. ☎ (541) 347-9616.
Beaverton. Beaverton Area Chamber of Commerce. 4800 Southwest Griffith Drive, #100, Beaverton, OR 97005. ☎ (503) 644-0123. 🖳 www.beaverton.org.

Beaverton. Washington County Visitors Association. 5075 Southwest Griffith Drive, #120, Beaverton, OR 97005. ☎ (503) 644-5555 or ☎ (800) 537-3149.

Bend. Bend Chamber of Commerce/Visitor and Convention Bureau. 63085 North Highway 97, Bend, OR 97701. ☎ (541) 382-3221 or ☎ (800) 905-2363. 🖳 www.emp net.com/bchamber.

Brookings. Brookings-Harbor Chamber of Commerce. Box 940, 16330 Lower Harbor Road, Brookings, OR 97415. ☎ (541) 469-3181 or ☎ (800) 535-9469. 🖳 www.wave. net/tsn/chamber/chamber.html.

Burns. Harney County Chamber of Commerce. 18 West D Street, Burns, OR 97720. ☎ (541) 573-2636. 🖳 www.eosc.osshe.edu/~jkraft/harneyco.htm.

Camp Sherman. Metolius Recreation Association. Box 64, Camp Sherman, OR 97730. ☎ (541) 595-6117.

Canby. Canby Area Chamber of Commerce. Box 35, 266 Northwest First, #C, Canby, OR 97013. ☎ (503) 266-4600.

Cannon Beach. Cannon Beach Chamber of Commerce. Box 64, Second and Spruce, Cannon Beach, OR 97110. ☎ (503) 436-2623.

Canyonville. Canyonville Information Center. Box 765, 250 Northwest Main, Canyonville, OR 97417. ☎ (541) 839-4258.

Cascade Locks. Port of Cascade Locks Visitors Center. Box 307, Marine Park Drive, Cascade Locks, OR 97014. ☎ (541) 374-8619.

Cave Junction. Illinois Valley Chamber of Commerce Visitor Information Center. Box 312, 201 Caves Highway, Cave Junction, OR 97523. ☎ (541) 592-2631 or 592-3326.

Charleston. Charleston Information Center. Box 5735, Charleston, OR 97420. ☎ (541) 888-2311 or ☎ (800) 824-8486.

Clatskanie. Clatskanie Chamber of Commerce. Box 635, 155 West Highway 30, Clatskanie, OR 97016. ☎ (503) 728-2502.

Cloverdale. Nestucca Valley Chamber of Commerce. Box 75, Cloverdale, OR 97112. ☎ (503) 392-3445.

Coos Bay. Bay Area Chamber of Commerce. Box 210, 50 East Central, Coos Bay, OR 97420. ☎ (541) 269-0215 or ☎ (800) 824-8486. 🖳 www.ucinet.com/~bacc.

Coquille. Coquille Chamber of Commerce. 119 North Birch, Coquille, OR 97423. ☎ (541) 396-3414. 🖳 www.coquille@mail.coos.or.us.

Corvallis. Corvallis Convention & Visitors Bureau. 420 Northwest Second Street, Corvallis, OR 97330. ☎ (541) 757-1544 or ☎ (800) 334-8118. 🖳 www.visitcorvallis.com/ccvb/.

Cottage Grove. Cottage Grove Chamber of Commerce. Box 587, 710 Row River Road, Cottage Grove, OR 97424. ☎ (541) 942-2411.

Creswell. Creswell Visitor Center. Box 577, 55 North Fifth Street, Creswell, OR 97426. ☎ (541) 895-5161.

Culver. Culver Visitors Information Center. Box 86, 411 First Street, Culver, OR 97734. ☎ (541) 546-6032.

Dalles. Dalles Area Chamber of Commerce. Box 377, 167 Southwest Academy, Dalles, OR 97338. ☎ (503) 623-2564. 🖳 www.thedalleschamber.com.

Depoe Bay. Depoe Bay Chamber of Commerce. Box 21, 630 Southeast Highway 101, Depoe Bay, OR 97341. ☎ (541) 765-2889.

Enterprise. Wallowa County Chamber of Commerce. Box 427, 107 Southwest First, Enterprise, OR 97828. ☎ (541) 426-4622 or ☎ (800) 585-4121.

Estacada. Estacada/Clackamas River Area Chamber of Commerce. Box 298, 313 Southwest Highway 224, Estacada, OR 97023. ☎ (503) 630-3483. 🖳 www.clackamas-oregon.com.

Eugene. Eugene/Convention & Visitors Association of Lane County. Box 10286, 115 West Eighth, Suite 190, Eugene, OR 97440. ☎ (541) 484-5307 or ☎ (800) 547-5445. 🖳 www.cvalco.org.

Florence. Florence Area Chamber of Commerce. Box 26000, 270 Highway 101, Florence, OR 97439. ☎ (541) 997-3128. 🖳 www.presys.com/wtc/discoverflorence.

Forest Grove. Forest Grove. Chamber of Commerce. 2417 Pacific Avenue, Forest Grove, OR 97116. ☎ (503) 357-3006.

Garibaldi. Garibaldi Chamber of Commerce. Box 915, 235 Garibaldi Avenue, Garibaldi, OR 97118. ☎ (503) 322-0301.

Glide. Colliding Rivers Information Center. 18782 North Umpqua Highway, Glide, OR 97443. ☎ (541) 496-0157.

Gold Beach. Gold Beach Chamber of Commerce Visitors Center. 29279 Ellensburg, Gold Beach, OR 97444. ☎ (541) 247-7526 or ☎ (800) 525-2334. 🖳 www.harborside. com/gb.

Grants Pass. Grants Pass Visitors and Convention Bureau. Box 1787, 1996 North-west Vine Street, Grants Pass, OR 97526. ☎ (541) 476-7717 or ☎ (800) 547-5927. 🖳 www.chatlink.com/~gpcoc/.

Gresham. Gresham Area Chamber of Commerce Visitors Information Center. Box 1768, 150 West Powell, Gresham, OR 97030. ☎ (503) 665-1131. 🖳 www.mecc.org.

Heppner. Heppner Chamber of Commerce. Box 1232, West May Street, Heppner, OR 97836. ☎ (541) 676-5536.

Hermiston. Greater Hermiston Chamber of Commerce. Box 185, 415 South High-way 395, Hermiston, OR 97838. ☎ (541) 567-6151.

Hillsboro. Greater Hillsboro Chamber of Commerce. 334 Southeast Fifth Avenue, Hillsboro, OR 97123. ☎ (503) 648-1102. 🖳 www.hilchamber.org.

Hood River. Hood River County Chamber of Commerce. 405 Portway Avenue, Hood River, OR 97031. ☎ (541) 386-2000 or ☎ (800) 366-3530.

Huntington. Huntington Chamber of Commerce. Box 280, Huntington, OR 97907. ☎ (541) 869-2019 or 869-2529.

Independence. Monmouth-Independence Chamber of Commerce. 148 Monmouth Street, Independence, OR 97351. ☎ (503) 838-4268 or ☎ (800) 772-2806.

Jacksonville. Jacksonville Chamber of Commerce. Box 33, 185 North Oregon Street, Jacksonville, OR 97530. ☎ (541) 899-8118. 🖳 www.wave.net/upg/juillechamber.

John Day. Grant County Chamber of Commerce. 281 West Main, John Day, OR 97845. ☎ (541) 575-0547 or ☎ (800) 769-5664. 🖳 www.grantcounty.cc.

Junction City. Junction City–Harrisburg Area Chamber of Commerce. Box 401, 620 Holly Street, Junction City, OR 97448. ☎ (541) 998-6154.

Klamath Falls. Klamath County Department of Tourism. Klamath County Museum, Box 1867, 1451 Main Street, Klamath Falls, OR 97601. ☎ (541) 884-0666 or ☎ (800) 445-6728. 🖳 www.sova.org.

LaGrande. LaGrande–Union County Chamber of Commerce Visitors and Conven-tion Bureau. 1912 Fourth Street, #200, LaGrande, OR 97850. ☎ (541) 963-8588 or ☎ (800) 848-9969. 🖳 www.ucinet.com/~lagrande.

Lake Oswego. Lake Oswego Chamber of Commerce. 242 B Avenue, Lake Oswego, OR 97034. ☎ (503) 636-3634.

Lakeview. Lake County Chamber of Commerce. 126 North E Street, Lakeview, OR 97630. ☎ (541) 947-6040. 🖳 www.triax.com/lakecounty/lakeco.htm.

LaPine. LaPine Chamber of Commerce. Box 616, LaPine, OR 97739. ☎ (541) 536-9771.

Leaburg. McKenzie River Chamber of Commerce. Box 1117, 44643 McKenzie Highway, Leaburg, OR 97489. ☎ (541) 896-3330. 🖳 www.el.com/to/mckenzierivervalley.

Lebanon. Lebanon Chamber of Commerce. 1040 Park Street, Lebanon, OR 97355. ☎ (541) 258-7164.

Lincoln City. Lincoln City Visitors and Convention Bureau. 801 Southwest High-way 101, #1, Lincoln City, OR 97367. ☎ (541) 994-8378 or ☎ (800) 452-2151. 🖳 www.peak.org/lincoln/html.

Madras. Madras–Jefferson County Chamber of Commerce. Box 770, 197 Southeast Fifth Street, Madras, OR 97741. ☎ (541) 475-2350 or ☎ (800) 967-3564. 🖳 www. madras.net.

Maupin. Greater Maupin Area Chamber of Commerce. Box 220, Maupin, OR 97037. ☎ (541) 395-2599.

McMinnville. McMinnville Chamber of Commerce. 417 North Adams, McMinnville, OR 97128. ☎ (503) 472-6196. 🖳 www.linfield.edu/mcminnville.

Medford. Medford Visitors & Convention Bureau. 101 East Eighth, Medford, OR 97501. ☎ (541) 779-4847 or ☎ (800) 469-6307. 🖳 www.visitmedford.org.

Medford. Southern Oregon Visitor's Association. 548 Business Park Drive, Medford, OR 97504. ☎ (541) 779-4691 or ☎ (800) 448-4856. 🖳 www.sova.org.

Mill City. North Santiam Chamber of Commerce Visitors Information Center. Box 222, Mill City, OR 97360. ☎ (503) 897-2865.

Milton-Freewater. Milton-Freewater Chamber of Commerce. Community Building, 505 Ward Street, Milton-Freewater, OR 97862. ☎ (541) 938-5563.

Milwaukie. North Clackamas County Chamber of Commerce. 7740 Southeast Harmony Road, Milwaukie, OR 97222. ☎ (503) 654-7777.

Molalla. Molalla Area Chamber of Commerce. Box 578, 103 South Molalla Avenue, Molalla, OR 97038. ☎ (503) 829-6941.

Moro. Sherman County Visitors Association. Box 173, Moro, OR 97039. ☎ (541) 565-3232.

Myrtle Point. Myrtle Point Chamber of Commerce. Box 265, 424 Fifth Street, Myrtle Point, OR 97458. ☎ (541) 572-2626.

Nehalem. Nehalem Bay Area Chamber of Commerce. Box 159, Eighth and Tohl Street, Nehalem, OR 97131. ☎ (503) 368-5100. 🖳 www.ohwy.com/or/n/nehalem.htm.

Newberg. Newberg Area Chamber of Commerce. 115 North Washington, Newberg, OR 97132. ☎ (503) 538-2014.

Newport. Greater Newport Chamber of Commerce. 555 Southwest Coast Highway, Newport, OR 97365. ☎ (541) 265-8801 or ☎ (800) 262-7844.

North Bend. North Bend Information Center. 1380 Sherman, North Bend, OR 97459. ☎ (541) 756-4613.

Nyassa. Nyssa Chamber of Commerce. & Agriculture. 14 South Third Street, Nyssa, OR 97913. ☎ (541) 372-3091.

Ontario. Ontario Chamber of Commerce Visitors & Convention Bureau. 88 Southwest Third Avenue, Ontario, OR 97914. ☎ (541) 889-8012 or ☎ (888) 889-8012.

Oregon City. Oregon City Chamber of Commerce. Box 226, Oregon City, OR 97045. ☎ (503) 656-1619 or ☎ (800) 424-3002.

Pacific City. Pacific City/Woods Chamber of Commerce. Box 331, Pacific City, OR 97135. ☎ (503) 965-6131 or ☎ (888) 549-2632. 🖳 www.oregoncoast.com/pac_city.

Pendleton. Pendleton Chamber of Commerce Visitors & Convention Bureau. 501 South Main, Pendleton, OR 97801. ☎ (541) 276-7411 or ☎ (800) 547-8911.

Philomath. Philomath Area Chamber of Commerce. Box 606, 2395 Main Street, Philomath, OR 97370. ☎ (541) 929-2454.

Port Orford. Port Orford Chamber of Commerce. Box 637, Battle Rock Park, Highway 101 South, Port Orford, OR 97465. ☎ (541) 332-8055.

Portland. Portland Oregon Visitors Association. 26 Southwest Salmon Street, Portland, OR 97204. ☎ (503) 222-2223 or ☎ (800) 962-3700.

Prineville. Prineville–Crook County Chamber of Commerce. 390 North Fairview, Prineville, OR 97754. ☎ (541) 447-6304.

Redmond. Redmond Chamber of Commerce. 446 Southwest Seventh, Redmond, OR 97756. ☎ (541) 923-5191.

Reedsport. Reedsport/Winchester Bay Chamber of Commerce. Box 11, 805 Highway Avenue, Reedsport, OR 97467. ☎ (541) 271-3495 or ☎ (800) 247-2155. 🖳 www.reedsportcc.org.

Rockaway Beach. Rockaway Beach Chamber of Commerce. Box 198, 103 South First Street, Rockaway Beach, OR 97136. ☎ (503) 355-8108.

Rogue River. Rogue River Chamber of Commerce. Box 457, 111 East Main Street, Rogue River, OR 97537. ☎ (541) 582-0242.

Roseburg. Roseburg Visitors Information Center. Box 1262/410 Southeast Spruce, Roseburg, OR 97470. ☎ (541) 672-9731 or ☎ (800) 444-9584.

Salem. Salem Convention & Visitors Association. 1313 Mill Street Southeast, Salem, OR 97301. ☎ (800) 874-7012. 🖳 www.scva.org.

Sandy. Sandy Area Chamber of Commerce. Box 536, 39260 Pioneer Boulevard, Sandy, OR 97055. ☎ (503) 668-4006.

Seaside. Seaside Chamber of Commerce. Box 7, 7 North Roosevelt, Seaside, OR 97138. ☎ (503) 738-6391 or ☎ (800) 444-6740.

Sheridan. West Valley Chamber of Commerce. Box 98, 147 West Main, Sheridan, OR 97378. ☎ (503) 843-4964.

Silverton. Silverton Area Chamber of Commerce. Box 257, 421 South Water, Silverton, OR 97381. ☎ (503) 873-5615.

Sisters. Sisters Area Visitor Information Center. Box 430, 352 East Hood Street, Suite D, Sisters, OR 97759. ☎ (541) 549-0251.

Springfield. Springfield Area Chamber of Commerce. Box 155, 101 South A Street, Springfield, OR 97477. ☎ (541) 746-1651.

Saint Helens. Saint Helens–Scappoose Chamber of Commerce. Box 1036, 1934 Columbia Boulevard, Saint Helens, OR 97051. ☎ (503) 397-0685.

Stayton. Stayton/Sublimity Chamber of Commerce. Box 121, 1203 North First Avenue, Stayton, OR 97383. ☎ (503) 769-3464.

Sunriver. Sunriver Area Chamber of Commerce. Box 3246, Sunriver Village, Building O, Sunriver, OR 97707. ☎ (541) 593-8149.

Sutherlin. Sutherlin Visitors Center. Box 327, 1470 West Central, Sutherlin, OR 97479. ☎ (541) 459-5829.

Sweet Home. Sweet Home Chamber of Commerce. 1575 Main Street, Sweet Home, OR 97386. ☎ (541) 367-6186.

The Dalles. The Dalles Area Chamber of Commerce. 404 West Second Street, The Dalles, OR 97058. ☎ (541) 296-2231 or ☎ (800) 255-3385. 💻 www.netcnct.net/chamberofcommerce.

Tigard. Tigard Chamber of Commerce. 12420 Southwest Main Street, Tigard, OR 97223. ☎ (503) 639-1656.

Tillamook. Tillamook Chamber of Commerce. 3705 Highway 101 North, Tillamook, OR 97141. ☎ (503) 842-7525.

Toledo. Toledo Chamber of Commerce. 311 Northeast First, Toledo, OR 97391. ☎ (541) 336-3183.

Troutdale. Troutdale Area Chamber of Commerce. Box 245, 338 East Historic Columbia River Highway, Troutdale, OR 97060. ☎ (503) 669-7473.

Tualatin. Tualatin Chamber of Commerce. Box 701, 8511 Southwest Tualatin Road, Tualatin, OR 97062. ☎ (503) 692-0780.

Umatilla. Umatilla Chamber of Commerce. Box 67, 1530 Sixth Street, Umatilla, OR 97882. ☎ (541) 922-4825 or ☎ (800) 542-4944.

Vale. Vale Chamber of Commerce. Box 661, 275 North Main Street, Vale, OR 97918. ☎ (541) 473-3800.

Waldport. Waldport Chamber of Commerce & Visitors Center. Box 669, 620 Northwest Spring Street, Waldport, OR 97394. ☎ (541) 563-2133.

Warrenton. Astoria-Warrenton Highway 101 Visitor Center. 143 South Highway 101, Warrenton, OR 97146. ☎ (503) 861-1031. 💻 www.el.com/to/astoria.

Welches. Mount Hood Information Center. Box 819, 65000 East Highway 26, Welches, OR 97067. ☎ (503) 622-4822.

Wilsonville. Wilsonville Chamber of Commerce. 8880 Southwest Wilsonville Road, Wilsonville, OR 97070. ☎ (503) 682-0411.

Woodburn. Woodburn Area Chamber of Commerce. Box 194, 2233 Country Club Road, Woodburn, OR 97071. ☎ (503) 982-8221.

Yachats. Yachats Area Chamber of Commerce Visitors Center. Box 728, 441 Highway 101, Yachats, OR 97498. ☎ (541) 547-3530.

Part III
Washington

Chapter 13
Introduction to Washington

Washington is all things to many people: mountains and big cities, wild ocean coast and gentle protected harbors, massive snowfalls and temperate rain forests, ever-frozen glaciers and fiery volcanoes.

It is an economy of basic farming and fishing, of aviation, and of the highest tech computer software and hardware.

Washington's Story

The original occupants of what is now the state of Washington were the Nez Percé, Spokane, Yakima, Cayuse, Okanogan, Walla Walla, and Colville peoples in the interior, and the Nooksak, Chinook, Nisqually, Clallam, Makah, Quinault, and Puyallup along the coast.

For European explorers, the original golden lure of the Pacific Northwest was fur, shipped back across the Atlantic to be made into clothing for the wealthy of Europe. In Washington, there was an abundance of sea otter.

Spanish explorer Bruno Heceta claimed the area for his country in 1775, but Spain was hard-pressed to support its would-be colony. In 1790, Britain and Spain negotiated the Nootka Sound Agreement, opening the coast from California and Alaska to trade and settlement by both nations.

Under that agreement, British naval officer George Vancouver made his extensive surveys of the coast, exploring Puget Sound in 1792. The first European settlements, though, were mostly established as the result of overland expeditions from the east; one of the most significant was the North West Company, a British fur trading company based in Montréal.

About the same time, American merchants from Boston and other New England ports explored the area; Robert Gray explored the Columbia River in 1792, more than a dozen years before the famed Lewis and Clark Expedition of 1804 to 1806.

In 1811 New York merchant John Jacob Astor established the American Fur Company and the Pacific Fur Company; the firm established a trading post near the mouth of the Columbia. Named after the founder, Astoria became an important commercial hub and his trading companies held a virtual monopoly

WASHINGTON

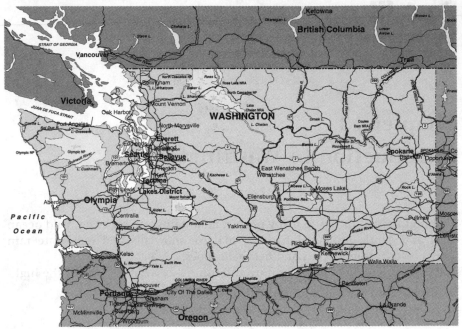

in the Pacific Northwest. At the time of his death in 1848, he was considered the wealthiest man in the United States. (Astor helped fund the predecessor of the New York Public Library and created the Astor House, which later became the Waldorf-Astoria in New York.)

From 1815, after the end of the War of 1812, there followed thirty years of uneasy peace between Great Britain and her former colony America, including a number of border disputes in eastern Canada.

In 1846, Britain and the United States settled the border between the United States and Canada. Two years later, Washington (named after the first president) became part of the American Territory of Oregon; Washington and Oregon became separate territories in 1853. At the time, Washington stretched from the Pacific Ocean to the Rocky Mountains with less than 4,000 pioneer residents.

In coming years, Native Americans were forced into treaties and resettlement, and from 1855 through 1858 there were outbreaks of war between Indian tribes and U.S. troops throughout the territory. It wasn't until 1886 that the Northern Pacific Railroad was able to complete a transcontinental link to the territory. Statehood followed soon afterwards, in 1889.

From the time of the first settlers, agriculture and fishing has been a major industry for Washington, lead by timber, apples, and wheat. But it was the military and aviation industry that helped build the modern economy. The Boeing Airplane Company was begun during World War I, producing wooden aircraft using the resources of the west. After the Depression, which hit the Pacific Northwest hard, Boeing went on to become the largest private employer in the state during World War II. In the years that followed, Boeing

Mount Adam, Columbia Gorge
Photo courtesy Washington Tourism Development

produced many of the military aircraft used by American and Allied forces, and after the war became the largest manufacturer of civilian airliners.

The availability of large quantities of inexpensive hydroelectric power allowed the growth of energy-intensive factories such as aluminum smelters, necessary for the aerospace industries.

In more recent times, Washington has thrived as the home of the highest of technology, including Microsoft. Youngsters will be duly impressed to learn that the state is also home to the American outpost of Japanese game king Nintendo.

About Washington

The Evergreen State, 71,302 square miles in size, is the eighteenth largest state in the nation. Spread across all of those miles is a population of about 5.5 million. Nearly a third of the land in the state is owned by the federal government, in national parks and forests, and military sites.

Washington's west coast is the Pacific Ocean. To the north is British Columbia, the east is Idaho, and the south is Oregon, with the southern border marked by the Columbia River.

The Pacific Coast is a mostly straight passage down from the Olympic Peninsula to the Oregon border. In the northwest, though, the Strait of Juan de Fuca, the Strait of Georgia, and Puget Sound are dotted with inlets and islands major and minor. Situated on Puget Sound are the major cities and ports of the state, including Seattle, Tacoma, and Everett.

The state's elevation ranges from sea level to 14,411 feet at the peak of Mount Rainier.

The western part of Washington is part of the Coast Ranges. At the southwest corner of the state near Oregon, the Willapa Hills mark the lowest segment of the Pacific Coast mountains, with a maximum elevation of about 3,110 feet. In the northwest, the snowcapped Olympic Mountains include Mount Olympus with a summit of 7,954 feet.

To the east of the Puget Trough, which includes Puget Sound, is the rugged Cascade Range, which features tall volcanoes Mount Rainier, Mount Adams, and Mount Saint Helens.

The southeastern part of Washington is built on the Columbia Plateau, a huge basin formed from vast lava flows. Over time, the Columbia and Snake rivers cut deep trenches in the Columbia Plateau. The Palouse Hills, covered by fertile, windblown dust known as loess, are one of the most fertile agricultural regions of the state.

The Columbia River, the longest river in the west, runs 1,243 miles from Columbia Lake in British Columbia down the center of Washington and then heads west past Portland Oregon to drain into the Pacific Ocean. Many of the numerous drops of the river are channeled through hydroelectric power plants.

The largest natural lake in the state is Lake Chelan, a long, narrow glacial lake in the Cascade Range. Other significant lakes include Franklin D. Roosevelt Lake, created by the Grand Coulee Dam, and Banks Lake, behind Dry Falls Dam.

Washington's Climate

It rains in Washington, but not all the time and not in every place.

East of the Cascade Range, the climate is predominately cool and dry.

To the west, temperatures are generally mild and conditions humid to wet. The coastal region is warmer than might be expected for its northern latitude, due to the warm North Pacific Current that passes offshore. The area experiences frequent cloud cover, considerable fog, and frequent rain or drizzles. The driest and fairest season is the summer.

The western portion of the Olympic Peninsula holds the dubious distinction of being the wettest area in the continental United States, receiving as much as 160 inches of precipitation annually. The western slopes of the Cascade Range are dumped with snow, in some seasons as much as 200 inches.

But not far away, in the rain shadow to the east of the Cascades, some regions receive only an average of six inches of precipitation each year.

And rumors of rain in Seattle are greatly exaggerated, according to tourism folk there. Seattle receives an average of thirty-six inches of rain, less than New York, Atlanta, or Boston. Seattle receives relatively few downpours, instead experiencing prolonged periods of drizzle or mist.

Chapter 14
Seattle: The Emerald City

Seattle can fairly well lay claim to one of its nicknames: The Emerald City. Like the capital of the Land of Oz, Seattle is a place of great wonder, mystery, manipulation, and enterprise.

Consider the leading business powers of the Seattle area, Everett, and Redmond: Microsoft, Nintendo, Boeing, and Starbucks. (Bill Gates, Mario and Luigi, a flying circus of jumbo jets, and an empire built on trendy cups of java.)

Consider the spread of scenery: a thriving downtown with a city population of 533,000 and a metropolitan area of three million residents set on the sparkling waters of Puget Sound, with the snow-capped volcano of Mount Rainier in the distance and almost untouched wilderness in Snoqualmie to the east.

The Story of Seattle

The small band of settlers from Illinois who landed on remote Alki Point on the exposed southwestern mouth of Puget Sound on cold and rainy November 13, 1851, named their tiny community of log cabins after a prosperous big city back east: New York. The name didn't last very long; the settlers changed the name to Duwamps and finally Seattle after local Chief Sealth, and they moved to the deep waters of Elliott Bay. (Alki, meaning "by and by," lives on as the official motto of Washington.)

The area of Puget Sound had been explored more than a half century earlier by British Royal Navy Captain George Vancouver and the crew of the HMS *Discovery.*

During the course of the last half of the nineteenth century, the little city on Puget Sound began to grow beyond its waterfront on the tidal flats and its mud streets to become a major port of call for ships moving up and down the Pacific Coast. The growth was helped greatly by the market for shiploads of lumber for burgeoning San Francisco and the California gold mines.

Seattle's beginnings include the original Skid Road (now Yesler Way), a path used to skid timber down from the hills to mills and ships at Elliott Bay. South of the path were the brothels and saloons; the respectable part of town began north of Skid Road.

Seattle Skyline
Photo courtesy Washington Tourism Development

The Northern Pacific Railroad arrived in Tacoma in 1887, connecting Puget Sound to the markets and the immigrants of the East. The competing Great Northern Railroad made it to Seattle five years later.

In 1889 a calamitous fire burned most of the city to the ground. In an early version of urban renewal, city engineers took the opportunity to raise downtown streets several feet above high tide level as part of the rebuilding. In doing so, they left an entire section of storefronts intact below the surface.

But the biggest spur to the growth of Seattle was the arrival in 1897 of the steamer *Portland* with a "ton of gold" from the Klondike. The resulting gold rush benefited Seattle as outfitter to the miners, ship builder, and transfer port for thousands of prospectors and millions of tons of goods heading north to Canada.

Seattle hosted the first of several world's fairs in 1909, with the Alaska-Yukon-Pacific Exhibition. Much of the present campus of the University of Washington is a legacy of that exhibition.

The city boomed again in World War II. Puget sound became a major naval base for the Pacific war. Tens of thousands of troops received their training at Fort Lewis and were shipped overseas from there.

The Boeing Company, a small airplane manufacturer founded in 1910, grew to become the primary manufacturer of the B-17 and B-29 heavy bombers flown by the U.S. Army Air Force.

After the war, in 1959, Boeing introduced the 707, the first American passenger jet. By that time, Boeing and its suppliers accounted for nearly half of the jobs in King County.

In 1962 the Seattle World's Fair marked the emergence of Seattle and the Pacific Northwest as a major tourist destination.

Seattle and the Klondike Gold Rush

In July of 1897 the steamship *Portland* arrived from Canada's Klondike with a cargo of gold.

In the ensuing Klondike Gold Rush, Seattle was a major provisioning center and port of embarkation for miners who arrived from around the world.

When the stampede began, merchants in Dawson City in Canada's Yukon were unprepared for the thousands of fortune seekers who passed through en route to the gold fields. When the Yukon River froze in the fall of 1897, there were worries that Dawson City would run out of food.

In January of 1898 the Northwest Mounted Police implemented the "One Ton Rule," a requirement that miners going north bring with them a year's supply of provisions, approximately one ton in weight.

Merchants in Seattle and elsewhere packaged goods to meet that rule. Seattle's merchants and its Chamber of Commerce spent thousands of dollars to advertise Seattle as an outfitting center. In addition to provisions, Seattle merchants sold horses and dogs as pack animals. Not all the animals were suited for conditions in the Klondike, and the market for dogs was so intense that city authorities warned residents to keep their pets inside.

By 1897 the transcontinental railroad reached to Seattle; trains went over the Cascade Mountains by the Great Northern and Northern Pacific Railroads, as well as north to Vancouver, British Columbia, and south to San Francisco and Los Angeles, California. Seattle was also home to the Pacific Coast Steamship Company, the North American Transportation and Trading Company and the Alaska Steamship Company.

Seattle was well prepared to serve the needs of the miners, with factories that produced clothing, shoes, wool blankets, and hardware as well as tents, portable stoves, and pack saddles. Companies made canned fruit and vegetables, cured meat, and evaporated dairy products.

The Chilkoot and White Pass Trails—the so-called poor man's routes—were the least expensive and most direct way to the gold fields, but also the most arduous. Miners left Seattle on an 800-mile voyage to Skagway and Dyea through the Inside Passage of Alaska. Once they were landed, the stampeders had to carry their ton of goods over the White Pass or Chilkoot Trails to the headwaters of the Yukon River. There they had to build their own boat or purchase an uncertain local vessel to make the final 500 miles by water.

A longer, all-water route was available, but at a cost few of the stampeders could afford. Ships sailed north from Seattle to the Bering Sea and the Yukon River delta, a distance of roughly 2,000 miles. Disembarking at Saint Michael, cargo was transferred to river steamers for a 1,700-mile journey of four to six weeks to Dawson City. The steamers only ran from about mid-June to mid-September; the rivers would freeze soon afterward.

Something like 100,000 gold-rushers passed through Seattle en route to the fields, but many never made it all the way to Canada's Yukon, and of those only a few dozen struck it rich. But one group that did make its fortune was the merchants of Seattle who sold about $25 million in supplies from 1897 to 1898.

As a result of the Gold Rush, Seattle earned a reputation as the commercial center of the Pacific Northwest. The population doubled and the city expanded during the decade that followed the rush. Tax revenues paid for water and sewage systems, the locks between Lake Washington and Lake Union, and the regrading of the steep hills and wetlands in downtown. In 1909 Seattle celebrated its success and recent history with the Alaska-Yukon-Pacific Exposition.

Tacoma was Seattle's closest competitor, but merchants failed to capitalize on the opportunity. Tacoma had grown when the Northern Pacific Railroad picked the city as its western terminus, but the collapse of that railroad after the Panic of 1893 ended dreams of its becoming the commercial center of the northwest.

Tougher competition was found in Canada in Victoria and Vancouver, less than 100 miles to the north. At the start of the gold rush, these cities fell behind Seattle because they lacked regular steamship service north. But they gained an advantage through the use of tariffs applied to American goods brought into Canada; stampeders could shop in Victoria or Canada and pass through Alaska with their goods under bond and avoid paying taxes when they re-entered Canada for the gold fields.

In downtown, the **Klondike Gold Rush Historic Park** is the Seattle unit of a national historic park dedicated to gold rush history. The small visitor center includes films, historic photographs, and an exhibit of just what a required year's worth of supplies looked like.

The park, located at 117 South Main Street, is open daily from 9 A.M. to 5 P.M. Admission: free. For information, call ☎ (206) 553-7220, or you can consult ▣ www.nps.gov/klgo/ or ▣ www.nps.gov./klse/.

The second half of the Klondike park is located in Skagway, Alaska.

In the summer, park rangers conduct ninety-minute walking tours of Pioneer Square, and gold-panning demonstrations in the afternoon. There is also a schedule of movies about Seattle and the Gold Rush in the Klondike.

Getting Around Seattle

The narrow city of Seattle is bracketed on the east by freshwater Lake Washington and on the west by the salt waters of Puget Sound.

Much of downtown Seattle and its attractions can be explored on foot.

Bus service within the central business district is free. Beneath the streets, Metro operates buses through a 1.3-mile transit tunnel running from the international District to Westlake Center and the convention center train stations in less than ten minutes. Dual-power vehicles operate with electric power inside the tunnel, changing over to diesel power on surface roads.

The Seattle Center Monorail speeds between downtown and the Seattle Center, home of the 605-foot-tall Space Needle. The tower, the best-recognized symbol of the city, is a legacy of the 1962 World's Fair. For most of the year, and especially in the peak season between April and October, the center is home to festivals, concerts, and special events.

Pike Place Market in downtown is one of the last authentic farmers' markets, a cornucopia of seafood, fruit, and vegetable displays, accented with spice dealers and the ubiquitous Seattle coffee stands (including the original Starbucks).

SEATTLE METROPOLITAN AREA

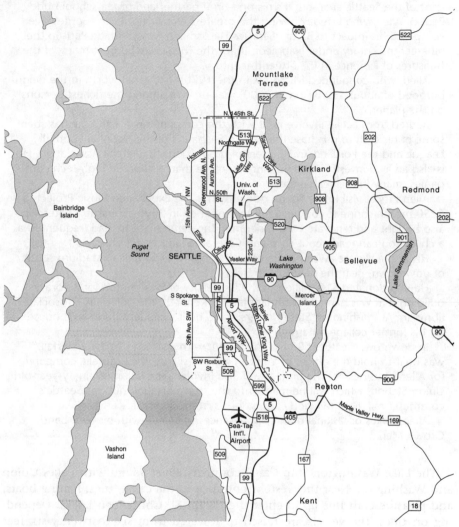

The Seattle Art Museum makes a striking pose in downtown, home to a renowned collection of African and Native American art, regional artists, Renaissance and Impressionist paintings, and ancient Greek coins and pottery.

At the south end of downtown is Pioneer Square, an area of lovingly preserved old homes and buildings. Today you'll find intriguing shops and dining. You can also take an unusual underground tour that ventures beneath the modern-day surface of Pioneer Square to view a section of Seattle frozen in time to about 1890, when the street levels were raised.

Today Fisherman's Terminal is home to hundreds of purse seine and gill net fishing boats. There's room to stroll along the piers to watch the fishermen at work and watch the comings and goings of seagoing vessels and ferries.

Modern patron. Microsoft billionaire Bill Gates may be the best-known resident of the Seattle area, but it's his one-time partner and grade-school buddy, Paul G. Allen, who is today having the greatest effect on the city. Some have compared his impact to Baron Georges Haussmann, who remade Paris in the nineteenth century under Napoleon III, or the Medicis, who built many of the treasures of Florence in the fifteenth century.

Allen, who co-founded Microsoft in the 1970s, had a net worth in the neighborhood of about $30 billion in 2000, making him among the richest persons on the planet.

Retired from active involvement with the company since 1983, he has spent some of his cash to purchase the Seattle Seahawks of the National Football League and the Portland Trail Blazers of the National Basketball Association. He is also an avid investor, with holdings in more than a hundred high-tech companies, many in the Seattle area.

Allen's most visible impact on downtown is the Experience Music Project, a $250 million shrine to rock and roll that opened in 2000 at Seattle Center. He also bought and renovated the Cinerama Theater, a place he had frequented as a child. You can read about EMP and Cinerama later in this chapter.

His Seahawks are awaiting the completion of a $450 million stadium south of downtown, near the new Safeco Field.

He also donated $10 million to the University of Washington for a library building that was named for his late father, Kenneth, the university's associate librarian. At Washington State University, he built a modern, high-tech house for his former college fraternity.

In downtown Seattle, 505 Union Station, with a striking "glass waterfall," was built to hold the offices of Vulcan Northwest Inc., the umbrella company for Allen's businesses. The project will also involve renovation of ninety-year-old Union Station, which will be made into the transportation hub for Seattle's commuter rail, light rail, and express bus systems.

Allen makes occasional public appearances in Seattle with his rock band, Grown Men.

The Lake Washington Ship Canal connects Puget Sound with Lakes Union and Washington. Near the western entrance to the canal, tugs, fishing boats, and pleasure craft line up to enter the Hiram M. Chittenden Locks. Depending on tides, the vessels are raised or lowered from six to twenty-six feet between fresh and saltwater.

You can get out on the water on one of many harbor tour boats, and on more extensive cruises through the ship canal to Lake Washington. You can also make a day trip to the San Juan Islands in the summer or travel across the Strait of Juan de Fuca to Victoria, British Columbia.

The least expensive way to see the harbor, the city skyline, and some of the residential districts is to take one of the big green-and-white Washington State Ferries across Puget Sound. The trip from Pier 52 in Seattle to Bremerton is fifty minutes each way; to Bainbridge Island, thirty-five minutes.

Washington State Ferries is the nation's largest ferry system, serving ten routes with twenty-seven vessels, which range from small, high-speed passenger boats to mammoth ferries that can carry 2,500 passengers and 218 automobiles.

Among the most popular and scenic routes are ones that depart from Seattle's waterfront. Car ferries go to Bremerton on the Olympic Peninsula and Bainbridge Island, and passenger-only ferries service Bremerton and Vashon Island.

The base fare for ferries is about $6.25 for auto and driver, and about $3.60 for passengers. A surcharge is applied to all vehicle fares from mid-May to mid-October. Other routes on Puget Sound include Mukilteo to Clinton on Whidbey Island and Edmonds to Kingston.

For information, call ☎ (206) 464-6400 or consult the Internet at 💻 www. wsdot.wa.gov.

Downtown Seattle

At the heart of downtown Seattle is the **Pike Place Market**, the oldest continually operating farmers market in the country, dating back to 1907.

This is living history, saved from the wrecking ball by a public referendum in 1971. Salmon fly through the air from cooler to stand; fruits and vegetables are presented as works of art. Dozens of interesting food stalls offer fare from around the world. And fans of a cuppa Joe may want to make a pilgrimage to the original Starbucks coffee store, still open within the market.

The Pike Market, at the end of Pike Street, consists of several hulking buildings that include the Main and North Arcades, which are worthwhile starting points. Across from the Main Arcade is the Sanitary Market, which received its name because it was the first building in the complex that barred live animals; within are some of the best food stalls, including the **Three Sisters Bakery**.

Outside are views of ships in the bay below, with entertainment provided by street performers. Parts of the area around the market are rather seedy, but the good news is that the comeback of the market in recent years has pushed most of the undesirable trade farther and farther from Pike Street.

Open daily, the market can become uncomfortably crowded on summer weekends, so a midweek visit may be more enjoyable. Early risers find smaller crowds and the best offerings; late visitors will find slim pickings but the best prices.

Pike Place Market
Photo by Corey Sandler

And now, ladies and gentlemen, we've got a really big shoe for you. The **Giant Shoe Museum**, which is exactly what its name suggests: a celebration of extra-large footwear, from merely large to the truly colossal: a five-foot-long black leather wingtip from the 1920s. Most of the shoes were created as advertising come-ons for shoe stores, although some come from circuses or from exhibitions such as the 1893 Chicago World's Fair.

The footwear fetish is the work of Dan Eskenazi, who earned an early fascination with oversized shoes at his grandfather's shoe repair shop, home of a pair of size 37AA shoes that belonged to Robert Wadlow, an 8'11" giant of the 1930s. Wadlow's shoes have disappeared, but this museum marches on.

The museum, on the second level of Down Under at the Pike Place Market at First Avenue and Pike Street, is open during the hours of the market, generally daily 10 A.M. to 6 P.M. Admission: free, but some display windows open only when a coin is paid. For information, call ☎ (206) 623-2870.

The **Hillclimb** stairs descend from the Pike Place Market to the waterfront near the Seattle Aquarium and surrounding piers.

Above the market is the commercial heart of Seattle, including Westlake Park and the Convention Center. The Monorail runs from Westlake Center to Seattle Center, about a mile northwest of downtown.

The **Washington State Convention & Trade Center** straddles Interstate 5, within walking distance of hotel rooms and most of downtown.

On University Street, the mammoth sculpture "Hammering Man" strikes a heroic pose outside the **Seattle Art Museum**. Within, a grand staircase opens on a collection that includes more than 21,000 art objects such as Northwest Native American art, African masks, paintings by the old masters, and contemporary art. The modern design of the museum is a celebrated work by architect Robert Venturi.

The museum is affiliated with the Seattle Asian Art Museum in Volunteer Park in Capitol Hill; same-day tickets are valid at both museums.

The museum, located at 100 University Street, is open daily except Monday from 10 A.M. to 5 P.M., and until 9 P.M. on Thursday. Admission: adult, ❸. For information, call ☎ (206) 654-3100.

The **Denny Regrade**, also known as **Belltown**, is at the cutting edge of the Seattle scene, with nightclubs, restaurants, boutiques, and condominiums reclaiming a long-neglected area. The area was once the site of Denny Hill, which was taken down in the name of development (regraded, actually), hence its unusual name.

One of the nice things about being a billionaire (I guess) is that there are always a few spare millions in your pocket to indulge your latest fancy. That was the case for Microsoft co-founder Paul G. Allen in 1998, when he purchased the original **Cinerama Theater** after developers began to consider alternate plans to convert the building into a dinner theater or climbing club. Allen (also responsible for the Experience Music Project at Seattle Center) had attended grand cinema events at the theater at its heyday in the '60s.

Allen's company has poured millions into the restoration of the 808-seat theater, bringing it back to its 1963 "space-age modern" décor, a place where George Jetson would feel right at home.

The restoration brought back the purple and green walls and red seats, and extended even to the popcorn boxes and signage within. New technology, though, includes digital surround-sound audio and state-of-the-art acoustics. Up front there's a completely restored curved Cinerama screen for special presentations of 70mm Cinerama classics; the ninety-foot-long, thirty-foot-high screen is constructed of 2,000 independently angled louvered strips and provides a clear, brilliant picture for patrons sitting anywhere in the theatre.

As befits a pet project of a high-tech billionaire, the theater has also been wired with video servers and broadband fiber-optic connections to feed digitized motion pictures to projectors, a future technology that could eventually replace movies on film.

Plans call for the return of three special movie projectors to present true Cinerama pictures—such as *This Is Cinerama*—as they were originally intended to be experienced. Once complete, Seattle's Cinerama will be one of only three theatres in the world capable of showing three-panel Cinerama films.

Talking coffee. They drink an awful lot of latté (and other forms of coffee) in Seattle, and they take their java seriously. Here's a guide to some of the terms of art:

Latté. Espresso with steamed milk and topped by thick foam.

Americano. Espresso diluted with hot water.

Mocha. Chocolate with coffee, or the other way around. Made with mocha syrup, espresso, whipped cream, and cocoa powder.

Skinny. A non-fat modifier to any drink. A latté skinny, for example, is made with non-fat or skim milk.

For screenings of modern first-run movies, architects developed a second screen that sits immediately in front of its massive counterpart. The modular screen breaks down in a matter of hours in preparation for special Cinerama presentations on the larger screen.

The original concept for Cinerama dates back to the 1939 World's Fair in New York, where inventor Fred Waller demonstrated an experimental motion picture process that used eleven different movie cameras to film the same shot from slightly different angles. The resulting films were projected on a dome-shaped screen using eleven separate projectors, creating a "virtual reality" well before anyone coined that term.

An adaptation of Waller's device was used during World War II by the United States military to help train airplane ball turret gunners.

After the war, Waller simplified his system to just three cameras, and added advanced stereo sound. In 1952, after several years of difficult production, the first feature-length Hollywood film, *This Is Cinerama*, premiered in New York. The film began with curtains framing an ordinary-size screen. After an uninspiring black-and-white introduction, the narrator declares, "And this is Cinerama!" and the curtains pull back to a wall-to-wall, floor-to-ceiling screen and vivid color. Among the scenes was a trip on a roller coaster.

In the next decade, five more Cinerama movies were made: *Seven Wonders of the World, Search for Paradise, South Seas Adventure, The Wonderful World of the Brothers Grimm*, and *How the West Was Won*.

By 1963 more than 160 American theaters were adapted to show Cinerama films. However, huge production costs for the complex three-camera films lead Hollywood to seek a less-expensive alternative. In 1964 movies shot with a single camera on large 70mm film were marketed as the next version of Cinerama; as spectacular as they were, they did not quite pack the punch of the original process. Among the first big hits was Stanley Kubrick's *2001: A Space Odyssey*.

By the 1970s even 70mm Cinerama films were deemed too expensive to make, and one by one, theaters removed their huge screens and specialized projectors. (Today's IMAX films are a derivative of the large-screen process, shot with a single specialized camera and presented in dedicated theaters.)

With the return of Seattle's showplace, there are now three theaters in the world capable of projecting three-panel Cinerama films; the others are in Dayton, Ohio, and Bradford, England.

The Cinerama Theater is located on Fourth Avenue at Blanchard Street. For information, call ☎ (206) 441-3080, or consult 🖳 www.cinerama.com.

Seattle Pioneer Square

In 1851 loggers built a path along Yesler Way to skid logs downhill to a steam-powered sawmill on the waterfront; it was named Skid Road. The collection of bars and brothels nearby the pathway gave rise to the meaning of skid road or skid row as the shady side of town.

In June of 1889 a pot of glue caught fire in a furniture maker's store and virtually all the flimsy, wooden town of Seattle burned to the ground.

Nearly all of what is now Pioneer Square rose from the ashes during the next five years; today it is here where you'll find the nation's largest concentration of buildings from the 1890s.

The Pioneer Building, constructed in 1892, dominated Seattle's skyline and the local Gold Rush economy. It was voted the "finest building west of Chicago" by the American Institute of Architects in 1892. Between 1897 and 1908, it was home to forty-eight mining companies.

The triangular park at **Pioneer Place** was the center of Seattle's first permanent settlement. The totem pole in the square was first put in place in 1890 when a drunken expedition stole it from a Tlingit village north of Seattle; when an arsonist destroyed the pole in 1938, the city sent a $5,000 check for a replacement. According to urban legend, the check was cashed and returned with a note thanking the city for finally paying for the original pole. The ornate cast iron pergola in the square was added in 1905 to shelter patrons waiting for the cablecar that ran up Yesler Way.

Nearby, the **Smith Tower** was the tallest building in the world outside New York City when it opened in 1914. It was built by Cornelius Smith, who made his fortune as a typewriter producer and gun manufacturer. The cut glass pyramid at the top is illuminated at night; the brass elevators within the 522-foot-high building are still run by uniformed operators.

The area, within walking distance of the International District and Safeco Field, includes shops, restaurants, and galleries, most of them small and fiercely independent.

Pioneer Square is also home to the Elliott Bay Book Co., a mecca for book lovers, located at 101 South Main Street. For information, call ☎ (206) 624-6600 or ☎ (800) 962-5311. You can also consult 💻 www.elliottbaybook.com/ ebbco/.

For information about the area, you can consult a website put together by the local business association: 💻 www.pioneersquarebia.org.

A quiet park on South Main Street is inhabited by life-sized bronze sculptures at the **Fallen Firefighters Memorial**. Granite slabs list the names of thirty-four Seattle firefighters who have died in the line of duty.

Have a heart. Seattle claims to be the best U.S. city in which to have a heart attack; the city's emergency response system was the first of its kind and remains one of the fastest. Response time for emergency units averages between three and five minutes.

And, more than half the adult population of Seattle and King County is estimated to have had some CPR training.

Waterfall Park, at Main and Second streets, is a quiet respite from downtown at the site of the original offices of United Parcel Service. The company was founded here in 1907 by an enterprising 19-year-old, James E. Casey, who borrowed $100 from a friend to establish a bicycle service, the American Messenger Company. With a handful of other teenagers, including his brother George, the company was run from a humble office located under the sidewalk.

An unusual way to explore the area is to take an **Underground Tour**, a walk through the history of Pioneer Square and Seattle that includes passage into the abandoned sunken storefronts and sidewalks of the area, frozen in time from about 1907 when the area was rebuilt.

The original city of Seattle was handicapped by some incomplete planning, including the fact that the lower part of town was built on a mud flat; all of the detritus of the upper hill, including early rudimentary sewage lines, flowed downhill toward the docks.

Around the end of the nineteenth century, British plumbing manufacturer Thomas Crapper popularized the first flush toilet, sold as Crapper's Valveless Waste Preventer. When the first devices arrived in Seattle, the low mud flats at the base of the city caused sewer pipes to backflow with the incoming tide. The solution was to regrade the hill.

The streets in Seattle were raised, some by as much as twenty feet; at first, the sidewalks and storefronts were left at their original level, resulting in awkward situations that included steep ladders at intersections and a number of plunges by drunken or otherwise inattentive pedestrians; the coroner ruled some of their deaths to be "involuntary suicide."

By 1907 the sunken sidewalks were covered over by new walkways, submerging old storefronts and walkways. Today, most of the old buildings in Pioneer Square have one or two stories of offices or storage areas that are below street level, and about twenty-five square blocks have hollow sidewalks.

Local historian and author Bill Speidel wrote a book about the area, which became the source material for guided tours. Underground Seattle tours begin at Doc Maynard's Tavern on the ground floor of the historic Pioneer Building. Guides escort walking groups of about forty along today's sidewalks to obscure openings in old buildings that lead below ground into the original 1890s storefronts. The right of way to the underground is that of the landlords; the city owns the sidewalks above.

You'll see the ruins of an old clothing store, a few bars, and some unusual views of the sidewalk above through glass brick.

The tour is among the most popular attractions in town; some come just for the many wonderfully awful puns that are at the heart of the guides' spiels.

Tours begin at 608 First Avenue in Pioneer Square, between Cherry Street and Yesler Way. The walk covers about five city blocks and includes six flights of stairs.

The ninety-minute tours run year-round, with a dozen or more per day in July and August, and several per day in the winter. Admission: adult, ❷; senior (60+) ❷; student, ❷; and child (7–12), ❶.

For information and reservations, call ☎ (206) 682-4646. You can also consult 🖳 www.UndergroundTour.com.

The National Park Service also offers free ninety-minute above-ground tours of Pioneer Square, concentrating on Gold Rush history.

Seattle Waterfront

More than a century ago, Seattle's waterfront was the last stop on the U.S. mainland for frenzied prospectors heading north to Alaska; it was known as Gold Rush Strip. The main road along the piers is still known as Alaskan Way.

At the heart of the modern rebirth of the waterfront are the **Harbor Steps**, a grand staircase/park that links Western Avenue along the water to First Avenue and the Seattle Art Museum above. The steps, which include eight waterfall fountains, has become one of the most popular gathering places in Seattle.

The district stretches from Pier 48 on the south, below Pioneer Square, to Pier 70 on the north, a half mile below the Space Needle and Seattle Center.

Pier 48. Boats to Victoria, B.C., in summer.

Pier 52. Washington State Ferries to Bainbridge Island, Bremerton, and other destinations.

Pier 54. Ye Old Curiosity Shop specializes in souvenirs and oddities, including a pair of mummies, Sylvester and Sylvia.

Pier 55. Argosy Tours of the harbor.

Pier 56. Gateway to Tillicum Village.

Pier 57. Amusement pier, including an antique carousel, dining, and shops. Also home to Waterfront Park, which includes a public fishing pier, fish and chip bars, and import houses that offer items from around the world. Tour boats depart from Piers 56 and 57, offering narrated cruises of Elliott Bay's waterfront and the Lake Washington Ship Canal. You can also take a ferry across Puget Sound to Bainbridge Island, about a thirty-five-minute cruise, or to Bremerton, about fifty minutes away.

Pier 59. Seattle Aquarium and Omnidome.

Piers 62 and 63. Outdoor performance area on the water.

Pier 66. Marina, Odyssey Maritime Discovery Center, and Anthony's Pier 66 restaurant.

Pier 69. Headquarters of the Port of Seattle. Boats and ferries to Victoria, B.C., year-round.

Pier 70. Shops and restaurants. The *Spirit of Puget Sound* lunch and dinner cruises.

Norwegian Cruise Line's *Norwegian Sky* sails a schedule of week-long summer cruises from Seattle to Alaska and back, with a stop in Vancouver or Victoria. Seattle is the only U.S. homeport to serve Alaska on a regular basis; most other cruises depart from Vancouver.

Royal Caribbean International is expected to base its new 2,100-passenger *Radiance of the Seas* in Seattle during the summer of 2001, sailing a set of fourteen three- and four-day cruises from Seattle to Victoria and Vancouver.

Seattle Metro Waterfront Streetcar

Two 1927 Australian streetcars began service along the Seattle waterfront in 1982; three more joined the fleet in 1990 as tracks were extended into the International District.

The Waterfront Streetcar runs along Alaskan Way from Broad Street near Seattle Center, past the piers, below Pike Place Market, and on to Pioneer Square and the International District.

Jackson Street Station. (Chinatown/International District.) Wing Luke Asian Museum, Safeco Field (five blocks), and Metro Tunnel entrance for bus service.

Occidental Park Station. (Pioneer Square.) Klondike Gold Rush Museum, Undergound Tour.

Washington Street Station. (South End of Alaskan Way.) *Princess Marguerite* ferry to Victoria.

Madison Street Station. (Waterfront Piers 48–55.) Washington State Ferries terminal, Ye Olde Curiosity Shop.

University Street Station. (Waterfront Piers 56–57.) Argosy Cruises, Tillicum Village Tours, Harbor Steps to downtown Seattle.

Pike Street Station. (Waterfront Pier 59.) Waterfront Park, Seattle Aquarium, Omnidome, Hillclimb Steps to Pike Place Market and downtown Seattle.

Bell Street Station. (Waterfront Pier 66.) Bell Street Pier, Belltown.

Vine Street Station. (Waterfront Piers 67–69). *Victoria Clipper.*

Broad Street Station. (Waterfront Pier 70.) Myrtle Edwards Park, Seattle Center (five blocks), Pier 70 restaurants and shops, *Spirit of Puget Sound* harbor cruises.

The cars, built for the Melbourne transit system, are appointed with Tasmanian mahogany and white ash woodwork. Each car can accommodate fifty-two seated passengers and forty standees. Cars run about every twenty minutes.

Streetcar conductors do not carry cash; you'll need to deposit exact fare. Travel during peak weekday hours is adult, $1.25, and child (5–17), 75 cents. Adult fares drop to $1 in off-hour periods.

When you board, you can ask for a transfer; the pass allows you to reboard the trolley within ninety minutes.

An all-day adult pass for Saturday, Sunday, and holidays is $2. On Sunday and holidays, four children ages 17 and younger can ride with one adult who has paid full fare.

For more information about Metro operations, call ☎ (206) 553-3000 or ☎ (800) 542-7876; you can also consult 🖳 http://transit.metrokc.gov.

Argosy Cruises operates a fleet of tour boats from Piers 55 and 57 and other locations, including Lake Union and Lake Washington.

For more than fifty years, guests have taken an Argosy trip into Elliott Bay and the Seattle harbor. The one-hour harbor cruise offers four to six departures daily most of the year; in winter from November through the end of March only one or two cruises are scheduled. Tickets: adult, ❶; senior, ❶; child (5–12), ❸.

Another cruise visits the houseboats on Lake Union and Portage Bay, past Husky Stadium into Lake Washington. Boats depart AGC Marina on Lake Union in downtown Seattle, at 1200 Westlake Avenue North. Two-hour cruises are offered year-round. Tickets: adult, ❶+; senior, ❶+; child (5–12), ❶.

The Locks Cruise departs from Pier 57 for a two-and-a-half hour trip from Elliott Bay and Puget Sound and through the Hiram Chittenden Locks into Lake Union. The cruise offers a glimpse of the houseboat community made famous in the film *Sleepless in Seattle*. Boats depart several times a day year-round, with as many as six departures in July and August. Tickets: adult, ❶+; senior, ❶+; child, ❶.

In 2000 the company launched the *Royal Argosy*, a new, old-style packet boat, run with one of Seattle's best groups of restaurants. The 180-foot-long ship carries as many as six hundred guests in on two- to three-hour scenic lunch or dinner cruises around Elliott Bay and Puget Sound.

At night, the ship heads out just before sunset in the summer and returns in the dark, the sparkling lights of Seattle off the port side.

Consolidated Restaurants is the owner and operator of some of Seattle's best-known restaurants, including Elliott's Oyster House, The Metropolitan Grill, Union Square Grill, Hiram's at the Locks, and Coconut Beach Grill.

Dinner cruises, featuring Dungeness crab, Chinook salmon, and other offerings from Thursday to Saturday are priced at adult $79, child (4–12) $53, and senior, $74. Rates are slightly less from Sunday to Wednesday. Weekend lunch cruises cost adult, $43; child (4–12), $27; and senior, $40. Weekday rates are slightly less.

For information and reservations, call (206) 623-1445, or consult ▣ www.argosycruises.com.

The Omnidome Film Experience in Pier 59's Waterfront Park features IMAX films on a dome screen; shows are offered daily from 10 A.M. For information, call ☎ (206) 622-1868.

Also on Pier 59 is the **Seattle Aquarium**, at 1483 Alaskan Way. The museum includes award-winning exhibits of aquatic life, including a Pacific coral reef, a working salmon ladder, and recreated Puget Sound habitats. Marine mammals on display include sea otters Kenai, Lootas, and Kodiak, and river otters Skykomish, Sammamish, and Skookumchuck. You can explore Puget Sound in the Underwater Dome where you are surrounded by 400,000 gallons of sea water; divers feed the animals there at 1:30 P.M. each day. The Pacific Coral Reef includes a group of black-tipped reef sharks.

The aquarium is open from 10 A.M. to 7 P.M. from Memorial Day to Labor Day, and until 5 P.M. at other times of the year. For information, call ☎ (206) 386-4300 or ☎ (206) 386-4320 for recorded information. You can also consult ▣ www.seattleaquarium.org.

Admission: adult, ❸; senior, ❸; youth (6–18), ❷; child (3–5), ❷. Combination Aquarium and Omnidome (one film) tickets: adult, ❸; senior, ❸; youth (6–18), ❸; child (3–5), free. Each additional film, ❶. Combination Aquarium & Odyssey Combination: adult, ❹; senior, ❹; youth (6–18), ❹; child (5 and younger), ❷; child (3–4), free.

> **One size fits all.** CityPass is a six-in-one ticket to some of Seattle's best museums that costs about half the price of individual admissions.
>
> The pass is valid at the Space Needle, Pacific Science Center, Seattle Aquarium, Museum of Flight, Seattle Art Museum, and Woodland Park Zoo. In 2000 prices were: adult, $28.25; senior (65+), $24.25, and youth (6–13), $16.50.
>
> You can purchase a CityPass at the ticket window of any of the six attractions; once you have the pass, you will not have to wait in line at the other museums. The pass can also be purchased by mail.
>
> Tickets are good for nine days from date of first use.
>
> For information, call ☎ (707) 256-0490 or consult ▣ www.citypass.net.

Inside the gates of the Coast Guard station on Pier 36 on Seattle's waterfront is a small but interesting collection of things nautical at the **Coast Guard Museum Northwest**.

You'll find photographs that tell the story of the Coast Guard in the Seattle area, artifacts from area lighthouses and navigational buoys, and assorted and fascinating odds and ends from a flag that traveled on the Space Shuttle to pieces of wood from the USS *Constitution* ("Old Ironsides").

The museum, at Pier 36, 1519 Alaskan Way South, is open Monday, Wednesday, and Friday from 9 A.M. to 3 P.M., and weekends from 1 P.M. to 5 P.M. Admission: free. For information, call ☎ (206) 217-6993.

Across the pier is the **Puget Sound Vessel Traffic Center**, a high-tech radar and radio communications center for ships in the coastal waters. Docked along-

Grave matters. Two of the most visited citizens of the Seattle area are not among the city's liveliest.

Martial arts film star Bruce Lee, who died under mysterious circumstances in 1973, and his actor son Brandon, who was killed in a freak accident on a film set in 1993, are buried at Lake View Cemetery, just north of Volunteer Park on Capitol Hill.

Legendary rock star Jimi Hendrix, a Seattle native, is buried in Greenwood Cemetery in suburban Renton, southeast of Bellevue and Seattle.

side are several Coast Guard cutters and ice-breakers. The ships are open for tours on the weekend when they are not in service. The traffic center is open for tours daily from 8 A.M. to 4 P.M. Admission: free. For information, call ☎ (206) 217-6050.

Ye Olde Curiosity Shop on Pier 54 is a monument to the strange, a gift shop built around a collection that began in Civil War times and has been protected and expanded by five generations of two families ever since.

Joseph Edward Standley, born February 24, 1854, in Steubenville, Ohio, was inspired by a schoolbook, *Wonders of Nature*. He explored Ohio riverbanks and the caves of West Virginia for Indian arrowheads and other items. In 1876, Standley moved to Denver where he got a job as a clerk in a grocery store, eventually starting his own store. He displayed the curios in his store, and they soon all but took over the space.

In late 1899 Standley packed up his family and his cherished collection of curios and opened a small shop near the Seattle waterfront, which was thriving during the Alaska Gold Rush. He named his store, "Ye Olde Curiosity Shop" after Charles Dickens' book; the shop's slogan became "Beats the Dickens."

Alaskan explorers, sea captains, and prospectors brought Standley rare Alaskan Indian and Eskimo carvings, ivories, baskets, tools, and weapons. Standley also sold items to museums around the world, including the Museum of the American Indian in New York in 1909. Private collectors included collector and author Robert L. Ripley. The shop has moved several times, most recently in 1988.

Today you'll find jokes and gags, souvenirs, and collectibles. The shop is located at 1001 Alaskan Way. For information, call ☎ (206) 682-5844 or consult 🖳 www.yeoldecuriosityshop.com.

Ferries depart from Piers 55–56 to the **Tillicum Village Restaurant and Northwest Coast Indian Cultural Center** on Blake Island Marine State Park, eight miles off the coast of downtown Seattle.

Blake Island, believed to be the birthplace of Chief Seattle, became a state park in 1959. The park offers magnificent views of the Olympic Mountains, Mount Rainier, Mount Baker, and the Seattle skyline.

A four-hour tour from the pier includes a narrated harbor tour, salmon dinner cooked in Pacific Northwest Coast Indian style, a stage show, and other activities. The *Dance on the Wind* show explores customs, beliefs, and dances of the Northwest Coast Indians.

Dances in the thirty-minute production include the Paddle Dance, Ancestral Mask Dance, Lummi Blanket Dance, Dance of the Terrible Beast, Raven Steals the Light, and the Ceremony of the Masks.

Tickets for the boat ride and tour: adult, about $55.25; senior (60+), about $49.72; child (5–12), about $22. For information, call ☎ (800) 426-1205 or ☎ (206) 443-1244 or consult 🖳 www.tillicumvillage.com.

Seafaring continues to be a major part of today's Seattle. At **Odyssey: The Maritime Discovery Center**, unusual exhibits let you try your hand at the simulation of navigating a freighter through busy Elliott Bay, listening in on Coast Guard and shipping radio communications, exploring a fishing boat, and otherwise gaining an understanding of the ways maritime commerce contributes to the local and global economy.

The museum, at Pier 66, 2205 Alaskan Way, is open in summer from Sunday to Wednesday from 10 A.M. to 9 P.M., and Thursday to Saturday from 10 A.M. to 5 P.M. For the remainder of the year, the museum is open daily from 10 A.M. to 5 P.M. Admission: adult, ❸; student (5–18), ❷; senior (62+), ❷. For information, call ☎ (206) 374-4000, or consult 🖳 www.ody.org.

Seattle's fascination with high-speed boats goes back at least half a century. The **Hydroplane and Raceboat Museum** includes a display of some of the best-known racing hulls, including more than a dozen winners of the Gold Cup. Other exhibits celebrate well-known drivers and display memorabilia that include trophies, programs, and artifacts from racing boats.

The museum, located at 1605 South Ninety-Third Street, Building E-D, is open from June to August on Tuesday from 10 A.M. to 5 P.M., Thursday from 10 A.M. to 10 P.M., and Saturday from 10 A.M. to 4:30 P.M. For the remainder of the year, the museum is open on Thursday and Saturday only, on the same hourly schedule as the summer. Admission: free. For information, call ☎ (206) 764-9452.

Oddly enough, the famed *Miss Bardahl* racing boat is not at the hydroplane museum. Instead, it is on display at the very casual **Memory Lane Museum**, which is located at the Seattle Goodwill facility at 1400 South Lane Street. The charity displays some of the more unusual items that were given as donations including a stuffed brown bear and vintage clothing. The collection is on display weekdays from 10 A.M. to 8 P.M., Saturday from 9 A.M. to 8 P.M., and Sunday from 11 A.M. to 6 P.M. Admission: free. For information, call ☎ (206) 329-1000.

Chinatown and International District

Up the hill from Pioneer Square and just past Union Station, a small neighborhood has been the traditional first step into Seattle for immigrants from Asia for decades.

Known first as Chinatown, and successively updated with new areas that include Japantown and Manilatown, in more recent years there have been large influxes from Southeast Asia, Korea, and the Pacific Islands.

Today the ethnographically correct label is the Chinatown/International District.

The area, located east of the Kingdome/Safeco Stadium area, includes a wide variety of restaurants, small shops, and exotic grocery stores. At the heart of the district is **Uwajimaya**, at 519 Sixth Avenue South, which offers authentic Japanese foods, arts and crafts, magazines, and books. Established in 1928, Uwajimaya has grown into the largest Asian store in the Northwest. For information, call ☎ (206) 340-6411.

Urban parks include Hing Hay ("park for pleasurable gatherings") with its dramatic pagoda donated by the city of Taipei; Kobe Terrace (named for Seattle's sister city in Japan), featuring an 8,000-pound stone lantern; and a children's park with a playful dragon sculpture.

The district's cultural life is centered on the Nippon Kan Theatre, a National Historic Landmark built in 1909.

The **Wing Luke Asian Museum**, at 407 Seventh Avenue South, is the country's only museum devoted to recounting Asian American history from the difficulties of arrival, the unhappy story of Japanese internment during World War II, and the accomplishments of more recent years. The museum is open daily except Monday, from 11 A.M. to 4:30 P.M. Admission: adult, ❶; senior and student, ❶; and child (5–12), ❶. For information, call ☎ (206) 623-5124.

Chinatown Discovery's Asian Cultural Tour includes a sit-down presentation and a leisurely guided walking tour. In 2000, there were four different tours offered. A Touch of Chinatown is ninety minutes long; admission: adult, ❹; child (5–11), ❷. Chinatown by Day is three hours long and includes a six-course Dim-Sum lunch; admission: adult, ❹+; child (5–11), ❹. Nibble Your Way Through Chinatown is two hours long; admission: adult, ❹; child (5–11), ❹. Chinatown by Night includes an eight-course banquet; this event is three hours long; admission prices in 2000 were adult, $36.95; child (5–11), $20.95. For information, call ☎ (425) 885-3085, or consult 🖳 www.seattlechamber.com/china towntour.

For information about Chinatown and walking tours of the area, call ☎ (425) 885-3085 or consult 🖳 www.seattlechamber.com/chinatowntour.

The **Frye Art Museum** is a rich but intimate art museum featuring American and European paintings, built upon a platform of American beef.

The original collection was established by Charles Frye, who made his fortune in meat packing and other businesses in Seattle and nearby Western states. The Frye-Bruhn Meat Packing Co. was a major beneficiary of the 1898 Klondike Gold Rush, providing provisions for many of the miners. Frye expanded his wealth with real estate, farms and ranches, gold mines, and oil wells in the 1920s and 1930s.

Charles and his wife Emma purchased their first European painting at the Chicago World's Fair in 1893; their collection eventually grew to more than 230 works that covered the walls of their mansion on Seattle's First Hill. The core collection concentrated on classical American, French, and German works; today featured artists include Winslow Homer, John Singer Sargent, and Andrew Wyeth.

Before he died in 1940, Charles Frye provided for the creation of a free public art museum to house and display his collection. The museum opened in 1952 and has been expanded since.

Watch your step. Jaywalking is taken seriously in Seattle, with citations routinely issued.

The museum, at 704 Terry Avenue, just east of downtown, is open Tuesday to Saturday 10 A.M. to 5 P.M. and Thursday until 9 P.M. Open Sunday noon to 5 P.M. Admission: free. For information, call ☎ (206) 622-9250, or consult 🖳 www.fryeart.org.

Founded in 1914, the **Museum of History and Industry** is now the largest private heritage organization in Washington, preserving the rich history of the Pacific Northwest from the 1780s to modern times.

The collection extends from ship's wheels to evening gowns, gramophones to baby carriages, time clocks to crosscut saws.

Accidents Happen, a computerized multimedia center, displays photographs of the 1889 Seattle fire. Salmon Stakes (their pun, not mine) tells the story of the important fishing industry of the northwest, including some hands-on demonstrations of the difficult work of catching and canning the fish.

Included in the archives are some 800,000 books, photographs, maps, and manuscripts. The museum, at 2700 Twenty-Fourth Avenue East, is open weekdays 11 A.M. to 5 P.M., weekends 10 A.M. to 5 P.M. Admission: adult, ❷; senior (55+), ❷; youth (6–12), ❷. For information, call ☎ (206) 324-1126, or consult 🖳 www.his torymuse-nw.org/.

The museum was due to move to the Convention Center area in late 2000.

Seattle Center

The seventy-four-acre park at **Seattle Center** was the site of the 1962 World's Fair and today is home to the city landmark Space Needle, the Seattle Children's Museum, and the Pacific Science Center/IMAX Theatre.

The most recognizable symbol of the Emerald City, built as the centerpiece of the 1962 Seattle World's Fair, the 605-foot-tall **Space Needle** stands atop an elegant concrete "X." (Early plans ranged from a tethered balloon to a flying saucer.)

The observation deck offers a jaw-dropping view of the city and Puget Sound; on a clear day, views from the top extend from downtown Seattle to Mount Rainier, Elliott Bay, Lake Union, and the Olympic and Cascade Mountain ranges. The Compass Northwest exhibit on the observation platform points out things to see and do in the area.

Elevators whisk thirty visitors at a time to the observation platform in about forty-three seconds; within the core are 832 steps to the top. The Space Needle Restaurant and the Emerald Suite on the 500-foot level make one complete revolution every fifty-eight minutes. Down at the 100-foot level, the Skyline restaurant is used for banquets and private functions.

Both of the revolving restaurants feature Northwest cuisine that includes seafood, steaks, and the decadent Lunar Orbiter dessert. The Emerald Suite is a more formal setting, while the Space Needle Restaurant is a casual room appropriate for families.

Breakfast is served daily and brunch is offered on Sunday. Lunch and dinner are offered daily.

The structure is planted on a 30-foot-deep, 120-foot-across foundation that weighs as much as the Needle itself. The carefully balanced top-level restaurants rotate with just a one-horsepower electric motor.

Built to withstand a wind velocity of 200 miles per hour, the Space Needle has been forced to close only a few times in its history, including the "Inauguration Day" storm of 1993, when winds reached ninety miles per hour, and in December of 1996, when a severe snowstorm built up snow on the tower. The tower has also handled several earthquakes including a 1965 tremor that measured 6.5 on the Richter scale; the tower was undamaged but swayed enough to spill water in toilet bowls.

The Space Needle is located at 219 Fourth Avenue North. The observation deck is open from 8 A.M. to midnight Monday through Saturday, and from 8 A.M. to midnight on Sunday. For information, call ☎ (206) 443-2111, or consult 🖳 www.spaceneedle.com.

Admission: adult, ❹; senior, ❸; child (5–12), ❷. Special deals include night and day tickets, and frequent rider passes. There is no charge to ride the elevator for those dining at the Space Needle Restaurant.

At the base of the Space Needle is the **Seattle Center**, an indoor gathering of shops, restaurants, and performance spaces. The area is home to a roster of annual festivals, including Bumbershoot, Folklife, and the Bite of Seattle fest.

There's also the permanent carnival of the **Fun Forest Amusement Park at Seattle Center**. Located between First and Fifth Avenue North and Denny Way and Mercer Street; for information and hours, call ☎ (206) 728-1586.

The **Seattle Center Monorail** was also built for the 1962 fair, linking the site to downtown; today it connects Seattle Center to Westlake Center at Fifth and Pine streets in about ninety seconds.

The 250-passenger monorails run along sixty-two concrete piers, traveling just short of a mile at a top speed of fifty miles per hour, making it the fastest full-sized monorail system in the country.

The Seattle Center Monorail is open weekdays from 7:30 A.M. to 11 P.M., and weekends from 9 A.M. to 11 P.M. The trains make at least one round trip every fifteen minutes. Round trip fares: adult, ❶; youth (5–12), ❶; and senior (65+), ❶. Several downtown parking garages offer special rates for monorail riders during major festivals at Seattle Center and for Seattle Supersonics basketball games. For information, call (206) 448-3481 or consult 🖳 www.seattlemonorail.com.

Yet another vestige of the World's Fair is the **Pacific Science Center/IMAX Theatre**, located in a former pavilion of the 1962 exposition. The hands-on learning center includes a Tropical Butterfly House, Tech Zone, robotic dinosaurs, and much more.

At Tech Zone, you can experience virtual reality, interact with robots, and try out computer applications; exhibits include virtual basketball. You can also put on a high-tech helmet and hang glide in a virtual city, play tic-tac-toe against a ten-foot-tall robot, and even create your own cartoon.

The museum's lush, semitropical Mesozoic environment is home to a quintet of recreated dinosaurs: Pachycephalosaurus ("thick-headed lizard"), Tyrannosaurus rex ("tyrant king lizard"), Triceratops ("three-horned face"), Stegosaurus ("plated lizard"), and Apatosaurus ("deceptive lizard").

Kids Works mixes fun and education for children of all ages, with areas named Water Play, Sound Sensations, Video Vibrations, Just for Tots, Animal Attractions, and the Rocket Climb.

Animal attractions at the center include a six-foot boa constrictor and a community of naked mole-rats, a strange breed that is classified as mammal; cold-blooded like reptiles, they live in a colony like some insects. Naked mole-rats, originally from Kenya, are neither naked, nor moles, nor rats. They belong to the rodent family, but are more closely related to porcupines, chinchillas, and guinea pigs. They are the only known cold-blooded mammal in the animal kingdom.

Water Works, an outdoor exhibit, allows you to power a water wheel with your body, play with a water arcade, and maneuver a two-ton granite ball suspended on a thin film of water.

The museum and IMAX theater, located at 200 Second Avenue North, is open weekdays from 10 A.M. to 5 P.M., and until 6 P.M. on weekends. For information, call ☎ (206) 443-2001 or ☎ (206) 443-4629 for IMAX schedules. You can also consult 🖳 www.pacsci.org.

Admission includes five buildings of exhibits, a free planetarium show, and demonstrations. Exhibits only: adult, ❸; senior (65+), ❷; junior (3–13), ❷. Exhibits and IMAX film: adult, ❹; senior (65+), ❹; junior (3–13), ❹. Exhibits and IMAX 3-D film, ❶ additional.

Admission to IMAX film only: adult, ❸; senior (65+), ❷; junior (3–13), ❷. Double feature: ❷ additional. IMAX 3D film only: adult, ❷; senior (65+), ❸; junior (3–13), ❸. Exhibits and matinee laser show: adult, ❹; senior (65+), ❸; junior (3–13), ❸. Evening laser rock shows: Tuesday, ❷; Wednesday–Sunday, ❸.

For children of all ages, the **Seattle Children's Museum** is a chance to travel through Japan on a virtual subway; explore a whale—outside and inside—at Discovery Bay; travel to an ancient marketplace in a Time Trek to ancient China, Greece, and the Mayan civilization; and work with others at Cog City to move balls through pipe mazes using pulleys, levers, cranks, and puffs of air.

The museum, at 305 Harrison Street on the first level of Center House at Seattle Center, is open daily from mid-June to Labor Day from 10 A.M. to 6 P.M., and until 7 P.M. on Saturday. For the remainder of the year, the museum is open weekdays from 10 A.M. to 5 P.M. and weekends until 6 P.M. As befits a museum aimed at children, the admission prices begin with the young. Admission: adult (13+), ❷; child (1–12), free. For more information, call ☎ (206) 441-1768, or consult 🖳 www.thechildrensmuseum.org.

Just like rock and roll, Seattle's new **Experience Music Project** is something that not everyone is capable of appreciating. Looking like the aftermath of a terrible accident at a guitar factory, the museum sits near the base of the Space Needle, its crazy quilt roof changing colors with the shifting Seattle sky.

The museum was a gift to the city by Microsoft co-founder Paul Allen, a serious amateur musician and collector of artifacts of Seattle's Jimi Hendrix; EMP draws its name from Hendrix's signature song, "Are You Experienced?"

The innovative museum celebrates Seattle musical heroes, which include Hendrix, Heart, Nirvana, Pearl Jam, Paul Revere and the Raiders, Ernestine Anderson, and many others.

It's a reverent, almost churchlike atmosphere within, except for the rooms where visitors can try their hands at computer-assisted rock and roll drums, lead guitar, or bass.

Architect Frank O. Gehry, a classical music fan, was commissioned to design the museum. Gehry is world-renowned for his unusual designs, including the Guggenheim Museum in Bilbao, Spain, the Temporary Contemporary Museum in Los Angeles, and the Frederick R. Weisman Art Museum in Minneapolis.

In interviews, Gehry said he purchased several electric guitars and cut them apart; the pieces formed the building blocks for the early design of the museum.

The exterior of the museum is made up of stainless steel and painted aluminum shingles, each individually cut and shaped. The steel has three finishes: mirrored purple, lightly brushed silver, and bead-blasted gold. The aluminum sections are painted red and blue. The colors of the building change with the angle and lighting.

Visitors enter into the Sky Church, lit by the world's largest indoor video screen. Through a corner window you can see the monorail arriving at the Space Needle station. By night, the room transforms into a live performance and event venue. Local bands make regular appearances and the museum hints that major stars may drop by when they are in town.

Guitar Gallery: The Quest for Volume presents the history of the guitar, beginning with an Italian instrument from the 1770s and moving on to today's high-tech axes. Among the stars of the collection: Rampa Red's National steel

The Guitar Gallery at EMP
Photo courtesy Experience Music Project

guitar from 1928; an Audiovox electric lap steel guitar made in Seattle in 1935; a Gibson Flying V prototype from 1957; and a 1964 Rickenbacker twelve-string, formerly owned by Roger McGuinn of The Byrds.

Northwest Passage highlights the development of the musical scene in the Northwest. Treasures include Quincy Jones's original trumpet from his Seattle days in the 1940s; Ray Charles's debut recording, "Confession Blues," made in Seattle in 1948; the Kingsmen's original Stratocaster guitar used on "Louie, Louie" in 1962, along with the FBI file investigating the lyrics of the mumbled song; original stage uniforms and instruments from Paul Revere and the Raiders from about 1965; stage apparel and equipment from Heart in the 1970s; and handwritten song lyrics by Nirvana's Kurt Cobain, Soundgarden's Chris Cornell, and The Presidents of the United States of America.

The **Jimi Hendrix Gallery** is based on Paul Allen's original collection. Items on display include a shard from the guitar Hendrix played and then smashed and burned at the Monterery International Pop Festival in 1967, his signed contract and the Fender Stratocaster he played at Woodstock in 1969, and handwritten lyrics.

Other treats include Bob Dylan's harmonica and guitar, floral bell-bottom pants worn by Janis Joplin, one of Elvis Presley's black leather jackets, and more recent artifacts from the stars of punk and hip-hop.

For many, the thrill will arrive at the **Sound Lab**, where visitors can try their hands and feet on computer-assisted musical instruments. In the center of the gallery, the futuristic Jam-O-Drum circle glows and pulsates to the rhythms played on its surface; with each beat, the giant drumhead reacts with images that light up the surface and project up onto the ceiling.

On Stage is a theatrical re-enactment of a large arena performance where visitors can play drums, guitars, and keyboards and sing in front of a virtual audience. Instruments are programmed to react to the novice player and correct mistakes; experts can show off their skills.

Nearby are three musical instrument platforms with guitar, bass, keyboard, and drums where guests can learn to play and jam with other visitors. Lining the room are twelve sound pods, acoustically isolated rooms where visitors can work on their chops in isolation.

Most visitors are locked into their private worlds like a teenager with a Walkman, attached to their personal electronic tour guide. You can point the hand-held device at symbols on exhibits to listen to music and description of the items; the display screen includes hyperlinks to other screens, and you can also bookmark items of interest and consult them on the Internet at home using your ticket number to retrieve your personal notes.

On the second level of the museum is **Artist's Journey**, an unusual simulator that invites visitors to "ride the music." The video includes a computer-enhanced, rejuvenated James Brown.

The museum has a capacity of about two thousand; a busy weekend or holiday may see long lines in the afternoon and evening.

EMP is located at 325 Fifth Avenue North at Seattle Center. For information, call ☎ (206) 367-5483 or ☎ (877) 367-5483. 🖳 www.emplive.com.

Open daily year-round, hours from Memorial Day to Labor Day are 9 A.M. to 11 P.M.; for the remainder of the year, the museum is open Sunday to Thursday from 10 A.M. to 6 P.M., and Friday and Saturday from 10 A.M. to 11 P.M. In winter only, the Artist's Journey show is also available as a separate admission nightly from 6 P.M. to 11 P.M. during the week and from 11 P.M. to 1:30 A.M. on Friday and Saturday.

Admission: adult, ❹; senior (65+) and student (13–17), ❹; child (7–12), ❹. Admission in the winter to Artist's Journey only, ❸.

And for something completely different, you can climb aboard a Duck and drive into the harbor. **Ride the Ducks of Seattle** sends its Army surplus amphibious vehicles on an expedition on the streets of Seattle and then, with a splash, out into the water.

The tour is launched from a parking space near the Ducks' ticket booth located between the Space Needle and the Monorail station.

The Duck (DUKW in military parlance) was an amphibious landing craft developed by the United States Army during World War II to deliver twenty-five fully equipped troops, or more than 5,000 pounds of cargo, from ships at sea directly to the shore. The DUKW could climb a 60 percent grade and broach an eighteen-inch-high obstacle, with a fifty-mile range in water.

The vessels were first used in the assault on Sicily and performed in other engagements in Italy; in the Pacific they were used in the invasion of the Philippines, the landing on Iwo Jima, and the final battle on Okinawa. Near the end of the war in Europe some 370 DUKWs were involved in the crossing of the Rhine River in March of 1945.

Some of the vessels were called back for service in the Korean War, but most were retired and many have found their way into use with police and fire departments, and in tourist operations.

In Seattle the ninety-minute harbor tours are offered year-round; in summer from 9:30 A.M. to 7 P.M., and in winter from 11 A.M. to 4 P.M. Tickets: adult, ❹; child (10+), ❸; child (10–younger), free.

For information, call ☎ (206) 441-3825 or ☎ (800) 817-1116, or consult 💻 www.RidetheDucksofSeattle.com.

Outlying Neighborhoods of Seattle

Alongside Seattle Center and climbing the steep hill to the north is the **Queen Anne** neighborhood.

In a city where there are more oohs and aahs to the mile than most anywhere else, this is the place to take your camera. **Kerry Park** on West Highland Drive is the place where the picture-postcard photographers set up their tripods. On a clear day or at sunset, you'll see the Space Needle in the foreground, the skyscrapers of Seattle and the busy harbor behind, and Mount Rainier in the distance.

That view has also created some of the city's most desirable places to live. The small-town atmosphere within the city limits features interesting shops and restaurants.

Nearby, the community of Magnolia has gorgeous views as well and also offers the mostly untouched Discovery Park, 400 acres of windswept bluff and broad sand beach. Bald eagles often come here to nest; the Daybreak Star Arts and Cultural Center celebrates Native American life in the area.

There's no state capitol on **Capitol Hill**; the name was the result of wishful thinkers more than a century ago. The capitol ended up in Olympia to the south, but in some ways the neighborhood of Capitol Hill lives on as a colony independent of the rest of the world.

Broadway is the central lifeline to a community that includes gays and lesbians, the rock music scene, and various other lively and fiercely independent folk. Longtime residents are ensconced in the historic mansions, elegant old homes, and classic apartment houses of Capitol Hill.

Volunteer Park at the north end of Capitol Hill was the original home of the Seattle Art Museum. The handsome building was restored as the home of the Seattle Asian Art Museum. The park also includes a conservatory and an imposing water tower that boasts, at the top of 108 steps, one of the best views of the city short of the Space Needle—and certainly the best view that includes the Space Needle.

The **Volunteer Park Conservatory**, a smaller tribute to the Crystal Palace in London, was built in 1912; the designers were the famed park architects John Olmstead and Frederick Law Olmstead Jr.

The original conservatory, now the central Palm House that links the two

The Volunteer Park Conservatory
Photo by Corey Sandler

wings of the building, was manufactured in New York at a cost of $5,000, and shipped to Seattle where it was assembled by the Seattle Parks Department.

Today, the Palm House is based around an orchid collection that dates back to a 1922 donation; plants come from Hawaii, Asia, and Costa Rica. One of the stars of the Cactus House is a century-old jade tree.

The conservatory is located at 1400 East Galer Street. For information, call ☎ (206) 684-4743. Open 10 A.M. to 4 P.M. daily; in summer until 7 P.M. Admission: donations accepted.

The park, which dates to the 1870s, was given its present name in honor of volunteers for the Spanish-American War of 1898, a brief war that took place mostly in the waters around Cuba and the Philippines.

Outside the conservatory is a statue of William Henry Seward, the former governor of New York who went on to the U.S. Senate and who was a fierce opponent of slavery. He later served as secretary of state in the cabinets of Abraham Lincoln and Andrew Johnson, and is best remembered for his negotiations of the treaty that purchased Alaska from Russia in 1867.

Not surprisingly, Capitol Hill includes a large college community with Seattle University, Seattle Central Community College, and Cornish College of the Arts located in the area.

Along Broadway are movie theaters, clubs, and taverns; dance steps are embedded in the sidewalk. There is also what some claim to be the largest concentration of Thai restaurants outside of Bangkok.

Just north of Volunteer Park is historic **Lake View Cemetery**, the scenic final resting place for many of Seattle's pioneers. But many visitors bypass the graves of pioneers "Doc" Maynard, Arthur Denny, or Henry Yesler to pay respects at the graves of Bruce and Brandon Lee, the martial arts film star who died under mysterious circumstances in 1973, and his young actor son who was killed in a freak accident on a film set in 1993.

(The grave of rock legend Jimi Hendrix, in Greenwood Cemetery in suburban Renton, prompts the same sort of devoted pilgrimages.)

The **Seattle Asian Art Museum**, considered one of the top collections of Asian art outside of Asia, is located in Volunteer Park at 1400 East Prospect Street. The museum, affiliated with the Seattle Art Museum, has a collection that includes works from Japan, China, Korea, India, the Himalayas, and Southeast Asia. The museum also presents musical performances, tea, and gifts. Open daily except Monday from 10 A.M. to 5 P.M., and until 9 P.M. on Thursday. For information, call ☎ (206) 654-3100 or consult 🖳 www.seattleartmuseum.org.

The **University District** is located across Union Bay from Washington Park. Centered around the University of Washington is a lively neighborhood of shops, restaurants, coffeehouses, theaters, and galleries.

From the dinosaurs to volcanoes to Native American art, the **Burke Museum of Natural History and Culture** on the University of Washington campus explores the natural and cultural history of the Pacific Northwest. Only a tiny portion of the huge collection of artifacts, fossils, and specimens is on display.

Seattle Asian Art Museum in Volunteer Park
Photo by Corey Sandler

The Life and Times of Washington State tells the dramatic story of the state, stretching back eons from the emergence of the land from the sea to the arrival of the dinosaurs, the Ice Age, and into modern times. Along the way you'll find some amazing skeletons of ancient creatures.

Kids can climb around within replicas of some of the dinosaur skeletons and explore a model of a volcano.

An exhibit on the cultures of Washington ranges from Native American clothing and ceremonial objects to items from more than a dozen Pacific Rim cultures that have contributed to the story of modern Washington, from Chinese and Japanese workers to more modern influences from Hawaii, Polynesia, Vietnam, Laos, the Philippines, and elsewhere.

The museum, at Seventeenth Avenue Northeast and Northeast Forty-Fifth Street on the University of Washington campus in Seattle, is open daily from 10 A.M. to 5 P.M., and until 8 P.M. on Thursday. Admission: the museum requests donations. Adult, ❷; senior, ❷; and student, ❶. For information, call ☎ (206) 543-5590 or consult 🖳 www.washington.edu/burkemuseum.

You can also purchase a discount ticket that includes same-day admission to the Burke and the **Henry Art Gallery**, also on the campus.

The heart of the collection includes paintings and prints by classic artists including Winslow Homer, Rembrandt, Daumier, and others. Modern artists and photographers include Stuart Davis, Robert Motherwell, Morris Graves, Diane Arbus, Ansel Adams, Imogen Cunningham, Man Ray, and Garry Winogrand.

The original old-style museum, dating back to 1927, was expanded in recent years with a modernistic set of galleries that include spaces for video and digital art and an outdoor sculpture garden.

The gallery, located at Fifteenth Avenue Northeast and Northeast Forty-First Street on the University of Washington campus, is open daily except Monday from 11 A.M. to 5 P.M., and on Thursday at 8 P.M. Admission: adult, ❷; senior (62+), ❷. Free admission Thursday 5 to 8 P.M. For information, call ☎ (206) 543-2280 or consult 📖 www.henryart.org.

Lake Union

The houseboat communities of **Lake Union** were made semi-famous in the film *Sleepless in Seattle*. The boats are mostly along Eastlake and Westlake avenues.

The lake itself is a beehive of activity, with seaplanes taking off and landing on trips to the San Juan Islands and British Columbia, and cruise and tour boats passing by. Small restaurants dot the shoreline with views of the activities on the water.

The **Northwest Seaport Maritime Heritage Center** is a home for a number of worthy old ships. Among the treasures here is the coastal schooner *Wauvona,* built in 1897 to haul lumber. She served in World War II carrying spruce for aircraft factories.

The 165-foot-long ship is undergoing a long and painstaking restoration.

Buildings at the center display nautical artifacts from sailing ships, fishing boats, and more modern vessels.

The center, on the shores of Lake Union, at 1002 Valley Street, is open from Memorial Day to early September Monday to Saturday from 10 A.M. to 5 P.M., and Sunday from noon to 5 P.M. For the remainder of the year, the center follows the same schedule of days, closing at 4 P.M. Admission: donation requested. For information, call ☎ (206) 447-9800.

Next door to the Northwest Seaport, the **Center For Wooden Boats** is home to more than a hundred wooden boats, from Native American and Polynesian canoes to more modern designs. Many of the vessels are in the water, and some can be rented for excursions on Lake Union.

The collection, at 1010 Valley Street, is open daily except Tuesday from 11 A.M. to 5 P.M. Admission: donations accepted. For information, call ☎ (206) 382-2628.

Alki Point

In 1851 a group of about two dozen rowed ashore to Alki Point from the schooner *Exact*, making the first settlement in the area. The **Log House Museum, Birthplace of Seattle** commemorates the place where the Denny party set up camp.

The restored log house at the site is actually from the late 1890s. It was moved to the location and furnished with artifacts of Native American culture as well as that of the settlers; there are also remembrances of the huge amusement park, dubbed the Coney Island of the West, that occupied the area in the early 1900s.

Located at 3003 Sixty-First Avenue Southwest, the museum run by the Southwest Seattle Historical Society is open Thursday noon to 6 P.M., Friday 10 A.M. to 3 P.M., and Saturday and Sunday noon to 3 P.M. Admission: donations accepted. For information, call ☎ (206) 938-5293.

Many thousands of Scandinavians made it all the way from their homes in Denmark, Norway, Sweden, Finland, and Iceland to the Pacific Northwest in the mid-1800s in search of jobs and inexpensive but fertile land. The **Nordic Heritage Museum** tells the story of the role immigrants played as farmers, loggers, and fishermen.

One section of the museum, a converted 1907 elementary school, is devoted to rooms about each of the Nordic nations.

The museum is in the Ballard neighborhood, the historic center of the Scandinavian community in the Seattle area.

Located at 3014 Northwest Sixty-Seventh Street, the museum is open Tuesday to Saturday 10 A.M. to 4 P.M., and Sunday noon to 4 P.M. For information, call ☎ (206) 789-5707.

The **Ballard** district has a long link to the sea. Each year, much of the Alaskan fishing fleet winters over at Fishermen's Terminal. A memorial in the neighborhood commemorates the lives of those lost at sea.

Ballard is also home to the **Hiram M. Chittenden Locks**, a watery elevator used to lift vessels from the saltwater of Puget Sound to freshwater levels of the lake, or return them to sea level. Ships progress across the eight-mile-long **Lake Washington Ship Canal**. The canal was constructed in 1917; today more than 100,000 boats per year pass through the locks.

A visitors center is open in summer daily from 10 A.M. to 6 P.M., and other times of the

Seattle hotel hotline. The Seattle–King County Convention & Visitors Bureau operates the Seattle Hotel Hotline, a free booking service at more than forty area hotels. The hotline is at ☎ (800) 535-7071 or ☎ (206) 461-5882.

Many area hotels participate in a program known as the Seattle Super Saver Package, offering reductions of as much as 50 percent on hotel rooms in downtown from November through March. In January, February, and March, visitors are also given a coupon book with discounts on dining, shopping, and attractions. The package is offered through the Seattle Hotel Hotline and by individual hotels.

Visitor Information Office 520 Pike Street, Suite 1300, Seattle, WA 98101 (206) 461-5840 year daily except Tuesday from 10 A.M. to 4 P.M. For information and schedules for free organized tours, call ☎ (206) 783-7059.

Along the southern side of the canal is a fish ladder to help salmon make their way to the headwaters of the Sammamish River, one of the tributaries of Lake Washington. A viewing port gives you an upclose (and dry) view of the fish, and sometimes of the sea lions hanging around in search of an easy luncheon of fresh salmon.

Other Major Museums in Seattle

The **Washington Park Arboretum** is an urban oasis on the shores of Lake Washington just east of downtown Seattle; within its 200 acres are worlds of oak, conifers, camellias, Japanese maples, and hollies recognized as among the best on the planet.

The arboretum was developed in the 1930s as a WPA project. Plantings include more than 40,000 trees, shrubs, and vines. More than 100 plants are on the endangered species list.

The University of Washington manages the Arboretum for the City of Seattle's Department of Parks and Recreation.

Located at 2300 Arboretum Drive East, the grounds and trails are open daily from 7 A.M. to dusk. The Donald G. Graham Visitors Center is open every day from 10 A.M. to 4 P.M. Admission is free to the grounds; a donation is asked for entrance to the Japanese Garden. For information, call ☎ (206) 543-8800 or consult 🖳 http://depts.washington.edu/wpa/.

As befits one of the world's commercial aircraft centers, the **Museum of Flight** at Seattle's historic Boeing Field includes an incredible collection of planes, almost all of them in near-mint flyable condition.

In the soaring Great Gallery, dozens of aircraft are suspended in formation above. You can watch jumbo jets and private planes take off and land at Boeing Field from an air traffic control tower exhibit. And you can step back in time to the days of early aviation at the restored Red Barn, birthplace of The Boeing Company.

Parked outside is Air Force One, SAM 970. This 1959 VC-137B, a military version of the Boeing 707, carried President Dwight D. Eisenhower on several international trips, and continued in service through the Kennedy and Nixon administrations. It was not officially decommissioned until 1996.

You can walk through the plane to view the galley, staff and press sections, and the flying Oval Office.

Other treasures of the collection include:

• 1926 Swallow. Flown by Varney Air Lines, which operated the nation's first contract airmail service from Pasco, Washington, to Boise, Idaho, and on to Elko, Nevada, a 460-mile route known as the "Route to Nowhere."

• 1933 Boeing 247D. The first modern airliner. One of only four known to exist today, the museum's plane is the only one still capable of flight.

• 1926 Ryan M-1. One of sixteen built, this light passenger-cargo plane was the basis for the design of Charles Lindbergh's Spirit of Saint Louis. The plane on display crashed in 1932 and sat untouched for nearly fifty years.

An Aerocar III at the Museum of Flight
Photo by Corey Sandler

• 1968 Boeing 747-100. A prototype of the world's first jumbo jet, a 231-foot-long monster.

• 1902 Wright Glider. A reconstructed version of the glider that was used by the Wright brothers as the basis for their first powered aircraft.

• 1968 Aerocar III. A flying car, or perhaps an airplane that could drive on the roads. First sold in 1950, Aerocars that had detachable wings and tail assemblies were aimed at returning pilots from World War II; they were never a commercial success.

• 1945 B-29 Superfortress. One of the most important bombers of World War II, a B-29 (not this particular one) was used to drop the atomic bombs on Japan.

• 1967 MiG-21 PFM. The best-known Soviet aircraft, well regarded for their speed, maneuverability, and inexpensive maintenance. This aircraft came to the museum from the Czech Republic.

• 1963 M-21 Blackbird. A Mach 3 successor to the U-2 spy plane, these are the fastest and highest-flying aircraft other than a spacecraft ever built.

The museum, located at 9404 East Marginal Way South at Boeing Field, is open daily from 10 A.M. to 5 P.M., and until 9 P.M. on Thursday. Admission: adult, ❸; senior (65+), ❸; child (6–15), ❷. For information, call ☎ (206) 764-5720 or consult 🖳 www.museumofflight.org.

Boeing Field, south of Seattle, is a busy private airport used by the aircraft manufacturer as well as corporate and private planes.

Shopping in Seattle

The **Pine Street Shopping District** is the heart of Seattle's retail district. The area between the Bon Marché and Westlake Center at Fourth and Pine to

Pacific Place and Old Navy at Sixth and Pine streets in downtown Seattle has undergone a major revitalization in recent years.

The **Westlake Center** is an urban mall. For information, call ☎ (206) 467-1600. Across from Westlake Center at Fifth and Pine is the **Nordstrom Flagship Store**, the largest in the Nordstrom chain. It features a doorman at the entrance, a day spa, shoe museum, and aquariums in the children's department.

Pacific Place is a newer urban shopping center with high-end retailers that include Cartier and Tiffany & Co. and six restaurants. The center is connected to Nordstrom via a skywalk over Sixth Avenue. The five-level mall at Seventh Avenue and Pine Street also offers fine dining at Jeremiah Tower's Stars, Gordon Biersch Brewing Company, and Il Fornaio. For information, call ☎ (206) 405-2655.

Seattle-based **Recreational Equipment, Inc., (REI)**, a national retailer of outdoor gear and clothing, opened its flagship retail store downtown at 222 Yale Avenue North. In addition to shopping for clothing and equipment, visitors can climb the nation's tallest free-standing indoor climbing wall, try out a mountain bike on the outdoor bike test track, or walk the outdoor hiking trail landscaped with native Northwest plants and featuring a pond and waterfall. For information, call ☎ (206) 223-1944 or ☎ (888) 873-1938, or consult www.REI.com.

Two notable shopping areas are within the **Seattle Waterfront**. On Pier 57, at 1301 Alaskan Way, **The Bay Pavilion** is a refurbished 1890s Gold Rush pier with dining, shopping, and a vintage carousel. For information, call ☎ (206) 623-8600.

The **Bell Street Pier Fish Market** is along the water at 2221 Alaskan Way.

Outlying Shopping Malls

Bellevue Square. Northeast Eighth & Bellevue Way, Bellevue. ☎ (425) 454-2431.

SeaTac Mall. 1928 South SeaTac Mall, Federal Way. ☎ (253) 839-6151. 🖳 www.seatac mall.com. Four major department stores and 115 specialty shops and restaurants.

Southcenter Mall. Junction I-5 and I-405, Seattle. ☎ (206) 246-7400. 🖳 www.ShopYourMall.com. Seattle's largest shopping center with Nordstrom, The Bon Marche, JCPenney, Mervyn's, Sears, and more than 150 specialty stores.

SuperMall of the Great Northwest. 1101 SuperMall Way, Auburn. ☎ (253) 833-9500 or ☎ (800) 729-8258. More than 100 stores.

Redmond Town Center. 16495 Northeast Seventy-Fourth Street, Redmond. ☎ (425) 867-0808. 🖳 www.shopredmontowncenter.com. Outdoor shopping center with some 100 stores.

Northgate Mall. 555 Northgate Mall, Seattle. ☎ (206) 362-4777. Nordstrom, The Bon Marche, others.

Prime Outlets at Burlington. 448 Fashion Way, Burlington. ☎ (360) 757-3549. Liz Claiborne, J. Crew, Jones New York, Casual Corner, TAG Designer Fashion Outlet, Dress Barn, Tommy Hilfiger.

Centralia Factory Outlets. 1342 Lum Road, Centralia. ☎ (360) 736-3327.

🖳 www.centraliafactoryoutlet.com. Helly Hansen, VF Factory Outlets, Levi's, London Fog, Bass Shoe, L'eggs, Van Heusen, Corning Revere, Casual Corner.

Seattle Theater

A Contemporary Theatre (ACT). 700 Union Street. ☎ (206) 292-7676. 🖳 www.acttheatre.org.

Cabaret de Paris (Crepe de Paris). Second level, Rainier Square, 1333 Fifth Avenue ☎ (206) 623-4111. Cabaret dinner theater.

Civic Light Opera. 11051 Thirty-Fourth Street Northeast. ☎ (206) 363-2809.

Empty Space Theatre. 3509 Fremont Avenue North. ☎ (206) 547-7500, 🖳 www.emptyspace.org.

Fifth Avenue Musical Theatre. 1308 Fifth Avenue ☎ (206) 625-1900. 🖳 www.5thavenuetheatre.org. Free tours of the ornate Chinese interior of the historic Fifth Avenue Theater are offered by appointment.

Intiman Theatre. 201 Mercer Street. ☎ (206) 269-1900.

The Moore Theatre. 1932 Second Avenue ☎ (206) 467-5510, 🖳 www.the moore.com.

Northwest Asian American Theatre. 409 Seventh Avenue South ☎ (206) 340-1445. 🖳 www.nwaat.org.

Pacific Northwest Ballet. 301 Mercer Street, Seattle. ☎ (206) 441-9411.

Paramount Theatre. 911 Pine Street. ☎ (206) 467-5510. 🖳 www.thepara mount.com. Home to the Paramount's Broadway Series, concerts, and other performance events.

Seattle Children's Theatre. The Charlotte Martin Theatre, Second Avenue North and Thomas Street, Seattle Center. ☎ (206) 441-3322, 🖳 www.sct.org.

Seattle Opera. 1020 John Street. ☎ (206) 389-7676. 🖳 www.seattleopera.org.

Seattle Repertory Theatre. Bagley Wright Theatre, 115 Mercer Street, Seattle Center. ☎ (206) 443-2222.

Seattle Symphony. 200 University Street. ☎ (206) 215-4747. 🖳 www.seattle symphony.org.

Taproot Theatre Company. 204 North Eighty-Fifth Street. ☎ (206) 781-9707, 🖳 www.taproottheatre.org.

University of Washington School of Drama. ☎ (206) 543-4880.

Village Theatre. 303 Front Street North, Issaquah. ☎ (425) 392-2202.

Ticket Outlets

Pacific Northwest Ticket Service. First-class tickets for local and national sporting events, concerts, theater, opera, and symphony, sold at a premium above-list price. Located on Mercer Island at 9727 Mercerwood Drive. For information, call ☎ (206) 232-0150.

Ticket/Ticket. Half-price, day-of-show tickets to theater, music, comedy, and dance events. Ticket booths at Broadway Market at 401 Broadway East and at Pike Place Market Information Booth, First and Pike streets. For information, call ☎ (206) 324-2744.

Ticketmaster Northwest. Ticketing for major sports, concerts, theater, and performing arts events in Western Washington. For information, call ☎ (206) 628-0888. 🖳 www.ticketmaster.com.

Nightclubs

Bohemian Café. 111 Yesler Way, Seattle. (206) 447-1514. Reggae and dance.

Dimitriou's Jazz Alley. 2033 Sixth Avenue and Lenora Street, Seattle. ☎ (206) 441-9729. 🖳 www.jazzalley.org.

Seattle Music

Bellevue Philharmonic. Westminster Chapel, 13646 Northeast Twenty-Fourth Street, Bellevue. ☎ (425) 455-4171. 🖳 www.bellevuephilharmonic.com.

Cathedral Associates. Saint Mark's Cathedral, 1245 Tenth Avenue East. ☎ (206) 323-1040.

Centrum. Fort Worden State Park, Port Townsend. ☎ (800) 733-3608. 🖳 www.centrum.org.

Early Music Guild. 2366 Eastlake Avenue East, Seattle. ☎ (206) 325-7066. 🖳 www.halcyon.com/emg/.

Northwest Chamber Orchestra. Benaroya Hall Recital Hall, 200 University Street. ☎ (206) 343-0445. 🖳 www.nwco.org.

Northwest Seaport. 1002 Valley Street. ☎ (206) 447-9800. Monthly concerts of maritime music onboard the historic schooner *Wawona* from April to October.

Seattle Chamber Music Festival. Lakeside School, 14050 First Avenue Northeast. ☎ (206) 283-8808.

Seattle Choral Company. Various locations. ☎ (206) 363-1100. 🖳 www.seattle choralcompany.org.

Seattle Men's Chorus. Various locations. ☎ (206) 323-2992, 🖳 www.seattle menschorus.org.

Seattle Opera. Seattle Center Opera House. ☎ (206) 389-7600. 🖳 www.seattle opera.org.

Seattle Philharmonic Orchestra. Meany Hall, University of Washington Campus. ☎ (206) 528-6878.

Seattle Symphony. Benaroya Hall, 200 University Street. ☎ (206) 215-4747 or 🖳 www.seattlesymphony.org.

Seattle Youth Symphony Orchestras. Benaroya Hall, 200 University Street. ☎ (206) 362-2300.

University of Washington School of Music. Meany Theater, Fifteenth Northeast and Fortieth streets. ☎ (206) 543-4880 or ☎ (800) 859-5342.

Vashon Island Meadow Music. Various locations. ☎ (206) 463-2592.

Art Galleries and Antiques

Asian Art Association. 104 West Roy Street. ☎ (206) 298-9425. Fine Asian art from China, Japan, Korea, and Southeast Asia.

Carolyn Staley Fine Prints. 313 First Avenue South. ☎ (206) 621-1888. 🖳 www.carolynstaleyprints.com

The Crane Gallery. 104 West Roy Street. ☎ (206) 298-9425.

Davidson Galleries. 313 Occidental Avenue South. ☎ (206) 624-6700.

Eyre/Moore Gallery. 913 Western Avenue ☎ (206) 624-5596.

Flury & Company. 322 First Avenue South. ☎ (206) 587-0260. ⬛ www.hal cyon.com/curtis. Photography by Edward South Curtis, antique Native American art.

Foster/White Gallery. 123 South Jackson Street. ☎ (206) 622-2833. ⬛ www.fosterwhite.com. Northwest masters and Pilchuck glass.

Francine Seders Gallery. 6701 Greenwood Avenue North. ☎ (206) 782-0355.

Friesen Gallery. 1210 Second Avenue ☎ (206) 628-9501.

Frye Art Museum. 704 Terry Street. ☎ (206) 622-9250.

Glasshouse Studio. 311 Occidental South. ☎ (206) 682-9939.

Greg Kucera Gallery. 212 Third Avenue South. ☎ (206) 624-0770. ⬛ www.greg kucera.com.

Henry Art Gallery. Fifteenth Avenue Northeast at Northeast Forty-First Street. ☎ (206) 543-2280.

Kirkland Gallery Association. 120 Park Lane, Kirkland. ☎ (425) 889-8212. A group of fourteen nearby art, glassware, jewelry, and furniture dealers.

The Legacy Ltd. 1003 First Avenue. ☎ (206) 624-6350 or ☎ (800) 729-1562. ⬛ www.thelegacyltd.com. Historic and contemporary Northwest Coast Indian and Alaskan Eskimo art.

Martin-Zambito Fine Art. 721 East Pike. ☎ (206) 726-9509.

Nelson/Rovzar Gallery. 118 Central Way, Kirkland. ☎ (425) 889-4627.

Nordic Heritage Museum. 3014 Northwest Sixty-Seventh Street. ☎ (206) 789-5707.

Seafirst Gallery. 701 Fifth Avenue, Floor 3. ☎ (206) 585-3200.

Tukan–South American Art Gallery. 218 Pike Street. ☎ (206) 624-6890. Exotic butterflies, spiders, and bugs from around the world, plus ceramics and sculptures.

Casinos

Big Al's Casino. 12715 Fourth Avenue West, Everett. ☎ (425) 347-1669 or ☎ (877) 244-2577.

Clearwater Casino. 15347 Suquamish Way Northeast, Suquamish. ☎ (360) 598-6889 or ☎ (800) 375-6073.

Diamond Lil's Card Casino. 361 Rainier Avenue South, Renton. ☎ (425) 226-2763.

Drift On Inn Roadhouse Casino. 16708 Aurora Avenue North, Shoreline. ☎ (206) 546-8040.

Emerald Queen Casino & Night Club. 2102 Alexander Avenue, Tacoma. ☎ (888) 831-7655.

Freddie's Club Casino. 111 South Third Street, Renton. ☎ (425) 228-0908.

Muckleshoot Casino. 2402 Auburn Way South, Auburn. ☎ (253) 804-4444 or ☎ (800) 804-4944.

Parkers Casino & Sports Bar. 17001 Aurora Avenue North, Shoreline. ☎ (206) 546-6161.

Pete's Flying Aces Casino & Sports Bar. 14101 Pacific Highway South, Tukwila. ☎ (206) 248-1224.

Red Wind Casino. 12819 Yelm Highway, Olympia. ☎ (360) 412-5000.

Silver Dollar Casino. 14027 Interurban Avenue South, Tukwila. ☎ (206) 241-9526.

Skagit Valley Casino Resort. 5984 Darrk Lane, Bow. ☎ (360) 724-7777 or ☎ (877) 275-2448.

Swinomish Casino & Bingo. 12885 Casino Drive, Anacortes. ☎ (360) 293-2691. 💻 www.swinomishcasino.com.

Tulalip Casino Bingo. 6410 Thirty-Third Avenue Northeast, Marysville. ☎ · (360) 651-1111 or ☎ (888) 272-1111.

Sports Teams

Seattle Mariners Baseball Club. The American League team plays its home games at Safeco Field, located at First Avenue South and Atlantic Street. For information, call ☎ (206) 346-4001, or for tickets, call ☎ (206) 622-4487. You can also consult 💻 www.mariners.org.

The new home of the Seattle Mariners opened in 1999, becoming an immediate hit with fans and visitors. Safeco Field, named after an insurance company, replaced the aging and awkward indoor Kingdome.

The stadium features real grass and fresh air, at least when it's not raining; the most notable feature of the new field is its retractable roof, a gigantic twenty-two-million–pound structure that rolls east to west on tracks from right field. The entire stadium can be covered with the push of a button in less than twenty minutes. The roof covers but does not completely enclose the park, allowing fresh air to come in from the sides.

Tickets for the Mariners range from about $5 for centerfield bleachers to $32 for lower box and Terrace Club seats. The stadium seats 47,116 for baseball.

Seats in the lower boxes and the upper decks between the left and right foul poles offer excellent sight lines. The unusual design of the park includes some unusual seats way, way up high over the right field fence, as well as centerfield bleachers that are almost in another county. The bleachers in right field are in permanent shade, sitting under the lip of the accordioned roof.

Ground rules for the park say that if a game is begun with the roof closed, it will remain so for the duration of the game. If the weather changes during a game, the roof can be put in place without interrupting the game.

The main scoreboard in centerfield features a huge video screen for display of graphics and animation. Along the first and third-base lines are play-by-play boards that display running summaries of each inning to help fans follow the action. And with a nod to baseball history, the small scoreboard in left field is hand-operated, with changeable numbers.

And just as Pike Market is a whole lot more than a mere roadside fruit stand and Seattle coffee is much more than mud in a cup, the food service at Safeco field is several cuts above a slimy hot dog and a warm beer. Under the stands are outposts of several Seattle landmarks, including Ivar's Fish & Chips, Tully's Coffee, and Porter's Place barbeque. As I wandered, I also found stands that offer Japanese noodle soup, kosher frankfurters, and salmon sandwiches. The Bullpen Pub above the leftfield scoreboard includes pub fare, table seats, and

The Seattle Mariners at Safeco Field
Photo by Corey Sandler

views into the visitor's bullpen. The Hit It Here Café in right field offers full-service dining.

The stadium also allows guests to bring their own food to the game; vendors surround the field and area restaurants offer all manner of culinary enticements for fans on their way into the field.

The Bullpen market in left field offers interactive games and activities from batting cages to Nintendo games. Lookout Landing, at the end of the left field line on the upper deck, provides spectacular views inside and outside the park.

And another unusual feature of the park is the promenade that circles the stadium at the back of the lower boxes. Fans can make a complete circle of the ballpark on the main concourse while still watching the game.

Safeco Field will be home to the 2001 All-Star Game on July 10, 2001. Tickets will be very difficult to obtain, but visitors should be able to attend a week-long series of special events, including the All-Star FanFest, All-Star Workout Day, the Home Run Derby, and All-Star Sunday, which includes the All-Star Futures Game, a showcase for up-and-coming stars of the minor leagues.

Only a few thousand parking spaces are available in garages near the stadium. There are private lots in the area (charging steep rates of up to $20) and the park is within walking distance of Pioneer Square and the International District. The Metro offers service on First, Second, and Third avenues nearby.

When the Mariners are not in town, you can take a guided tour, including areas of the ballpark that are not normally open to the public such as the press box, luxury suites, and the visitor's clubhouse. You can also set foot in one of the dugouts and step onto the field itself. Tours last about an hour and cover a walking distance of about a mile; the tour is wheelchair accessible.

During the baseball season, from April 1 to the end of October, tours are offered at 10:30 A.M., 12:30 P.M., and 2:30 P.M. on non-day games. If there is a night game, only the first two tours are given. For the remainder of the year, tours are offered Tuesday through Sunday at 12:30 and 2:30 P.M.

Tours depart from the Team Store, located on the First Avenue South side of Safeco Field. A limited number of walk-up tickets are sold at the store; advance tickets can also be purchased from Ticketmaster, at ☎ (206) 622-4487. Admission: adult, ❸; senior (65+), ❷; child (3–12), ❷.

Seattle Seahawks. For tickets and information about the National Football League team, call ☎ (425) 827-9777.

In the fall of 2002 the **Seattle Seahawks** will gain a new stadium that will sit just beyond the left field wall of Safeco Field. The stadium will block a portion of the spectacular view of downtown from the lower boxes, but visitors in the upper seats will be able to look over its roof to Seattle.

The 72,000-seat stadium will be used for NFL and collegiate football, as well as professional and amateur soccer and other events. Developers, lead by Paul G. Allen, also hope to stage outdoor music concerts and dangle the possibility of use of the stadium for a future Olympics. About 70 percent of the seats will be sheltered beneath overhangs.

The $360 million stadium will have an open corridor down the center (north-south), with stands rising up on the east and west sides; seats will be sheltered with overhangs.

Once the new football stadium is completed, local ordinances will require that both fields are not in use at the same time, a situation that would overwhelm limited parking and traffic options in the area.

Between the baseball and football stadiums is a new 196,000-square-foot exhibition hall.

Seattle SuperSonics. The National Basketball Association team plays at Key Arena at Seattle Center. For information, call ☎ (206) 281-5800. 🖳 www.super sonics.com.

Seattle Thunderbirds Hockey Club. The Western Hockey League team plays at Key Arena at Seattle Center. For tickets, call ☎ (206) 448-7825 or Ticketmaster at ☎ (206) 628-0888.

University of Washington. ☎ (206) 543-2200, or 🖳 www.gohuskies.com.

Race Tracks

Emerald Downs. 2300 Emerald Downs Drive, Auburn. ☎ (253) 288-7000 or ☎ (888) 931-8400 or consult 🖳 www.emdowns.com. Horse racing.

Seattle International Raceway. 31001 144th Avenue Southeast, Kent. ☎ (253) 631-1550. Drag racing.

Adventure Tours

Beamers Hells Canyon Tours & Excursions. 1451 Bridge Street, Clarkston. ☎ (509) 758-4800 or ☎ (800) 522-6966. Jet boat tours through Hells Canyon, North America's deepest gorge.

Biplane Tours. Galvin Flying Service, 7001 Perimeter Road, Seattle. ☎ (206) 730-1412. 🖳 www.oldethymeaviation.com. Scenic rides from Boeing Field in three-seat biplane (pilot plus two passengers).

Over the Rainbow Balloon Flights. Woodinville. ☎ (206) 364-0995. Panoramic views of Seattle, Mount Rainier, and Puget Sound from a hot air balloon.

Spirit of Washington Dinner Train. 625 South Fourth Street, Renton. ☎ (425) 227-7245 or ☎ (800) 876-7245. Gourmet cuisine and Northwest wines served in restored rail cars.

Seattle Transport

Seattle is well served by a comprehensive bus system, plus specialty rail service—the Seattle Monorail and the Waterfront Streetcar.

Exploring downtown is easy—and free—within **Metro Transit's Ride Free Zone** for Metro Buses. Going beyond the downtown area, the fare is ❶ adults and ❶ for children during peak hours; off-peak rates in the evening and weekends are 25 cents less. You can also purchase all-day passes.

Travel in the mile-long underground tunnel from the International District to the Convention Center is free during the day; after 7 P.M. regular bus fares apply.

The **Seattle Monorail** runs from downtown at the Westlake Center to the Seattle Center near the Space Needle. A round-trip ticket is ❶ for adults and ❶ for children.

Metro Transit maintains a twenty-four-hour information line at ☎ (206) 553-3000.

Sound Transit and ST Express buses service the major urban centers of King, Pierce, and Snohomish counties. Buses pick up passengers at local stops with the Sound Transit logo. For information, call ☎ (800) 201-4900 or ☎ (888) 889-6368.

The **Waterfront Streetcar** provides a connection from Seattle's International District through historic Pioneer Square, ending at Myrtle Edwards Park at the end the of Alaskan Way. Fares: adult, ❶; child, ❶; and senior and/or disabled, ❶. You can obtain a transfer that allows you to get on and off the streetcar to explore different areas.

The **Washington Department of Transportation** maintains a web page with information about automobile traffic, ferries, and train service. You'll also find traffic cams with views of mountain passes. To check up on traffic, consult 🖳 www.wsdot.wa.gov/traveler.htm.

SeaTac International Airport

Seattle-Tacoma International airport includes a main terminal and two satellite terminals. Access to all gates is through the main terminal building. You can expect the airport to be uncommonly chaotic until sometime in 2003, when a reconstruction of Concourse A is expected to be completed.

Amtrak

In early 1999 Amtrak debuted new Talgo European-style passenger trains on the 466-mile Pacific Northwest Rail Corridor from Eugene to Vancouver, B.C., including Seattle-Portland and Seattle-Vancouver runs. The new trains can reach speeds of about 80 mph; further improvements to the tracks will allow even speedier service in years to come.

For information and reservations, call ☎ (800) 872-7245.

Washington State Ferries

The largest ferry system in the country, carrying more than 25 million passengers each year on twenty-seven vessels on ten routes.

The queens of the fleet are the giant Mark II ferries that can carry 218 cars and 2,500 passengers.

The ferries are at their busiest inbound (east) during the weekday commute each morning and outbound (west) each late afternoon. Ferries can also be crowded on weekends in both directions.

For general information on ferries, call ☎ (206) 464-6400. For customer service and reservations, call ☎ (888) 808-7977.

Ferries to British Columbia

One of the prettiest routes to Vancouver Island is onboard a Washington State Ferry from Anacortes through the San Juan Islands to Victoria. The big ships thread their way through the islands, pass secluded coves and uninhabited islands, making stops at Lopez, Shaw, Orcas, and San Juan Islands. Car-carrying ferries are often fully booked in the summer for the three-hour passage. For information, call ☎ (800) 843-3779.

The *Victoria Clipper* high-speed catamaran makes several round-trips from Seattle to Victoria, British Columbia, daily; round trip tickets for the two-hour trip range from about $59 to $89, depending on the season.

Clipper Navigation also offers car ferry service between Seattle and Victoria on the *Princess Marguerite III*, a 200-vehicle, 1,070-passenger vessel that seasonally travels between Pier 48 in Seattle and Victoria's Ogden Point.

For information, call ☎ (800) 888-2535 or ☎ (206) 448-5000 or consult 🖳 www.victoriaclipper.com.

From May to October, Victoria–San Juan Cruises sails between Bellingham and Victoria's Inner Harbour, winding through the scenic San Juan Islands with a brief stop at Roche Harbor. A round-trip fare is about $89. For information, call ☎ (800) 443-4552.

Two ferries operate between Port Angeles on the Olympic Peninsula and Victoria.

Blackball Transport operates the auto/passenger ferry MV *Coho*. A passenger round-trip ticket is about $15, and an auto and driver ticket costs about $59 round-trip. For information, call ☎ (206) 622-2222 in Seattle or ☎ (360) 457-4491 in Port Angeles.

From mid-spring through early fall, Victoria Rapid Transport offers the *Vic-*

toria Express, a passenger-only ferry from Port Angeles. Call ☎ (360) 452-8088 for information.

Once you are in Victoria or elsewhere on Vancouver Island, you can catch a BC Ferry across the strait to the city of Vancouver and mainland British Columbia.

Cruise Lines

In 2000, **Norwegian Cruise Line** began seven-day round-trip summer cruises to Alaska from the Seattle waterfront with its new 848-foot-long, 2,000-passenger *Norwegian Sky.* For information, call ☎ (800) 327-7030 or consult 💻 www.ncl.com.

The Port of Seattle built a $12.7 million cruise terminal at the Bell Street Pier on the Seattle Waterfront to accommodate cruise ships.

Alaska Sightseeing Tours/Cruise West offers overnight and lengthy cruises from Seattle through the San Juan Islands, the Gulf Islands, Vancouver, Princess Louisa Inlet, Juneau, and Glacier Bay, as well as up the Columbia and Snake Rivers. Call ☎ (800) 426-7702 for information.

Another small cruise line is **Catalyst Cruises,** which offers six- to fourteen–day cruises from Seattle/Tacoma to the San Juan Islands of British Columbia and up the Inside Passage toward Alaska. For information, call ☎ (800) 670-7678 or ☎ (253) 537-7678.

Alaska Sea Adventures operates small cruise ships from Tacoma in Puget Sound to Alaska. For information, call ☎ (206) 938-1662 or consult 💻 www. Alaska-Sea-Adventures.com.

Alaska Marine Highway operates auto and passenger ferries year-round between Bellingham and several Alaskan ports. Fares vary depending on the season and destination. For information, call ☎ (800) 642-0066 or ☎ (907) 465-3941.

Harbor Cruises

The Spirit of Puget Sound departs from Pier 70 for lunch and dinner harbor cruises with live entertainment. Tickets range from about $28 to $33 for lunch cruises and $57 to $62 for dinner cruises. For information, call ☎ (206) 674-3499 or consult 💻 www.spiritcruises.com.

Argosy runs hour-long tours of Elliott Bay as well as longer cruises from Pier 57 in downtown through the Hiram M. Chittenden Locks. Prices range from about $14 to $21.50. In summer the company also offers ninety-minute cruises on Lake Washington, departing from the Kirkland waterfront. In 2000 prices were: adult, $24; child (4–12), $12. For information, call ☎ (206) 623-4252 or consult 💻 www.argosycruises.com.

And for a step back into Seattle's past, Tall Ship Tours and the Gray's Harbor Historical Seaport have in recent years offered two-hour sailing excursions and sunset trips on the *Lady Washington,* a full-sized replica of the first American vessel to explore the Pacific Northwest Coast. For information, call ☎ (360) 532-8611.

Seattle Hotels

Seattle Hotel Hotline, a hotel reservation service operated by the Seattle–King

County Convention & Visitors Bureau, includes more than fifty places to stay in the Greater Seattle area.

The hotline is at ☎ (800) 535-7071 or ☎ (206) 461-5882. It is available weekdays from 8:30 A.M. to 5 P.M. Pacific time. For more detailed visitor information, call ☎ (206) 461-5840.

New hotels in Seattle include the tony W Seattle Hotel, the first of a new brand of hotels from Starwood Lodging Corporation. The twenty-seven-story, 426-room hotel includes several upscale restaurants, including Earth and Ocean, run by the operators of Nobu, Montrachet, and Tribeca Grill in New York and Rubicon in San Francisco.

The expansion of the Washington State Convention & Trade Center will include The Elliott, a 450-room hotel; the project is expected to open in mid-2001.

At SeaTac Airport, a new Westin Hotel will add 384 rooms by the summer of 2001; the building will be connected to the airport terminal and parking garage.

In the historic Lower Queen Anne neighborhood near the Seattle Center, the MarQueen Hotel restored a 1918 three-story former apartment building into a fifty-room hotel with large guest suites and a grand lobby.

Seattle Breweries

Hedges Cellars. 195 Northeast Gilman Boulevard, Issaquah. ☎ (425) 391-6056 or ☎ (800) 859-9463. 🖳 www.hedgescellars.com.

The Pike Pub and Brewery. 1415 First Avenue. ☎ (206) 622-6044.

Pyramid Brewery & Alehouse. 1201 First Avenue South. ☎ (206) 682-3377. 🖳 www.PyramidBrew.com.

Redhook Ale Brewery. 3400 Phinney Avenue North. ☎ (206) 548-8000.

Chapter 15
Around Seattle: East, North, West

Across Lake Washington to the East of Seattle, **Bellevue** has grown from a bedroom community to the state's fifth largest city with its own impressive skyline. **Kirkland** is a lively alternative community on the lake. And **Redmond** has flourished as the home of Microsoft and many of the software millionaires that company created. Up in the hills is the spectacular and quirky **Snoqualmie Falls**.

The road to the eastside runs across one of two floating bridges. The Evergreen Point Bridge (Highway 520) skirts the University of Washington and the Arboretum on its way to Bellevue; the I-90 Bridge connects Mercer Island.

Heading north leads to **Everett**, home of Boeing's huge factory for jumbo jets, and one of the area's leading unnatural attractions.

To the west across Puget Sound is **Bremerton** and the maritime Kitsap Peninsula.

Bellevue

The **Bellevue Art Museum** is located across the street from the tony Bellevue Square shopping mall, which says something about something.

Issaquah, along Interstate 90, offers a handsome beach at Lake Sammamish State Park, and popular hiking trails in the Cascades Mountain foothills known as the "Issaquah Alps."

The **Bellevue Art Museum** devotes its space to a changing series of exhibits from collections around the region and the world. BAM is located four miles east of downtown Seattle. The museum reopened in 2001 after an extensive renovation.

Located at the corner of Bellevue Way and Northeast Sixth Street, information and ticket prices for the new facility can be obtained by calling the museum directly. For information, call ☎ (425) 454-3322 or consult 🖳 www.bellevueart.org.

From priceless antiques to Barbie and GI Joe, and just about everything in between, the **Rosalie Whyel Museum of Doll Art** is set within an oversized Victorian dollhouse. The collection also includes nineteenth century French and German dolls, and it is based around the private stock of Rosalie Whyel, whose family wealth comes from Alaskan coal.

Most of the several thousand pieces are European dolls from the Victorian era and American toys, but you'll also find some ancient Egyptian tomb dolls.

For those who are serious about their toys, the museum also offers seminars on doll collecting, restoration, and other subjects.

The museum, located at 1116 108th Avenue Northeast in Bellevue, is open daily from 10 A.M. to 5 P.M., and on Sunday from 1 P.M. to 5 P.M. Admission: adult, ❸; senior, ❷; child (5–17), ❷. For information, call ☎ (206) 455-1116 or consult 🖳 www.dollart.com/dollart.

Chateau Ste. Michelle to the north in Woodinville is the largest and oldest winery in the state; free guided tours of the vineyard, winery, and an impressive French-style chateau with meticulously landscaped grounds are offered daily from 10 A.M. to 4:30 P.M. The winery is located at 14111 Northeast 145th Street. For more information, call ☎ (425) 488-1133 (weekdays) or ☎ (425) 415-3632 (weekends) or consult 🖳 www.ste-michelle.com.

You can also inquire about the **Spirit of Washington Dinner Train**, vintage railroad cars that travel along the eastern shore of Lake Washington to Chateau Ste. Michelle Winery. Gourmet dinner is offered daily, plus Saturday lunch and Sunday brunch.

The train departs from the Renton Depot at Fourth and Burnett streets; Renton is about half an hour south of Seattle.

The train runs on the tracks of the Burlington Northern Santa Fe Railway Company, on a three-hour, forty-four mile round trip from Renton to the Columbia Winery in Woodinville. Portions of the track parallel the east shore of Lake Washington, providing brief glimpses of the water and homes along the way. It crosses the Wilburton trestle in Bellevue, the longest wooden trestle in the northwest, standing 102 feet above a ravine; built in 1891, it is 975 feet long.

The train began in Eastern Washington in 1988, using a leased set of antique diner cars from the Canadian Historical Society. In 1992 the train began a new service from Renton.

The seven vintage cars include a restored round-end observation car, three dome cars, and a set of diner cars. A three-course meal is provided along the way, with a break before dessert at the winery.

The **Columbia Winery** was founded in 1962 by ten friends, seven of whom were University of Washington professors and wine aficionados who were convinced that classic European vinifera vines could survive Washington's harsh winters. Today the winery produces more than 125,000 cases of wines based on grapes that include Semillon, Pinot Gris, Chardonnay, Riesling, Cabernet Sauvignon, and Merlot.

Guests on the train—as well as visitors who drive to Woodinville—can taste many of the winery's products and purchase bottles to bring home. Located at 14030 Northeast 145th Street, the winery is open daily from 10 A.M. to 7 P.M. For information, call ☎ (425) 488-2776.

The train operates year-round daily except Monday for dinner, plus Saturday lunch and Sunday Brunch. Prices in 2000 were $59 for dinner and $49 for lunch or brunch; seats in the dome car were $10 additional.

For information on the train call ☎ (800) 876-7245 or ☎ (206) 227-7245. You can also consult 💻 www.SpiritofWashingtonDinnerTrain.com.

Across the road is Chateau Ste. Michelle, founded in 1934, just after the repeal of Prohibition; Washington's bountiful fruit and berry harvests were waiting and ready to be turned to wine instead of jam. In the 1950s the company began planting classic vinifera grapes in the Columbia Valley, which lead to the first varietal wines under the Ste. Michelle label in 1967.

Visitors at the Columbia Winery in Woodinville
Photo by Corey Sandler

Snoqualmie Falls and the Salish Lodge
Photo by Corey Sandler

The Woodinville chateau produces white wine grapes on eighty-seven wooded acres originally part of the summer estate of Seattle lumber baron Frederick Stimson.

Snoqualmie

One of the more spectacular reasons to cross those floating bridges from Seattle is **Snoqualmie Falls**, about an hour east of Seattle and fifteen miles east of Bellevue just off I-90 on Highway 202. The dramatic 268-foot torrent is almost as big a draw as the **Salish Lodge**, perched on a rock precipice beside the falls. It was the setting for "Twin Peaks," the quirky television series of the early '90s. You will not be the first to ask for a slice of cherry pie, although the joke from the show—if not the pie—is a bit stale.

For information about the lodge, call ☎ (800) 826-6124 or ☎ (206) 888-2556.

Snoqualmie Pass nearby offers four winter ski areas for sports enthusiasts, on I-90 about fifty miles east of Seattle. The four areas in the pass (Alpental, Hyak, Ski Acres, and The Summit) are now run by the same company; a single ticket is good at all four, and shuttle buses link the base areas. Alpental is, overall, the most challenging of the areas; Hyak, on the east side of the pass, often has the best conditions. For more details, see the section on Washington ski resorts.

Snoqualmie Valley Railroad

The hills and mountains around Snoqualmie, east of Seattle, were once one of the major logging centers in the northwest; trees are still harvested, but today the area is a hotbed of housing developments and tourism.

Logging companies built railroads to haul timber from the otherwise inaccessible forests.

The Snoqualmie depot opened in 1890 and was used for passenger trains until 1920. Among its features were segregated waiting rooms; in the late nineteenth century, unescorted ladies did not mingle with men, especially loggers lacking in social graces.

Today train fanciers have restored a portion of the track. The Cascade Foothills Limited's diesel engine hauls antique passenger cars built in 1912 and 1915. Trips run on Sunday from early April through late October, and on Saturday from Memorial Day through the end of October, hourly from 11 A.M. to 4 P.M. During the holiday season, the reservations-only Santa Train also runs.

Five-mile, one-hour round-trips chug slowly through the upper Snoqualmie Valley, departing from the Snoqualmie depot to the North Bend station.

In 2000, round trip fares were adult, ❸; senior (62+), ❷; and child (3–12), ❷. For information, call ☎ (425) 888-3030 or consult 🖳 www.trainmuseum.org. From Seattle, take I-90 east to exit 27.

Just outside the station, toward Snoqualmie Falls, is an amazing collection of old logging locomotives and other equipment parked along the side of the road.

Redmond

Begun as a farming and logging center, the settlement was built around the original 1871 farm of Luke McRedmond east of the Sammamish River. The city of **Redmond** was incorporated on December 31, 1912, with just 303 residents.

In 1963 the Evergreen Point Floating Bridge was completed and by 1970 the population had grown to 11,020.

It was the arrival of high-tech in the 1980s that put Redmond on the map. The most famous corporate headquarters, of course, is software giant Microsoft. For some, though, Redmond is mecca because of the presence of game company Nintendo of America. It's also home to Eddie Bauer, Genie Industries, Allied Signal Avionics, and other modern-day powerhouses.

You can drive by the impressive corporate headquarters, but there's otherwise not much to see—these are factories of the mind. All of the assembly is done elsewhere.

Everett: A Jumbo Jet Town

Can you imagine a room so large that a dozen or so wide-body jets look like toys scattered on the floor of a kid's bedroom?

Boeing's Everett plant assembles wide-body 747, 767, and 777 jets in a massive building that is the largest structure in the world by volume. About 24,000 people work three shifts at the plant; there are 77,000 Boeing employees in Washington and 189,000 around the world.

The Everett facility, more than two miles around, encloses 472 million cubic feet of space. (By comparison, the huge Vehicle Assembly Building at Cape Canaveral in Florida encloses 228 million cubic feet; put another way, all of Disneyland would fit within the Everett building, with twelve acres left over for souvenir stands.)

The assembly plant is one of Washington's leading unnatural wonders, drawing about 140,000 visitors per year for tours that begin with a seven-minute video that shows a speeded-up assembly of a Boeing 747. From there, a bus takes visitors to an underground passage through a service tunnel beneath the factory and on to a freight elevator to a balcony over the 747 assembly area. On your way in, you'll pass a huge cross-section of a 747–100 that shows the

Boeing's Everett Assembly Plant
Photo courtesy of Boeing

passenger area, as well as the cargo area beneath. (The cross-section is twin to another display at the Museum of Science in London.)

The Everett factory can accommodate two 747 lines, one 767 line, and two 777 lines. Production rates vary, but have been as high as seven per month for the 747 and 777, and five per month for the 768.

Twenty-six overhead cranes travel on thirty-one miles of network track; the largest of the cranes can lift forty tons. On the current schedule, the first parts to go into the assembly process are the wing spars, internal beams that run the length of the wing. The spars are machined by Boeing in Puyallup, Washington; they arrive in Everett on a unique truck trailer that is so long its rear wheels must be steered by a driver who sits in a cab beneath the back of the trailer.

There is no provision for heating or cooling in the building. Warmth is provided by the machinery and lighting, and windows can be opened to cool the factory on uncommonly warm days.

The tour concludes with a bus trip onto the flight line, where completed jets are tested before they are delivered to customers.

Tickets, at ❶ each, are sold on a first-come, first-served basis beginning at 8 A.M.; if you want to call ahead to make a prepaid reservation the charge is ❷ per person. Boeing accommodates about one hundred guests per tour, and all participants must be at least fifty inches tall and able to deal with a walk of about a third of a mile and a few dozen steps.

You'll have to leave cameras, backpacks, and large purses in your car; they are not permitted on the tour.

The tour's busiest period is during the summer months. Tours are offered weekdays at 9, 10, and 11 A.M., and 1, 2, and 3 P.M. Additional tours are added as needed.

For information about the tour call ☎ (800) 464-1476 or ☎ (206) 544-1264. You can also consult a website at 🖳 www.boeing.com/companyoffices/about us/tours/background.html.

To get to Everett from Seattle, take I-5 north to exit 189, State Highway 526 west. Drive about three-and-a-half miles and follow signs to the tour center.

Tour companies offer bus service from Seattle. There is also limited public transportation from Seattle; call Metro at ☎ (206) 553-3000.

Bremerton

Bremerton, just west of Seattle, is the largest town on the Kitsap Peninsula, and was once one of the most important U.S. Navy ports.

A car and passenger ferry makes more than a dozen round-trips daily from Seattle's Pier 52. It's a pleasant hour-long cruise priced at about $3.50 each way for passengers, and ❸ for a car and driver.

The historic naval destroyer USS *Turner Joy* is on display in a waterfront park near the ferry terminal in Bremerton. It is located at 300 Washington Beach Avenue. For information, call ☎ (360) 792-2457 or consult the web at 🖳 www.apptechsys.com/kmag. Tours are offered from May to September daily from 10 A.M. to 5 P.M., from October to April from Thursday through Monday from 10 A.M. to 4 P.M. Admission: adult, ❸; senior, ❸; child, ❷.

Nearby, the Bremerton Historic Ships Association preserves some of the history of the United States Navy, focusing on the Puget Sound Naval Shipyard. Exhibits are open daily from 10 A.M. to 3 P.M. Admission: donations accepted.

The **Bremerton Naval Museum** includes exhibits depicting the Puget Sound Shipyard as it looked during World War II, a room full of ship's models, and various naval weapons, including an unexploded torpedo.

The museum, at 130 Washington Avenue, is open Memorial Day to Labor Day Monday to Saturday from 10 A.M. to 5 P.M., and Sunday from 1 to 5 P.M. For the remainder of the year, the museum is closed on Monday. For information, call ☎ (360) 479-7447.

You can also take to the sea for a tour of the **Puget Sound Naval Shipyard** and the **Mothball Fleet**, one of the largest concentrations of modern and mothballed aircraft carriers, battleships, nuclear submarines, cruisers, and other types of warships in the country. Mothballed ships are deactivated vessels kept afloat for possible reuse. Tour boats depart from the Bremerton Boardwalk hourly from 11 A.M. to 4 P.M. from May to September, and from 11 A.M. to 3

P.M. the remainder of the year. For information, call Kitsap Harbor Tours in Bremerton at ☎ (360) 377-8924.

The **Kitsap County Historical Museum** tells the story of Kitsap, from the time of Native Americans to modern days, including logging and farming, a street of recreated old storefronts, and military installations that include the nearby Puget Sound Naval Shipyard.

A special section for children includes a working telephone switchboard and old-time toys and games.

The museum, at 280 Fourth Street, is open daily from Memorial Day to Labor Day from 10 A.M. to 5 P.M.; for the remainder of the year, the museum is closed on Monday. Admission: donations accepted. For information, call ☎ (360) 479-6226 or consult 💻 www.waynes.net/kchsm/.

Chapter 16
Tacoma and Olympia

Tacoma

The third most populous metropolitan area in Washington State with more than 665,000 residents in the metropolitan area, Tacoma stretches from Commencement Bay on lower Puget Sound to Mount Rainier National Park in the western portion of the state.

Tacoma is about thirty-six miles south of Seattle; the Seattle-Tacoma International Airport, which sits between the two cities, is eighteen miles away.

The land reaches from sea level to 14,411 feet at the summit of Mount Rainier.

Major communities in Pierce County include Tacoma, Lakewood, Puyallup, Fife, and Gig Harbor.

Tacoma takes its name from the Indian word for Mount Rainier, "Tacobet," meaning "Mother of Waters." The town booster's motto, "City of Destiny," was adopted in 1873 when Tacoma was chosen over Seattle as the Northern Pacific Railroad's western terminus for its transcontinental route.

Tacoma Narrows Bridge

For many visitors, Tacoma may be best known as the home of a ghost of a bridge.

The **Tacoma Narrows Bridge**, at the time one of the world's longest suspension spans at 5,939 feet, opened on July 1, 1940, linking Tacoma and Gig Harbor. Almost immediately it picked up a nickname, Galloping Gertie, for its unusual, undulating motion in windy weather.

Drivers on the 2,800-foot center span sometimes felt like they were on a giant roller coaster, watching the cars ahead of them seem to drop into the trough of a wave.

The movement was considered somewhat of a novelty until four months later, on Nov. 7, 1940, when the bridge rocked and rolled out of control in a 42 mph windstorm and eventually collapsed.

Engineers determined that the design of the bridge allowed the wind to catch the steel girders and the solid roadbed rather than passing through harmlessly;

Tacoma waterfront
Photo courtesy Washington Tourism Development

they also found fault with the narrowness of the two-lane roadway, only twenty-six feet wide. The post-mortem also lead to some of the most important advances in bridge building in modern times.

A month after the collapse, Hallett French, representative of the Merchants Fire Assurance Corporation of New York, was arrested at his home near Seattle. French had sold an $800,000 policy to insure the bridge but failed to turn in the $1,217 premium to the home office; he was sentenced to jail for embezzlement.

For the next ten years, Tacoma and Gig Harbor were once again linked by ferries. A new bridge, built upon the undamaged piers of the original span, opened in 1950. The sunken remains of "Galloping Gertie" were placed on the National Register of Historic Places in 1992 to protect her from salvagers.

Downtown Tacoma

Tacoma was shaped by the coming of the railroads more than a century ago, an influence that continues in the modern day.

Tacoma's **Union Station** was once considered the grandest building north of San Francisco, a monument to the golden age of railroads.

In 1873 Tacoma was chosen as the western terminus of the Northern Pacific Railway, the place where "rail met sail" at Commencement Bay's deepwater port. Freight operations were moved to the site of Union Station in 1892, but it wasn't until 1906 that a passenger station was planned.

The building was designed by Reed & Stem, the architects of New York's Grand Central Station; it opened in 1911 with a total cost of just under $500,000. The building was considered a Romanesque revival design, with elements of the Pantheon in Rome and sixteenth century Italian baroque details. Inside, giant barrel ceilings extend out from a massive central dome; the exterior of the dome was covered in copper.

The building was the centerpiece of Tacoma for most of the twentieth century, but it began to fall into disrepair as the railroads went into decline. Amtrak moved its operations out of downtown in 1983, and the huge building became an abandoned derelict.

But in the late 1980s a community group was formed to save the station with the proviso that the central rotunda be maintained for public use. Restoration began in 1988, costing some $57 million.

Union Station reopened in 1992 as a federal courthouse, with a public display area in the rotunda. In recent years the area has been home to a massive display of sculptured glass art by renowned artist and native son Dale Chihuly. The space is under the domain of the Tacoma Art Museum.

The rotunda is open to the public Monday through Friday 10 A.M. to 4 P.M. After the Milwaukee, St. Paul and Pacific Railroad (the "Milwaukee Road") ceased operations in the Pacific Northwest in 1980, its immense Tacoma freighthouse was empty and abandoned. In 1987 private business converted it into a public market as **Freighthouse Square.**

The building houses more than seventy small businesses including fruit and vegetable stands, seafood stores, flower stalls, clothing, books, handicrafts, jewelry, and art galleries, plus an international food court.

The railroad is remembered with maps, photos, memorabilia, and paintings. Special events at the market include observances of Mardi Gras, Cinco de Mayo, Summerfest, and Octoberfest.

Freighthouse Square is located one block north of the Tacoma Dome at East Twenty-Fifth Street and East "D" Street. For more information, call ☎ (253) 305-0678. The market is open Monday through Saturday from 10 A.M. to 7 P.M. and Sunday from noon to 5 P.M.

Twenty ethnic art masks mounted on buildings tie Tacoma's 15-block business and theater districts together.

Near the **Broadway** theater district on Broadway between Seventh Street and Ninth Street is **Antique Row**, with more than a dozen shops that offer collectibles and vintage furniture. Most of the stores are open 10 A.M. to 5 P.M. weekdays, and from noon to 5 P.M. on Saturdays and Sundays.

The area is also home to a lively **Farmer's Market** open from June to mid-September, conducted every Thursday from 10 A.M. to 2 P.M.

You'll also find more than twenty art galleries on and near Broadway in downtown, showing everything from glass sculpture and classic art to neon and grunge. For a guided overview, you can join Tacoma's **Third Thursday Art Walk**, held the third Thursday evening of each month. Most of the galleries stay open until 8 P.M. on that day, and many use the occasion to premiere new exhibits. Walking-tour maps and exhibit schedules are available at participating galleries.

The bustling **Port of Tacoma** is the sixth largest container port in North America and among the top twenty-five container ports in the world. Tacoma handles more than 80 percent of all waterborne cargo shipped to Alaska from the lower forty-eight states, as well as freight to and from the Pacific Rim.

SEATTLE AND TACOMA

The port's **Observation Tower** offers spectacular views of the Sitcum Waterway, as well as information about the port and the city of Tacoma.

Overlooking the Port of Tacoma, **Fireman's Park** is home to the state's largest totem pole, a 105-foot-high work.

Long-term downtown development plans call for a pedestrian bridge across the I-705 freeway, linking downtown to the Thea Foss Waterway and new development along its shore. As part of the project, an **International Museum of Glass Art** would showcase local artist Dale Chihuly's famed creations, as well as works by other artists.

Art and Special Interest Museums

The **Tacoma Art Museum** collection is a wide-reaching one, encompassing rare Japanese woodblock prints, works of the French Impressionists such as Degas and Renoir, a display of sculptured glass by Tacoma artist Dale Chihuly, and works by other contemporary Northwest artists.

The museum is due to leave its home in a former bank sometime in 2001 for new quarters north of Union Station.

Located at 1123 Pacific Avenue, the museum is open 10 A.M. to 5 P.M. Tuesday through Saturday, and until 7 P.M. on Thursday. On Sunday, the museum is open noon to 5 P.M. Admission: adult, ❷; senior (65+), ❷; child (6–younger) free. For information, call ☎ (253) 272-4258, or consult 📖 www.tacomaart-museum.org.

The **Washington State History Museum** claims the largest collection of pioneer, Native American, and Alaskan artifacts on the Pacific Coast. But this modern museum also relies on state-of-the-art interactive computer, video, and audio systems to tell the story of the state.

The museum moved into impressive new quarters in 1996, next door to historic Union Station.

Exhibits explore the history of the Native Americans of the region, moving on to the arrival of the pioneers and logging, mining, fishing, and other industries. Recreated Coast Salish and pioneer homes are open for hands-on exploration.

Electronic journal monitors are hidden beneath many of the flip books of historical photos throughout the museum; the monitors tell stories of the development of the state, such as the journey to Washington by wagon train or the building of the Cascade Tunnel.

In the Hall of Washington History you can visit with Dave and Dandy, the two oxen that pulled Ezra Meeker's wagon on his retracing of the Oregon Trail in 1906. The animals lived for a short while in a pen alongside the original museum, and were stuffed for display when they died.

The museum, located at 1911 Pacific Avenue, is open from late March through Labor Day daily from 10 A.M. to 5 P.M., and 10 A.M. to 8 P.M. on Thursday. On Sunday, the museum is open from 11 A.M. to 5 P.M. The museum is closed on Monday from Labor day through March.

Admission: adult, ❸; senior (60+), ❸; student (6–18), ❷; youth (6–younger), free; Thursday 5 to 8 P.M., free. For information, call ☎ (888) 238-4373 or ☎ (253) 272-3500, or consult the web at 🖳 www.wshs.org.

The **Children's Museum of Tacoma** presents the world on a kid's-eye level, with hands-on learning experiences that include interactive computers, a gallery of children's art, and a recreated African village.

The museum, located at 936 Broadway, is open Tuesday to Saturday from 10 A.M. to 5 P.M. Admission: adult, ❷; child ❷; child (2–younger), free; free the first Friday of every month from 10 A.M. to 9 P.M. For information, call ☎ (253) 627-6031.

Karpeles Manuscript Library Museum, at 407 South G Street, is a private collection of handwritten drafts, letters, and documents of historical significance, part of a group of libraries established by the Karpeles family. Among the treasures of the collection is a draft version of the Bill of Rights, the Constitution of the Confederate States of America, Handel's *Messiah*, written in the hand of Beethoven, and a copy of Abraham Lincoln's Emancipation Proclamation. Call to check on changing exhibits.

"Baseball's Beginnings," the library's newest exhibit, opened in October 2000. The collection is filled with items from the first thirty-three years of baseball, including a $150-per-month major league player's contract; an 1866 scorecard; several letters of challenge exchanged between different ball clubs; and pre-Civil War baseballs from the 1833, 1855, and 1860 seasons.

The library is open weekdays from 9 A.M. to 4 P.M. Admission is free. For more information, call ☎ (253) 383-2575, or consult 🖳 www.rain.org/~karpeles.

The **Pioneer Farm Museum and Ohop Indian Village** is a hands-on museum that focuses on an 1887 homestead and native life. The museum is located at 7716 Ohop Valley Road in Eatonville. For information, call ☎ (360) 832-6300.

An impressive display of military hardware of the aerial sort can be seen at the **McChord Air Museum** at the McChord Air Force Base in Tacoma. Aircraft and memorabilia stretch from 1929 to modern times; planes on display include a Douglas B-18 bomber and a Douglas C-124C transport.

The museum is in Building 192 on the base. Admission is free, but you will need to display identification and vehicle registration to obtain a visitor's pass. The museum is open noon to 4 P.M. Tuesday through Sunday. For information, call ☎ (253) 984-2485, or consult 🖳 www.ohwy.com/wa/m/mcchoram.htm.

Tacoma's Green Gem

Point Defiance Park is one of the largest and most beautiful city parks in the world, including within its 698 acres natural forests, saltwater beaches, and spectacular views enjoyed by more than two million visitors each year.

In addition to walking spectacular old-growth forests and manicured gardens, you can also visit the animals at the Point Defiance Zoo & Aquarium, travel back in time at the Fort Nisqually restoration, and ride a train pulled by an antique locomotive at Camp 6 Logging Museum. You can rent a boat or go fishing at the Boathouse Marina. And youngsters can see some of their favorite nursery rhymes and story books come to life at Never Never Land.

Point Defiance Park was originally set aside as a military reservation by President Andrew Johnson in the aftermath of the U.S. Civil War. Never used for that purpose, in 1888 President Grover Cleveland approved a bill authorizing Tacoma to use the reserve as a public park.

Visitors came by streetcar in the 1890s to stroll through the developing gardens and dense forest. An octagonal waterfront pavilion was completed in 1903, and the southern end of the park became a "seaside resort" by 1907, offering a heated, saltwater bathing pavilion on the bluff above the boathouse, known as the Nereides Baths.

The lodge, the oldest existing original structure, was finished in 1898 and served as the park superintendent's home until 1980. The pagoda was completed in 1914 as a streetcar or trolley station. The pagoda and lodge were refurbished in 1988 and are now popular rentals for meetings, receptions, and weddings.

Specialty gardens within the park include the **Rose Garden**, with more than 1,500 bushes in bloom from about June through September; one acre of roses is in a section dating from 1895, and a second acre was planted in 1940. The **Dahlia Trial Garden** includes plants from the Americas, England, New Zealand, Australia, and other countries. The **Iris Garden** features more than 100 tall bearded iris, 80 Pacific Coast iris hybrids, and 26 iris tectorum. The **Herb Garden** has more than 150 Northwest perennial herbs. And the **Northwest Native Garden** is an acre-and-a-half field of indigenous plants from Northwest's six geographic and climatic zones. Finally, the **Rhododendron Garden** displays some 115 cultivated varieties and 29 species of rhododendrons in a five-acre area.

The park is open year-round from sunrise to sunset. Admission is free. For general information, consult 🖳 www.tacomaparks.com.

You can step back into history at **Fort Nisqually Historic Site**, a restored Hudson's Bay Company fur-trading post in Point Defiance Park.

The post was originally established in 1833, some seventeen miles south of Tacoma near DuPont; it was reconstructed at Point Defiance Park in the early 1930s on a site overlooking the Tacoma Narrows.

The Factor's House, a National Historic Monument, displays a collection of fur trade artifacts. The reconstructed trade store, blacksmith shop, laborer's dwelling, and bastions are furnished as they would have been about 1855.

The fort's gift shop includes replicas of items from the 1800s such as pottery, glass beads, and Hudson's Bay Company blankets.

Each fall, staff and volunteers take the parts of inhabitants of the fort for a series of Candlelight Tours; dressed in period clothing, they discuss the events and skills of their time, demonstrating crafts that include blacksmithing, spinning, and beadwork. Other annual events at Fort Nisqually include several living history days, a celebration of Queen Victoria's birthday in May, the Brigade Encampment in August, and a nineteenth century Christmas in December.

The fort museum and grounds are open daily 11 A.M. to 6 P.M. in June, July, and August, and Wednesday through Sunday 11 A.M. to 5 P.M. the rest of the year. A nominal admission fee is charged April through September.

The fort is located on Five Mile Drive. For information, call ☎ (253) 591-5339, or consult 🖳 www.tacomaparks.com.

The **Point Defiance Zoo & Aquarium** is a world-class zoo and aquarium, home to more than 5,000 animals with special emphasis on sharks, beluga whales, polar bears, and snow leopards.

A small zoo was installed at Point Defiance in 1890; in the 1960s, the zoo was expanded and an aquarium added. The facility has a Pacific Rim theme, with animals from the volcanic ("ring of fire") countries bordering the Pacific Ocean.

The 160,000-gallon North Pacific Aquarium features Pacific Northwest marine life from anemones to octopuses to wolf eels. The Simpson Marine Discovery Lab includes the Tidepool, a living replica of shallow Northwest coastlines.

Rocky Shores is a replica of the North Pacific's craggy coast, home to beluga whales, sea otters, puffins, seals, and walrus. At Penguin Point, Magellanic penguins swim, burrow, and nest in a recreation of their South American coastal habitat.

Among the most popular exhibits at the zoo is the Polar Bear Complex, a recreated setting from Point Hope, Alaska, including above and below-water viewing. The World of Adaptations showcases small mammals, birds, and reptiles such as aardvarks, porcupines, pythons, bats, Bali mynahs, golden lion tamarins, and black lemurs.

The Farm Zoo is a place for youngsters to pet llamas, goats, sheep, pigs, and rabbits.

Arctic Tundra is home to a herd of massive muskox, native Northern waterfowl, and arctic fox.

Located in Point Defiance Park; open daily 10 A.M. to 5 P.M.

For information, call ☎ (253) 591-5337 or consult 🖳 www.pdza.org.

Another facet of Washington's history is presented at **Camp 6 Logging Exhibit & Museum** within Point Defiance Park.

The museum explores steam-powered logging in Washington from 1880 to 1950, with treasures that include a vintage Dolbeer donkey engine and an immense 240-ton Lidgerwood Skidder.

The museum also includes the Point Defiance Quinault & Klickitat Railroad (the "mainline track"), the Quinault Railcar Camp, and the rustic Kapowsin Bunkhouses in which the loggers lived. Pacific Coast Shay No. 7, a geared ninety-ton logging locomotive that operated on the rough, unballasted track and steep grades of the Pacific Coast woods, now pulls passengers from April through the end of September, and on "Santa Train" rides during the first three weeks of December.

Volunteers transport and maintain equipment found at various defunct logging operations throughout the Northwest.

Open Wednesday to Sunday 10 A.M. to 5 P.M. from mid-January through the end of October. Admission: free. Small charge for vintage steam train rides during the summer. For information, call ☎ (253) 752-0047 or consult 💻 www.camp-6-museum.org.

For kiddies, **Never Never Land** is a summertime treat at Point Defiance—June through August only—presenting sculpted figurines from favorite children's stories. For information, call ☎ (253) 305-1000.

Another jewel of Tacoma is **Ruston Way**, a two-mile stretch of waterfront park along Commencement Bay, with beaches, grassy areas, and picnic spots. The park offers panoramic views of Commencement Bay, Vashon Island, the Olympic Mountains, and Northeast Tacoma.

For information call ☎ (253) 305-1000 or consult 💻 www.Tacoma parks.com.

Also located on Ruston Way is **Fireboat #1**, Tacoma's first fireboat, a National Historic Landmark. The vessel is open occasionally for free tours in the summer.

Scenic Gardens and Nature Parks in Tacoma–Pierce County

A forest on tabletops, the **Pacific Rim Bonsai Collection** features more than fifty meticulously cultivated bonsai from six Pacific Rim nations: Canada, China, Japan, Korea, Taiwan, and the United States.

The one-acre display area consists of a tropical conservatory and fifty outdoor tables in a landscaped setting; stucco walls behind each group of display tables improve viewing and photography.

The collection is owned by wood products giant Weyerhaeuser Company; it was created in honor of the company's trade relations with Pacific Rim nations and as a tribute to the Washington state centennial in 1989.

The exhibit is located twenty-three miles south of downtown Seattle and eight miles north of downtown Tacoma, at 33663 Weyerhaeuser Way South in Federal Way, off Interstate 5. Admission: free. From March through May the collection is open daily except Thursday from 10 A.M. to 4 P.M.; from June through February, hours are 11 A.M. to 4 P.M. daily except Thursday and Friday.

For information, call ☎ (253) 924-5206 or ☎ (800) 525-5440, ext. 5206, or consult 💻 www.weyerhaeuser.com/bonsai/.

Adjacent to the bonsai collection is the **Rhododendron Species Botanical Garden**, a twenty-two-acre garden home to more than 10,000 rhododendrons from 450 species, a pond garden, an alpine garden, and tree and fern collections.

The flowering season in western Washington begins in early January and continues through late July, with the majority of species in bloom from March to May in shades of pure white to soft pink, yellow, brilliant red, and deep violet.

Other plantings include primroses, iris, heathers, maples, magnolias, conifers, and many other exotic and unusual plants; the additional species are in bloom at other times of the year. The alpine area is built around 200 tons of granite from the nearby Cascade Mountains, designed to look like a Himalayan slope where tiny-leaved rhododendrons cling precariously against the wind and snow.

The garden is in Federal Way. In March, April, and May the garden is open daily except Thursday from 10 A.M. to 4 P.M. For the remainder of the year, the garden is open daily except Thursday and Friday from 11 A.M. to 4 P.M. Admission: adult, ❷; senior and student, ❶; child (12–younger), free. For information, call ☎ (253) 927-6960 or ☎ (253) 661-9377 or consult 💻 www.halcyon.com/rsf/.

One of only three Victorian-style conservatories on the West Coast, constructed in 1908, the **W. W. Seymour Botanical Conservatory** indoor garden sits beneath a 12-sided central dome with 12,000 panes of glass. Within are more than 500 species of exotic tropical foliage, flowers, and fruit trees, plus seasonal displays of spring bulbs, azaleas, Easter lilies, and poinsettias.

The conservatory is located at 316 South G Street in Tacoma. Open daily from 8 A.M. to 4:20 P.M. Admission: free. For information, call ☎ (253) 591-5330.

A former private estate designed by noted landscape architect Thomas Church, **Lakewold Gardens** includes one of the largest collections of rhododendrons and Japanese maples in the Northwest, plus roses, ferns, and alpines highlighted in individual gardens spread across 10 acres.

Located at 12317 Gravelly Lake Drive Southwest in Lakewood near Tacoma, the gardens are open from April through September from 10 A.M. to 4 P.M. Thursday to Monday, and from noon to 8 P.M. on Friday. From October to March, the gardens are open from 10 A.M. to 3 P.M. on Monday, Thursday, and Friday only. Admission: adult, ❷; senior and student, ❷; child (12–younger), free. For information, call ☎ (888) 858-4106 or ☎ (253) 584-4106 or consult 💻 www.lakewold.org.

The **Tacoma Nature Center** is a fifty-four-acre wooded wildlife preserve with an interpretive center, wetlands display, and nature trails including more than two miles of self-guided paths with wildlife observation shelters.

Located at 1919 South Tyler Street in Tacoma, the visitors' center is open Tuesday to Friday from 8 A.M. to 5 P.M.; the park is open daily until dusk. Admission: free. For information, call ☎ (253) 591-6439.

The **Gog-Le-Hi-Te Wetland** is a unique man-made wetland created by the Port of Tacoma in 1985 to replace a natural wetland area filled in for a container ter-

Key to Prices
❶ $3 and under
❷ $3 to $6
❸ $6 to $10
❹ $10 to $15
When prices are listed as a range, this indicates various combination options are available. Most attractions offer reduced-price tickets for children and many have family rates that include two adults and two or three children.

minal. The mix of salt water and fresh water environments provides a home for many plants, fish, waterfowl, and small animals; observers have recorded ninety-two types of migratory and resident birds. Gog-Le-Hi-Te means "where the land and waters meet" in the Puyallup tribal language.

The preserve is located off Lincoln Avenue adjacent to the Puyallup River on Port of Tacoma land. Open daily during daylight hours. Admission: free. For information, call ☎ (253) 383-5841.

A tradition in the Puyallup Valley since 1934, the family-owned **Van Lierop Bulb Farm** displays more than 150 varieties of daffodils, crocuses, hyacinths, tulips, and irises in bloom each spring. Flowers and bulbs are offered for sale.

The farm is located at 13407 Eightieth Street East in Puyallup. Open from September 15 to November 15, and January 15 to June 5, from 9 A.M. to 5 P.M. Monday to Saturday, and 11 A.M. to 5 P.M. Sunday. At other times, hours can be scheduled by appointment. Admission: free. For information, call ☎ (253) 848-7272 or consult 🖳 www.ohwy.com/wa/v/van-liero.htm.

One of the few remaining untouched river deltas in the country, the **Nisqually National Wildlife Refuge** preserves 2,948 acres of salt marsh, forested swamp, and wetland meadows; the area is home to 300 species of wildlife.

There are several walking trails to view birds, wildlife, and plants. Canoers, kayakers, and boaters can launch from nearby Luhr Beach to explore the area by water.

The refuge is located west of Interstate 5 on the Pierce-Thurston county line. Open daily during daylight hours. Admission: ❶ per family. For information, call ☎ (360) 753-9467.

The animals run free and the humans pass by in cages, or at least in motorized trams, at the sprawling **Northwest Trek Wildlife Park** in Eatonville near Tacoma.

The park is a 635-acre wildlife habitat dedicated to the flora and fauna of the Pacific Northwest; visitors take a one-hour, naturalist-guided tram tour through the home of free-roaming herds of bison, elk, moose, and caribou. There are walking paths into the natural habitats of wolves, grizzly bears, black cougars, birds of prey, and wetland dwellers.

The Forest Theater features a presentation on the history of the area and Northwest Trek. The Bear Exhibit offers the largest natural outdoor display of grizzly and black bears in a North American zoological facility.

The park was created in 1975 from land donated by Dr. David and Connie Hellyer; they began buying the land in 1937 when it was beginning to recover from a fire and extensive logging. Today Trek is run by Metro Parks Tacoma.

Northwest Trek Wildlife Park is located at 11610 Trek Drive East in Eatonville, about thirty-five miles southeast of Tacoma and seventeen miles south of Puyallup. Admission, including tram tour: adult, ❸; senior (62+), ❸;

youth (5–17), and tots (3–4), ❷. For information, call ☎ (800) 433-8735 or ☎ (360) 832-6117 or consult 🖳 www.nwtrek.org.

The park is open daily from March to October from 9:30 A.M., with closing times ranging from 3 to 6 P.M. depending on the month and time of sunset; early opening at 8:30 A.M. during July through Labor Day. The park is open Friday through Sunday and selected holidays November through February. Tram tours operate 11 A.M. to 4 P.M. weekdays and 10 A.M. to 5 P.M. weekends.

Fox Island

The small **Fox Island Historical Museum** chronicles local history with dioramas of Native American, early pioneers, and local notables including former governor Dixy Lee Ray. At the heart of the museum is a collection of restored farming equipment.

Fox Island is located across the Narrows Bridge from Tacoma. The museum, at 1017 Ninth Avenue on Fox Island, is open on Monday and Saturday from 1 P.M. to 4 P.M., and on Wednesday from 11 A.M. to 3 P.M. Admission: donation requested. For information, call ☎ (253) 549-2239.

South of Tacoma

DuPont was established in 1906 as a company town by explosives maker E. I. Du Pont de Nemours. For nearly seventy years, the main industry in town was the manufacture of dynamite, and most of the exhibits at the **Dupont Historical Museum** in the former city hall explore this touchy subject; artifacts include the machines used to mix and press dynamite into sticks and shell casings.

Another set of displays tells of Fort Nisqually, the Hudson's Bay Company trading post established here in 1833; that fort has been restored in Tacoma at Point Defiance.

The museum, located at 207 Barksdale Avenue in Dupont, is open year-round on Sunday from 1 to 4 P.M., and from June to August also on Wednesday from 7 P.M. to 9 P.M. Admission: donations accepted. For information, call ☎ (253) 964-2399.

South of Tacoma toward Olympia is Fort Lewis and the **Fort Lewis Military Museum.** Camp Lewis began as a training camp for Doughboys who were preparing to head overseas in World War I. Today, Fort Lewis is an active U.S. Army installation.

Items on display at the Fort Lewis Military Museum in the Red Shield Inn, constructed by the Salvation Army during World War I as a lodge and social center, include a dugout canoe of the sort used by Lewis and Clark's infantrymen on their explorations of the mouth of the Columbia River in 1804. Other artifacts include old uniforms, weapons, and equipment of the nineteenth and twentieth centuries.

Outside, the museum's parking lot includes tanks, missiles, cannons, and, in recent years, a few Iraqi military vehicles and tanks that were captured in Kuwait during Operation Desert Storm by the 864th Engineer Battalion based at Fort Lewis.

The museum, in Building 4320, Main Gate, in Fort Lewis, is open Wednesday through Sunday from noon to 4 P.M. Admission: free. Visitors must show identification and receive a pass to enter the base. For information, call ☎ (253) 967-7206 or consult 💻 www.ohwy.com/wa/f/ftlewimm.htm.

Gig Harbor

The little town of **Gig Harbor** usually comes with a "quaint" or a "picturesque" in front of its name, and not without reason. Gig Harbor is across the Tacoma Narrows.

The rich maritime history of the region is at the center of the collection at the **Gig Harbor Peninsula Historical Museum**. Artifacts include items related to shipbuilding, ferryboats, fishing, and the infamous Narrows Bridge. You can also learn about agriculture and logging on the peninsula.

Other treasures are truly local, including the winning entries from a fifty-year-old contest to locate the most perfectly round rocks. There's also household furniture and toys from long-ago residents and other mementos.

The museum, located at 4218 Harborview Drive in an old church in Gig Harbor, is open Tuesday to Saturday from 10 A.M. to 4 P.M. Admission: donations accepted. For information, call ☎ (253) 858-6722 or consult 💻 www.peninsula-art.com/ghphsm/ghphsm.html.

For information on the area, call the Gig Harbor Peninsula Area Chamber of Commerce at ☎ (253) 851-6865 or consult 💻 www.gigharbor.com.

Steilacoom

Steilacoom is Washington's oldest incorporated town, dating back to 1854, and the **Steilacoom Historical Museum** proudly displays a small collection of artifacts of pioneer life from about 1860 to 1900, including a blacksmith's shop, Victorian parlor, and a barbershop with an unusual collection of shaving mugs. Special events in October include an apple squeeze on old presses.

The museum, located at 112 Main Street below the Town Hall in Steilacoom, is open March to October daily except Monday from 1 to 4 P.M. Open Friday to Sunday only in November, December, and February. Closed in January. Admission: Donations accepted. For information, call ☎ (253) 584-4133.

You can step into a century-old general store at the **1895 Bair Drug & Hardware Museum**, where you'll find displays of original patent medicines and pharmacy bottles, hardware, and a nineteenth-century post office. A restaurant serves breakfast and lunch daily, and dinner on Friday, plus old-fashioned ice cream sodas and sarsaparilla at a 1906 soda fountain.

The museum, located at 1617 Lafayette Street in Steilacoom, is open weekdays from 9 A.M. to 4 P.M., weekends from 8 A.M. to 4 P.M., and Friday evenings from 6 to 9 P.M. Admission: free. For information, call ☎ (253) 588-9668.

Nearby, the **Steilacoom Tribal Cultural Center and Museum** offers exhibits on the history of the Steilacoom Indian Tribe and other Coast Salish tribes, the prehistory of their traditional homeland, the Tacoma Basin, and a changing exhibit on Native American themes.

An archeological dig at a Steilacoom village site has found bones dating back to the 1400s and buttons, beads, and other trading items from the early 1800s, the time of first contact with European traders.

The museum, at 1515 Lafayette Street in Steilacoom, is open Tuesday through Saturday from 10 A.M. to 4 P.M. For admission prices, call ☎ (253) 584-6308.

On Anderson Island, accessible only by ferry from Steilacoom, the **Anderson Island Historical Society Museum** includes the 1912 Johnston Farm with restored buildings and antique farm machinery. Open on Saturday and Sunday in summer only from 10 A.M. to 4 P.M. Admission: donations accepted. For information, call ☎ (253) 884-2135.

Puyallup

Each September, Puyallup (pronounced "pew-al-up") swells from a sleepy town of 25,000 to home base for more than 1.5 million partygoers at the **Western Washington Fair.** Puyallup is nine miles east of Tacoma, off Highway 512.

Better known as The Puyallup Fair, the event is the largest fair in the state and among the nation's top ten fairs in attendance. The fair begins on the Friday after Labor Day and lasts seventeen days.

The fair dates back to 1900, originally a basic agricultural showcase; an immediate success, it has grown in scope and attendance during the years.

Today there is a huge midway, major rides, and attractions, including a huge wooden roller coaster, grandstand shows by big-name performers, and free entertainment at four stages located around the fairgrounds. New in 1999 was the Extreme Scream, a twenty-story-tall space shot ride that sends twelve riders at a time shooting up the tower at a force of +3 gs and then lets them fall to earth at a rate of -1 g. The ride is the tallest structure in Puyallup.

Other major attractions include rodeo, horse, and livestock shows, harvest competitions, and a petting farm for children.

Culinary delights include such Washington specialties as the Walla Walla Sweet Onion Burger and Fair Scones.

Throughout the rest of the year, the fairground is home to various shows, seminars, and recreational events.

The fair is located at 110 Ninth Avenue Southwest. For information, call a twenty-four-hour information line at ☎ (253) 841-5045 or, during office hours, ☎ (253) 845-1771. You can also consult 💻 www.thefair.com.

The fair is open in September daily from 10 A.M. to 10 P.M., and until 11 P.M. on Friday and Saturday. Admission: adult, ❸; youth (6–18), ❷; and senior (62+), ❷.

Meeker's Mission

Ezra Meeker, a pioneer who made his fortune as the Hop King, selling the beer ingredient in Europe and elsewhere, turned his attention to the road already traveled. The first mayor of Puyallup became self-appointed champion of the preservation of parts of the Oregon Trail.

In 1906, at age 76, he drove a team of two oxen from his front yard to Washington, D.C., by way of New York City to re-mark the Oregon Trail, which was already being obliterated by civilization.

Meeker went on to make the journey by ox team a second time, then by automobile in 1915, and by airplane in 1924. He lived to the age of 98.

The fact that today you can still find traces of the Oregon Trail is due almost entirely to Ezra Meeker.

The **Ezra Meeker Mansion** in Puyallup preserves the seventeen-room Victorian mansion built in 1890 by Puyallup's founder. It features grand staircases, exotic woods, and hand-painted ceilings; the interior is furnished with period pieces and outside a formal rose garden is maintained. The Ezra Meeker Historical Society presents displays from its collection of artifacts.

The mansion is open for tours Wednesday to Sunday from 1 to 4 P.M. from mid-March to mid-December (including special Victorian Christmas festivities). Admission: adult, ❷; senior, ❷; child (12–younger), ❶. For information, call ☎ (253) 848-1770, or consult 💻 www.meekermansion.org.

Auburn

In Auburn, east of Tacoma, the **White River Valley Museum** is a small but rich museum that tells the story of the once-bustling farming, logging, and railroad town.

Displays include details of the Nikkei experience of Japanese Americans in the early part of the twentieth century, a re-creation of shops in downtown Auburn from about 1915, and the old Auburn Depot.

The museum, at 918 H Street Southeast in Les Gove Park off Auburn Way, is open daily except Monday and Tuesday. For information, call ☎ (253) 939-4523.

Performing Arts and Entertainment in Tacoma–Pierce County

The **Broadway Center for the Performing Arts**, located at 901 Broadway, includes nearby cultural treasures of the Pantages Theater, the Rialto Theater, and the Theatre on the Square. For information, call ☎ (253) 591-5890.

Pantages Theater. ☎ (253) 591-5894 or ☎ (253) 627-7789. Built in 1918 as a vaudeville house by theater impresario Alexander Pantages, this lavish structure was inspired by the theater in the opulent Palace of Versailles outside of Paris.

In its early years entertainment included variety shows starring W. C. Fields, Mae West, Charlie Chaplin, and the Marx Brothers; in 1932 it was converted into a movie theater.

After years of decline, in 1978 a community project was begun to restore the theater; the Pantages was reopened in 1983 for drama, comedy, and dance performances with 1,182 seats.

Among companies calling the Pantages home are **BalleTacoma**, which presents classic favorites (including *The Nutcracker* at Christmas) and avant garde performances. For information, call ☎ (253) 272-4219.

The **Tacoma Symphony** uses the Pantages for its series of shows; for information, call ☎ (253) 591-5894. And the **Tacoma Opera** also performs there; all its shows are presented in English. For information, call ☎ (253) 627-7789.

The **Rialto Theater** was also opened in 1918 with a lively Beaux Arts décor; it was renovated in 1991. The 742-seat theater is the home of the Tacoma Youth Symphony, drawing from eighty-five regional schools; it is also host to the

Northwest Sinfonietta chamber orchestra and Rialto Film Guild. For information, call ☎ (253) 591-5890.

The small **Theatre on the Square**, home of the Tacoma Actors Guild, opened alongside the Pantages Theater in 1993. The group produces half a dozen dramas, musicals, and comedies over the course of each year in the 302-seat theater. For information, call ☎ (253) 272-2145.

An important annual event is **Wintergrass—A Mid-Winter Bluegrass Festival**, which claims to be the world's largest indoor bluegrass soiree, with more than 100 performances by thirty bands on five stages. For information, call ☎ (253) 926-4164, or ☎ (253) 848-4523.

Community Theaters

Tacoma Little Theatre. ☎ (253) 272-2481. 210 North I Street. Six shows per year.

Paradise Theater. ☎ (253) 851-7529. Outdoor shows held in a meadow in Gig Harbor; in winter, shows are presented indoors at 9916 Peacock Hill Avenue Northwest.

Tacoma Master Chorale. ☎ (253) 565-6867. Choral concerts at various locations, including an annual Christmas Renaissance Madrigal Feast.

Tacoma Musical Playhouse. ☎ (253) 565-6867. 7116 Sixth Avenue. www.tmp.org.

AmphiTheater. ☎ (253) 848-3411. 14422 Meridian East. One of the more ambitious passion plays in the country, Jesus of Nazareth is presented at Puyallup's outdoor theater from July through Labor Day with a cast of more than 800 people, plus live animals.

Casinos

The **Emerald Queen Casino** offers a recreated riverboat setting; it is located at 2102 Alexander Avenue in Tacoma. For information, call ☎ (888) 831-7655 or ☎ (253) 594-7777.

In Olympia, there's the **Red Wind Casino** at 12819 Yelm Highway. For information, call ☎ (360) 412-5000.

Tacoma Spectator Sports

The **Tacoma Dome** is the world's largest wood-domed arena, which seems appropriate given the lumbering history of the northwest. The 530-foot-round, 152-foot-tall structure can seat as many as 28,000 spectators for events, including ice hockey, ice shows, basketball, football, soccer, tennis, boxing, wrestling, motor sports, circuses, rodeos, concerts, and major trade shows.

Built in 1981 with 1.6 million board feet—about eight miles—of lumber, the dome has over the years been used as home of the NBA Seattle Supersonics for one season, the U.S. Figure Skating Championships, the Goodwill Games, and other major events.

For information, call ☎ (253) 272-3663 or you can consult a web page at 🖳 www.ci.tacoma.wa.us/tdome/.

Tacoma Rainiers Baseball Club. Cheney Stadium. For information, call ☎ (800) 281-3834 or ☎ (253) 752-7707 or consult 🖳 www.rainiers.com.

The Rainiers of the AAA Pacific Coast league play seventy-two home games at outdoor Cheney Stadium from April to early September. In recent years, the team has been the top affiliate of the Seattle Mariners; at other times in its forty-year history the team has been affiliated with the Oakland As, Cleveland Indians, New York Yankees, Minnesota Twins, Chicago Cubs, and San Francisco Giants. Among current stars who apprenticed at Cheney Stadium are Mark McGwire and Jose Canseco.

When the stadium was first built in 1960, the light towers and seats were shipped from Seals Stadium in San Francisco; many are still in use today.

Tacoma Sabercats Hockey Club. For information, call ☎ (253) 627-2673 or consult 🖳 www.sabercats.com.

Winners of the West Coast Hockey League's Taylor Cup in 1999, the Sabercats play their home games at the Tacoma Dome. Ticket prices range from about $11.50 to $17.50.

Emerald Downs. 2300 Emerald Downs Drive, Auburn. For information, call ☎ (888) 931-8400 or ☎ (253) 288-7000 or consult 🖳 www.emdowns.com.

The thoroughbred racing season runs from late April to late September, daily from Wednesday or Thursday through Sunday, depending on the time of year. Weekday post time is 6 P.M.; weekends and holidays 1 P.M. General admission, ❷; reserved seats, ❷ for grandstand, ❷ for clubhouse.

Free tours of the stables are offered on the first Saturday of each month, departing from the north end of the grandstand at 10 A.M.; call ☎ (253) 288-7711 for required reservations.

Spanaway Speedway. 16413 Twenty-Second Avenue East, Spanaway. ☎ (253) 537-7551. Automobile racing Wednesday, Friday, and Saturday in summer.

Recreational Activities in Tacoma–Pierce County

Enchanted Park. 36201 Enchanted Parkway South, Federal Way. ☎ (253) 925-8000. Includes Enchanted Village and the Wild Waves water park. Enchanted Village operates from late March to mid-September; Wild Waves from mid-May to mid-September. Call for hours.

Grand Prix Raceway. 2105 Frank Albert Road East, Fife. Amusement park and indoor karting center. For information, call ☎ (253) 922-7722 or consult 🖳 www.karts.com/grandprix.

Northwest Passages Inc. 8811 North Harborview Drive, Gig Harbor. ☎ (253) 851-7987. 🖳 www.clearlight.com/kayak. Kayak sales and tours.

Wildwater River Tours. Federal Way. ☎ (253) 939-2151 or ☎ (800) 522-9453. Whitewater and scenic raft trips.

Tacoma Area Shopping

Freighthouse Square Tacoma's Market. 430 East Twenty-Fifth Street, Tacoma. ☎ (253) 305-0678. Specialty shops and eateries in a block-long former railroad warehouse.

Lakewood Mall. 10509 Gravelly Lake Dr. SW, Lakewood. ☎ (253) 984-6100. More than 160 stores.

South Hill Mall. 3500 South Meridian, Puyallup. ☎ (253) 840-2828. 120 stores.

Starlite Swap & Shop. 8327 South Tacoma Way, Tacoma. ☎ (253) 588-8090. The oldest indoor/outdoor marketplace in Tacoma. Open daily except Monday.

SuperMall of the Great Northwest. 1101 SuperMall Way, Auburn. ☎ (253) 833-9500. More than 100 stores.

Tacoma Mall. 4502 South Steele, Tacoma. ☎ (253) 475-4565. 135 stores.

Scenic Drive: The Kitsap Peninsula Loop

Tacoma to Olympia, Shelton, Port Ludlow, Poulsbo, Bremerton, Gig Harbor, and Back to Tacoma

Round-trip 205 miles. Allow at least five hours of driving, plus any side trips or stopovers.

Depart **Tacoma** heading south on Interstate 5 toward **Olympia**, twenty-nine miles away. Continue west past Olympia to Route 101, which heads north up the Olympic Peninsula. Just beyond **Quilcene** (121 miles from the start of this journey) leave the peninsula to go east on Route 104. At **Port Gamble** at the top of the Kitsap Peninsula, pick up Route 3 southbound to **Bremerton** (145 miles). At Bremerton, you can make a side trip to Bainbridge Island or take a ferry across Puget Sound to Seattle.

> **Tourism sites.** For information on the region, you can contact the **Tacoma–Pierce County Visitor & Convention Bureau** at ☎ (800) 272-2662 or ☎ (253) 627-2836 or consult 💻 www.tpc tourism.org. You can also obtain information on small bed and breakfast inns from **A Greater Tacoma Bed & Breakfast Reservation Service** at ☎ (800) 406-4088 or ☎ (253) 759-4088 or by consulting 💻 www.Tac oma-inns.org. You can also contact the **Bed & Breakfast Association of Tacoma & Mount Rainier** at ☎ (888) 593-6098 or ☎ (253) 593-6098 or by consulting 💻 www.bbonline.com/wa/ tacomainns/.

To continue on the Kitsap Peninsula Loop, stay on Route 3 south past Bremerton to **Port Orchard** and there join Route 16 to **Gig Harbor** and from there on to Tacoma.

For more information on the area, contact the Kitsap Peninsula Visitor and Convention Bureau at ☎ (800) 416-5615 or consult 💻 www.visitkitsap.com.

Olympia

A boulder in Sylvester Park in downtown Olympia marks the end of the southern fork of the Oregon-Cowlitz Trail. The town was little more than a muddy collection of shacks when thousands of emigrants arrived in the 1840s and 1850s. It wasn't much more than that in 1853 when it was chosen as the state capitol.

The roads are paved and the Washington State Capitol is an impressive campus. But Olympia has remained a relatively small and sleepy town, with a population of about 35,000.

The Story of Olympia

The native village at the southernmost point of Puget Sound was called "the black bear place"; the area was a common meeting place for many of the tribes of the region.

In 1792 Peter Puget of the British Vancouver Expedition visited the area, but it wasn't until 1846 that Levi Lathrop Smith and Edmund Sylvester claimed the townsite. Sylvester laid out the settlement like a New England village, with a town square and common lands. The town was given its name in recognition of the Olympic mountains in the distance.

There were less than 1,000 residents in 1853, but Olympia was the county seat and had the only newspaper in the Washington Territory; both were factors in the decision to place the territory's first capital there that year. The seat of government was a group of temporary buildings that were used until 1928 when a more significant structure was completed.

Meanwhile, the selection of Olympia as capital was challenged by other cities in coming years, including Vancouver, Steilacoom, Seattle, Port Townsend, and Tacoma.

When Washington Territory became a state in 1889, Olympia was ratified again as the capital. The shape of the city was markedly changed in 1912 when a major project to dredge the harbor to accommodate deep-draft ships was completed; most of the fill was added to the shallows to the north of the city, creating a new section of land.

The small town finally began to look like a state capital in 1927 with the completion of the Legislative Building, a grand design with a high stone dome in the style of London's famed Saint Paul's Cathedral and the U.S. Capitol in Washington, D.C. Many of the historic buildings in downtown were severely damaged or destroyed by a major earthquake in 1949; by the 1960s, the capital's campus of office buildings was near completion.

The Capital's Campus

The **Legislative Building** is open for tours daily from 10 A.M. to 3 P.M. Set on a bluff overlooking Puget Sound, forty-two broad granite steps lead to the entrance, symbolizing Washington's entrance as the forty-second state in the Union. Within, the amazing details include stone oxen circling the base of the dome in a commemoration of the ox-cart pioneers who first settled much of the state. The ceiling of each of the legislative chambers is decorated with elaborate plasterwork and gilded rosettes. Most of the lamps, sconces, and chandeliers were designed by famed artisan Louis Comfort Tiffany; included is a five-ton Angels of Mercy chandelier hanging from the dome on a 101-foot chain. The Legislative Building is open weekdays from 8 A.M. to 5 P.M., and weekends from 10 A.M. to 4 P.M. For information on free guided tours, call ☎ (360) 586-8687 or ☎ (360) 586-3460.

Tours of the governor's **Executive Mansion** are offered Wednesday by reservation only.

OLYMPIA

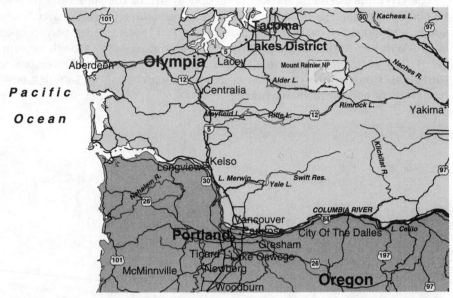

The **Capitol Conservatory** greenhouse, built by the Work Projects Administration in 1939, contains tropical plants and bedding plants for the capital's campus. Open for tours weekdays 8 A.M. to 3 P.M.

The **Old Capitol Building**, built in 1892 and used as the capitol from 1901 until 1928, is open for self-guided tours weekdays from 8 A.M. to 5 P.M.

The Washington State Supreme Court is housed within the **Temple of Justice**, completed in 1920. It is open weekdays from 8 A.M. to 5 P.M.

For information on tours of official buildings, call ☎ (360) 586-8687.

The **State Capital Museum** has exhibits on Northwest Indians, including cedar-bark baskets and a native winter house that has dried fish dangling from a smokehole overhead. The museum, located in the Lord Mansion south of the capitol's campus on Twenty-First Avenue, is open Tuesday to Friday from 10 A.M. to 4 P.M., and on weekends from noon to 4 P.M. For information, call ☎ (360) 753-2580.

Olympia Attractions

The **Washington Center for the Performing Arts** is home of the Olympia Symphony Orchestra, as well as a number of community theater, music, and dance groups. For box office information call ☎ (360) 753-8586 or consult 📖 www.washingtoncenter.com/.

The historic **Capital Theater**, at 206 Fifth Avenue Southeast, is used by the Olympia Film Society throughout the year, and for a film festival in November. For information, call ☎ (360) 754-6670.

Twice a year, Olympia's art community celebrates its accomplishments with **Art Walk**; the event is usually held on a Friday in April and again in October.

The **Olympia Farmers Market** is second in size in the state only to Seattle's Pike Place Market. Offerings include local vegetables, flowers, crafts, baked goods, and more. The market, in downtown at 700 North Capitol Way, is open on weekends in April; Thursday through Sunday from May through September; Friday through Sunday in October; and weekends from November to Christmas. Hours are 10 A.M. to 3 P.M. For information, call ☎ (360) 352-9096 or consult 💻 www.farmers-market.org/.

Chapter 17
Olympic Peninsula and Bremerton

The Olympic Peninsula in Washington is the most northwestern tip of the lower forty-eight states. With the Pacific Ocean to the west, the Strait of Juan de Fuca to the north, and Puget Sound to the east, it is among the most isolated areas of the United States.

Sometimes referred to as "the last frontier," the Olympic Peninsula was among the last major areas of the United States to be settled by white men.

The jewel of the region is the Olympic National Park: a world that includes rugged Pacific coastline, glacier-topped mountains, and paradisiacal temperate rain forests.

History of the Olympics

The creation of Mount Olympus dates back more than 35 million years ago. The rocks that were to form the mountains were on the ocean floor, built up by compressed sediment from shore and in huge underwater seamounts created by lava flows.

The geological plate moved eastward, with much of it sliding beneath the continental land mass. The irregular profile of the Olympic Mountains is the result of the tumbling forces of that movement.

At least six times ice covered much of the Olympic Peninsula, including the great Pleistocene Ice Age that moved down from Canada. The movement and recession of the ice carved and shaped Puget Sound, the Strait of Juan de Fuca, the mountains and valleys, and other features of the park.

Much of the ice retreated about 10,000 years ago. Today there are sixty named glaciers that continue to shape the area, including seven on Mount Olympus. Geologists say most of the glaciers likely date back only about 2,500 years, but the larger ones, such as Blue and Hoh Glaciers, may be survivors from a more ancient ice age.

The land and nearby waters teemed with fish, whales, and game. The first known human residents of the area were Northwest Coast peoples including members of the Skokomish, Quinault, Quileute, Hoh, Makah, Klallam, and Chehalis tribes.

Spanish explorer Juan Peréz sailed along the Olympic coast in 1774, naming the predominate peak Santa Rosalia. A year later several sailors from the Spanish ship *Sonora*, who went ashore near today's community of Kalaloch to gather water and firewood, were killed by Native Americans. The captain named a nearby island the Island of Sorrows.

After a group of English sailors were also killed by Native Americans near the same area in 1787, the island was renamed Destruction Island. The island can be seen from shore on U.S. 101 south of Ruby Beach.

The Spanish built the first European settlement on the Olympic Peninsula in 1792, but the settlement was abandoned after five difficult months.

In 1788 English explorer Captain John Meares, following Captain James Cook along the coast, spotted an impressive peak not far inland. Meares named it Olympus after the home of the Greek gods. "If that be not the home where dwell the Gods, it is beautiful enough to be, and I therefore call it Mount Olympus," he wrote.

Settlers began to move into the region in the middle of the nineteenth century to farm, fish, and harvest timber for the growing cities of California. Like the tribes before them, the American settlers mostly built their towns along the coasts, with Port Townsend the first permanent American settlement on the peninsula in 1851.

Port Angeles on the Strait of Juan de Fuca, which included a military reservation, customs house, and lighthouse, was designated as a federal reserve by President Abraham Lincoln, as the United States warily watched British activities in Canada. Illegal squatters moved into the area anyway.

Port Angeles was officially opened to settlers by President Grover Cleveland in 1891. Today it is the largest town on the peninsula, with a population of more than 17,000.

The rugged interior of the peninsula, though, remained mostly unexplored until near the end of the century. In 1885 and 1890, Lieutenant Joseph P. O'Neil of the U.S. Army led scientific survey trips near Mount Olympus; in the process, the soldiers cut a mule trail near what is now the road to Hurricane Ridge to the north, and across the southern section.

As timber interests began to harvest huge tracts of land in the area, O'Neil lead the early fight to protect the region. In response, President Grover Cleveland created the Olympic Forest Reserve in 1897, but that designation did not fully protect the land and its resources.

Partly in response to the near-extinction, by hunting and destruction of grazing areas, of a sub-species of elk that lived only in the area, President Theodore Roosevelt designated the area Mount Olympus National Monument in 1909. The deer were designated by naturalists as Roosevelt elk.

Again, though, the land was not protected from mining, timber, and hunting interests and the monument was reduced in size several times.

Finally, President Franklin D. Roosevelt visited the Olympic Peninsula in 1937 and declared his support for the creation of a national park. A year later, 898,000 acres were set aside as Olympic National Park. Most of the coastal wilderness was added to the park in 1953. And the 632,324-acre Olympic

National Forest, managed by the U.S. Forest Service, all but surrounds Olympic National Park.

The park was named as an International Biosphere Reserve in 1976 by UNESCO in recognition of the essentially untouched temperate rain forest. In 1981 Olympic was also recognized as a World Heritage Park, putting the park in company with Yellowstone National Park, Australia's Great Barrier Reef, and Tanzania's Serengeti National Park.

In 1988 95 percent of Olympic was officially designated as wilderness, banning road construction, motorized vehicles, mining, timber cutting, hunting, and other development and uses.

Olympic National Park

Today's **Olympic National Park** preserves some 922,651 acres; 95 percent of the land is designated as wilderness. The park includes sixty miles of coastline, the longest wilderness coast in the lower forty-eight states. There are 266 glaciers in the Olympic mountains.

Parts of the Olympic rain forest receive twelve to fourteen feet of rain every year. The temperate rain forest in the park has more than 500 tons of living biomass per acre, higher than any other place on earth, according to park naturalists. The park is home to more record-breaking trees than anywhere else in North America.

Naturalists have identified some 1,200 types of plants, 200 species of birds, and 70 types of mammals. At least eight plants and eighteen animals can be found nowhere else in the world.

The Olympics have nearly 900 miles of trails, about three-quarters of them within the National Park. The majority of the trails were constructed by the Forest Service before the land was transferred to the Park Service.

When it rains. The valleys on the western slopes of the Olympic Mountains receive an average of 120 to 167 inches of rain per year and the top of Mount Olympus some 200 inches, more than anywhere else in the continental United States.

The weather machine begins as moisture-laden clouds rise out of the Pacific Ocean and move eastward and inland. There they meet the wall of mountains, which forces them to rise sharply. As they do, they cool and release moisture in the form of rain or snow.

The mountains are so efficient at wringing moisture from the clouds, though, that there is a rain "shadow" on the northeastern side. The town of Sequim, about twenty-five miles from Mount Olympus, averages less than sixteen Inches of precipitation per year.

About four million visitors come to the park each year, with the busiest months December and January. The park is open year-round, although roads may be closed because of snow or flood in winter and spring.

The park contains three very distinct ecosystems: the glacier-covered mountains, old growth and temperate rainforest, and a long stretch of wild Pacific coast.

Headquarters for the park is in Port Angeles. For information, call the Visitors Center at ☎ (360) 452-4501 or the **Wilderness Information Phone** at ☎ (360) 452-0300.

Entrance to the park is ❹ per vehicle, ❷ per person for pedestrians, cyclists,

Hurricane Ridge, Olympic Peninsula
Photo courtesy Washington Tourism Development

and bus passengers; passes are valid for seven consecutive days. Fees are collected at Elwha, Hurricane Ridge, Hoh, Sol Duc, and Staircase entrance stations, May through September.

Visitors can also purchase an Olympic park pass for about $20, good for one calendar year. The Golden Eagle Passport annual pass, good in all federal recreation areas and national parks, is about $65 per year. The Golden Age Passport is available for a one-time charge of $10 to U.S. residents 62 years of age and older. Passes are available at entrance stations and Olympic Park visitor centers.

As you'll find throughout the Pacific Northwest, the weather is subject to change during the course of a day. Experienced travelers and locals learn to dress in layers and to pack a sweater and rain gear.

Summer is the warmest and driest season, with frequent fog banks and temperatures in the low 70s. Spring and fall are cool and wet. The greatest rainfall is in December and January, when daytime temperatures average in the 40s. Temperatures and rain and snow are more extreme in the mountains.

Tour of the Park

By car, there are a dozen or so spur roads off U.S. 101 that enter into sections of the park. Each of the roads comes to a dead end; access deeper into the park is on foot or by water. The spurs do not connect to each other; you'll have to backtrack to U.S. 101 to continue your circuit of the park.

Heading due south out of Port Angeles takes you to **Hurricane Ridge.** From the sea-level coastal plain of the Strait of Juan de Fuca, a seventeen-mile paved road enters the lowland forest at Olympic Park Visitor Center and makes its way to the high mountain ridges.

Hurricane Ridge offers unparalleled views of Mount Olympus and the glacier-covered heart of the Olympic Range to the south, the Strait of Juan de Fuca and Vancouver Island in Canada to the north.

In the spring and early summer Hurricane Ridge is carpeted with wildflowers and often populated by wildlife, including the Olympic marmot and black-tailed deer. In the winter the area is a popular destination for snowshoeing and cross-country skiing; the roads are sometimes closed after a heavy snowfall.

Obstruction Point Road, a steep eight-and-a-half-mile dirt road heading east from Hurricane Ridge, offers a spectacular view of Mount Olympus. The road is only open from mid-summer to early fall.

West of Port Angeles is **Lake Crescent**, a deep freshwater lake carved by glaciers, as much as 1,000 feet deep in places. The waters reflect the mountains around the eight-mile-long lake; a road circles the water and a former railroad grade on the north shore is a popular hiking and biking trail.

The lake is famed for Beardslee trout. Further along Highway 101 is Marymere Falls, where glacier melts drop ninety feet to a pool below.

A bit further westward, another spur road leads to **Sol Duc**. According to Native American legend, the hot springs at Sol Duc were formed when two dragons engaged in a great battle that lasted many years. The dragons knocked down the timber from the tops of the mountains and scattered boulders through the valleys. Their skin flew off and became the mosses and lichens hanging from the trees of the rain forest. The battle ended in a draw, with both wounded creatures crawling back to their caves. The hot tears they cried formed Sol Duc and Olympic hot springs.

Think of the legend in terms of a long-ago volcanic eruption and it begins to make sense.

Driving along the coast on U.S. 101 south of Forks, a road heads into the **Hoh Rain Forest.** This temperate zone, thirty miles east of the coastline, annually receives an average of 140 inches (nearly 12 feet) of rain.

The rain forest has the feel of another world of an ancient time. Most sounds are all but swallowed by the lush vegetation and the heavy, moist air. Overhead, Sitka spruce, western red cedar, and western hemlock grow to 200 feet or more, some of the world's largest trees. The trunks of the trees are shrouded in moss, and ferns arc from the forest floor into any available open space. The forest floor, soft and springy, is carpeted with berry plants, wildflowers, and other plants.

Other such zones are in the valleys of the Quinault and Queets rivers. Precipitation in the rainforests generally ranges from 140 to 167 inches (12 to 14 feet) per year, but some isolated sections may be drenched with as much as 250 inches per year.

The rain forests are protected from the extremes of weather by the overhanging Olympic Mountains, with temperatures rarely dropping below freezing or rising above 80 degrees Fahrenheit.

In the rainforests nearly everything is covered with luxuriant plant growth, including mosses, lichens, ferns, Oregon oxalis, salmonberries, and sorrels. The dense ground cover makes it difficult for tree seedlings to get a start; instead, seeds often germinate on the decaying remains of fallen trees, known as nurse trees. As the old tree decomposes, the young trees grow on the stilts of their roots that grew around the old tree.

Sitka Spruce and Western Hemlock are the most common species of tree in the forest, and can grow to sizes exceeding 300 feet in height and 23 feet in circumference. Other stands include Bigleaf Maple, Douglas Fir, Western Red Cedar, Red Alder, Vine Maple, and Black Cottonwood.

A visitor center introduces the area and leads to self-guided trails or ranger-led nature walks in the rain forest. The **Hall of Mosses Trail** offers a short introduction to the flora and ecology of the rain forest. The mile-long **Spruce Nature Trail** heads farther into the forest. And the **Hoh River Trail** leads deep into the primeval Hoh; the seventeen-mile trail continues on to **Glacier Meadows** and the **Blue Glacier** moraine.

Blue Glacier, one of six frozen rivers on Mount Olympus, is three miles long and 900 feet thick. Experienced mountaineers can hike the length of the glacier, the most direct route to the 7,965-foot peak of Mount Olympus.

Another rain forest, less often visited, is **Quinault**, reached from the southern perimeter of the park. You'll pass through the Quinault Indian Reservation en route to the spur road; you can obtain a fishing permit for Lake Quinault from reservation stores.

The Coastal Zone

Very different from the lush greenery and soaring peaks of the interior, the coastal zone of Olympic National Park extends more than fifty miles from Shi Shi Beach to Kalaloch. A notable feature of the undeveloped beaches are sea stacks, remnants of coastal cliffs eroded by the waves.

Most of the beaches are reachable only on foot or by boat. Highway 101 comes near the shore at the southwestern section of the park; to the northwest, routes 112, 113, and 110 branch off toward the ocean.

Paths lead down to six different beaches from Ruby Beach to Kalaloch. Information and maps are available at the Mora and Kalaloch ranger stations. In summer, park rangers lead guided walks to tidal pools and through coastal forests.

Ozette, in the northwest corner of the park, off Route 112, offers several beaches that have impressive sea stacks as well as Ozette Lake, the largest natural body of fresh water in Washington, just inland from the ocean.

Tribes of the Olympic Peninsula

The first residents of the Olympic Peninsula are believed to have arrived from Asia through Alaska.

They were mostly left alone until the United States and Canada finally established the border between the two nations in 1846. At the time of the treaty, there was not a white settlement anywhere on the peninsula.

Large numbers of Native Americans died in the nineteenth century, mostly as the result of diseases introduced by Europeans. Most of those who survived were forced to change their ways of life because of the encroachment of the settlers.

One of the most significant cultural customs of the tribes was the *potlatch*, a huge feast held to celebrate a chief's ascension or other important event. As many as a thousand guests were invited, including high-ranking members of other tribes, and the party could go on for several days.

Anthropologists say the potlatch seemed to date from around the time of first contact with Europeans in the 1800s, perhaps as the result of the arrival of manufactured goods. An important part of the ceremony involved the giving of gifts to the host and later to other invitees according to their status.

At the end of the gathering, the blanket on which the presents had rested was presented to one of the guests, and he was then expected to host a potlatch of his own in the following year.

Indian agents, representatives of the U.S. government, grew nervous about the huge gatherings in the late 1800s, and they attempted to ban the potlatches. Some of the tribes, though, were able to continue by adapting the gatherings into forms more like Western Christmas and birthday parties. Many tribes still have potlatches.

Today the region is home to the Hoh, Quileute, Makah, Lower Elwha S'Klallam, and Jamestown S'Klallam tribes. Other tribes, including the Chimakum, are gone.

The **Quileute** used to move around from various locations on the peninsula during the summer, ranging from Lake Ozette in the north to the Queets River in the south. In the winter, the three major bands often came together at the mouths of the Quileute and Hoh rivers and Goodman Creek.

Like the other peninsula tribes, the Quileute gave up vast tracts of land in the treaty of 1855 in exchange for fishing and hunting rights. The Quileute, though, refused to move to the Quinault reservation, a tribe with whom they had often clashed. Instead, the federal government set up a small reservation at La Push at the mouth of the Quileute river.

Today the Quileute have the only tribal school on the peninsula, and the Quileute language and traditions, including cedar canoe construction, are taught. The tribe also conducts an active tourism industry.

The **Hoh** are a separate band of the Quileute Indians to the north, who share the same language. Perhaps the smallest tribe on the peninsula, the tribe's fishing grounds stretch from Goodman Creek to the north to Kalaloch Creek to the south, centered around the Hoh River on the western coast. Their primary maritime crop is smelt.

In the 1855 Treaty of Neah Bay, the **Makah** gave up much of their land in exchange for permanent access to the sea and fishing rights from the Makah Reservation at the far Northwest tip of the Olympic Peninsula. About 2,000 people live on the forty-seven-square-mile reservation.

Neah Bay, Olympic Peninsula
Photo courtesy Washington Tourism Development

Included in the treaty was the right to hunt whales, the only tribe in the United States with this right. In 1999, following removal of Gray Whales from the endangered species list, tribal members conducted a hunt from a canoe; environmental and animal rights groups opposed the event.

The name Makah was bestowed by other tribes; it means "generous with food." The Makah called themselves Kwih-dich-chuh-ahtx, which means "people who live by the rocks and seagulls."

The 2,000-year-old Makah village of Ozette at Cape Alava was destroyed more than 300 years ago by a massive mudslide. Rediscovered in 1970 after a big storm, the site was excavated by Washington State University archeologists at the invitation of the Makah. Many of the well-preserved artifacts, including harpoons, carved figures, and household items, are on display at the **Makah Cultural and Research Center** in Neah Bay; the center is open daily in summer from 10 A.M. to 5 P.M. and daily except Monday and Tuesday the remainder of the year. For information, call ☎ (306) 645-2711.

The tribe hopes to build on a nascent tourism industry; the Makah offer a marina in Neah Bay facing the Strait of San Juan de Fuca and Vancouver Island.

The Makah once spread over all the north coast of the Olympic Peninsula and across the Strait of Juan de Fuca on Vancouver Island. Members of the tribe moved from one to another of some twenty-three villages following the fish and shellfish harvests.

Under terms of an 1855 treaty, the S'Klallam gave up their land in return for guaranteed fishing rights. In a story similar to that of the Makah, the tribe was told to move to the Skokomish reservation, a tribe with which they were enemies; they refused.

During the following years, the tribe split into three bands at Jamestown, Lower Elwha, and Port Gamble, without clear title to a homestead. In 1930 the

Jamestown S'Klallam were asked to move once more, this time to the Lower Elwha reservation; when they refused, all federal assistance to the tribe was ended and much of what little land the tribe had purchased in Jamestown was sold off.

The tribe began to push for renewed federal recognition in the 1960s, finally winning recognition once again in 1981. The tribe now owns about 188 acres, with a tiny reservation of 20 acres.

In modern times, though, the Jamestown S'Klallam have been very active in the local economy. In addition to fishing, the tribe owns a gambling casino.

Dungeness Spit

The **Sequim Dungeness Valley** on the Olympic Peninsula lies between the Strait of Juan de Fuca to the north and the Olympic Mountains to the south. New Dungeness Bay was given its name by Captain George Vancouver in 1792, after a section on the south coast of England.

Formed by the interaction between the waters of the Strait of Juan de Fuca and the Dungeness River, the main arm of the shoal extending from shore—known as a spit—is the longest natural spit in the world at more than five miles in length. In places it is as narrow as fifty feet, and it is regularly breached by high tides and rough seas.

A lighthouse, part of a four-light chain along the strait, was built at the end of the Dungeness Spit in 1857.

The branch from the main spit that goes toward the mainland is known as Graveyard Spit. Its name was derived from the Dungeness massacre of 1868, which was a surprise attack on a band of eighteen Tsinshian Indians (a Vancouver Island tribe) by a group of S'Klallam Indians. The lone survivor, a pregnant Tsinshian woman, was sheltered by the keeper of the lighthouse. Graveyard Spit, along with Cline Spit (the site of the original dock for the town of Dungeness), partially encloses Dungeness Bay and is the widest portion of the spit. Now part of the Dungeness Wildlife sanctuary, it is closed to visitors.

The area was declared a wild bird reservation by President Woodrow Wilson in 1915; and today it's part of the 631-acre Dungeness National Wildlife Refuge. Naturalists say the refuge is the permanent or temporary home to more than 250 species of bird, 41 species of land mammal, and 8 species of marine mammal.

The spit continues to change with the action of the waters of the strait and the Dungeness River. The lighthouse was originally built one-sixth of a mile from the tip of the spit but now sits about half a mile from the end.

The Dungeness River rises near Mystery Mountain, traveling thirty-two miles before emptying into the Strait of Juan de Fuca at New Dungeness Bay. The second steepest river in America, it drops 7,300 feet over the course of its journey, in some stretches dropping 1,000 feet in a mile.

Beginning in 1896, portions of the river were diverted into irrigation ditches for agriculture, helping the area become one of the leading dairy regions of the country; today, there are nearly one hundred miles of irrigation ditches providing water to the farmers and residents of the valley. Residents pay tribute to the river with an annual Irrigation Festival each spring, the oldest continuous community-based celebration in Washington, dating back to 1896.

The river supports four species of salmon, as well as steelhead trout. The Dungeness Fish Hatchery along the banks of the river helps preserve the native salmon population and its habitat. The valley also is home to the famed Dungeness Crab.

For information on events and attractions in the area, consult the Web at ☐ www.sequimonline.com.

Port Angeles

The northern gateway to the Olympic National Park is Port Angeles on the Olympic Peninsula. The town is also home to ferry service to Vancouver Island in British Columbia.

Billing itself as the "City of Flowers," the city decks itself with hanging baskets and planters in the spring and summer, especially along the waterfront.

The first residents of the area arrived from Asia through Alaska. The Indians mainly lived along the coast, using the dense forests for hunting.

The first confirmed report of the Strait of Juan de Fuca was made in 1787, although a Greek sailor of uncertain veracity named Apostolos Valerianus claimed to have found the strait in 1592; he called himself Juan de Fuca. An American, Captain John Kendrick, visited the strait in 1792 and reached back to Valerianus's claim to give it its name.

Port Angeles received its name in 1791 when Spanish explorer Francisco Eliza named the natural harbor El Puerto de Nuestra Senora de Los Angeles.

The peninsula was generally left to the Native Americans until the boundary between Canada and the United States was established by treaty in 1846. Settlers began to arrive in the 1850s, lured by the timber riches and the call of the last frontier in the lower forty-eight states. It wasn't until the 1880s that the first detailed explorations of the peninsula were undertaken, first by soldiers from Fort Townsend and later by civilian expeditions, including one in 1889 sponsored by a newspaper in Seattle.

In the 1920s and 1930s, the U.S. Navy's Pacific fleet used the harbor at Port Angeles as a port; that use ended by the 1980s, although naval ships occasionally return there today.

Getting to the Olympics

The park is about 90 miles from Seattle, and 120 miles from Tacoma, reachable by highway and by ferry service across Puget Sound.

U.S. 101 runs around the east, north, and west perimeters of the park.

The highway leads directly to northern entrances at Port Angeles (park headquarters), Hurricane Ridge, Elwha, Lake Crescent, and Sol Duc. (Sol Duc is closed in winter.)

Heading south from Port Angeles, the Pacific Coast area starts with a spur road off Highway 112 to Ozette. Other coastal areas are accessed from U.S. 101. A spur road leads to Mora's Rialto Beach, another goes inland to the Hoh Rain Forest, and Kalaloch Beach is on U.S. 101.

Rialto Beach is one of few easily accessible portions of the Pacific coastline in the Olympic National Park; it can be reached by car along a thirteen-mile paved road. The rocky beaches include tidepools at low tide. Rialto Beach is a popular starting point for backpackers.

Hiking access to Second and Third Beaches and the South Wilderness Coast is also available from the nearby town of La Push on the Quileute Indian Reservation.

From the south, spur roads lead into the **Queets** and **Quinault Valleys** and to **Lake Quinault**. A spur road from U.S. 101 leads to Staircase, a southeast entrance to the park.

On the east side, a spur road from U.S. 101 leads to **Dosewallips**; that entrance is also closed in winter.

You can fly into Fairchild International Airport in Port Angeles on commuter carriers, including Horizon Air. The closest major airport is Seattle-Tacoma International Airport, 120 miles away.

Olympic Bus Lines & Tours serves Port Angeles from Seattle; for Olympic Bus Lines information, call ☎ (360) 417-0700; for Olympic Tours information, call ☎ (360) 452-3858. Gray Line of Seattle offers bus tours around the Olympic Peninsula in the summer; call ☎ (800) 426-7532 or consult 🖳 www.grayline ofseattle.com.

Washington State Ferries offers year-round service across Puget Sound and between Port Townsend and Whidbey Island, Edmonds and Kingston, and Seattle and Bainbridge Island. For information, call ☎ (206) 464-6400.

Black Ball Transport offers passenger and car ferry service for much of the year between Port Angeles and Victoria, British Columbia; for information, call ☎ (360) 457-4491.

Victoria Express operates a passenger ferry from Port Angeles to Victoria from mid-May to mid-October. For information, call ☎ (360) 452-8088.

Wineries of the Olympic Peninsula and Puget Sound Islands

Many Washington wines are made on the "wet" west side of the Cascades from grapes raised on the "dry" east side. Each season, harvested grapes are trucked to the wineries that benefit from moderating ocean breezes on the Strait of Juan de Fuca.

Port Angeles

Black Diamond Winery. 2976 Black Diamond Road, Port Angeles. ☎ (360) 457-0748. 🖳 www.wineryloop.com/blackdiamond.html.

Open April through October, Thursday through Sunday from 10 A.M. to 4 P.M. Winter hours November through March, Saturday only 10 A.M. to 4 P.M.

Located about three miles from downtown Port Angeles off Bridge Street, the winery sits in a small valley in the foothills of the Olympic mountains overlooking Tumwater creek.

The new winery opened on May 1, 2000, offering rhubarb, strawberry rhubarb wine, Shiro Plum, apricot, from locally grown fruit; and a selection of regional pinot gris, white reisling, Muscat Ottonel, and Syrah grapes.

Camaraderie Cellars. 334 Benson Road, Port Angeles. ☎ (360) 452-4964. 🖳 www.wineryloop.com/camaraderie.html. Open by appointment.

Located five minutes west of downtown Port Angeles, just south of Highway 101 at 334 Benson Road.

Producing about 1,000 cases per year, some of the wines use grapes from well-regarded sources including Artz Vineyards on Red Mountain and Mercer Ranch. The winery specializes in full-flavored red and white Bordeaux grape varieties. A proprietary red blend is of Cabernet Sauvignon, Merlot, and Cabernet.

Olympic Cellars. 255410 Highway 101 East, Port Angeles. ☎ (360) 452-0160 🖳 www.olympiccellars.com.

Open mid-April to mid-October daily from 9:30 A.M. to 5:30 P.M.; remainder of the year Wednesday through Sunday, noon to 5:30 P.M.

Located in a huge old barn on Highway 101, nine miles west of Sequim, the small winery uses grapes from two of Washington's premier "old-wine" vineyards to produce limited quantities of varietals and the Dungeness series of custom-blended, semi-dry wines.

Bainbridge Island

Bainbridge Island Vineyards & Winery. 602 Street Highway 305 Northeast, Bainbridge Island. ☎ (206) 842-9463. 🖳 www.wineryloop.com/bainbridge.html.

Open Wednesday through Sunday from noon to 5 P.M.

Located a half-mile from the Bainbridge Island ferry terminal on Highway 305. The winery produces about 2,000 cases per year from cool-climate French and German Vinifera grapes from its own vineyards, plus fruit wines.

Sequim

Lost Mountain Winery. 3174 Lost Mountain Road, Sequim. ☎ (360) 683-5229. 🖳 www.lostmountain.com.

Open April to May and September to November from 11 A.M. to 5 P.M. on weekends only; from Memorial Day to Labor Day open 11 A.M. to 5 P.M. daily. Open by appointment only from December to March.

Appropriate for its name, Lost Mountain Winery is almost hidden in the forested foothills above Sequim, off Highway 101 West, south to Taylor Cut-Off Road and up the hill on Lost Mountain Road.

Wines are handcrafted in small lots, with a specialty in Cabernet Sauvignon, Merlot, and Pinot Noir grapes; the winery's Poetry Series features local poets on the labels of blended vintage. In addition to the quality wines, the winery, whose family roots reach back to Italy, also produces Lost Mountain Red. Made from a third-generation recipe, it's a Zinfandel-based blend that is referred to by the family as "Our Distinguished Dago Red."

Port Townsend

FairWinds Winery. 1984 Hastings Avenue West, Port Townsend. ☎ (360) 385-1368. 🖳 www.fairwindswinery.com.

Open Saturday and Sunday 1 P.M. to 5 P.M.

The winery, in a former horse stable, is located off State Route 20 just outside the Port Townsend city limits; head west on Jacob Miller Road to Hastings Avenue West, and right on Hastings.

Varietals include Lemberger, aged in American Oak barrels; Gewurztraminer, Cabernet Sauvignon, and Aligoté, a white wine from the Burgundy area.

Sorensen Cellars. 234 "G" Otto Street, Port Townsend. ☎ (360) 379-6416. 🖳 www.wineryloop.com/sorensen.html.

Open in summer on Friday, Saturday, and Sunday from 11 A.M. to 4 P.M.; at other times by appointment.

The winery is about a mile south of Port Townsend, off Highway 20 in the Glen Cove Industrial Park. The small family-owned winery concentrates on premium wines, using selected grapes from small vineyards of Eastern Washington.

Whidbey Island

Whidbey Island Greenbank Farm. Greenbank, Whidbey Island. ☎ (360) 678-7700. 🖳 www.greenbankfarm.com.

Open daily from 10 A.M. to 5 P.M.

Located at the center of Whidbey Island, just off Highway 525 and Wonn Road, the winery is within an historic 1904 farm on 522 acres of what was once the world's largest loganberry farm. Not surprisingly, the signature product is loganberry wine, as well as varietal grape wines.

Whidbey Island Winery & Vineyards. 5237 South Langley Road, Langley. ☎ (360) 221-2040. 🖳 www.wineryloop.com/whidbey.html.

Open daily, except Tuesday in July and August, from 11 A.M. to 5 P.M.; remainder of the year open Thursday through Sunday 11 A.M. to 5 P.M.

The winery produces small lots of wine from island-grown whites and reds from eastern Washington; another specialty is rhubarb wine. Local grapes are harvested in September and October by volunteer pickets.

The company is located thirty-five miles south of Oak Harbor off Highway 20/525 on Langley Road.

Scenic Drive: The Olympic Peninsula Loop

Seattle to Tacoma, Olympia, Hoquiam, Quinault, Kalaloch, Forks, Port Angeles, Sequim, Seattle

Round-trip 372 miles. Allow at least eight hours of driving, plus any side trips or stopovers.

Depart Seattle on Interstate 5 toward Olympia, about twenty-nine miles south. Continue on to Olympia (sixty-two miles from the beginning of this journey) and pick up State Route 8 to Elma (ninety miles). At Elma, take Route 12 to where it joins Route 101 into Hoquiam (119 miles).

From Hoquiam, head north on Route 101 to Forks (238 miles). Along this stretch of the road are spurs into the Olympic National Park, including the Hoh Rain Forest. At Forks, a road heads west to the Pacific Coast at La Push.

Route 101 continues across the top of the peninsula. You can head south on a spur road to the Sol Duc Hot Springs. A bit further along, at Port Angeles, you can catch a ferry to Victoria on Canada's Vancouver Island.

At Sequim (195 miles), head south on Route 101 toward Poulsbo, picking up State Route 104, then State Route 3 to Poulsbo, and finally State Route 305 to Winslow and the ferry across Puget Sound to Seattle.

For more information, contact the North Olympic Peninsula Visitor and Convention Bureau at ☎ (800) 942-4042 or consult 📖 www.northolympic.com.

Lodging in the Olympic National Park

There are a handful of historic and rustic lodges around the edges of the park. Many are fully booked well in advance of the peak summer season; seek reservations early.

Kalaloch Lodge on the coast in the southwest corner of the park has forty cabins, including a dozen or so on a bluff overlooking the Pacific Ocean. The lodge was built in 1953. A restaurant in the lodge is open for breakfast, lunch, and dinner. For information and reservations, call ☎ (360) 962-2271.

The **Lake Crescent Lodge**, twenty-one miles west of Port Angeles, is at the base of Mount Storm King among the giant hemlock and fir trees of Lake Crescent. The main lodge, built in 1916, has five rooms; there are also more modern rooms in an outbuilding, and there are fifteen cottages. President Franklin D. Roosevelt stayed here in 1938. The lodge is open from late April through late October; a lakeside restaurant is open for breakfast, lunch, and dinner. For information and reservations, call ☎ (360) 928-3211.

Nearby, the **Log Cabin Resort** on the northeast shore of Lake Crescent has been the site of a visitor's lodge since 1885. The present lodge and surrounding buildings date back as far as the late 1920s. The lodge is open from May through September; breakfast and dinner are served at a restaurant at the resort. For information and reservations, call ☎ (360) 928-3325.

There has been a resort at the mineral springs here since 1914; the present **Sol Duc Hot Springs Resort** dates back to the 1960s. Located about forty miles west of Port Angeles in the Sol Duc River Valley, the resort offers thirty-two cabins. Visitors can soak in three mineral pools, which have water temperatures up to 105 degrees Fahrenheit. The resort is open from the beginning of April to late September; the restaurant is open for breakfast and dinner. For information and reservations, call ☎ (360) 327-3583.

At the south end of the park, on the shores of Lake Quinault, the **Lake Quinault Lodge** has been in operation since 1926. The timber lodge, furnished with wicker furniture and decorated with Native American designs, was another stop on President Franklin D. Roosevelt's tour in 1938. The lodge and restaurant is open year-round. For information and reservations, call ☎ (800) 562-6672 or ☎ (360) 288-2900.

For information on accommodations in nearby communities, write to the Olympic Peninsula Resort and Hotel Association, Colman Ferry Terminal, Seattle, WA 98104. Information is also available through the Seattle Visitors Bureau at ☎ (206) 461-5800. You can also contact the chambers of commerce in Forks at ☎ (360) 374-2531; Port Angeles at ☎ (360) 452-2363; Port Townsend at ☎ (360) 385-2722; or Sequim at ☎ (360) 683-6197.

Chapter 18
The Volcanoes: Rainier, Saint Helens, Baker

Mount Rainier

Mount Rainier, seventy-four miles southeast of Tacoma, is the highest peak in the state of Washington and one of the tallest in the lower forty-eight states at 14,411 feet.

The national park was created by Congress in 1899, the fifth largest in the nation. The 378-square-mile Mount Rainier National Park includes 27 named glaciers (the largest single glacial system in the continental United States), 35 square miles of ice and snow, and 305 miles of hiking and nature trails. There are thirty-four waterfalls and sixty-two lakes in the park. The lowest elevation in the park is 1,880 feet in the Carbon River rain forest, nearly two and a half miles below the summit.

Among the accessible wonders of the park are the **Nisqually Glacier and Icefall.** The icefall is a jumble of refrigerator-sized chunks of ice frozen in a perpetual slow-motion tumble down the glacier. The glacier itself moves as much as three feet a day.

The park is home to more than 700 species of flowering plants, including meadows of wildflowers in the sub-alpine regions in the summer. Mount Rainier's forests are home to several species of hemlock, cedar, fir, and pine, including many trees that are more than 600 years old.

More than 130 species of birds and 50 species of wild animals dwell in the park, including mountain goat, elk, deer, bear, beaver, marmots, and raccoons; the most-observed birds are eagles, stellar jays, Oregon jays, and Clark's nutcrackers.

Mount Rainier creates its own weather. The mountain impedes the flow of warm, moisture-laden marine air from the Pacific Ocean and cools it, creating rain and snowfall. During the winter

How tall? The highest mountain in the United States and Canada is Mount McKinley in Alaska, at 20,320 feet, followed by Mount Logan in Canada's Yukon at 19,850 feet.

The tallest peak in the lower 48 states is Mount Whitney in California, at 14,494 feet. Washington's Mount Rainier is the fifth highest peak on that list.

Mount Rainier
Photo courtesy Washington Tourism Development

of 1971–72, more than 1,220 inches of snow (101 feet) fell at Paradise Lodge on the mountain's southern flank, setting a world's record. Total precipitation annually averages 100 inches at Paradise.

The Rainier Story

The Taidnapam, Upper Cowlitz, Yakama, Nisqually, and Puyallup tribes lived in the foothills of the mountain they called Tahoma for several thousand years before the arrival of the white explorers and settlers. Members of the tribe hunted, fished, and gathered food on the mountain's lower slopes; out of reverence for Tahoma, they apparently never went near the summit.

The Puyallup and Nisqually Indian tribes called the mountain "Tacobet" or "Tahoma." That didn't matter to Captain George Vancouver of the Royal British Navy, who named it in 1792 in honor of his friend Rear Admiral Peter Rainier. (Rainier never visited the peak that bore his name.)

The first Europeans and Americans brought diseases that ravaged the tribes in the 1700s; only small groups of natives still survived when American settlers set up homesteads near the peak in the 1800s.

In the late 1850s, James Longmire, a settler who had a farm near Yelm Prairie, created the rough Packwood Trail, which served as the first route for many mountain climbers from the Pacific Coast to Mount Rainier's slopes.

In 1857 Army Lieutenant August Valentine Kautz and his party came within 400 feet of the summit, suffering from snow-blindness and other discomforts before giving up. The first documented climb to the top occurred in 1870.

In 1884 Longmire built Mineral Springs Resort, the first hotel on Mount Rainier, near the site of a mineral spring on the south flank.

President McKinley established Mount Rainier as the nation's fifth national park in 1899; in 1911 President William H. Taft traveled to Paradise in the first automobile to reach the area. It must have been quite a sight: President Taft was a huge man of more than 300 pounds; the auto was unable to continue and had to be towed by horses the last several miles.

In 1916 a trail system that encircles the mountain was put into place; the system is known today as the Wonderland Trail. During the Depression of the 1930s the Civilian Conservation Corps built or expanded many of the park buildings, trails, and bridges that are still in use today.

During World War II the U.S. Army's 10th Mountain Ski Division trained for winter operations on Mount Rainier. In 1962, the peak was a training ground for the successful American expedition to Mount Everest.

The Geology of Rainier

Mount Rainier is a dormant volcano, part of the Ring of Fire of volcanic ranges that nearly circle the Pacific Ocean. Included in the ring are the Aleutian islands, the western coast of North and South America, Antarctica, eastern Indonesia, the Philippines, and Japan.

Mount Rainier is the highest volcanic peak in the Cascades, a mountain range that stretches from Mount Garibaldi in British Columbia to Lassen Peak in northern California.

The creation of Rainier dates back about 12 million years ago when magma from the earth's core built layers of rock below the surface. About one million years ago, molten rock broke through a weak spot in the earth's crust; lava oozed out of the hole while rock and pumice spewed out violently, building a volcanic cone.

During the course of its creation, Mount Rainier grew to about 16,000 feet above sea level.

Then, about 5,800 years ago, the pressures within Mount Rainier reached the breaking point and the mountain blew its top, sending huge amounts of rock, mud, and debris down its northeast flank. Scientists estimate that a wall of mud 100 feet high spread like a river of wet cement across 125 square miles.

The mud slide reached all the way to today's Puget Sound. Geologists call the resulting deposit of dirt the Osceola Mudflow; the modern towns of Kent, Sumner, Auburn, and Puyallup are built on top of the flow.

Rainier's 16,000-foot summit was destroyed, leaving a two-mile depression on the east side of the mountain.

The most recent major eruption came about 2,500 years ago, which created a second volcanic cone at the summit. The remains of the older, higher cone are seen in Liberty Cap and Point Success. The two craters overlap at the mountain's summit, 14,411-foot Columbia Crest.

Based on their studies, scientists believe Mount Rainier's volcanic activity is on a cycle of about 3,000 years between major eruptions, which would schedule the next big bang for sometime in the next few hundred years or so. A small eruption occurred about 150 years ago and occasional ash and steam issue forth from the mountain.

Park pass. A Mount Rainier park pass, good for one calendar year, is offered for about $20. The Golden Eagle Passport annual pass, good in all federal recreation areas and national parks, is about $65. The Golden Age Passport is available for a one-time fee of about $10 to U.S. residents or citizens 62 years of age and older. Golden Eagle and Golden Age Passports are available at park entrance stations. For information, call the National Park Service at ☎ (360) 569-2211, or consult 🖳 www.American ParkNetwork.com.

The Glaciers Move In

Volcanic forces built Mount Rainier, but over the eons it has been glaciers that have shaped it.

Glaciers are created in areas where the snowfall of winter is greater than the summer snowmelt. The top layer of a glacier is snow; below that is mixed snow and ice, and at the bottom the snow is compacted into glacier ice.

These "rivers of ice" move down steep mountain valleys to the point where the "snout" or end of the glacier melts or breaks away. Mount Rainier's glaciers move from one to two feet per day, depending on the steepness of the slope.

Glaciers tend to lengthen or recede, depending on climatic conditions; in the modern era of global warming, most are receding. During the last Ice Age, the valley glaciers of Mount Rainier were fifteen to forty miles long. At that time, the area that is now Seattle was buried under 4,000 feet of ice that moved south from Canada.

Rainier's thirty-four square miles of glaciers radiate out from the summit, the largest collection of glaciers on one peak in the contiguous United States. There are twenty-five named glaciers and fifty smaller, unnamed glaciers and ice fields.

Getting to the Park

More than 2.2 million visitors enter the park each year. There are three areas with tourist facilities: Paradise (at elevation 5,400 feet) and Longmire (2,700 feet), which offer accommodations, restaurants, and gift shops, and Sunrise (6,400 feet), which has only day facilities.

The park is open year-round; call for weather and road conditions. Entrance fees for the park are ➍ per vehicle; ➋ per person for pedestrians and cyclists.

Be sure to stop at one of the Visitor Centers on arrival for current maps, copies of *Tahoma* or *Snowdrift*, the park newspapers, and advice on conditions and events, including National Park Service naturalist walks.

The entrance to the park is about eighty-seven miles by car from Seattle or sixty-five miles from Tacoma. Take I-5 south to Highway 512 east, then drive south on Highway 7; turn east on Highway 706 at Elbe and continue on to the Nisqually Entrance.

From Portland, Oregon, about 136 miles away, take I-5 north to U.S. 12 east, then Highway 7 north to Morton; turn east on Highway 706 at Elbe and continue on to the Nisqually Entrance.

The Nisqually Entrance is the only road open year-round. In the winter, all park roads are closed except the stretch between Nisqually and Paradise and the road from the park boundary to the Ohanapecosh ranger station.

To use the east (Stevens Canyon) entrance, from Yakima, take Highway 12 west, then Highway 123 north. For the northeast (White River) entrance, take Highway 410 south from Seattle and Tacoma. From Yakima to the northeast entrance, take Highway 410 north. For the Northwest (Carbon River) entrance, take Highway 165 south.

One of the best views of Mount Rainier is from Highway 410, which approaches the mountain from the White River Valley, connecting the Puget Sound with the Yakima Valley.

The road, also known as the Stephen Mather Memorial Parkway, was improved in the 1930s by the Civilian Conservation Corps. Sections are still bordered by original stone guardrails. Highway 410 over Chinook Pass is closed in the winter.

Several private carriers offer ground transportation to the park. Gray Line Tours of Seattle offers scheduled bus tours into the park from mid-spring through mid-fall. For information, call ☎ (800) 426-7532 or ☎ (206) 626-5208. Other tour companies include **Rainier Shuttle,** ☎ (360) 569-2331, and **Scenic Tours,** ☎ (888) 293-1404.

The **Henry M. Jackson Memorial Visitor Center,** located at Paradise, is open daily from early May to mid-October and on weekends and holidays from mid-October to early May. The center offers exhibits on geology, glaciers, flora, fauna, and mountain climbing. For information, call ☎ (360) 569-2211, ext. 2328.

Ohanapecosh Visitor Center, at Ohanapecosh on Highway 123, is open weekends late May to mid-June, and daily mid-June to early October. You'll find exhibits on wildlife, old-growth forests, and local history. For information, call ☎ (360) 494-2229.

Sunrise Visitor Center, at the end of Sunrise Road, has displays, walks led by naturalists, and programs on Mount Rainier's subalpine ecology and alpine life zones. Telescopes permit a close-up view of the mountain's slopes and glaciers. The center is open daily from July through mid-September. For information, call ☎ (360) 663-2425.

Longmire Hiker Information Center and the **White River Hiker Information Center** offer trail information and backcountry permits. Both are open in summer only. For information, call ☎ (360) 569-2211, ext. 2356.

Lodging Within the Park

There are two small inns within the park. Reservations are very difficult to obtain, especially in summer; book as far in advance as possible.

The 126-room **Paradise Inn** offers spectacular views of Mount Rainier and Nisqually Glacier. Open from mid-May through early October, this is your basic massive wooden national park lodge, built in 1917. Afternoon tea is served in the oversized lobby, which has a pair of massive stone fireplaces.

The dining room serves breakfast, lunch, and dinner; Sunday brunch is served in the heart of the summer season. For information, call ☎ (360) 569-2413.

The cozy **National Park Inn** is nestled in the forest at Longmire, offering just twenty-five rooms without benefit of televisions and most other modern trappings. But there is that unbelievable view of Mount Rainier from the north porch. A gen-

Rainier weather. Prepare for a variety of conditions, with great variation over the course of summer and winter days. Dress in layers and carry a sweater and rain gear. Summer temperatures average in the mid-70s; winter temperatures average in the mid-20s.

eral store is located in a 1911 log cabin nearby. The inn is open year-round, and cross-country skis and snowshoes are available for rent in the winter. For information, call ☎ (360) 569-2411.

For reservations at either of the lodges, contact Mount Rainier Guest Services in Ashford, at ☎ (360) 569-2275.

You can also find places to stay in some of the surrounding towns. And you can consult the Mount Rainier Business Association at 🖳 www. mt-rainier.com. You can also call the Seattle Visitors Bureau at ☎ (206) 461-5800.

Exploring the Park

Longmire is the oldest developed area in the park, the site of mineral springs found by James Longmire in 1883 and the park's first hotel, the Mineral Springs Resort. Access to the Longmire area, in the southwestern corner of the park, is via a road through the forest from the Nisqually Entrance.

Paradise, named for the heavenly appearance of the lush meadows in summer, is a very different place in the winter. More than a mile above sea level, Paradise averages more than 600 inches of snowfall annually—more than 50 feet!

At the **Narada Falls**, the Paradise River drops 168 feet off a ledge.

The **Glacier View** outlook on the road from Bisqually to Paradise is about a mile from the snout of **Nisqually Glacier**.

The **Grove of the Patriarchs** trail heads to a stand of old-growth Douglas fir, western red cedar, and western hemlock, some more than a thousand years old. The forest is along the Ohanapecosh River in the southeastern corner of the park.

The highest point in the park accessible by car is **Sunrise**, located in the northeastern area of the park at 6,400 feet. From the point, there are views of the dormant volcanoes of the Cascades: Rainier, Hood, Baker, and Adams.

The rocky summit of Little Tahoma Peak is visible to the left of Rainier as seen from Sunrise. Native American legend says Little Tahoma is the son of Mount Rainier and sits on her shoulder. Also in view on the eastern slope of Rainier is Emmons Glacier, the largest glacier in the contiguous United States, covering more than four square miles.

Sunrise is on Mount Rainier's dry east side, receiving much less precipitation than Paradise.

The **Carbon River** area in the northwest corner of the park, named for the deposit of coal in the area, includes the only rain forest in the region. There's also Carbon Glacier, which descends to a lower elevation than any other glacier in the lower forty-eight states.

If you can bring yourself to take your eyes off the spectacular natural beauty of the park for a moment, head inside the doors of the small **Longmire Museum** just inside the Nisqually Gate entrance at the south end of the park across from the administration building. The collection sets the scene for Mount Rainier, including the natural history and geology of the park, the story of Native Americans of the area, and a collection of taxidermied animals taken from the park over the years—including cougar, bobcat, and porcupine.

The museum is located on State Route 706 in Ashford. For information, call ☎ (360) 569-2211 or consult 📖 www.nps.gov/mora/interp.htm. Admission is included with the park entry. For visits of seven days or more, admission is ❹ per car; the museum is open daily from 9 A.M. to 5 P.M.

Mount Rainier Scenic Railroad

The Mount Rainier Scenic Railroad travels back in time to one of the most spectacular natural beauties of the Pacific Northwest.

The company's vintage steam locomotive makes a fourteen-mile round trip from Elbe to Mineral Lake and back from Memorial Day through the end of September. The ninety-minute tours are offered daily from mid-June through Labor Day and on weekends at the beginning and end of the season.

The 1920s-era oil-fired Mikado-type steam engine operates on the track of the former Chicago, Milwaukee, Saint Paul, and Pacific Railroad (better known to some as the Milwaukee Road).

The Elbe station is about fifty miles south of Tacoma, off Highway 7. Admission: adult, ❹; senior, ❸; junior (12–17), ❸; child, ❸. For information, call ☎ (888) 783-2611 or ☎ (360) 569-2588 or consult 📖 www.mrsr.com/.

The railway also operates the **Lewiston Excursion Dinner Train**, a four-hour, forty-mile excursion from Elbe to the Morton Depot and back. Meals are served in two seatings in an authentic dining car, with live music.

The dinner train operates on Saturday and Sunday from Memorial Day to Labor Day, and Sunday only during spring and fall months. Tickets are about $65, and advance reservations are required. For information on the dinner train, call ☎ (888) 773-4637.

Scenic Drive: The Volcano Loop

Yakima to White Pass, Castle Rock, Vancouver, White Salmon, Goldendale, and Back to Yakima

370 miles round-trip. The tour encloses Mount Saint Helens and Mount Adams and comes to access points north to Mount Rainier and south to Mount Hood. Allow at least nine hours of driving plus any side trips or stopovers. Be sure to check on road conditions any time of the year.

Depart Yakima westbound toward White Pass, about eighty miles away. This town and Packwood, on the other side of the pass, are jumping-off points to Mount Rainier to the north.

There are many lakes and recreational opportunities in this area, fed by runoff from snowfall in the late spring and summer. Check with local ranger stations for conditions at any of the numerous waterfalls in the region.

As you pass Randle, Mount Saint Helens is in the distance to the southwest; it will stay mostly to your left as you pass through Morton and Mossyrock. There are three entries to the Mount Saint Helens National Volcanic Monument. From Randle, you can head south on Route 99 and National Forest Road 25 to the Windy Ridge Viewpoint. Check on conditions before heading down the road.

Mayfield Lake, near Mossyrock, is a popular spot for water sports.

Route 12 meets Interstate 5 near Napavine, and from there the loop heads south on the high-speed road. The western entrance to the Mount Saint Helens National Volcanic Monument branches off I-5 at Toledo to State Route 505 and 504, leading to the Coldwater Ridge Visitor Center.

A southern entrance to Mount Saint Helens National Volcanic Monument leaves I-5 at Woodland to State Route 503 to Cougar.

Leave the interstate at Exit 1 at Vancouver and take Route 14 east along the Washington side of the Columbia River Gorge, including the Bonneville Dam. At White Salmon, Route 141 heads north to the end of the road at the Mount Adams Wilderness. Heading the other direction at White Salmon, a toll bridge crosses the Columbia River Gorge to Hood River; there, Route 35 leads south to Mount Hood.

Near Wishram, south of Goldendale, is the respected Maryhill Museum. A few miles further east, Route 97 heads north across the Yakama Indian Reservation to Toppenish and on to Yakima.

For information on this region, you can call the Yakima Valley Visitors and Convention Bureau at ☎ (800) 221-0751 or consult ▤ www.visityakima.com, or the Columbia River Gorge Visitor Association at ☎ (800) 984-6743 or consult ▤ www.gorge.net/crgva.

Mount Saint Helens

Before its eruption in 1980, the symmetrical snow-capped Mount Saint Helens was sometimes referred to as the "Fujiyama of America." The mountain and other active Cascade volcanoes, together with volcanoes in Alaska, make up the North American segment of the "Ring of Fire" that surrounds the Pacific Basin.

Geologists classify Mount Saint Helens as a *composite* or *stratovolcano*, a term for an inherently unstable construction of steep cones made up of alternating layers of lava flows, ash, and other volcanic debris. Composite volcanoes tend to erupt explosively, as opposed to more gently sloping volcanoes such as those in Hawaii, which more typically disgorge fluid lava that travels relatively slowly and predictably.

Geologists have found evidence of ash deposits at least 40,000 years old on top of even-older volcanic rock. The volcano seems to have gone through at least ten periods of activity since then, with dormant periods of as much as 15,000 years and as little as 150 years.

Some of the Indian tribes of the area referred to the peak as "Louwala-Clough," or "smoking mountain."

Just as with mounts Baker, Hood, and Rainier, Mount Saint Helens received its modern name in 1792 from Captain George Vancouver of the British Royal

Navy; Vancouver bestowed names on geographical features throughout the area to honor friends and supporters. In this instance, the mountain was named for Alleyne Fitzherbert, the British Ambassador to Spain and holder of the title of Baron Saint Helens.

The Smoking Mountain was particularly active in the early days of the settlement of the Pacific Northwest, with a series of recorded eruptions from 1831 to 1857; scientists believe there were other, unobserved explosions or eruptions dating back to about 1800.

Although there were occasional steam explosions in the early part of the twentieth century, modern-day residents had little reason to think of the mountain as posing a threat. Spirit Lake, at the base of the northern flank of the mountain, was a popular recreational area for hiking, camping, fishing, swimming, and boating.

Mount Saint Helens awoke from a 123-year sleep on March 20, 1980, with a moderate earthquake. Hundreds of smaller temblors followed until a week later, when a steam explosion blasted a 250-foot-wide crater through the ice cap at the top. Dozens of later explosions expanded the new crater to more than 1,000 feet in diameter.

By mid-May, a mile-and-half wide section of the mountain had been pushed out 450 feet. Geologists determined the "bulge" had been caused by the rise of molten rock, pushing aside older rocks inside the volcano.

During the two-month period, about 10,000 earthquakes of varying magnitude were recorded, mostly in an area just below the bulge on the north flank of the mountain. And then finally, on May 18, 1980, the mountain violently exploded. The explosion, ash fall, and mud slides resulted in the worst volcanic disaster in the recorded history of the United States. Despite two months of warnings, fifty-seven people were killed; some were scientists studying the volcano, others were emergency workers, and the rest were residents of the surrounding area who refused to evacuate.

Most of the avalanche of volcanic debris, glacier ice, mud, and water flowed westward into the upper North Fork of the Toutle River; the flow had enough force to flow up and over a 1,150-foot-high ridge about four miles north of the summit. Part of the avalanche surged into and across Spirit Lake, destroying virtually all structures in the area.

The debris avalanche filled the Toutle valley to an average depth of about 150 feet, dumping nearly a cubic mile of material. The bottom of Spirit Lake was raised by about 295 feet; the water level was increased by about 200 feet. More than 185 miles of roads and bridges, 15 miles of railway track, and tens of thousands of acres of forest were flattened. Interstate 90 from Seattle to Spokane was closed for a week, and air transportation was disrupted for as much as two weeks because of poor visibility and ash in the air, which was dangerous to aircraft engines.

Scientists estimate that the initial velocity of the explosive blast reached to about 670 miles per hour. The sound of the explosion was heard hundreds of miles away in the Pacific Northwest, including parts of British Columbia, Montana, Idaho, and northern California.

A plume of ash reached as much as twelve miles into the sky. Moving in the atmosphere at about sixty miles per hour, the cloud reached Yakima, Washington, in about two hours and Spokane, Washington, in four hours. The cloud was dense enough to block the sunlight, and street lamps came on in the two cities. The eruption continued for more than nine hours. Some of the ash drifted around the globe within about two weeks. The heaviest ash deposits occurred within 60 miles downwind of the volcano, but there was as much as two inches of ash deposited near Ritzville in eastern Washington, about 195 miles from the volcano.

After the eruption, the volcano stood 8,364 feet high, or 1,313 feet lower than the former summit elevation.

Game wardens estimated that nearly 7,000 big game animals, primarily deer, elk, and bear, were killed, along with uncounted numbers of birds and many small mammals. An estimated twelve million Chinook and Coho salmon fingerlings were killed when hatcheries were destroyed.

In the years that have followed, much of the area has made a remarkable recovery. Burrowing rodents, frogs, salamanders, and crawfish were among the survivors, which were protected because they were either underground or underwater at the time of the explosion and flow. Other animals have come back as the area has been reforested; and the ash deposits have brought some necessary nutrients to the soil.

Cowlitz County covers 1,144 square miles in southwest Washington. Once known as the "Timber Capital of the World," the region is still home to abundant stands of Douglas fir, hemlock, and western cedar.

Mount Saint Helens National Volcanic Monument

Today the story of the volcano is explored at four visitor centers along the Spirit Lake Memorial Highway, State Route 504.

The first of three U.S. Forest Service facilities is the Mount Saint Helens Visitor Center, five miles off Interstate 5 on Route 504. Here you'll find videos and exhibits that offer a good introduction to the story of the area and the 1980 eruption. In addition to seismographs recording the activities beneath the volcano, there is also a display where you can see the effects of your own footsteps on one of the sensitive instruments.

The Coldwater Ridge Visitor Center, at milepost 43, concentrates on the environmental effects of the eruption, showing the amazing recovery of plants and animals in the area, as well as how Mount Saint Helens has changed the ecology.

At the end of Route 504, at milepost 52, the Johnston Ridge Observatory tells the geological story of the mountain, with spectacular views of the crater and lava dome; a film and a high-tech model of the volcano explain the events of 1980. Along SR-504 on the west side of the volcano, the scars of the eruption are still evident. Tourism operators offer wildlife viewing tours, sightseeing, hiking, mountain biking, helicopter tours, and camping in the area.

SR-503, Lewis River Road, follows the Lewis River Valley toward the south side of Mount Saint Helens. Forests, foliage, and lakes have recovered here.

A single admission fee covers entrance to all three Forest Service facilities. For information and hours, call Mount Saint Helens, ☎ (360) 274-2100; Coldwater Ridge Visitor Center, ☎ (360) 274-2131, or Johnson Ridge Observatory, ☎ (360) 274-2140. You can also consult 🖳 www.fs.fed.us/gpnf/mshnvm. For information and a live view of the mountain, you can consult 🖳 www.mount-st-helens.com.

To enter into the Mount Saint Helens National Volcanic Monument by car, you'll need to purchase a vehicle pass. In late 2000 the Northwest Forest Pass sold for $5 for one day or $30 for one year.

Admission fees for each of the observatories were adult, ❶; and youth (5–15), ❶. You could also purchase a Site Day Pass for all three monuments plus Ape Cave for adult, ❷; and youth, ❶.

The **Forest Learning Center**, located at milepost 33, is run by the huge Weyerhauser Company, which had extensive timberlands in the region. You'll learn about the effects of the blast on the trees and about the amazing reforestation efforts now underway. A multimedia exhibit allows you to feel as though you're flying over the tree plantings. Admission: free. For information and hours, call ☎ (360) 414-3439.

Mount Saint Helens Visitor Center at Silver Lake. A view across Silver Lake toward the western flank of the volcano; the center is about five miles off exit 49 of I-5. ☎ (360) 274-2100.

Coldwater Visitor Center. Views farther away down the scarred Toutle River Valley, at Milepost 43. Open year-round. ☎ (360) 274-2131.

Johnston Ridge Observatory. The closest viewpoint of the mountain, the bunker-like structure offers views of the smoldering crater six miles away. ☎ (360) 274-2140.

The Weyerhauser Company, a major forest products company, operates the Forest Learning Center at milepost 33 on SR-504 in conjunction with the Washington State Department of Transportation and the Rocky Mountain Elk Foundation. The center offers information on the eruption as well as efforts by the logging industry to speed the area's recovery. A multimedia exhibit allows you to feel as though you're flying over the tree plantings. Open daily from May through October, admission is free. ☎ (360) 414-3439. 🖳 www.weyerhaeuser.com/sthelens/.

The Hoffstadt Bluffs Visitor Center is operated by Cowlitz County, offering views of the mountain as well as commercial tours by helicopter. ☎ (360) 274-7750.

On the other side of the volcano, Forest Roads 25 and 99 enter into the area of blown-down forest and Spirit Lake. The roads are usually open from Memorial Day until they are blocked by winter snows.

The Cowlitz Valley Ranger Station, one mile east of Randle on Highway 12, is open to visitors from 8 A.M. to 4:30 P.M. daily during the summer season, from late May to early September.

On the south side of Mount Saint Helens, Forest Road 83 crosses lava and mudflows from earlier eruptions en route to the Pine Creek Information Station; roads are open from about Memorial Day until winter snowfall.

In this area is **Ape Cave**, a 2,000-year-old lava tube formed by an ancient eruption. At Ape's Headquarters on Forest Road 8303, three miles north of the junction of Forest Roads 83/90, you can rent a lantern to explore the tube. The facility is open from about June 1 to the end of September.

Mount Baker

The twin peaks of 10,778-foot **Mount Baker** and her sister, **Mount Shuksan** (9,038 feet), to the east are among the most-photographed sites in the world. Heather Meadows sits between the twin snowcaps, a green accent in the summer.

Mount Baker is located about three hours north of Seattle or one hour east of Bellingham; the north end of the Mount Baker National Recreation Area sits on the border with Canada's British Columbia.

In winter, Mount Baker typically receives more than 600 inches of snow—50 feet—and has the longest ski season in the state. In the amazing winter of 1998–99, though, Mount Baker set a record for the most snowfall ever measured in the United States in a single season. During the course of the season, the Mount Baker Ski Area received 1,140 inches of snow: 95 feet of the white stuff.

The previous U.S. record was 1,122 inches, set during the 1971–72 snowfall season at Mount Rainier/Paradise, a station located at 5,500 feet on the slopes of Mount Rainier, about 150 miles south of Mount Baker.

The dormant volcano, topped by a plume of steam through its snow cap, can be seen on a clear day from as far away as Victoria, B.C., or Seattle.

The biggest draw of the mountain is the Mount Baker Ski Area. Hikers, campers, and experienced climbers treasure Baker and Shuksan. A good source for maps and information on trails is the U.S. Forest Service Glacier Public Service Center at ☎ (360) 599-2714; the center is on State Route 542 (Mount Baker Highway), a mile east of Glacier.

Note that many trails are not accessible until July or August in many years because of snow accumulation.

Trailhead parking for the Mount Baker–Snoqualmie National Forest is ❷ per day or about $25 for the season. Vehicles heading to Heather Meadows, the 5,100-foot-high alpine area, which includes the Mount Baker Ski Area lodge and Picture Lake, are charged ❷ for a three-day pass or ❹ for an annual pass. Fees are collected at the Forest Service's Glacier Public Service Center, at automated machines in the park, or by mail.

Sites Within the Forest

Route 542 runs across the top of the forest, due east from Bellingham along the Nooksack River Valley. The forty-five-mile trip from Bellingham is about an hour.

Seven miles east of Glacier, at the entrance to the forest, is **Nooksack Falls**, a 170-foot cataract. The **Grove of the Druids** at the thirty-seven–mile marker, includes a stand of lofty Douglas fir trees that are at least 600 years old.

Picture Lake, famous for the stunning reflection of the mountain in its waters, is just below the ski lodge. **Artist Point** is the base for several popular hiking trails and also offers several short, paved trails.

Chapter 19
Vancouver, Washington

Vancouver, Washington, is on the north bank of the Columbia River, directly across from Portland, Oregon, and about ninety miles inland from the Pacific Coast.

The Cascade Mountain Range rises on the east, including the spectacular Columbia River Gorge National Scenic Area, thirty minutes away. Mount St. Helens National Volcanic Monument and Mount Hood are less than two hours away.

The city of more than 132,000 draws its name from Captain George Vancouver, also honored at British Columbia's largest city.

Vancouver enjoys mild weather with less average annual rainfall than Boston, Washington, D.C., or Atlanta. Summer temperatures generally reach the 80s, while in winter the nights rarely fall below 30 degrees Fahrenheit. Average snowfall is less than seven inches.

The Vancouver Story

In May of 1792 American trader and sailor Robert Gray became the first outsider to enter the Columbia River, the fabled "Great River of the West." Later that year, British Lieutenant William Broughton, serving under Captain George Vancouver, explored 100 miles upriver; along the way, he named a point of land along the shore in honor of his commander.

In 1806 American explorers Lewis and Clark, returning from their expedition west, made their camp near that point of land. Lewis declared the area "the only desired situation for settlement west of the Rocky Mountains."

In 1825 the Hudson's Bay Company decided to move its northwest headquarters from Astoria to a more favorable setting upriver; the site was named after Point Vancouver on Broughton's original map.

Fort Vancouver was developed by the Hudson's Bay Company from 1825 through 1846, one of the more important outposts of Western civilization and a center for the fur trade in the Pacific Northwest.

With Fort Vancouver as its regional headquarters, the Hudson's Bay Company controlled thirty-four forts and posts in a territory that encompasses today's British Columbia, Washington, Oregon, Idaho, western Montana, and the Hawaiian Islands.

VANCOUVER, WASHINGTON

As representative of a British trading company, the fort became the heart of British claims to the Oregon Territory. In the mid-nineteenth century, though, Great Britain, France, and Russia were all preoccupied with European disputes and wars, and their claims to territory in America were abandoned or sold off.

In 1846 an uneasy standoff with British Canada was settled, for the time being, and American control was extended north to the 49th parallel. The northwest became part of the United States. In 1849 American troops arrived to establish Columbia (later Vancouver) Barracks. It served as military headquarters for much of the Pacific Northwest. The neighboring settlement was named "the City of Columbia." The City of Vancouver was incorporated in 1857.

Fort Vancouver

The **Vancouver National Historic Reserve** includes the Fort Vancouver National Historic Site, Pearson Field, Vancouver Barracks, Officers Row, and portions of the Columbia shoreline and Marine Park.

The homes along the tree-lined northern edge of Evergreen Boulevard at Vancouver Barracks, made up the **Officers Row**. The oldest homes on the Row date to the early days of the barracks in the mid-1800s. Declared as surplus by the U.S. Army in 1980, the homes were rehabilitated as housing and public monuments by the city of Vancouver.

Officers Row today includes fifty-one residential units, office space, and the restored Grant, Marshall, and Howard houses.

The **George C. Marshall House** was built in 1886. This Queen Anne Victorian was home for the commanding officer of the Department of the Columbia. Marshall was commanding officer at Vancouver Barracks from 1936 to 1938; he went on to become U.S. Army Chief of Staff during World War II, Secretary of State, and Secretary of Defense.

Marshall was author of the Marshall Plan, which helped rebuild the economies of Western Europe and the Pacific nations after World War II; he was awarded the Nobel Peace Prize in 1952 in recognition of his efforts.

Today the Marshall House is decorated with antiques from the 1880s and houses a Victorian Gift Shop.

For information on visiting hours, call ☎ (360) 693-3103.

The **General O. O. Howard House** was named for its first inhabitant, Oliver Otis Howard (1830–1909). Recipient of the Congressional Medal of Honor in the Civil War, Howard was the first head of the Freedman's Bureau, established in 1865 to aid former slaves. Howard University in Washington, D.C., was named in recognition of his work.

Gen. Howard was Commander of the U.S. Army's Department of the Columbia from 1874–1880.

The house, built in 1879 in Italianate-style architecture, serves as a visitor information center for the Vancouver National Historic Reserve and features exhibits on the area's history from the mid-nineteenth century to the 1930s.

Ulysses S. Grant was stationed at Vancouver garrison in the 1850s as a quartermaster. He returned as a visitor to Vancouver Barracks in 1879, after serving two terms as President of the United States. The **Ulysses S. Grant House**, constructed as the commanding officer's quarters, was the first house built on Officers' Row. Though Grant never lived in the house, it was renamed in Grant's honor after he achieved his military and political success.

The oldest building remaining at Vancouver Barracks, the Grant House later served as an officers club for more than a quarter of a century. Today, the building houses the Grant House Folk Art Center and a café. For more information, call ☎ (360) 694-5252.

Extensive archaeological documentation of the Fort Vancouver site has allowed reconstruction of the Chief Factor's House, bakery, blacksmith shop, central stores, and fur storage facility. Ongoing explorations continue to yield important details.

The site was designated a National Historic Monument by Congress in 1948, and was expanded and renamed Fort Vancouver National Historic Site in 1961. Fort Vancouver National Historic Site is administered by the National Park Service. Winter hours are 9 A.M. to 4 P.M. Summer hours are 9 A.M. to 5 P.M. For more information, call ☎ (360) 696-7655.

Pearson Field, one of the oldest continuously operating airfields in the United States, was used as far back as the early 1800s when it operated as a farm for adjacent Fort Vancouver.

When the U.S. Army came to Vancouver in the mid-1800s, the area was used for storage of ammunition. In 1905, Lincoln Beachey piloted the dirigible *Gelatine* to Vancouver Barracks in the first aerial crossing of the Columbia River. And in 1911 the field's first airplane landed there.

During World War I a spruce mill was established for mass production of wood components for military aircraft. From 1923 to 1941, the field was home to the U.S. Army Air Service. One of its first commanders, Lieutenant Oakley Kelly, made the first non-stop transcontinental flight in 1923. A year later, the landing strip was a stopover on the army's first round-the-world flight.

In 1925 the field was named in honor of Lieutenant Alexander Pearson, winner of the first cross-country air race in 1919; he died while preparing for an air race in 1924.

Soviet aviator Valeri Chkalov and crew landed at the field at the end of the first nonstop trans-polar flight in 1937. During the years the field was visited by notable aviators, including Charles Lindbergh, Jimmy Doolittle, and Eddie Rickenbacker. Two companies at an adjacent commercial field, Pacific Air Transport and Varney Airlines, later joined with two other companies to form United Airlines.

After World War II, the airfield was sold to the City of Vancouver. In more recent years, Vancouver and the National Park Service agreed on a long-term plan that will transition Pearson from predominantly general aviation to historic aircraft by 2022. This came about as a resolution of a conflict regarding a portion of Pearson's runway that sits on land once occupied by historic Fort Vancouver and now owned by the National Park Service.

Getting Around Vancouver

C-TRAN operates thirty-seven bus routes in Clark County and the surrounding area, including Vancouver, Battle Ground, Camas, La Center, Ridgefield, Washougal, Yacolt, and commuter service to Portland. For information, call ☎ (360) 695-0123.

Chapter 20
Eastern Washington

The current course of the Columbia River was bulldozed by the glaciers and floods of the last Ice Age. The river enters into a chasm that forms the border between Washington and Oregon below Richland, heading mostly westward to Portland and then making a jog north toward Mount Saint Helens before resuming its march westward to the sea.

The famed Columbia River still rolls on, tamed by a series of dams for most of its length from Canada across Washington and out into the Pacific near Astoria.

The only free-running stretch of the river is the Hanford Reach, north of the Tri Cities of Richland, Pasco, and Kennewick in southeastern Washington. The Hanford Reach runs along the eastern border of the U.S. Department of Energy Hanford Site, a troubled uranium reprocessing facility.

In northeastern Washington, the Grand Coulee Dam regulates the upper Columbia. The dam, completed in 1941, created two bodies of water—Franklin D. Roosevelt Lake above the dam and Banks Lake below—providing hydroelectric power, irrigation, and recreation.

Banks Lake, held in check by the smaller Dry Falls Dam, fills a channel left dry when floods of the Ice Age forced the Columbia to reroute.

The Grand Coulee Dam

The **Grand Coulee Dam** was a triumph of engineering over nature. It helped control the fast-running Columbia River, it diverted rivers of water to 500,000 acres of fertile but dry fields in the Columbia Basin of eastern Washington, and as a bonus, it produces a huge amount of electricity that is transmitted to eleven western states.

The canal, completed in 1942 after nine years of work, blocks much of the flow of the Columbia River in northeastern Washington, diverting much of its flow south into the channel of the Grand Coulee River.

The resulting structure is today the largest concrete dam in North America, and the third-largest hydroelectric plant in the world. Stretching nearly a mile, 5,223 feet, it rises 500 feet above the bedrock of the river.

EASTERN WASHINGTON

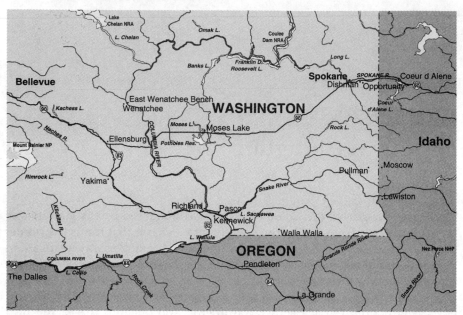

Within the dam are four power plants and thirty-three generators (the Bonneville Dam has two plants and twenty-one generators).

Guided tours are offered daily, on the hour, at the pumping plant from 10
A.M. to 5 P.M., and at the incline elevator from 10 A.M. to 8 P.M.

The visitor center on Highway 155 is open daily. From late May to late July,
the center is open from 8:30 A.M. to 11 P.M., with a laser show nightly at 10 P.M.
In August, the center is open from 8:30 A.M. to 10:30 P.M., with a 9:30 P.M.
show. In September, the center is open from 8:30 A.M. to 9:30 P.M., with an 8:30
P.M. show.

And for the remainder of the year, from October through late May, the center is open 9 A.M. to 5 P.M.; no laser light show is presented in the off-season.

For information on the dam, call the visitor center at ☎ (509) 633-9265 or
consult ▤ www.grandcouleedam.org.

Yakima Valley

The state's highest percentage of vineyard plantings can be found in the fertile valley between the eastern foothills of the Cascades and the Kiona Hills of
the Yakima Valley.

Although there have been stands of grapes cultivated in the area back to the
1930s, it was only in the 1960s that European stock was established in the area
and fine wines resulted. Experts say the harsh winters and the hot summers
combine to stress the vines and make them yield strong flavors.

You can obtain a free guide and map to twenty-seven wineries of the Yakima
Valley by calling the Yakima Valley Wine Growers at ☎ (800) 258-7270.

Covey Run. 1500 Vintage Road, Zillah. Tastings daily in summer from 10 A.M. to 5 P.M.; in winter, on weekends only from noon to 4:30 P.M. For information, call ☎ (509) 829-6235.

Eaton Hill Winery. 530 Gurley Road, Granger. Open daily for wine tasting except Thursday from 10 A.M. to 5 P.M.; in winter, from noon to 4 P.M. For information, call ☎ (509) 854-2220.

A dozen wineries are located in and around the Tri Cities of Kennewick, Pasco, and Richland.

One of the better known is **Columbia Crest Winery** in Paterson. Located on Highway 221, Columbia Crest Drive, the winery is open daily from 10 A.M. to 4 P.M. Tours and tastings offered. For information, call ☎ (888) 309-9463.

Chapter 21
Bellingham

Bellingham, set on Bellingham Bay with Mount Baker in the background, is the last major city on the West Coast short of the Canadian border.

Located about ninety minutes north of Seattle and an hour south of Vancouver, B.C., the area is linked by ferry to the nearby San Juan Islands and Victoria on Vancouver Island. Alaska Marine Highway System ferries depart from the Bellingham Cruise Terminal in the historic Fairhaven District. And boats also depart for area tours and whalewatching expeditions.

The active port is home to fishing vessels, boat building, and shipping. **Squalicum Harbor** is the second largest in Puget Sound, with about 2,000 pleasure and commercial boats moored. Many of the buildings are Victorian designs, frozen in time and restored as shops, restaurants, and galleries.

Ferndale, just north of Bellingham, claims one of the largest collections of original log cabins in the United States.

Further north, just short of the Canadian border, is Lynden, the state's largest Dutch settlement, which celebrates its heritage with Dutch-style architecture and cultural festivals.

An hour east of Bellingham is **Mount Baker**, a ski area that generally delivers the state's longest season. In the summer and fall you can hike the trails.

The Story of Bellingham

The first inhabitants of Northwest Washington and Whatcom County were Northwest Coast Indians, including Lummi, Semiahmoo, and Nooksack tribes. Their history goes back thousands of years.

Living in substantial cedar homes, they traveled by dugout canoes on the sound and inland on rivers in search of fish, shellfish, wild plants, and animals. Populations were never large, probably less than 3,000 people.

The Lummi roamed some of the San Juan Islands and most of the shoreline from south of Bellingham to Birch Bay. Semiahmoo territory included the shoreline from Birch Bay to Blaine and some distance inland. The Nooksacks lived almost entirely inland on the Nooksacks River, with saltwater gathering grounds reaching into Bellingham Bay and Chuckanut Bay.

BELLINGHAM AND NORTHWEST WASHINGTON

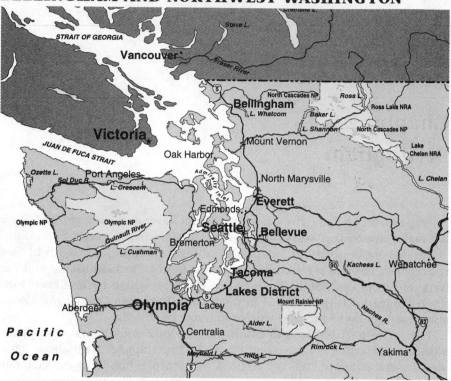

Archeologists and anthropologists say there were no permanent Indian settlements on Bellingham Bay itself; the first encampments there came with the arrival of the Europeans after the establishment of the United States on the East Coast.

The first formal exploration of Bellingham Bay was made by Captain George Vancouver in 1792; he came to Puget Sound as part of an effort to strengthen Great Britain's claims in the area and to weaken the claims made by Spain and Russia.

Vancouver's small oceangoing sailing ships were still too large to explore all of the bays, inlets, and channels of the North Sound. Instead, the ships anchored in Birch Bay and launches or rowboats were sent out.

Two launches commanded by Lieutenant Joseph Whidbey rowed into Bellingham bay on June 15, 1792. Vancouver named Whidbey's discovery after Sir William Bellingham, controller of the storekeeper's accounts for the British Navy at the time. (Perhaps he hoped for better treatment when he next provisioned his ship.)

Vancouver named Whidbey Island after his lieutenant, and gave names to Puget Sound, Birch Bay, Mount Baker, and many other local landmarks.

By the middle of the nineteenth century, there were many outsiders passing through the area or settling; one influx was due to miners who came to California during the gold rush of 1849 and stayed behind after the frenzy subsided.

The boom town of San Francisco demanded large amounts of lumber for its construction and for reconstruction after numerous fires, outstripping local supplies in California.

Two former gold miners, Henry Roeder and Russell Peabody, came to Washington in search of a site for a lumber mill that had a waterfall to power a waterwheel for saws and was near the coast so the product could be transported out by ship.

The two men were brought to the right place by Lummi Indians, who helped them build the mill at Bellingham Bay on North Puget Sound. They named the town that grew up around the mill Whatcom, after the Indian name for the waterfall, which meant "noisy waters" or "noisy all the time."

The Fraser River Gold Rush in Canada in 1858 brought more than 10,000 people to the bay area and Whatcom boomed as a tent city and center where would-be miners shopped for their grubstake before heading into the wilderness. But the population all but vanished overnight when the British Colombian government passed regulations requiring that miners report to Victoria before heading to the diggings.

About the same time, coal was discovered on Sehome Hill to the south of Whatcom; a San Francisco mining syndicate built a dock, homes, and stores for 125 miners. A fleet of sailing schooners transported Bellingham Bay coal to California. The company town of Sehome was the second town on Bellingham Bay. The Roeder Mill suffered from an uneven lumber market and was shut for long periods of time; it finally was destroyed by fire in 1873.

Similarly, the coal mine suffered from cave-ins, fires, floods, and the booms and busts of the West Coast economy; it closed in 1878.

A new town, Bellingham, was laid out in 1871 in hopes of becoming the West Coast terminal of the Northern Pacific Railroad, but the railroad went elsewhere. By the early 1880s the population on Bellingham Bay dropped to less than a hundred.

Another attempt at launching a local economy came in the 1890s when boom times in the developing big cities of the East Coast brought an influx of investment to the West. Wealthy outsiders promoted the new town of Fairhaven at the south end of Bellingham Bay; they put in hotels, banks, shops, power plants, streetcar lines, and other infrastructures to support docks, mills, and mines in the area.

A railroad was built southward into Skagit County, and another line was added from Sehome north to British Columbia. Again there were hopes for the creation of a terminus for a transcontinental line, the Great Northern Railroad.

By now the population around the bay had grown to several thousand.

But in 1893 a nationwide depression cut off the sources of investment. At the same time, railroad surveyors gave up on the idea of cutting through the mountains to bring a line through to Bellingham Bay; instead the railroad met the coast farther south.

With the dawn of the twentieth century the flow of capital returned. Bellingham grew with new lumber mills, salmon canneries, shipyards and other industries. Fairhaven became the largest salmon canning outfit in the world.

With development, the four towns began to grow together. The town of Bellingham was purchased by a wealthy developer and incorporated into Fairhaven in 1890. Sehome merged with Whatcom that same year. In 1903

Key to Prices
❶ $3 and under
❷ $3 to $6
❸ $6 to $10
❹ $10 to $15

When prices are listed as a range, this indicates various combination options are available. Most attractions offer reduced-price tickets for children and many have family rates that include two adults and two or three children.

Whatcom and Fairhaven voted for consolidation but could not agree on a name; so, they reached back to the earlier name of Bellingham.

The town of Whatcom has disappeared, but the name lives on in Whatcom County and Whatcom Creek, the source of the water for Whatcom Falls.

Museums and Attractions of Bellingham

The **Whatcom Museum of History and Art** resides in an imposing brick main building originally built in 1892 as the city hall; three other buildings make up the museum campus, all located on Prospect Street between Champion Street and Central Avenue.

The Main Building includes changing local history exhibits, contemporary art, and Victorian clothing, woodworking tools, and toys. The Syre Education Center features Victorian era period rooms and a staggering collection of taxidermied birds from wild ducks to owls and eagles, and exhibits on Northwest Coast First Nations and Inuit peoples. The Arco Exhibits Building presents changing exhibitions of contemporary art, history, and topical issues.

The Northwest First Nations Ethnography Collection includes carvings, masks, tools, garments, and basketry. The History Collection comprises more than 10,000 examples of garments, textiles, decorative arts, tools, and Victorian furniture.

The Archives include the renowned Darius Kinsey Collection of thousands of images of Northwest landscape.

The three buildings are open daily except Monday from noon to 5 P.M. Admission: free. For information, call ☎ (360) 676-6981 or consult the web at 🖳 www.cob.org/museum.htm.

The fourth building in the campus is the Whatcom Children's Museum, a hands-on museum for young children that features interactive exhibits.

The children's museum is open Sunday, Tuesday, and Wednesday from noon to 5 P.M. and Thursday through Saturday from 10 A.M. to 5 P.M. It is closed Monday. Admission: ❶. For information, call ☎ (360) 733-8769.

One man's obsession with old-time radios has become a treasure trove of the **Bellingham Antique Radio Museum** in a downtown Bellingham storefront. The space is crammed with old devices, from crystal sets to early military and consumer radios, and all manner of other pieces of early technology. Most were gathered by Jonathan Winter, who oversees his collection.

The museum, at 1315 Railroad Avenue, is open Wednesday through Saturday from 11 A.M. to 4 P.M. Admission: donations welcome. For information, call ☎ (360) 671-4663.

And now for something completely different: **Mindport Exhibits** is dedicated to the proposition that the best way to learn about something—from science to art—is to play. This place just about defies description, which may be its greatest strength; make a visit to discover things you may not have known you were looking for.

Recent exhibits have included Backwards Speech, where visitors speak into a receiver and then listen to their words repeated backwards; the challenge is to try to speak backwards so it comes out forwards. The Line-Following Robot will chase a white string you lay down on a black background. At the Eye Mirror, a small mirror offers a close inspection of the interior of your eyes.

The exhibit, located at 111 Grand Avenue in downtown Bellingham, is opened daily Wednesday to Saturday from 10 A.M. to 5 P.M., and Sunday from noon to 4 P.M. It is closed on Monday and Tuesday. Admission: donations welcome. For information, call ☎ (360) 647-5614, or consult 🖳 www.mindport.org/.

Transport in and Around Bellingham

Bellingham is the southernmost terminus of the **Alaska Marine Highway System**, with service up the Inside Passage to coastal Alaska.

The Bellingham Cruise Terminal and visitor information center are adjacent to the historic Fairhaven district, at 355 Harris Avenue. The terminal offers train, bus, and ferry service to Alaska, Victoria, and the San Juan Islands. Shuttle services are available for travel between the terminal and major airports.

For information about the Bellingham terminal, call ☎ (360) 676-2500, or consult www.portofbellingham.com.

Adjacent to the Bellingham Cruise Terminal is Fairhaven Station, an historical waterfront building restored as Bellingham's Amtrak station. In addition to Amtrak, Fairhaven Station is a terminal for Greyhound bus, public transit, taxi, and shuttle services. The two terminals are linked by a covered walkway and are just a short distance from shopping and dining in the historic Fairhaven District.

Alaska Marine Highway System. ☎ (800) 642-0066. 🖳 www.dot.state.ak.us/exter nal/amhs/home.html.

Amtrak. ☎ (800) 872-7245. 🖳 www.amtrak.com

Greyhound Bus Lines. ☎ (360) 733-5251. 🖳 www.greyhound.com/.

San Juan Island Shuttle Express. ☎ (360) 671-1137. 🖳 www.orcawhales.com.

Victoria–San Juan Cruises. ☎ (800) 443-4552. 🖳 www.whales.com.

Bellingham International Airport, off Interstate 5, offers commuter service to Seattle-Tacoma Airport and connections beyond, and to the San Juan Islands.

For information on the airport, call ☎ (360) 671-5674. Carriers include Horizon Airlines, ☎ (800) 547-9308 or 🖳 www.horizonair.com; United Express, ☎ (800) 241-6522 or 🖳 www.ual.com; and West Isle Air, ☎ (800) 874-4434.

Chapter 22
Ski Resorts in Washington

Washington's ski resorts are not as well known as those in Oregon or British Columbia, but there are a few hills worth a trip from most anywhere. The two big ones are The Summit at Snoqualmie, with more than sixty-five trails spread across four ski areas, and Crystal Mountain, with fifty trails all by itself.

Organized winter recreation on **Snoqualmie Pass** began in the 1920s, when Seattle-area adventurers would climb the hills for ski jumping and racing. Hyak, which has operated since the early 1930s, is the oldest area at The Summit. The first lift was a rope tow at Snoqualmie Summit in 1937; in 1945, that area introduced the first night skiing in the country.

The four areas in the pass were brought together in 1997 by Booth Creek, under the name of The Summit at Snoqualmie. Alpental is now known as Alpental at the Summit; Snoqualmie became The Summit West; Ski Acres is now The Summit Central; and Hyak, The Summit East. Tickets are interchangeable among the resorts.

During the next ten years, Booth Creek plans to connect the resorts with trails, build a new central resort for the area, and add sixteen quad chairs.

Crystal Mountain is now part of the Boyne family (together with Boyne Mountain in Michigan, Big Sky in Montana, and Brighton in Utah), and the new owner has grand plans for expansion during the next decade. Perhaps in celebration, the snow gods delivered massive amounts of snow to the area in the 1998 and 1999 seasons, more than fifty feet each year.

★★★ Crystal Mountain Resort

1 Crystal Mountain Boulevard, Crystal Mountain, WA 98022. Information: ☎ (360) 663-2265. 🖳 www.skicrystal.com. Ski conditions: ☎ (888) 754-6199. Central lodging: ☎ (360) 663-2265. Typical season: Mid-November to mid-April.

Peak: 7,012. Base: 4,400. Vertical: 3,100.

Trails: 50. Skiable acres: 2,300. Average natural snowfall: 340 inches. Snowmaking: 2%. Longest trail: 3.5 miles. Trail rating: 13% Novice, 57% Intermediate, 30% Expert.

Lifts: 10 (2 six-seat high-speed chairs, 1 high-speed quad, 2 triples, 4 doubles, 1 surface tow).

Recent prices: all-day adult, $40; youth, $35

★★ 49° North

Box 166, 3311 Flowery Trail Road, Chewelah, WA 99109-0166. Information: ☎ (509) 935-6649. 🖳 www.ski49n.com. Ski conditions: ☎ (509) 935-6649. Typical season: Late November to early April.

Peak: 5,774. Base: 3,956. Vertical: 1,851.

Trails: 43. Skiable acres: 1,100. Average natural snowfall: 240 inches. Snowmaking: 0%. Longest trail: 3 miles. Trail rating: 30% Novice, 40% Intermediate, 30% Expert. Features: 16 km cross-country trails.

Lifts: 5 (4 doubles, 1 surface tow).

Recent prices: weekend adult, $32; junior, $24; senior, $25

★★ Mission Ridge Ski Area

7500 Mission Ridge Road, Wenatchee, WA 98807-1668. Information: ☎ (509) 663-6543. 🖳 www.missionridge.com. Ski conditions: ☎ (800) 374-1693. Central lodging: ☎ (888) 757-4343. Typical season: Late November to mid-April.

Peak: 6,770. Base: 4,570. Vertical: 2,200.

Trails: 35. Skiable acres: 2,000. Average natural snowfall: 200 inches. Snowmaking: 10%. Longest trail: 2 miles. Trail rating: 10% Novice, 60% Intermediate, 30% Expert.

Lifts: 6 (4 doubles, 2 surface).

Recent prices: weekend adult, $34; student/senior, $19

★★★ Mount Baker Ski Area

1017 Iowa Street, Bellingham, WA 98226. Information: ☎ (360) 734-6771. 🖳 www.mtbakerskiarea.com. Ski conditions: ☎ (360) 671-0211. Typical season: Mid-November to end of April.

Peak: 5,050. Base: 3,500. Vertical: 1,550.

Trails: 38. Skiable acres: 1,000. Average natural snowfall: 615 inches. Snowmaking: 0%. Longest trail: 1.75 miles. Trail rating: 30% Novice, 42% Intermediate, 28% Expert. Features: 4 km cross-country trails.

Lifts: 10 (2 quads, 6 doubles, 2 surface).

Recent prices: weekend adult, $33; youth, $23; senior, $26

★★★ Mount Spokane

State Hightway 206, Mead, WA 99021. Information: ☎ (509) 238-2220. 🖳 www.mtspokane.com. Ski conditions: ☎ (509) 443-1397. Typical season: Early December to early April.

Peak: 5,883. Base: 3,818. Vertical: 2,065.

Trails: 38. Skiable acres: 547. Average natural snowfall: 423 inches. Snowmaking: 0%. Longest trail: 2.25 miles. Trail rating: 35% Novice, 40% Intermediate, 25% Expert.

Lifts: 5 (5 doubles).
Recent prices: weekend adult, $29; youth, $23; senior/young adult, $27

★★ Ski Bluewood

North Touchet Road, Dayton, WA 99328. Information: ☎ (509) 382-4725. 🖳 www.skiwashington.com. Ski conditions: ☎ (509) 382-2877. Typical season: Late November to late March.

Peak: 5,670. Base: 4,445. Vertical: 1,125.

Trails: 21. Skiable acres: 430. Average natural snowfall: 300 inches. Snowmaking: 0%. Longest trail: 2.25 miles. Trail rating: 25% Novice, 39% Intermediate, 36% Expert.

Lifts: 3 (2 triples, 1 surface tow).

Recent prices: all-day adult, $27; child, $20; senior/student, $23

★★ Stevens Pass Ski Area

Summit Stevens Pass, Snohomish, WA 98288. Information: ☎ (360) 973-2441. Typical season: Thanksgiving to mid-April.

Peak: 5,845. Base: 4,061. Vertical: 1,784.

Trails: 37. Skiable acres: 1,125. Average natural snowfall: 415 inches. Snowmaking: 0%. Longest trail: 1.5 mile. Trail rating: 11% Novice, 54% Intermediate, 35% Expert. Features: 25 km cross-country trails.

Lifts: 10 (2 high-speed quads, 1 quad, 3 triples, 4 doubles).

Recent prices: adult, $41; child, $26; senior, $29

★★★ The Summit at Snoqualmie (Alpental, Summit West, Summit Central, Summit East)

Hyak, WA 98068. Information: ☎ (425) 434-7669. 🖳 www.summit-at-snowqualmie.com. Ski conditions: ☎ (425) 434-7669. Central lodging: ☎ (800) 557-7829. Typical season: Mid-November to late April.

Peak: 5,400. Base: 3,000. Shortest vertical: 2,200.

Trails: 65. Skiable acres: 1,916. Average natural snowfall: 379 inches. Snowmaking: 0%. Longest trail: 1.3 miles. Trail rating: 30% Novice, 42% Intermediate, 28% Expert. Features: 55 km cross-country trails.

Lifts: 27 (2 high-speed quads, 2 quads, 4 triples, 12 doubles, 7 surface).

Recent prices: weekend adult, $37; senior/youth, $24; child, $7

★★ White Pass Ski Area

Highway 12, White Pass, WA 98937. Information: ☎ (509) 672-3101. 🖳 www.skiwhitepass.com. Ski conditions: ☎ (509) 672-3100. Typical season: Mid-November to late April.

Peak: 6,000. Base: 4,500. Vertical: 1,500.

Trails: 32. Skiable acres: 638. Average natural snowfall: 300 inches. Snowmaking: 25%. Longest trail: 2.5 miles. Trail rating: 20% Novice, 60% Intermediate, 20% Expert. Features: 18 km cross-country trails.

Lifts: 5 (1 high-speed quad, 3 doubles, 1 surface tow).

Recent prices: weekend and holiday adult, $34; senior/junior, $21

Cross-Country Skiing

Colville Ranger District. ☎ (509) 684-7000.
   Cowlitz Valley Ranger District. ☎ (360) 497-1100.
   Echo Valley. ☎ (509) 682-4002.
   Hurricane Ridge. ☎ (360) 452-0330.
   Lake Easton State Park. ☎ (509) 656-2230.
   Lake Wenatchee State Park. ☎ (509) 763-3101.
   Leavenworth Ski Hill. ☎ (509) 548-5115.
   Loup Loup Ski Bowl. ☎ (509) 826-2720.
   Methow Valley Sport Trails Association. ☎ (509) 996-3287.
   Mount Adams Ranger District. ☎ (509) 395-3400.
   Mount Saint Helens NVM. ☎ (360) 247-3900.
   Mount Rainier National Park. ☎ (360) 569-2211.
   Mount Spokane State Park. ☎ (509) 238-4258.
   Mount Tahoma Trails Association. ☎ (360) 569-2451.
   Newport Ranger District. ☎ (509) 447-7300.
   Omak Visitor Information Center. ☎ (800) 225-6625.
   Republic Ranger District. ☎ (509) 775-3305.
   Sitzmark. ☎ (509) 485-3343.
   Ski Acres/Hyak Cross-Country Center. ☎ (206) 236-7277.
   Stehekin Valley Recreation Area. ☎ (509) 682-4494.
   Stevens Pass Nordic Center. ☎ (360) 973-2441.
   White Pass Cross-Country Area. ☎ (509) 672-3100.

Other Ski and Winter Sports Resources

North Cascades Heli-Skiing. ☎ (800) 494-4354.
   Washington State Snowmobile Association. ☎ (800) 784-9772.
   Trail Grooming Report. ☎ (800) 233-0321.
   Washington Ski and Snowboard Industries. ☎ (206) 623-3777 or ☎ (800) 278-7669. You can also consult 🖳 www.skiwashington.com.
   The state's extensive system of Sno-Parks includes many miles of trails that are maintained for cross-country skiing and snowmobiling. Users must purchase a permit to use the trails, and snowmobiles must be registered with county auditors. Permits are sold at retail locations across Washington or through the Washington State Parks Winter Recreation Office. For information, call ☎ (360) 902-8552.

Chapter 23
Washington Events and Festivals

Seattle and Western Washington

January

Upper Skagit Bald Eagle Festival. Marblemount. ☎ (360) 853-7009. Early.
    Art is for Everyone. Everett. ☎ (425) 257-8380. Mid-January to mid-February.
    Jumpernite Horse Jumping. Tumwater. ☎ (253) 584-9219. Mid-January to mid-February.
    Kids & Critters Naturefest. Eatonville. ☎ (360) 832-6117. Mid.
    Martin Luther King Jr. Day. Seattle. ☎ (206) 684-7200 or ☎ (206) 684-8582. Mid.
    Seattle International Boat Show. Seattle. ☎ (206) 634-0911. Mid.
    Upper Skagit Bald Eagle Festival. Concrete and Rockport. ☎ (360) 853-7009. Late.

February

Chinese New Year. Seattle, International District. ☎ (206) 223-0623. Varies.
    Quilt Show. Castle Rock. ☎ (360) 274-6603.
    Ethnic Celebration. Olympia. ☎ (360) 753-8380. Early.
    Winter Visuals. Gig Harbor. ☎ (253) 851-9462. Early.
    Festival Sundiata. Seattle. ☎ (206) 329-8086. African-American arts and culture. Mid.
    Northwest Flower and Garden Show. Seattle. ☎ (206) 789-5333. Mid.
    February Fling Celtic Dance. Tacoma. ☎ (253) 939-8413. Late.
    Tet Festival Vietnamese Cultural Festival. Seattle. ☎ (206) 684-7200. Late.
    Wintergrass. Tacoma. ☎ (253) 926-4164. Bluegrass festival. Late.

March

Country Elegance Bazaar. Bothell. ☎ (425) 483-1191. Early.
    Floral Display, Seymour Botanical Conservatory. Tacoma. ☎ (253) 591-5330.
    Peak Bloom, Rhododendron Species Botanical Gardens. Tacoma. ☎ (253) 661-9377.
    A Country Collection Craft & Antique. Lynden. ☎ (360) 966-5573. Mid.
    Annual Oyster Olympics. Shilshole Bay. ☎ (206) 283-7566. Mid.
    Antique Show and Sale. Tacoma. ☎ (253) 572-3663. Mid.
    Confections Fun & Fashions. Chehalis. ☎ (360) 740-5299. Mid.
    Fringe Theatre Festival. Seattle, Capitol Hill neighborhood. ☎ (206) 443-9809. Mid.
    Gray Whalewatch. Seattle. ☎ (800) 325-6122. Mid- to late March.
    Gallery Walk. Pioneer Square. ☎ (206) 622-6235. Early.
    Irish Cottage Fair. Olympia. ☎ (360) 753-8380. Mid.
    Irish Week Festival. Seattle. ☎ (206) 329-7224. Mid.
    Jumpernite Horse Jumping. Spanaway. ☎ (253) 584-9219. Mid.

Keeper Tours & Free Roaming Area Photo Tours, Northwest Trek Wildlife Park.
Eatonville. ☎ (360) 832-7182. Mid.
   Lawn and Garden Show. Chehalis. ☎ (800) 525-3323. Mid.
   Old-Time Music Festival. Tenino. ☎ (360) 273-5360. Mid.
   TrailsFest. Seattle. ☎ (206) 625-1367. Mid.
   Capital Food & Wine Festival. Lacey. ☎ (360) 438-4366. Late.
   Boat Show. Tacoma Dome. ☎ (253) 756-2121. Late.
   International Wine Fair. Union Station. ☎ (206) 937-2965. Late.
   Model A Swapmeet. Puyallup. ☎ (253) 841-5045. Late.
   Whirligig. Seattle. ☎ (206) 684-7200. Kids festival. Late March to mid-April.

April
Annual Quilt Show. Anacortes. ☎ (360) 299-8117. Early.
   Bellingham Children's Theatre. Bellingham. ☎ (360) 734-5468. April.
   Camano Island Quilters Show. Camano Island. ☎ (425) 348-3486. Early.
   Easter Breakfast. Seattle, Woodland Park Zoo. ☎ (206) 684-4800. Early.
   Easter Egg Hunt. Seattle, Pike Place Market. ☎ (206) 587-0351. Early.
   Easter Eggstravaganza. Federal Way, Enchanted Parks. ☎ (253) 661-8001. Early.
   First Thursday Art Walk. Seattle, Pioneer Square. ☎ (206) 622-6235. Early.
   Free Roaming Areas Photo Tours, Northwest Trek Wildlife Park. Eatonville. ☎
(360) 832-7182. Early.
   Junior Daffodil Parade. Tacoma. ☎ (253) 627-6176. Early.
   Mount Rainier Family Activity Day. Tacoma, Washington State History Museum.
☎ (888) 238-4373. Early.
   Mount Baker Rock & Gem Club. Bellingham. ☎ (360) 384-3169. Early.
   The Nisqually Mission Anniversary. Du Pont. ☎ (253) 964-3492. Early.
   Northwest Guitar Festival. Bellingham. ☎ (360) 650-7712. Early.
   Skagit Valley Tulip Festival. La Conner and Mount Vernon. ☎ (360) 428-5959. 🖳
www.tulipfest ival.org/. Early.
   Snohomish Easter Parade. Snohomish. ☎ (360) 568-2526. Early.
   Spring Fling. Vashon Island. ☎ (206) 463-6217. Early.
   Spring Plant Sale. Federal Way, Rhododendron Species Botanical Garden. ☎ (253)
661-9377. Early.
   Arts Walk. Olympia. ☎ (360) 753-8380, Mid.
   Cherry Blossom/Japanese Cultural Festival. Seattle. ☎ (206) 684-7200. Mid.
   Daffodil Grand Floral Parade. Orting. ☎ (253) 627-6176. Mid.
   Daffodil Grand Floral Parade. Puyallup. ☎ (253) 627-6176. Mid.
   Daffodil Grand Floral Parade. Sumner. ☎ (253) 627-6176. Mid.
   Daffodil Grand Floral Parade. Tacoma. ☎ (253) 627-6176. Mid.
   Earth Day Celebration. Longview. ☎ (360) 577-3345. Mid.
   Floral Marine Parade. Tacoma. ☎ (253) 752-3555. Mid.
   Hulda Klager Lilac Festival. Woodland. ☎ (360) 225-8996. Mid-April to mid-May.
   Keeper Tours, Northwest Trek Wildlife Park. Eatonville. ☎ (360) 832-7182. Mid.
   Little Puyallup Spring Fair. Puyallup. ☎ (253) 841-5045, Mid.
   Living History Day. Fort Nisqually, Tacoma. ☎ (253) 591-5339. Mid.
   Living with Wildlife: Earth Week Celebration, Northwest Trek Wildlife
Park. Eatonville. ☎ (800) 433-8735. Mid.
   Meerkerk Magic. Greenbank. ☎ (360) 678-1912. 🖳 www.whidbey.net/meerkerk/gar
dens.html. Mid.
   Taste Washington: A Celebration of Wine and Food. Seattle. ☎ (206) 667-9463.
🖳 www.washington wine.org/. Mid.
   Zoobotanica. Seattle, Woodland Park Zoo. ☎ (206) 684-4800. Mid.
   American Rhododendron Society Convention. Bellevue. ☎ (425) 837-8760. 🖳
www.rhododen dron.org/. Late.

Artspring. Seattle. ☎ (206) 684-7200. Late.
Bellevue Parks Wild n' Wooly Sheep Shearing. Bellevue. ☎ (425) 452-6881. Late.
Best of the Northwest Crafts Fair. Seattle. ☎ (360) 221-6191. Late April to early May.
Discovery Walk Festival. Vancouver. ☎ (360) 892-6758. Late.
Festival of the Rain. Stevenson. ☎ (800) 989-9178. Late.
Holland Days. Lynden. ☎ (360) 354-5995. Late.
Holland Happening. Oak Harbor. ☎ (360) 675-3535. Late.
International Horse Drawn Plowing Match. Lynden. ☎ (360) 354-4111. Late.
Keeper Tours. Eatonville. ☎ (360) 832-7182. Late.
Northshore Seniors Plant Sale. Bothell. ☎ (425) 483-2250. Late April to early May.
Seattle Regional Rhododendron Flower Show. Bellevue. ☎ (360) 678-1912. Late.
Spring Opening. Vashon Island. ☎ (206) 463-6217. Late.
Spring Youth Fair. Chehalis. ☎ (360) 748-0280. Late April to early May.
Worldfest. Seattle. ☎ (206) 443-1410. Late.

May

Bainbridge Island Home Tour. Bainbridge Island. ☎ (206) 842-8569 Early.
Bellevue Botanical Garden Plant Sale. Bellevue. ☎ (425) 452-2750. Early.
Blossoms & Burgers. Seattle, Mercer Island. ☎ (206) 236-3545 Early.
Cascade Wine Country's Spring Barrel Tasting. Seattle, Columbia Winery. ☎ (425) 488-2776. Early.
Community Day. Eatonville. ☎ (360) 832-3551. Early.
Community Wide Garage Sale. Ferndale. ☎ (360) 384-3042. Early.
First Thursday Art Walk. Seattle, Pioneer Square. ☎ (206) 622-6235. Early.
Gig Harbor's Farmers Market. Gig Harbor. ☎ (253) 884-2496. Early to late May.
Hovander Open House & FFA Day. Ferndale. ☎ (360) 384-3444. Early.
International Sculpture Exhibition. Blaine. ☎ (360) 332-7165. Early May to late September.
Mom & Me at the Zoo. Seattle, Woodland Park Zoo. ☎ (206) 684-4800 Early.
Mother's Day at Rhododendron Species Botanical Garden. Federal Way. ☎ (253) 661-9377. Early.
Mother's Day Breakfast. Seattle, Woodland Park Zoo. ☎ (206) 684-4800 Early.
Mother's Day Open House at the Bellevue Botanical Garden. Bellevue. ☎ (425) 452-2750. Early.
Native Plant Society Sale at the Bellevue Botanical Garden. Bellevue. ☎ (425) 452-2750. Early.
Puyallup Farmers Market. Puyallup. ☎ (253) 845-6755. Early May to early June.
Return of the Orcas Festival. Roche Harbor. ☎ (360) 378-6545. Early.
Sculptor's Workshop Semi Annual Pottery Sale. Edmonds. ☎ (425) 774-8282. Early.
Seattle Airline Collectibles Show. Seattle, Museum of Flight. ☎ (425) 485-8780 Early.
Wooden Boat Fair. Olympia. ☎ (360) 943-5404. Early.
Anacortes Waterfront Festival & Boat Show. Anacortes. ☎ (360) 293-7911. Mid.
Art Fest. Puyallup. ☎ (253) 840-6015. Mid.
Herb Festival. Yacolt. ☎ (360) 686-3537. Mid.
Maritime Tug Boat Races Special. Seattle. ☎ (206) 674-3499. Mid.
Mutual of Enumclaw Stage Race. Enumclaw. ☎ (360) 802-9038. Mid.
Seattle International Children's Festival. Seattle. ☎ (206) 684-7346. Mid.
Seattle International Film Festival. Seattle. ☎ (206) 324-9996. Mid-May to early June.
Seattle Maritime Festival. Seattle. ☎ (206) 282-6858. Mid.
Woodfest. Sedro-Woolley. ☎ (888) 225-8365. Mid.
Block Party. Bellingham. ☎ (360) 734-2500. Late.
Civil War Battle & Reenactment. Lakewood. ☎ (253) 756-3928. Late.
Civil War Reenactment. Tacoma. ☎ (800) 260-5997. Late.
Custom Car, Truck & Bicycle Show. Chehalis. ☎ (206) 772-6963. Late.
Gallery Walk. Edmonds. ☎ (425) 670-1496. Late.

International Festival. Longview. ☎ (360) 636-2791. Late.
It All Ends in Fairhaven Festival. Bellingham. ☎ (360) 671-6745. Late.
Langley Antique Extravaganza. Langley. ☎ (360) 221-7797. Late.
Memorial Day Parade. Coupeville. ☎ (360) 678-5434. Late.
Northwest Folklife Festival. Seattle. ☎ (206) 684-7300. Late.
Pike Place Market Festival. Seattle. ☎ (206) 587-0351. Late.
Queen Victoria's Birthday Celebration. Tacoma. ☎ (253) 591-5339. Late.
Queen Victoria's Birthday Celebration. Vancouver. ☎ (360) 696-7655. Late.
Ski to Sea Festival. Bellingham. ☎ (360) 734-1330. Late.
The Edmonds Waterfront Festival. Edmonds. ☎ (425) 771-1744. Late.
Whidbey Island Garden Tour. Freeland. ☎ (360) 321-0358. Late.
World Music and Dance Festival. Tukwila. ☎ (206) 443-1410. 📖 www.cultural.
org/ehc/. Late.

June

Antique Auto Show. Bellingham. ☎ (360) 734-1330. Early.
   Bamboo Festival & Plant Sale. Seattle. ☎ (206) 242-8848. Early.
   Blast from the Past. Sedro-Woolley. ☎ (360) 855-1841. Early.
   Columbia Summerfest. Seattle, Columbia Winery. ☎ (425) 488-2776. Early.
   Deming Logging Show. Deming. ☎ (360) 592-3051. Early.
   Farmer's Day Parade. Lynden. ☎ (360) 354-5995. Early.
   Filmmaker's Forum/SIFF. Seattle. ☎ (206) 324-9996. Early.
   First Thursday Art Walk. Seattle, Pioneer Square. ☎ (206) 622-6235. Early.
   Free Roaming Areas Photo Tours. Eatonville, Northwest Trek Wildlife Park. ☎
(360) 832-6117. Early.
   Greenbank Artists Art Show. Greenbank. ☎ (360) 678-0960. Early.
   Keeper Tours. Eatonville, Northwest Trek Wildlife Park. ☎ (360) 832-7182. Early.
   Maritime Gig. Gig Harbor. ☎ (253) 851-6865. Early.
   Pagdiriwang Philippine Cultural Festival. Seattle. ☎ (206) 684-7200. Early.
   Pioneer Square Fire Festival. Seattle. ☎ (206) 622-6235. Early.
   Roy Pioneer Rodeo. Roy. ☎ (253) 843-1113. Early.
   Salty Sea Days. Everett. ☎ (425) 339-1113. Early.
   Scottish Highland Games. Ferndale. ☎ (360) 384-3444. Early.
   Seattle Area Open Gardens Day. Seattle. ☎ (845) 265-5384. Early.
   Studebaker Car Club Show. Seattle. ☎ (206) 684-7200. Early.
   Tastin' n Racin'. Issaquah. ☎ (425) 427-9828. Early.
   University District Farmers Market. Seattle. ☎ (206) 547-2278. Early.
   Washington Women in Timber, Woods Tour. Deming. ☎ (360) 733-8349. Early.
   All Breed Dog Show. Puyallup. ☎ (253) 841-5045. Mid.
   Antique Farm & Tractor Fair. Ferndale. ☎ (360) 384-3444. Mid.
   Edmonds Arts Festival. Edmonds. ☎ (425) 771-6412. Mid.
   Fall City Days Community Festival. Fall City. ☎ (425) 222-4572. 📖 www.fallcity
days.com/. Mid.
   Father's Day at Rhododendron Species Botanical Garden. Federal Way. ☎ (253)
661-9377. Mid.
   Father's Day Breakfast with the Beasts. Eatonville, Northwest Trek Wildlife Park.
☎ (360) 832-6117. Mid.
   Flag Day Celebration. Tacoma, Never Never Land, Point Defiance Park. ☎ (253) 305-
1000. Mid.
   Fremont Fair. Fremont. ☎ (206) 726-2623. Mid.
   Fremont Fun Run & Briefcase Relay. Seattle. ☎ (206) 632-1500. Mid.
   Gig Harbor Garden Tour. Gig Harbor. ☎ (253) 851-3776. Mid.
   Juneteenth Festival. Seattle. ☎ (206) 322-8296 or ☎ (206) 325-2864. Mid.
   Marysville Strawberry Festival. Marysville. ☎ (360) 659-7664. Mid.

Meeker Days Hoe-Down & Bluegrass Festival. Puyallup. ☎ (253) 840-2631. Mid.
Nugget Hunt on the Beach. Birch Bay. ☎ (360) 371-5004. Mid.
Picnic in the Park. Fremont. ☎ (206) 632-1500. Mid.
Pops on Us. Snoqualmie, Northwest Railway Museum. ☎ (425) 746-4025. Mid.
Solstice Parade. Fremont. ☎ (206) 547-7440. Mid.
Tour de Blast. Toutle. ☎ (360) 749-2192. Mid.
Wildflower Festival. Darrington. ☎ (888) 338-0976. Mid.
Winlock Egg Days. Winlock. ☎ (360) 785-4377. Mid.
Woodland Planters Days. Woodland. ☎ (360) 225-8450. Mid.
Darrington Rodeo. Darrington. ☎ (360) 436-1831. Late.
All Breed Dog Show. Mount Vernon. ☎ (425) 334-7396. Late.
Annual Gardens of Tacoma Tours. Tacoma. ☎ (253) 474-0400. Late.
Annual Tour of Private Gardens. Bellingham. ☎ (360) 738-6833. Late.
Berry Dairy Days Celebration. Burlington. ☎ (360) 757-0994. Late June or early July.
Buckley Log Show. Buckley. ☎ (360) 829-1921. Late.
City of SeaTac International Festival. SeaTac. ☎ (206) 241-9100. Late.
Corvette & High Performance Expo. Puyallup. ☎ (253) 841-5045. Late.
Day of the Accordion Festival & Competition. Seattle. ☎ (206) 684-7225. Late.
Doll & Teddy Bear Show. Puyallup. ☎ (503) 284-4062. Late.
Sandcastle Contest. Birch Bay. ☎ (360) 371-2070. Late.
Skamania Brewfest. Stevenson. ☎ (800) 989-9178. Late.
Sumas Community Days. Sumas. ☎ (360) 988-2104. Late.
Tacoma Highland Games. Graham. ☎ (253) 535-0887. Late.
Welcome to Summer. Eatonville, Northwest Trek Wildlife Park. ☎ (360) 832-6117. Late.

July

4th of July Extravaganza. Anacortes. ☎ (360) 293-5380.
4th of July Extravaganza. Blaine. ☎ (360) 371-2000.
4th of July Family Celebration & Fireworks. Bellevue. ☎ (425) 452-6885.
4th of July Parade. Eatonville. ☎ (360) 832-6206.
4th of July Parade. Tumwater. ☎ (360) 754-4160.
Annual Naturalization Ceremony. Seattle. ☎ (206) 443-1410. July 4.
Blast over Bellingham Bay. Bellingham. ☎ (360) 734-1330. July 4.
Burien 4th of July Parade. Burien. ☎ (800) 638-8613.
Bursts Over Port Gardner Bay. Everett. ☎ (425) 339-1113.
Family Fourth Fireworks. Lake Union. ☎ (206) 281-8111.
Fourth of Jul-Ivar's. Seattle. ☎ (206) 587-6500.
Fourth of July on the Water. Kirkland. ☎ (206) 623-1445.
Fourth of July Splash. Lake Meridan, Kent. Seattle Symphony. ☎ (253) 859-3991.
Grand Old Fourth Parade & Street Fair. Bainbridge Island. ☎ (206) 842-3700.
Independence Day Parade & Ice Cream Social. Stanwood. ☎ (360) 629-6110.
Old-Fashioned 4th of July. Oak Harbor. ☎ (360) 675-3535.
Paddle, Pedal, Puff Triathlon. Arlington. ☎ (360) 435-3708. July 4.
Ridgefield Celebrates the 4th of July. Ridgefield. ☎ (360) 887-0703.
Summerfest 4th of July. Chehalis. ☎ (800) 525-3323.
Summerfest–Independence Day Parade. Centralia. ☎ (800) 525-3323.
4th of July Parade. Burien. ☎ (206) 575-1633.
Antique Gas Engine & Tractor Show. Roy. ☎ (360) 357-4709. Early.
Arlington Festival. Arlington. ☎ (360) 435-3708. Early.
Book Signings & Food Demonstrations. Seattle, Columbia Winery. ☎ (425) 488-2776.
Chinatown International District Festival. Seattle. ☎ (206) 382-1197. Early.
Chuckanut Foot Race. Bellingham. ☎ (360) 650-8258. 🖳 www.bellingham.org. Early.
Dam Rod Run. Mossyrock. ☎ (360) 983-3511. Early.

Edmonds Museum Summer Market. Edmonds. ☎ (425) 775-5650. Early July to Late September.
Everson-Nooksack Summer Festival. Everson. ☎ (360) 966-3407. Early.
First Thursday Art Walk. Seattle, Pioneer Square. ☎ (206) 622-6235. Early.
Flyerworks Aerial Parade. Seattle, Museum of Flight. ☎ (206) 764-5720. Early.
Gorge Games. Stevenson. ☎ (541) 386-7774. Early.
Heritage Festival. Marymoor Park, Redmond. ☎ (206) 296-2964. Early.
Heritage Festival. Seattle. ☎ (206) 296-4528. Early.
Highland Games and Scottish Faire. Mount Vernon. ☎ (360) 416-4934. 🔲 www.celticarts.org/. Early.
Island Days. Bainbridge Island. ☎ (206) 842-2982. Early.
Kirkland Arts Center's Summerfest. Kirkland. ☎ (425) 822-7161. Early.
Marysville Sites & Bites Festival. Marysville. ☎ (360) 653-1269. Early.
Music in the Park. Bothell. ☎ (425) 486-7430. Early July to mid-August.
Outrigger Canoe and Paddle Races. Stevenson. ☎ (541) 386-7774. Early.
Redmond Derby Days. Redmond. ☎ (425) 885-4014. Early.
Seafair. Seattle. ☎ (206) 728-0123. 🔲 www.seafair.com/. Races, airshows, parades. Early July to early August.
Seafirst Freedom Fair. Tacoma. ☎ (253) 761-9433. Early.
Emerald Queen of Tacoma. Tacoma. ☎ (206) 232-2982. Early.
Slug Festival. Eatonville. ☎ (360) 832-6117. Early.
Steilacoom Apple Squeeze. Steilacoom. ☎ (253) 584-4133. Early.
Street Dance. Bainbridge Island. ☎ (206) 842-2982. Early.
Sultan Summer Shindig. Sultan. ☎ (360) 793-0983. Early.
Summer Celebration. Mercer Island. ☎ (206) 236-7285. Early.
Toledo Cheese Days. Toledo. ☎ (360) 864-4564. Early.
West Seattle Street Festival. Seattle. ☎ (206) 935-9966. Early.
ZooTunes. Seattle, Woodland Park Zoo. ☎ (206) 684-4800.
Ha Ya Days. Snohomish. ☎ (360) 568-4084. Family festival. Mid.
Bainbridge In Bloom. Bainbridge Island. ☎ (206) 842-7901. Mid.
Big Birthday Cake Bash, Northwest Trek Wildlife Park. Eatonville. ☎ (360) 832-6117. Mid.
Birch Bay Discovery Days. Birch Bay. ☎ (360) 371-5004. Mid.
Bite of Seattle. Seattle Center. ☎ (206) 232-2982. Mid.
Bluegrass Festival. Darrington. ☎ (888) 338-0976. Mid.
Brigade Encampment. Vancouver. ☎ (360) 696-7655. Mid.
Capital Lakefair. Olympia. ☎ (360) 943-7344. 🔲 www.lakefair.org/. Mid.
Children's Art Festival. Mount Vernon. ☎ (360) 336-6215. Mid.
Chinatown International District Summer Festival. Seattle. ☎ (206) 382-1197. Mid.
Cornucopia Sidewalk Sale. Kent. ☎ (253) 373-7697. Mid.
Fire in the Sky. Snohomish. ☎ (360) 568-4084. Mid.
Frontier Days Rodeo and Celebration. Springdale. ☎ (509) 258-4548. Mid.
Gig Harbor Art Festival. Gig Harbor. ☎ (253) 851-9346. Mid.
Harvest Days. Battle Ground. ☎ (360) 687-1510. Mid.
July Jubilee Days. White Center. ☎ (206) 763-4196. Mid.
Kalama Fair. Kalama. ☎ (360) 673-5323. Mid.
Kent Cornucopia Days. Kent. ☎ (253) 852-5466. Mid.
Lakewood Summerfest. Lakewood. ☎ (253) 582-9400. Mid.
Lewis County Roundup Rodeo. Centralia. ☎ (360) 330-2088. Mid.
Loganberry Festival. Greenbank. ☎ (360) 678-7700. Mid.
McPhail Raspberry Farm Festival. Lynden. ☎ (360) 354-5936. Mid.
Out of This World for Kids. Seattle, Museum of Flight. ☎ (206) 764-5715. Mid.
Rod, Custom & Classic Car Show. Snohomish. ☎ (360) 568-4084. Mid.
Shipwreck Day & Flea Market. Anacortes. ☎ (360) 293-7911. Mid.
South Puget Sound Air Show. Olympia and Tumwater. ☎ (360) 754-0793. Mid.

Vashon Island Strawberry Festival. Vashon. ☎ (206) 463-6217. Mid.
Whidbey Island Race Week. Oak Harbor. ☎ (360) 679-6399. Mid.
Aquafest. Lake Stevens. ☎ (425) 397-2344. Late.
Ballard Seafood Festival. Ballard. ☎ (206) 784-9705. Late.
Beethoven in Bellingham. Bellingham. ☎ (800) 335-5550. Late.
Brewster's Backyard Blues Picnic. Point Roberts. ☎ (360) 945-4545. Late.
Camas Days. Camas. ☎ (360) 834-2472. Late.
Castle Rock Fair. Castle Rock. ☎ (360) 274-8422. Late.
Celebrate Olympia. Olympia. ☎ (360) 753-8380. Late.
Centralia Antique Festival. Centralia. ☎ (360) 736-8730. Late.
Columbia Gorge Bluegrass Festival. Stevenson. ☎ (509) 427-8928. Late.
Cruise the Narrows. Gig Harbor. ☎ (253) 265-3648. Cars, airplanes, helicopters. Late.
Eatonville Arts Festival. Eatonville. ☎ (360) 832-3202. Late July to early August.
Enumclaw Street Fair. Enumclaw. ☎ (360) 825-1448. Late.
Festival of Music. Bellingham. ☎ (360) 676-5997 or ☎ (800) 335-5550. Late.
Garden Tour. Snohomish. ☎ (360) 568-7913. Late.
Jr. Grand Seafair Parade. Seattle. ☎ (206) 547-4417. Late.
King County Fair. Enumclaw. ☎ (206) 296-8888. Late.
Klickitat Canyon Days. Klickitat. ☎ (509) 369-2322. Late.
Music and Art Festival. Chehalis. ☎ (800) 525-3323. Late.
Music in the Park. Olympia. ☎ (360) 357-8948. Late.
Nubian Jam Community Festival. Everett. ☎ (425) 356-8082. Late.
Old-Time Fiddlers Stage Show & Campout. Stanwood. ☎ (360) 435-5848. Late.
Oregon Trail Days. Tenino. ☎ (360) 264-5075. Late.
Pacific Northwest Arts Fair. Bellevue, Bellevue Art Museum. ☎ (425) 454-3322. 🖳 www.bellevueart.org/. Late.
Pacific Northwest Scottish Highland Games. Enumclaw, King County Fairgrounds. ☎ (206) 522-2541. Late.
Renaissance Faire & Gothic Fantasy. Gig Harbor. ☎ (800) 359-5948. Late.
Rest of the Best Fest. Seattle. ☎ (206) 363-2048. Late.
Salmon Bake. Steilacoom. ☎ (253) 584-9410. Late.
San Juan Island Jazz Festival. Friday Harbor. ☎ (360) 378-5509. Late.
Sandcastle Contest. Birch Bay. ☎ (360) 371-2070. Late.
Seafair Indian Days Pow Wow. Seattle. ☎ (206) 285-4425. Late.
Sixth Street Fair & Taste of Bellevue. Bellevue. ☎ (425) 453-1223. Late.
Snoqualmie Railroad Days. Snoqualmie. ☎ (425) 888-0021. 🖳 www.trainmuseum.org. Late.
Street Fair. Enumclaw. ☎ (360) 825-1448. Late.
Waterland Festival. Des Moines. ☎ (206) 878-7000. Late.
Whatcom County Old Settlers Picnic. Ferndale. ☎ (360) 384-1866. Late.

August

Anacortes Arts Festival. Anacortes. ☎ (360) 293-6211. 🖳 www.cnw.com/~aaf/. Early.
   Brigade Encampment. Tacoma. ☎ (253) 591-5339. Early.
   Civil War Reenactment. Ferndale. ☎ (800) 260-5997. Early.
   Clark County Fair. Ridgefield. ☎ (360) 397-6180. Early.
   Cowlitz County Fair and Thunder Mountain Pro Rodeo. Longview. ☎ (360) 577-3121. Early.
   First Thursday Art Walk. Seattle, Pioneer Square. ☎ (206) 622-6235. Early.
   Festival of Fun. University Place. ☎ (253) 460-2500. Early.
   Greater Bothell Arts Fair. Bothell. ☎ (425) 821-1127. Early.
   Greenbank Artists Art Show. Greenbank. ☎ (360) 678-9970. Early.
   Heritage Art Festival. Tumwater. ☎ (360) 943-1805. Early.
   Kids Day. Fremont. ☎ (206) 632-1500. Early.
   Lake City Pioneer Days. Lake City. ☎ (206) 363-3287. Early.
   Pioneer Day. Key Center. ☎ (253) 884-3304. Early.

Proctor Summer Arts Festival. Tacoma. ☎ (253) 272-5767. Early.
Puget Sound Antique Tractor & Machinery. Lynden. ☎ (360) 354-3754. Early.
Railroad Days. Snoqualmie, Northwest Railway Museum. ☎ (425) 746-4025. Early.
Renaissance Faire. Olympia. ☎ (360) 943-9492. Early.
Show and Shine. Granite Falls. ☎ (360) 691-5244. Car show. Early.
Stanwood-Camano Community Fair. Stanwood. ☎ (360) 445-2806. Early.
Sumner Summer Festival. Sumner. ☎ (253) 863-8300. Early.
TibetFest. Seattle. ☎ (206) 684-7200. Early.
Washington Shakespeare Festival. Olympia. ☎ (360) 943-9492.
Zoo Tunes. Seattle, Woodland Park Zoo. ☎ (206) 684-4800.
A Taste of Edmonds. Edmonds. ☎ (425) 670-9112. Mid.
Alpine Days. Snoqualmie, Northwest Railway Museum. ☎ (425) 746-4025. Mid.
Arts and Crafts Festival. Coupeville. ☎ (360) 678-5116. Mid.
Bubble Festival. Seattle. ☎ (206) 443-2001. 🖳 www.pacsci.org/. Mid.
Garlic Festival. Arlington. ☎ (360) 403-8714. Mid.
Hopefest. Darrington. ☎ (800) 965-4673. Mid.
Hot Air Balloon/Folk Festival–Civil War Reenactment. Ferndale. ☎ (360) 384-3042. Mid.
Island County Fair. Langley. ☎ (360) 221-4677. Mid.
Kent Summer Concert Series. Kent. ☎ (253) 859-3991. Mid.
Kidsfair. Seattle. ☎ (206) 684-7200. Mid.
Morton Loggers Jubilee. Morton. ☎ (360) 498-5250. Mid.
North Whidbey Lions Club Old Car Show. Oak Harbor. ☎ (360) 675-5628. 🖳 www.whidbeynet.net/ nwlions/carshow.htm. Mid.
Northwest Washington Fair. Lynden. ☎ (360) 354-4111. Mid.
Pierce County Fair. Graham. ☎ (253) 843-1173. Mid.
Sandcastle Contest. Birch Bay. ☎ (360) 371-2070. Mid.
Skagit County Fair. Mount Vernon. ☎ (360) 336-9453. Mid.
Skamania County Fair. Stevenson. ☎ (509) 427-5588. Mid.
Southwest Washington Fair. Chehalis. ☎ (360) 736-6072. Mid.
Taste of Edmonds. Edmonds. ☎ (425) 670-9112. Mid.
Threshing Bee and Antique Tractor Show. Monroe. ☎ (360) 794-0189. Mid.
World Famous Salmon Bar-B-Que. Anacortes. ☎ (360) 293-3012. Mid.
All Breed Dog Show. Enumclaw, King County Fairgrounds. ☎ (206) 878-3891/☎ (360) 598-5645. Late.
Antique Aircraft Fly-In. Vancouver. ☎ (360) 892-2155. Late.
Art in the Park. Monroe. ☎ (360) 794-0364. Late.
Art Walk. Centralia. ☎ (360) 748-0291. Late.
Bigfoot Daze. Carson. ☎ (509) 427-4441. Late.
Canterbury Faire. Kent. ☎ (253) 859-3991. Late.
Celebrate Shoreline. Shoreline. ☎ (206) 546-5041. Late.
Evergreen State Fair. Monroe. ☎ (425) 339-3309. Late.
Festival of the River. Arlington. ☎ (360) 435-2755. Late.
Fife Community Festival. Fife. ☎ (253) 761-9433. Late.
Founder's Day. Vancouver. ☎ (360) 696-7655. Late.
Good Olde Days. Concrete. ☎ (360) 853-7042. Late.
Hub City Car Show. Centralia. ☎ (800) 525-3323. Late.
Kalama Car Show. Kalama. ☎ (360) 578-9303. Late.
Lynnwood Trolley Days. Lynnwood. ☎ (425) 712-1800. 🖳 www.trolleydays.org/. Late.
Mukilteo Lighthouse Festival. Mukilteo. ☎ (425) 355-2514. Late.
Old Timers' Day. Longbranch. ☎ (253) 884-4440. Late.
Rainier Valley Heritage Festival. Seattle. ☎ (206) 725-2010. Late.
Steam Threshing and Gas Show. Toledo. ☎ (360) 864-4917. Late.
Sunshine Hill Garlic Fest. Chehalis. ☎ (360) 740-4411. Late.
Three Rivers Air Show. Kelso. ☎ (360) ☎ (425) 3688. Late.
Unique Tin Car Show and Cruise. Longview. ☎ (360) 636-1969. Late.

September

Bumbershoot. Seattle. ☎ (206) 684-7200. 💻 www.bumbershoot.org. Arts and music. Early.

   Duck Race. Enumclaw. ☎ (360) 825-2505. Early.

   Fall Festival. Everson. ☎ (360) 966-3407. Early.

   First Thursday Art Walk. Seattle, Pioneer Square. ☎ (206) 622-6235. Early.

   Foofaraw. Olympia. ☎ (360) 357-3362. Military appreciation day. Early.

   Harbor Days. Olympia. ☎ (800) 788-8847. Early.

   Highlander Festival. Kelso. ☎ (360) 423-0900. Early.

   Salmon Homecoming Celebration. Seattle. ☎ (206) 386-4315. 💻 www.seattleaquar
ium.org/. Early.

   SausageFest. Vancouver. ☎ (360) 696-4407. Early.

   Sedro-Woolley Founders' Day. Sedro-Woolley. ☎ (888) 225-8365. Early.

   Sumas Junior Rodeo. Sumas. ☎ (360) 988-2104. Early.

   Western Washington Fair. Puyallup. ☎ (253) 841-5045. Early to late September.

   Art & Soul, the Vancouver Arts Festival. Vancouver. ☎ (360) 693-2978. Mid.

   Commencement Bay Maritime Fest. Tacoma. ☎ (253) 272-1005. Mid.

   Fall Plant Sale. Federal Way, Rhododendron Species Botanical Garden. ☎ (253) 661-
9377. Mid.

   Fiestas Patrias—Hispanic Cultural Festival. Seattle. ☎ (206) 706-7775. Mid.

   Fort Vancouver Candlelight Tour. Vancouver. ☎ (360) 696-7655. Mid.

   Historic Home Tour. Snohomish. ☎ (360) 568-2526. Mid.

   Pacific Rim Art Exposition. Seattle Center. ☎ (253) 761-9510. Late.

   Pedals-n-Paws Bike & Dog Parade. Kirkland. ☎ (425) 822-7066. Mid.

   Puyallup Fair. Puyallup. One of the largest fairs in the country. ☎ (253) 841-5045. Mid.

   Taste! Kirkland. Kirkland. ☎ (425) 822-7066. Mid.

   Thunder Mountain Motor Madness. Enumclaw. ☎ (360) 825-7666. Mid.

   Tilth Organic Harvest Fair. Seattle. ☎ (206) 633-0451. Mid.

   Victory Music's Great Northwest Shanty Sing-Off. Tacoma. ☎ (253) 428-0832. Mid.

   Arts of the Terrace. Mountlake Terrace. ☎ (425) 776-9173. Late.

   Classic Car and Hot Rod Display. Snohomish. ☎ (360) 568-2526. Late.

   Harvest Swap Meet. Chehalis. ☎ (360) 273-6961.

   NWCHA Futurity and Derby. Camas. ☎ (360) 834-0984. Cutting horses. Late.

   Vancouver Wine & Jazz Festival. Vancouver. ☎ (360) 906-0441. 💻 www.vancouver
winejazz.com/. Late.

   Washington Draft Horse and Mule Extravaganza. Monroe. ☎ (206) 246-3671. Late.

October

Artists in the Gorge Series. Stevenson. ☎ (509) 427-5471.

   Candlelight Tour. Tacoma. ☎ (253) 591-5339. Early.

   Children's Day. Olympia. ☎ (360) 753-8380. Early.

   Cider Fest. Key Center. ☎ (253) 396-6812. Early.

   Cloud Mountain Farm Fruit Festival. Everson. ☎ (360) 966-5859. Early.

   Coffee Fest Seattle. Seattle, Washington State Convention & Trade Center. ☎ (206)
232-2982. Early.

   Deming Oktoberfest. Deming. ☎ (360) 592-3051. Early.

   Everett Sausage Fest. Everett. ☎ (425) 349-7014. Early.

   Fall Bulb Sale. Seattle, Arboretum Foundation. ☎ (206) 325-4510. Early.

   Fall Color. Federal Way, Rhododendron Species Botanical Garden. ☎ (253) 661-9377.

   Festa Italiana. Seattle. ☎ (206) 282-0627. Early.

   First Thursday Art Walk. Seattle, Pioneer Square. ☎ (206) 622-6235. Early.

   Fremont Oktoberfest. Fremont. ☎ (206) 632-1500. Early.

   Harvest at Stoney Ridge Farm. Everson. ☎ (360) 966-3919. Early.

   Harvest Days Celebration. Centralia. ☎ (800) 525-3323. Early.

   International Travel Expo. Seattle, Seattle Center. ☎ (206) 382-0067. Early.

   Lakewood Crazy Days. Lakewood. ☎ (360) 652-8642. Early.

   Lark at the Mountain Festival. Ashford. ☎ (360) 569-0910. Early.

Lynden Lions Club Model Train Show. Lynden. ☎ (360) 354-2993. Early.
Oktoberfest. Vashon Island. ☎ (206) 463-6217. Early.
Old Apple Tree Celebration. Vancouver. ☎ (360) 696-8171. Early.
Railroad Days. Granite Falls. ☎ (360) 691-6441. Early.
Rain Fest. Longview. ☎ (360) 423-8400. Early.
Salmon Days Festival. Issaquah. ☎ (206) 270-2532. Early.
Seattle Airline Collectibles Show. Museum of Flight. ☎ (425) 485-8780. Early.
Uniquely Whidbey Showcase. Coupeville. ☎ (360) 678-5434. Early.
University Place Cider Squeeze. University Place. ☎ (253) 460-2530. Early.
Wild Mushroom Show. Seattle. ☎ (206) 522-6031. Early.
Winter Woodlands Quilt Show. Renton. ☎ (253) 631-3546. Early.
A Country Collection Craft & Antique. Lynden. ☎ (360) 966-5573. Mid.
Harvest Festival. Lynden. ☎ (360) 354-5995. Mid.
Pumpkin Fest. Custer. ☎ (360) 366-4372. Mid.
Skandia Ball. Seattle. ☎ (206) 784-7470. Mid.
Bug-a-Boo. Seattle, Woodland Park Zoo. ☎ (206) 684-4800. Late.
Columbia River Pow Wow. Roosevelt. ☎ (541) 296-8816. Late.
Enumclaw Merchants Halloween. Enumclaw. ☎ (360) 825-1448. Late.
Halloween Fun Fest. Battle Ground. ☎ (360) 687-1510.
Halloween Hoot 'n Howl. Eatonville. ☎ (360) 832-6117.
Halloween Parade. Sedro-Woolley. ☎ (888) 225-8365.
Halloween Train. Snoqualmie, Northwest Railway Museum. ☎ (425) 746-4025.
Halloween Trick or Treating. Seattle, Pike Place Market. ☎ (206) 587-0351.
Halloween. Vashon Island. ☎ (206) 463-6217.
Harvest Festival/Pumpkin Contest. Ferndale. ☎ (360) 384-3042. Late.
Hillcrest Haunted Forest. Mount Vernon. ☎ (360) 336-6215. Late.
Kent Parks Halloween Party. Kent. ☎ (253) 859-3991. Late.
Merchants' Halloween. Enumclaw. ☎ (360) 825-1448. October 31.
Northwest Bookfest. Seattle. ☎ (206) 378-1883. Late.
Seattle Cooks! Seattle. ☎ (206) 516-3052. Gourmet food and kitchen show. Late.
Trick 'R Treat Scavenger Hunt. Kent. ☎ (253) 813-6976. Late.
Trick or Treat on the Waterfront. Seattle. ☎ (206) 386-4320. 🔲 www.seattleaquar ium.org/. Late.
Trick-or-Treat in Fremont. Fremont. ☎ (206) 632-1500. October 31.

November

Central Whidbey Dance Bonanza. Greenbank. ☎ (360) 678-5434. Early.
Hmong New Year Celebration. Seattle. ☎ (206) 684-7200. Early.
A Cloth Doll's Christmas. Bellevue. ☎ (425) 455-1116. Mid.
Cultural Crossroads. Bellevue. ☎ (206) 443-1410. Mid.
Home for the Holidays. Bellingham. ☎ (360) 676-1891.
Sculptor's Workshop Semi Annual Pottery Sale. Edmonds. ☎ (425) 774-8282.
Seattle International Auto Show. Seattle. ☎ (206) 542-3551. 🔲 www.seattleauto show.com. Mid.
Whatcom Art Guild Holiday Show and Sale. Bellingham. ☎ (360) 398-1411.
Bellevue: The Magic Season. Bellevue. ☎ (425) 453-1223. Late.
Christmas Tree Lighting and Santa's Visit. Edmonds. ☎ (425) 776-6711. Late.
Christmas Tree Lighting. Granite Falls. ☎ (360) 691-6441. Late.
Dickens of a Christmas. Centralia. ☎ (800) 525-3323. Late.
Fantasy Lights. Tacoma. ☎ (253) 798-4176 or ☎ (253) 798-3330. Drive-through display. Late.
Opening Night, Santa Comes to Town. Snohomish. ☎ (360) 568-2526. Late.
Proctor Holiday Express. Tacoma. ☎ (253) 272-5767. Model trains and railroad memorabilia. Late.
Winterfest. Gig Harbor. ☎ (253) 857-3530. Late.
Zoolights. Tacoma. ☎ (253) 591-5337. Late.

December

Winterfest. Seattle Center. ☎ (206) 684-7200.
  A Victorian Country Christmas. Puyallup. ☎ (253) 770-0777. Early.
  Annual Tree Lighting. Tenino. ☎ (360) 264-5075. Early.
  Argosy **Christmas Ship Festival.** Seattle. ☎ (206) 623-1445. Early.
  Chehalis Santa Parade. Chehalis. ☎ (800) 525-3323. Early.
  Christmas at Fort Vancouver. Vancouver. ☎ (360) 696-7655. Early.
  Christmas Celebration. Battle Ground. ☎ (360) 687-1510. Early.
  Christmas Festivities. Mossyrock. ☎ (360) 983-8470. Early.
  Christmas in Kalama. Kalama. ☎ (360) 673-6299. Early.
  Christmas in the Gorge. Stevenson. ☎ (800) 989-9178. Early.
  Christmas Parade & Tree Lighting. Longview. ☎ (360) 577-2557. Early.
  Christmas Parade. Auburn. ☎ (253) 833-0700. Early.
  Christmas Parade. Eatonville. ☎ (360) 832-4000. Early.
  Christmas Tree Lighting. Burlington. ☎ (360) 757-0994. Early.
  Dickens Dinner. Coupeville. ☎ (800) 366-4097. 📖 www.captainwhidbey.com/dick
ens.htm. Early.
  Historic Holiday Home Tour. Coupeville. ☎ (360) 678-3310. Early.
  Holiday Bed & Breakfast Tour. Langley. ☎ (360) 221-6765. Early.
  Holiday Port. Bellingham. ☎ (360) 734-1330. Early.
  It's All Happening Downtown. Vancouver. ☎ (360) 693-2978. Early.
  Jingle Bell Run/Walk. Bellingham. ☎ (800) 542-0295. Early.
  Lighted Christmas Parade. Enumclaw. ☎ (360) 825-7666. Early.
  Look-a-Rama. Mossyrock. ☎ (360) 983-3702. Early.
  Merrysville for the Holidays. Marysville. ☎ (360) 651-5085. Early.
  Old-Fashioned Christmas. Ferndale. ☎ (360) 384-6416. Early.
  Ridgefield Hometown Celebration. Ridgefield. ☎ (360) 887-0703. Early.
  Santa Parade. Puyallup. ☎ (253) 840-2631. Early.
  Santa's City of Light Christmas Parade. Sedro-Woolley. ☎ (888) 225-8365. Early.
  Sinterklaas Lighted Christmas Parade. Lynden. ☎ (360) 354-5995. Early.
  The Lights of Christmas. Stanwood. ☎ (800) 228-6724. December.
  The Magic of Christmas. Chehalis. ☎ (360) 736-6486. Early.
  Tidefest. Gig Harbor. ☎ (253) 851-6131. Early.
  University Place Holiday Tree Lighting. University Place. ☎ (253) 460-2500. Early.
  Uptown Gallery Walk. Bellingham. ☎ (360) 647-6772. Early.
  Winter on Whidbey. Greenbank. ☎ (360) 678-7700.
  World Market. Seattle. ☎ (206) 443-1410.
  Christmas Lighting Contest. Birch Bay. ☎ (360) 371-5004. Mid- to late December.
  Christmas Parlor Tour. Snohomish. ☎ (360) 568-2526. Mid.
  Scandinavian Christmas Festival. Bellingham. ☎ (360) 733-5597. Mid.
  Festival of Trees. Castle Rock. ☎ (360) 274-6603. Late.
  Seattle Christmas Ships. Various locations. ☎ (206) 461-5840. Late.

Coastal Washington

January

Student Art Show. Port Orchard. ☎ (360) 876-3693. Mid.

February

Bainbridge Island Quarterly Arts Walk. Bainbridge Island. ☎ (206) 842-0985. Early.
  Taste of the North Beach. Ocean Shores. ☎ (800) 874-6737. Early.
  Viking Jazz Festival. Poulsbo. ☎ (360) 598-8472. Early.
  Art on the Hill. Forks. ☎ (800) 443-6757 Mid.
  Chilly Hilly Bicycle Ride. Bainbridge Island. ☎ (206) 522-2453. Late.
  Kitsap Quilters Show. Poulsbo. ☎ (360) 779-4848. Late.

March

Beachcomber's Fun Fair. Ocean Shores. ☎ (800) 874-6737. Early.
  Elegant Flea. Sequim. ☎ (360) 683-8110. Antiques and collectibles. Early.
  Environmental Explorations. Belfair. ☎ (360) 275-0373. Early.
  Annual Beachcombers Driftwood Show. Grayland. ☎ (800) 473-6018. Mid.
  Grays Harbor Indoor Pro Rodeo. Elma. ☎ (360) 482-2734. Mid.
  St. Patrick's Day Parade. Bainbridge Island. ☎ (206) 842-2982. Mid.
  Port Townsend Marine Science Center Boat Tours. Port Townsend. ☎ (360) 385-5582. Late.
  Port Townsend Victorian Festival. Port Townsend. ☎ (888) 698-1116. Late.

April

Art Guild Display. Bremerton. ☎ (360) 478-7934. April.
  Old Time Fiddlers Fest. Shelton. ☎ (800) 576-2021. Early.
  Seagull Calling Contest. Port Orchard. ☎ (800) 982-8139. Early.
  Sequim Open Aire Market. Sequim. ☎ (360) 683-9446. April through October.
  Shoalwater Bay Sobriety Pow-Wow. Westport. ☎ (360) 267-6766. Early.
  Bed and Breakfast Tour. Kitsap Peninsula. ☎ (360) 297-8200. Mid.
  Ragtime Rhode Dixieland Jazz Festival. Long Beach. ☎ (800) 451-2542. Mid.
  Rainfest. Forks. ☎ (800) 443-6757. Mid.
  Shellfish Shindig. Hood Canal. ☎ (360) 796-4415. Mid.
  World Class Crab Races & Crab Feed. Westport. ☎ (800) 345-6223. Mid.
  Antique/Collectible Show & Gem Show. Elma. ☎ (360) 482-2651. Late.
  Bonsai Show. Sequim. ☎ (360) 683-7712. Late April to early May.

May

Bainbridge Island Quarterly Arts Walk. Bainbridge Island. ☎ (206) 842-0985. Early.
  Bronze Works Art Fair. Shelton. ☎ (800) 576-2021. Early.
  Discovery Days. Aberdeen. ☎ (800) 200-5239. Early.
  Festival of Colors. Ocean Shores. ☎ (800) 762-3224. Early.
  Grapeview Day. Grapeview. ☎ (360) 275-4542. Early.
  Hoodsport Oyster Bite. Hoodsport. ☎ (360) 877-9474. Early.
  Irrigation Festival. Sequim. ☎ (360) 683-6197. Early.
  Loyalty Day Celebration. Long Beach Peninsula. ☎ (800) 451-2542. Early.
  Matlock Old Timers' Historical Fair & Exhibition. Matlock. ☎ (800) 576-2021. Early.
  Olympia Dog Fanciers Show. Elma. ☎ (360) 482-2651. Early.
  Rhododendron Show. Shelton. ☎ (800) 576-2021. Early.
  Armed Forces Festival and Parade. Bremerton. ☎ (360) 479-3579. Mid.
  Rhododendron Festival. Port Townsend. ☎ (888) 365-6978. Mid.
  Mason County Forest Festival. Shelton. ☎ (800) 576-2021. Late.
  Oyster Stampede. South Bend. ☎ (360) 942-5572. Late.
  Shepherd's Festival. Sequim. ☎ (360) 683-6495. Late.
  World's Longest Garage Sale. Long Beach Peninsula. ☎ (800) 451-2542. Late.

June

Art Guild Display. Bremerton. ☎ (360) 478-7934. June.
  Associated Arts Photography & Fine Arts Shows. Ocean Shores. ☎ (800) 762-3224. Early.
  Classic Car/Motorcycle Show and BBQ. Skamokawa. ☎ (360) 795-8107. Early.
  International Kite Challenge. Ocean Shores. ☎ (800) 762-3224. Early.
  June Faire. Silverdale. ☎ (360) 479-3499. Early.
  Medieval Faire. Bremerton. ☎ (360) 297-4751. 🔖 http://lazarusfire.net/junefaire/. Early.
  Poulsbo Gallery Walk. Poulsbo. ☎ (360) 779-4848. Early.
  Trawlerfest. Poulsbo. ☎ (360) 775-4848. Early.
  Chautauqua and Opening of Farmers Market. Raymond. ☎ (360) 942-5419. Mid.

Duck Derby. Port Angeles. ☎ (360) 683-3840. Mid.
Grandmother's Club Strawberry Festival. Poulsbo. ☎ (360) 779-5209. Mid.
Northwest Garlic Festival. Ocean Park. ☎ (800) 451-2542. ▣ www.opwa.com/garlic/. Mid.
Olympic Music Festival. Quilcene. ☎ (206) 527-8839. Mid-June to mid-July.
Art Show. Belfair. ☎ (360) 895-1338. Late.
Blessing of the Fleet. Westport. ☎ (800) 345-6223. Late.
Centrum's Festival of American Fiddle Tunes Workshop. Port Townsend. ☎ (360) 385-3102. ▣ www.centrum.org/. Late.
Centrum's Port Townsend Country Blues Workshop. Port Townsend. ☎ (360) 385-3102. ▣ www.cen trum.org/. Late.
Fathers Day Salmon Bake. Manchester. ☎ (360) 871-3921. Late.
Fathoms O'Fun Grand Parade & Carnival. Port Orchard. ☎ (800) 982-8139. Late.
International Elwha River Pow Wow. Port Angeles. ☎ (360) 457-4196. Late.
Island Days & Street Dance. Bainbridge Island. ☎ (206) 842-2982. Late June to mid-July.
Leap for Learning. Shelton. ☎ (425) 882-0820. Parachute festival. Late.
NW Stunt Kite Championships. Long Beach. ☎ (800) 451-2542. Late.
Pacific Days Arts & Music Festival. Pacific. ☎ (253) 929-1100. Late.
Puget Sound Sea Kayak Festival. Poulsbo. ☎ (360) 697-6095. Late.
Sand & Sawdust at the Shore. Ocean Shores. ☎ (800) 762-3224. Late.
Skandia Midsommerfest. Poulsbo. ☎ (206) 784-7470. Late.
Strawberry Festival. Bainbridge Island. ☎ (206) 780-2313. Late.
SummerFest. Belfair. ☎ (877) 484-7486. Late.
Sunbonnet Sue's Quilt Show. Sequim. ☎ (360) 681-4530. Late.
Swede Day Midsummer. Rochester. ☎ (360) 273-8949. Late.

July

4th of July Street Fair & Parade. Ocean Park. ☎ (800) 451-2542. ▣ www.opwa.com/events.html.
Bainbridge in Bloom. Bainbridge Island. ☎ (206) 842-7901. Early.
Celebrate Hoodsport. Hoodsport. ☎ (800) 576-2021. July 4.
Centrum's Festival of American Fiddle Tunes. Port Townsend. ☎ (360) 385-3102. ▣ www.cen trum.org/. Early.
Clallam Bay/Sekiu Fun Days. Clallam Bay. ☎ (360) 963-2346. Early.
Fathoms O'Fun Fireworks Show. Port Orchard. ☎ (800) 982-8139. July 4.
Fire O'er the Water. Ocean City. ☎ (800) 286-4552. Early.
Forks Old-Fashioned 4th of July. Forks. ☎ (800) 443-6757.
Grand Old 4th & Parade. Bainbridge Island. ☎ (206) 842-3700.
Husum Days. Husum. ☎ (509) 493-2996. Early.
Independence Day Celebration. Sequim. ☎ (360) 683-8110.
Independence Day Fireworks. Long Beach. ☎ (800) 451-2542.
Jefferson Days. Port Hadlock. ☎ (360) 379-5380. Early.
Kite Festival. Westport. ☎ (800) 345-6223. Early.
McCleary Bear Festival. McCleary. ☎ (360) 495-4425. Early.
Ol' Fashioned 4th. Westport. ☎ (800) 473-6018.
Old-Fashioned 4th of July. Kingston. ☎ (360) 297-3813.
Poulsbo's 3rd of July. Poulsbo. ☎ (360) 779-8018.
Tahuya Day. Tahuya. ☎ (800) 576-2021. Early.
Theler Children's Fair. Belfair. ☎ (360) 275-4898. Early.
Tokeland Parade. Tokeland. ☎ (360) 267-7006. Early.
Voyages of Rediscovery. Tall Ship *Lady Washington*. Aberdeen. ☎ (800) 200-5239.
Allyn Days/Salmon Bake. Allyn. ☎ (360) 275-5002. Mid.
Bald Eagle Festival. Cathlamet. ☎ (360) 795-3545. Mid.
Gorge Games. Hood River. ☎ (541) 386-7774. Week-long sports and music festival at Washington and Oregon sides of the Columbia River. Mid.

Harrison Foundation Golf Classic. Bremerton. ☎ (360) 792-6760. Mid.
Lavender Festival. Sequim. ☎ (360) 683-6197. Mid.
Quileute Days. La Push. ☎ (800) 443-6757. Mid.
Wooden Boat Festival. Cathlamet. ☎ (360) 795-3420. Mid.
Arts in Action. Port Angeles. ☎ (360) 452-2363. Late.
Centrum's Airtouch Jazz Port Townsend. Port Townsend. ☎ (360) 385-3102. 💻
www.centrum.org/. Late.
   Forks Fly-In. Forks. Aircraft and festivals. ☎ (800) 443-6757. Late.
   Grapeview Water Festival. Grapeview. ☎ (360) 275-2587. Late.
   Mason County Fair. Shelton. ☎ (800) 576-2021. Late.
   North Kitsap Arts & Crafts Festival. Port Gamble. ☎ (360) 697-2735. Late.
   Perch Fishing Derby. Pacific Beach. ☎ (800) 286-4552. Late July to early August.
   Poulsbo Boat Rendezvous. Poulsbo. ☎ (360) 373-6154. Wooden boats. Late.
   Sandsations Sand Sculpture Contest. Long Beach. ☎ (800) 451-2542. Late.
   Sun & Surf Run (H.O.G.S.). Ocean Shores. ☎ (800) 762-3224. Harley Davidsons and
more. Late.

August

Bainbridge Island Quarterly Arts Walk. Bainbridge Island. ☎ (206) 842-0985. Early.
   Copalis Heritage Days. Copalis Beach. ☎ (360) 289-0528. Early.
   International Nautical Chainsaw Carving. Grayland. ☎ (800) 572-0177. Early.
   International Nautical Chainsaw Carving. Westport. ☎ (800) 572-0177. Early.
   Joyce Daze Wild Blackberry Festival. Joyce. ☎ (360) 928-3892. Early.
   Marrowstone Music Festival Workshops. Port Townsend. ☎ (360) 385-3102. 💻
www.centrum.org/. August.
   Mustangs by the Bay. Port Orchard. ☎ (800) 982-8139. Car show. Early.
   NRA-Sanctioned Rodeo. Long Beach. ☎ (800) 451-2542. Early.
   Rotary Salmon Bake. Sequim. ☎ (360) 683-3840. Early.
   Surf Festival and Long Board Contest. Westport. ☎ (800) 345-6223. Early.
   The Cruz. Port Orchard. ☎ (800) 982-8139. Custom cars and hot rods. Early.
   Willipa Harbor Festival. Raymond. ☎ (360) 942-5419. Early.
   Crosby Days. Seabeck. ☎ (360) 830-4270. Mid.
   Filipino-American Day. Bainbridge Island. ☎ (206) 780-2313. Mid.
   Grays Harbor County Fair. Elma. ☎ (360) 482-2651. Mid.
   Jazz and Oysters. Oysterville. ☎ (800) 451-2542. Mid.
   Jefferson County Fair. Port Townsend. ☎ (888) 365-6978. Mid.
   Swing City Arts and Crafts Show. Bremerton. ☎ (360) 377-8888. Mid.
   Touch a Truck. Poulsbo. ☎ (360) 779-4848. Mid.
   Wahkiakum County Fair. Skamokawa. ☎ (360) 795-3480. Mid.
   Washington State International Kite Festival. Long Beach. ☎ (800) 451-2542. 💻
www.kitefestival. com/. Mid.
   World of Outlaws Northwest Tour. Elma. ☎ (360) 568-2529. Sprint Cars. Mid.
   Arts by the Bay. Poulsbo. ☎ (360) 697-1397. Late.
   Chief Seattle Days. Suquamish. ☎ (360) 598-3311. Late.
   Clallam County Fair. Port Angeles. ☎ (360) 452-2363. Late.
   Kids' Daze. Port Orchard. ☎ (800) 982-8139. Late.
   Kiwanis' Classic Car Show. Port Townsend. ☎ (888) 365-6978. Late.
   Makah Days. Neah Bay. ☎ (360) 645-2201. Late.
   Olalla Bluegrass Festival. Olalla. ☎ (253) 857-5285. Late.
   Pacific County Fair. Menlo. ☎ (360) 934-5412. Late.
   Peninsula Junior Rodeo. Port Angeles. ☎ (360) 452-6260. Late.
   Polynesian Luau & Heritage Fair. Shelton. ☎ (800) 576-2021. Late.
   Seattle Symphony. Port Townsend. ☎ (360) 385-3102. 💻 www.centrum.org/. Late.

September

Art Guild Display. Bremerton. ☎ (360) 478-7934.
    Arts & Craft Show. Ocean Shores. ☎ (800) 762-3224. Early.
    Blue Grass Festival. Port Angeles. ☎ (360) 417-8878. Early.
    Bluegrass Festival. Kingston. ☎ (360) 297-3813. Early.
    Bremerton Blackberry Festival. Bremerton. ☎ (360) 377-3041. Early.
    Come and Play on Labor Day. South Bend. ☎ (360) 875-5533. Early.
    Festival in the Park. Ocean Park. ☎ (800) 451-2542. 🖳 www.opwa.com/events.html. Early.
    Kelper Parade and Shake Rat Olympics. Pacific Beach. ☎ (360) 276-4525. Early.
    Rod Run to the End of the World. Ocean Park. ☎ (800) 451-2542. Classic cars. Early.
    Seafood Festival. Westport. ☎ (800) 345-6223. Early.
    Up Your Wind Kite Festival. Pacific Beach. ☎ (360) 276-4525. Early.
    Wooden Boat Festival. Port Townsend. ☎ (360) 385-3628. Early.
    Fall Historic Homes Tour. Port Townsend. ☎ (888) 365-6978. Mid.
    Forest Storytelling Festival. Port Angeles. ☎ (360) 457-3169. Mid.
    Operation Shore Patrol. Westport. ☎ (800) 345-6223. Thirty miles of garage sales. Mid.
    Sand Castle & Sculpture Contest. Pacific Beach. ☎ (360) 276-4525. Mid.
    Septemberfest. Poulsbo. ☎ (360) 779-4848. Mid.
    Longest Beach Cribbage Classic. Long Beach. ☎ (800) 451-2542. Late.
    Oyster Open Surf Kayak Festival. Westport. ☎ (360) 697-6095. Late.

October

Cranberrian Festival. Ilwaco. ☎ (800) 451-2542. Early.
    Great Kinetic Sculpture Race. Port Townsend. ☎ (888) 365-6978. Early.
    Hickory Shirt/Heritage Days. Forks. ☎ (800) 443-6757. Early.
    Oysterfest. Shelton. ☎ (800) 576-2021. Early.
    Scandia Valley Pumpkin Tours. Poulsbo. ☎ (360) 779-3353.
    Marang African Music and Dance Ensemble. Port Angeles. ☎ (360) 457-5411. Early.
    First Lutheran Church Annual Lutefisk Dinner. Poulsbo. ☎ (360) 779-2622. Mid.
    Halloween Costume and Picture Hunt Parade. Kingston. ☎ (360) 297-3813.
    Pumpkin Festival. Port Orchard. ☎ (800) 982-8139. Late.
    Water Music Festival. Long Beach Peninsula. (800) 451-2542. 🖳 www.watermusic festival.com. ☎ Late.

November

Art Guild Display. Bremerton. ☎ (360) 478-7934.
    Arts and Crafts Sale. Sequim. ☎ (360) 683-8110. Early.
    Bainbridge Island Quarterly Arts Walk. Bainbridge Island. ☎ (206) 842-0985. Early.
    Christmas Cottage Crafts Fair. Port Angeles. ☎ (360) 452-3543. Early.
    Cranberry Harvest Festival. Grayland. ☎ (800) 473-6018. Early.
    Dixieland Jazz Festival. Ocean Shores. ☎ (800) 762-3224. Early.
    Holiday Bazaar. Ilwaco. ☎ (800) 541-2542. Early.
    North Kitsap Holiday Fest. Poulsbo. ☎ (360) 779-4408. Early.
    Wine, Brew & Cheese Tasting. Forks. ☎ (800) 443-6757. Mid.
    Festival of Trees. Bremerton. ☎ (360) 792-6760. Late.
    Festival of Trees. Port Angeles. ☎ (360) 457-3141. Late.
    Holiday Heritage House. Poulsbo. ☎ (360) 799-4848. Late.
    Santa Arrives on the Peninsula. Long Beach. ☎ (800) 541-2542. Late.
    Winter Fan-ta-Sea Arts & Crafts Show. Ocean Shores. ☎ (800) 762-3224. Late.

December

B & B Holiday Open Parlor. Port Townsend. ☎ (360) 385-7911. Early.
    Bainbridge Studio Tours. Bainbridge Island. ☎ (206) 842-7901. Early.

Christmas in the Country. Bainbridge Island. ☎ (206) 842-6883. Early.
Christmas Parade and Tree Lighting. Raymond. ☎ (360) 942-5419. Early.
Community Christmas Concert. Sequim. ☎ (360) 683-6197. Early.
Grayland Christmas Tree Lighting. Grayland. ☎ (800) 473-6018. Early.
Kingston Country Christmas. Kingston. ☎ (360) 297-3813. Early.
Lighted Boat Parade. Poulsbo. ☎ (360) 779-4848. Early.
Nautical Christmas Lane. Port Orchard. ☎ (800) 982-8139. Early.
Port Gamble Country Christmas. Port Gamble. ☎ (360) 598-5591. Early.
Santa By the Sea. Westport. ☎ (800) 345-6223. Early.
Shelton Shines at Christmastime. Shelton. ☎ (800) 576-2021. Early.
Victorian Holidays. Port Townsend. ☎ (888) 365-6978. Early.
Yule Fest. Poulsbo. ☎ (360) 779-5209. Early.
Elma Christmas Parade. Elma. ☎ (360) 482-0129. Mid.
Lucia Festival of Light. Rochester. ☎ (360) 273-8949. Traditional Swedish Christmas pageant. Mid.

Eastern Washington

January

A Joyful Noise. Wenatchee. ☎ (509) 664-3340. Early.
Columbia River Circuit Rodeo Finals. Yakima. ☎ (509) 454-3663. Early.
Mid Columbia Farm Forum & Ag Show. Pasco. ☎ (509) 547-9755. Early.
Bavarian Ice Fest. Leavenworth. ☎ (509) 548-5807. Mid.
Deer Park Winter Festival. Deer Park. ☎ (509) 276-5900. Mid.
Snow Days. Conconully. ☎ (509) 826-1037. Includes outhouse race on skis on Main Street. Mid.
Snowshoe Festival. Mazama. ☎ (509) 996-3287. Mid.
Winterfest Carnival. Republic. ☎ (509) 775-2704. Mid.
Winterfest. Chelan. ☎ (800) 424-3526. Mid.
Chocolate Affair. Wenatchee. ☎ (509) 664-3340. Late.
Rendezvous Mountain Tour. Mazama. ☎ (509) 996-3287. Late.

February

Fasching. Leavenworth. ☎ (509) 548-5807. Early.
Langlauf Cross-Country Ski Race. Spokane. ☎ (509) 458-8880. Race and festival. Early.
Cowboy Poetry Gathering. Toppenish. ☎ (800) 569-3982. Mid.
Fudge Mountain Mania. Zillah. ☎ (800) 454-7623. Mid.
Motorsports Monster Jam. Spokane. ☎ (800) 325-7328. Mid.
President's Day Celebration. George. ☎ (509) 785-3831. Mid.
Red Wine and Chocolate. Yakima. ☎ (800) 258-7270. Mid.
Washington Birthday Celebration & Pow Wow. Toppenish. ☎ (509) 865-5121. Mid.
Yakima Greenway Winterwalk. Yakima. ☎ (509) 453-8280. Mid.
Antiques Show and Sale. Yakima. ☎ (415) 441-4290. Late.
Doll, Toy & Teddy Bear Show. Yakima. ☎ (509) 452-4485. Late.
Snowshoe Festival. Mazama. ☎ (509) 996-3287. Late.
White Pass Winter Carnival. White Pass. ☎ (509) 453-8731. Late.

March

Anniversary Celebration. Moses Lake. ☎ (509) 345-0101. Early.
Bacchus Wine & Food Festival. Richland. ☎ (509) 946-1651. Early.
Golden Eagles Senior Pow Wow. Toppenish. ☎ (509) 865-5121. Early.
Spring Arts & Crafts Show. Spokane. ☎ (509) 924-0588. Early.
Chelan County Centennial Ball. Wenatchee. ☎ (509) 664-3340. Mid.
Chocolate Fantasy. Yakima. ☎ (509) 966-6309. Mid.

Speelyi-Mi Indian Arts & Crafts Fair. Toppenish. ☎ (509) 865-5121. Mid.
St. Patrick's Day Parade. Wenatchee. ☎ (509) 662-0059. Mid.
Valley Pride Auction. Chelan. ☎ (800) 424-3526. Mid.
Anniversary Celebration. East Wenatchee. ☎ (509) 663-2395. Late.
Annual Quilt Show. Pasco. ☎ (509) 582-3257. Late.
Canal Caper. Ephrata. ☎ (509) 754-5506. Late.
Ephrata Canal Caper. Ephrata. ☎ (509) 754-5506. Late.
Sandhill Crane Festival. Othello. ☎ (800) 684-2556. 🖳 www.othello-wa.com. Late.

April

Anniversary Celebration. Ephrata. ☎ (509) 754-3025. Early.
Artistry in Wood Show and Sale. Yakima. ☎ (509) 697-4143. Early.
Community vs. Campus Olympic Games. Walla Walla. ☎ (509) 529-8755. Early.
Dogwood Festival. Clarkston. ☎ (509) 758-7712. April.
Great Downtown Easter Basket Hunt. Wenatchee. ☎ (509) 662-0059. Early.
Spring Garden Fair. Manson. ☎ (800) 424-3526. Early.
Waitsburg Jr. Livestock Show. Waitsburg. ☎ (509) 337-6207. Early.
Antique and Collectibles Show. Pasco. ☎ (509) 924-0588. Mid.
Professional Bull Riders. Spokane. ☎ (800) 325-7328. Mid.
Spring Antique and Collectors Sale. Pasco. ☎ (509) 924-0588. Mid.
Tri-Cities Farm Fair. Pasco. ☎ (509) 547-9755. Mid.
Apple Blossom Weekend. Cashmere. ☎ (509) 782-2123. Late April to early May.
Arbor Day Celebration. Spokane. ☎ (509) 624-4832. Late.
Arts & Crafts/Opening of Fishing. Conconully. ☎ (509) 826-1154. Late.
Asotin County Fair. Asotin. ☎ (509) 758-7712. Late.
Blossom Daze Festival. Clarkston. ☎ (509) 758-5872. Late April to early May.
Classy Chassis Car Show and Parade. East Wenatchee. ☎ (509) 884-2514. Late.
Earth Day Fair. Chelan. ☎ (800) 424-3526. Late.
Gem & Craft Show. Yakima. ☎ (509) 248-6401. Late.
Granger Cherry Festival. Granger. ☎ (509) 854-2130. Late April to early May.
Northwest Action Chess Championship: Maryhill Museum of Art. Goldendale.
☎ (509) 773-3733. 🖳 www.maryhillmuseum.org/. Late.
Palouse Duck Dash. Colfax. ☎ (509) 397-3712. Late.
Ponies on the Mall. Union Gap. ☎ (509) 697-7891. Car show. Late.
Seaport River Run. Clarkston. ☎ (509) 758-7712. Late.
Spring Antique & Collectors Show. Spokane. ☎ (509) 924-0588. Late.
Spring Barrel Tasting. Yakima. ☎ (800) 258-7270. Late.
Spring Fling and Quilt Show. Odessa. ☎ (509) 982-0049. Late.
Tri-Cities Ala Carte Festival. Tri-Cities. ☎ (800) 254-5824. Late April to early May.
Washington State Apple Blossom Festival. Wenatchee. ☎ (509) 662-3616. Late.
Washington State Asparagus Festival. Sunnyside. ☎ (800) 814-7004. Late.

May

49er Days. Winthrop. ☎ (509) 996-2125. Early.
Art in the Park. Leavenworth. ☎ (509) 548-5807. May through October.
Balloon Stampede. Walla Walla. ☎ (509) 525-0850. Early.
Bloomsday Race. Spokane. ☎ (509) 838-1579. Early.
Central Washington Jr. Livestock Show. Toppenish. ☎ (800) 569-3982. Early.
Cinco de Mayo Fiesta Days. Sunnyside. ☎ (800) 457-8089. Early.
Cinco de Mayo. Chelan. ☎ (800) 424-3526. Early.
Cinco de Mayo. Pasco. ☎ (509) 545-0738. Early.
Colorama Festival and PWRA Rodeo. Grand Coulee Dam area. ☎ (800) 268-5332. Early.
Entiat Hydroplane Regatta. Entiat. ☎ (509) 784-7117. Early.
Kids Day in the Japanese Garden. Spokane. ☎ (509) 456-8038. Early.

Kittitas County Farmers Market. Ellensburg. ☎ (509) 925-3137. May through late October.
Maifest. Leavenworth. ☎ (509) 548-5807. Early.
Manson Apple Blossom Festival. Manson. ☎ (800) 424-3526. Early.
Oroville May Day Festival. Oroville. ☎ (509) 476-2739. Early.
Pedal Power Days. Palouse. ☎ (509) 878-1735. Early.
Pomeroy Civic Theatre. Pomeroy. ☎ (509) 843-1211. May through end of September.
Ritzville Quilters Guild Show. Ritzville. ☎ (509) 659-1370. Early.
Satus Longhouse Pow Wow. Satus. ☎ (509) 865-5121. Early.
Spokane Lilac Festival. Spokane. ☎ (509) 326-3339. Early to mid-May.
Spring Barrel Tasting. Spokane. ☎ (509) 926-0164. Early.
Sunflower Relay & Iron Run. Twisp. ☎ (509) 996-3287. Early.
Apple Cup Regional Aerobatics Contest. Ephrata. ☎ (360) 245-3948. Mid.
Civil War Reenactment. Spokane. ☎ (800) 260-5997. Mid.
Columbia Gorge Challenge. Lyle. ☎ (509) 365-3245. Mid.
Friendly OK Car Club Swap Meet and Car Show. Okanogan. ☎ (509) 826-3154. Mid.
May Festival. White Salmon. ☎ (509) 493-3630. Mid.
Mayfly Fun Run. Chewelah. ☎ (509) 935-8991. Mid.
National Western Art Show & Auction. Ellensburg. ☎ (509) 962-2934. Mid.
Salmon Derby. Lake Chelan. ☎ (509) 682-2802. Mid.
Selah Community Days. Selah. ☎ (509) 697-5545. Mid.
Sunbanks Blues Festival. Grand Coulee Dam area. ☎ (800) 268-5332 or ☎ (509) 633-3786. Mid.
Wild Goose Bill Days. Wilbur. ☎ (509) 647-5551. Mid.
10K Fun Run/Pancake Breakfast. Mazama. ☎ (509) 996-3287. Late.
Baker Boyer Ducky Derby. Walla Walla. ☎ (509) 525-2000. Late.
Coulee City Last Stand PRCA Rodeo. Coulee City. ☎ (509) 632-5497. Late.
Dayton Days. Dayton. ☎ (800) 882-6299. Late.
Laser Light Festival. Grand Coulee Dam area. ☎ (800) 268-5332. Late.
Laser Light Show on the Grand Coulee Dam. Grand Coulee Dam area. ☎ (800) 268-5332. 🖳 www.grandcouleedam.org/. Half-hour laser light show. Late.
Memorial Day Rodeo. Winthrop. ☎ (509) 996-2125. Late.
Moses Lake Spring Festival. Moses Lake. ☎ (509) 765-8248. Late.
Muzzle Loader Rendezvous. Asotin. ☎ (509) 758-4342. Late.
Nostalgia Days. Chewelah. ☎ (509) 935-8991. Late.
Wenatchee Valley Garden Tour. Wenatchee. ☎ (509) 662-9577. Late.

June
Alder Creek Rodeo. Bickleton. ☎ (509) 896-2351. Early.
ArtFest. Spokane. ☎ (509) 456-3931. Early.
Bridgeport Daze. Bridgeport. ☎ (509) 686-4101. Early.
Craft Fair. Leavenworth. ☎ (509) 548-5807. Early.
Curlew Barrel Derby. Curlew. ☎ (509) 779-4490. Early.
Dixieland Jazz Festival. Spokane. ☎ (509) 235-4401. Early.
Fairfield Flag Day Celebration. Fairfield. ☎ (509) 283-2590. Early.
Folk Music Festival. Cashmere. ☎ (509) 782-3230. Early.
Lewis & Clark Festival. Walla Walla. ☎ (509) 525-7703. Early.
Manly Men Festival. Roslyn. ☎ (509) 674-5958. Mid.
Mill Creek Gospel Festival. Pomeroy. ☎ (509) 843-1211.
Mural-in-a-Day, Arts, Crafts, Food Fair. Toppenish. ☎ (800) 569-3982. Early.
Okanogan Days. Okanogan. ☎ (509) 422-9882. Early.
Pioneer Day Celebration. Pomeroy. ☎ (509) 843-1211. Early.
Pony Express Ride. Tonasket. ☎ (509) 486-4297. Early.
Prospector Days. Republic. ☎ (509) 775-2704. Early.
Quest for Summer Cruise. Goldendale. ☎ (800) 573-3793. Early.

Rosalia Battle Days. Rosalia. ☎ (509) 523-3311. Early.
Summer Fun Day Parade. Richland. ☎ (509) 946-1651. Early.
Thursday Market Downtown. Wenatchee. ☎ (509) 662-0059. Early.
Tonasket Founders Day Rodeo. Tonasket. ☎ (509) 486-4297. Early.
Town and Country Days. Kettle Falls. ☎ (509) 738-2300. Early.
Tri-Cities Wineries Barrel Tasting. Tri-Cities. ☎ (509) 588-6716. Early.
Trout Derby-Free Fishing Weekend. Conconully. ☎ (509) 826-0813. Early.
Washington State High School Rodeo. Pasco. ☎ (509) 545-1914. Early.
Yakima Nation Treaty Day Commemoration. Toppenish. ☎ (509) 865-5121. Early.
Yakima Nation Treaty Day Commemoration. White Swan. ☎ (509) 865-5121. Early.
All Wheels Weekend. Dayton. ☎ (800) 882-6299. Mid.
Alpine Square Dance Festival. Colville. ☎ (509) 684-2408. Mid.
Art in the Park. Omak. ☎ (509) 826-4218. Mid.
Arts & Crafts Fair. Chelan. ☎ (800) 424-3526. Mid.
Colville PRCA Rodeo. Colville. ☎ (509) 684-4849. Mid.
Cool Desert Nights. Richland. ☎ (509) 946-1651. Mid.
IMAX Film Festival & Summer Celebration. Spokane. ☎ (509) 625-6624. Mid.
International Accordion Celebration & Folk Dance Performance. Leavenworth. ☎ (509) 548-5807. Mid.
Kinderfest. Leavenworth. ☎ (509) 548-5807. Mid.
Lind Rodeo and Combine Demolition Derby. Lind. ☎ (509) 677-3655. Mid.
Living Museum. Ephrata. ☎ (509) 754-3334. Mid.
Sage n' Sun Festival. Ephrata. ☎ (509) 754-4656. Mid.
Square & Round Dance Festival. Wenatchee. ☎ (800) 842-0977. Mid.
Tonasket Father's Day Fly In. Tonasket. ☎ (509) 486-2295. Mid.
Anatone Days. Anatone. ☎ (509) 256-3331. Late.
Classic Car Show. Chelan. ☎ (800) 424-3526. Late.
Family Fun Day: Maryhill Museum of Art. Goldendale. ☎ (509) 773-3733. 🖳 www.maryhillmuseum.org/. Late.
Founders' Day. Cashmere. ☎ (509) 782-7404. Late.
Glenwood Rodeo. Glenwood. ☎ (509) 364-3355. 🖳 www.gorge.net/glenwoodrodeo/. Late.
Longest Day of the Year Barbecue. Sunnyside. ☎ (800) 814-7004. Late.
Newport PWRA Rodeo. Newport. ☎ (509) 447-5812. Late.
North Country Car Show. Tonasket. ☎ (509) 486-1222. Late.
Save Our Salmon Derby. East Wenatchee. ☎ (509) 884-2514. Late.
Slippery Gulch Days. Tekoa. ☎ (509) 284-3861. Late.
Taste of Chelan Street Fair. Chelan. ☎ (800) 424-3526. Late.

July

4th of July Celebration. Chelan. ☎ (800) 424-3526.
4th of July Celebration. George. ☎ (509) 785-3831.
4th of July Celebration. Manson. ☎ (800) 424-3526.
4th of July Festival at Grand Coulee Dam. Grand Coulee Dam area. ☎ (800) 268-5332.
4th of July in the Park. Walla Walla. ☎ (509) 525-3300.
Deer Park Fireworks Display. Deer Park. ☎ (509) 276-8802. July 4.
Fireworks Cruise. Chelan. ☎ (800) 424-3526. July 4.
Grand Ole Fourth Celebration. Pasco. ☎ (509) 547-9755.🖳 http://visittri-cities.com/.
Old-Fashioned 4th of July. Kennewick. ☎ (509) 735-8486. 🖳 www.visittri-cities.com/.
Old-Fashioned Fourth of July. Prosser. ☎ (800) 408-1517.
Old-Fashioned Independence Day at the Park. Pomeroy. ☎ (509) 843-1211.
Bach Feste. Lake Chelan. ☎ (800) 424-3526. Early to mid-July.
Blues Festival. Ritzville. ☎ (509) 659-1936. Early.

Chataqua. Chewelah. ☎ (509) 935-8991. Early.
Cheney Rodeo Days. Cheney. ☎ (509) 235-8480. Early.
Colville Confederated Tribes Pow Wow. Nespelem. ☎ (509) 633-0751. Early.
Community Days. Royal City. ☎ (509) 346-9264. Early.
Community Spirit Fire Works Display. Clarkston. ☎ (509) 758-7712. Early.
Concrete River Festival. Colfax. ☎ (509) 397-3712. Early.
Creating Memories and Treasures. Yakima. ☎ (509) 698-3827. Early.
Custom Car, Truck & Bicycle Show. Yakima. ☎ (206) 772-6963. Early.
Happy Days Car Rally. Omak. ☎ (509) 826-1880. Early.
Icicle Creek Music Center Summer Music Festival. Leavenworth. ☎ (509) 548-5807.
Leavenworth Summer Theater Presents. Leavenworth. ☎ (509) 548-5807. July and August.
Northwest Flinters. Asotin. ☎ (509) 758-2661. Early.
Pend Oreille County Pioneer Weekend. Newport. ☎ (509) 447-5388. Early.
Pioneer Days. Cle Elum. ☎ (509) 674-5958. Early.
Pioneer Days. Roslyn. ☎ (509) 674-5958. Early.
Smokiam Days. Soap Lake. ☎ (509) 246-1821. Early.
Spokane American Music Festival. Spokane. ☎ (509) 921-5579. Early.
Sunfaire. Othello. ☎ (800) 684-2556. Early.
The Great Canoe Race. Soap Lake. ☎ (509) 246-1821. Early.
Toppenish Pow Wow & Rodeo. Toppenish. ☎ (509) 865-5313. Early.
Tumbleweed Festival. Pomeroy. ☎ (509) 843-1211. Early.
Walla Walla Sweet Onion Blues Fest. Walla Walla. ☎ (877) 998-4748. 🖳 www.wwchamber.com/wwsoblues fest.htm. Early.
Waterville Days. Waterville. ☎ (509) 745-8871. Early.
Wenatchee Youth Circus. Wenatchee. ☎ (509) 662-0722. Early.
Wild West Parade. Toppenish. ☎ (800) 569-3982. Early.
Yakima Folklife Festival. Yakima. ☎ (509) 248-0747. Early.
Civil War Reenactment. Cle Elum. ☎ (509) 674-5958. Mid.
Civil War Reenactment. Roslyn. ☎ (509) 674-5958. Mid.
Concert Under the Stars. ☎ (509) 328-3263. Mid.
Croatian Picnic. Roslyn. ☎ (509) 649-2714. Mid.
Draft Horse Show. Republic. ☎ (509) 634-4388. Mid.
Dream Riders Junior Rodeo. Newport. ☎ (509) 447-2095. Mid.
Eagles Junior Rodeo. Toppenish. ☎ (800) 569-3982. Mid.
Festival at the Depot. Dayton. ☎ (800) 882-6299. Mid.
Napavine Funtime Festival. Napavine. ☎ (360) 262-3887. Mid.
Pend Oreille River Poker Paddle. Newport. ☎ (509) 447-5812. Mid.
Pioneer Days. Davenport. ☎ (509) 725-0101. Mid.
Rhythm & Blues Festival. Winthrop. ☎ (509) 997-2541. Mid.
Trout Lake Festival of the Arts. Trout Lake. ☎ (509) 493-2294. Mid.
Allied Arts Sidewalk Show. Richland. ☎ (509) 943-9815. 🖳 http://visittri-cities.com/. Late.
Chelan County Centennial Champagne Cruise. Chelan. ☎ (800) 424-3526. Late.
Down River Days. Ione. ☎ (509) 446-3028. Late.
Hydroplane Races. Kennewick. ☎ (509) 735-8486. 🖳 www.visittri-cities.com/. Late.
Jazz in the Valley. Ellensburg. ☎ (509) 925-2002. 🖳 www.jazzinthevalley.com/.Late.
Moose Days. Roslyn. ☎ (509) 649-3080. 🖳 www.moosefest.com/. Northern Exposure festival. Late.
Old Schoolhouse Summer Festival. Loon Lake. ☎ (509) 233-2829. Late July to early August.
Royal Fireworks Festival & Concert. Spokane. ☎ (800) 248-3230. 🖳 www.allegro baroque.org/. Late.
Tri-County Settlers Celebration and Rodeo. Deer Park. ☎ (509) 276-5900. Late.
U.S. Team Roping Championship. Spokane. ☎ (509) 922-3863. Late.
WPRA Rodeo. Chelan. ☎ (800) 424-3526. Late.

August

Alpo Frisbee Disc Championship. Spokane. ☎ (509) 625-6200. Canine athletes. Early.

    Colville Rendezvous. Colville. ☎ (509) 684-5973. Early.

    Concert Under the Pines. Spokane. ☎ (509) 328-3263. Early.

    Fabulous 50's Car Show and Swap Meet. Newport. ☎ (509) 447-2729. Early.

    Methow Music Festival. Mazama. ☎ (800) 340-1458. www.methow.com/mmf/. Early.

    Moxee Hop Festival. Moxee. ☎ (509) 457-6670. Early.

    Old-Fashioned Ice Cream Social. Goldendale. ☎ (509) 773-4487. Early.

    Omak Native & Western Arts Show. Omak. ☎ (509) 826-1880. Early.

    Omak Stampede & Suicide Race. Omak. ☎ (509) 826-1983. Early.

    Scottish Highland Games. Spokane. ☎ (509) 489-4516. Early.

    Traditional Salish Fair. Usk. ☎ (509) 445-1147. Early.

    Trout Lake Community Fair Days. Trout Lake. ☎ (509) 395-2900. Early.

    A Case of the Blues and All That Jazz. Yakima. ☎ (509) 453-8280. Mid.

    Asotin Days. Asotin. ☎ (509) 243-4411. Mid.

    Columbia Basin Farmers Market. Moses Lake. ☎ (509) 346-2060. Mid.

    County Fair and Rodeo. Cusick. ☎ (509) 445-1128. Mid.

    Cruise to Cle Elum. Cle Elum. ☎ (509) 674-5958. Mid.

    Grant County Fair. Moses Lake.☎ (509) 765-3581. www.grantcountyfair.com/. Mid.

    Hot Summer Nights and Crazy Days. Wenatchee. ☎ (509) 662-0059. Mid.

    Kids Day. Spokane. ☎ (509) 625-6440. Mid.

    Moses Lake Roundup Rodeo. Moses Lake. ☎ (509) 765-6393. Mid.

    NE Washington Fiddle Contest. Republic. ☎ (509) 775-3819. Mid.

    Pig Feed and Rod Run. Soap Lake. ☎ (509) 246-0524. Mid.

    Senior Games. Spokane. ☎ (509) 625-6546. Mid.

    Sprint Boat Races. Clarkston. ☎ (509) 758-7712. Mid.

    Sunflower Days. Clarkston. ☎ (509) 758-7712. Mid.

    Valley Community Fair. Valley. ☎ (509) 937-2054. Mid.

    Wine and Food Fair. Prosser. ☎ (800) 408-1517. Mid.

    Allied Arts Festival of the Arts. Yakima. ☎ (509) 966-0930. Late.

    Benton Franklin County Fair. Kennewick. ☎ (509) 586-9211. � www.visittri-cities.com/. Late.

    Chewelah Basin Blues & Jazz Festival. Chewelah. ☎ (509) 935-6649. Late.

    Children's Festival of the Arts. Othello. ☎ (800) 684-2556. Late.

    Contemporary Gospel Concert. Pomeroy. ☎ (509) 843-1211. Late.

    Cowboy Poetry Performance. Toppenish. ☎ (800) 569-3982. Late.

    Deer Park Fair & Pee Wee Rodeo. Deer Park. ☎ (509) 276-2444. Late.

    Entiat Valley Bluegrass/Ol' Time Country Music Heritage Festival. Entiat. ☎ (509) 784-7117. Late.

    Hunters Community Fair. Hunters. ☎ (509) 722-4020. Late.

    Klickitat County Fair & Rodeo. Goldendale. ☎ (509) 364-3325. Late.

    Lake Osoyoos International Bin Boat Regatta. Oroville. ☎ (509) 476-2739. Late.

    Lincoln County Fair. Davenport. ☎ (509) 725-5161. Late.

    National Lentil Festival. Pullman. ☎ (800) 365-6948. Late.

    NCW District Fair. Waterville. ☎ (509) 745-8480. Late.

    Riverwalk Fine Arts Show. Chelan. ☎ (800) 424-3526. Late.

    Spokane Falls NW Native American Encampment & Pow Wow. Spokane. ☎ (509) 535-0886. Late.

    Summer Eve in the Park. Grandview. ☎ (509) 882-2100. Late.

    Toppenish Western Art Show. Toppenish. ☎ (800) 569-3982. Late.

    Wanderer's Car Club Rally–James Dean Days. Chewelah. ☎ (509) 935-8991. Late.

    Washington State Pioneer Power Show. Union Gap. ☎ (509) 453-2395. Late.

    Yakima Valley Rail & Transportation Show. Toppenish. ☎ (800) 569-3982. Late.

September

An Affair on Main Street. Metaline Falls. ☎ (509) 446-2429. Early.

Antique Auto Rally. Winthrop. ☎ (888) 463-8469. Early.
Bluebird Flitter. Bickleton. ☎ (509) 896-5281. Early.
Chelan County Fair and Rodeo. Cashmere. ☎ (509) 782-3232. Early.
Coal Miner's Festival. Roslyn. ☎ (509) 649-2795. Early.
Connell Fall Festival. Connell. ☎ (509) 234-8731. Early.
Ellensburg Rodeo. Ellensburg. ☎ (800) 637-2444. Early.
Farmer-Consumer Awareness Day. Quincy. ☎ (509) 787-2140. Early.
Farmers Market & Harvest Festival. West Richland. ☎ (509) 967-3431. Early.
Ferry County Fair. Republic. ☎ (509) 775-2704. Early.
Huckleberry Festival. Bingen. ☎ (509) 493-3630. Early.
Kittitas County Fair. Ellensburg. ☎ (800) 426-5340. Early.
Labor Day Rodeo. Winthrop. ☎ (509) 996-2125. Early.
Leavenworth Annual Quilt Show. Leavenworth. ☎ (509) 548-5807. Early.
Northeast Washington Fair. Colville. ☎ (509) 684-2585. Early.
One World One Valley. Yakima. ☎ (509) 248-7160. Early.
Pig Out in the Park. Spokane. ☎ (509) 625-6624. Early.
Ritzville Rodeo & Parade. Ritzville. ☎ (509) 659-1936. Early.
Riverwalk Arts & Crafts Marketplace. Chelan. ☎ (800) 424-3526. Early.
Sportsman's Days. Naches. ☎ (509) 653-2647. Early.
States Day. Prosser. ☎ (800) 408-1517. Early.
Train Rides. Harrah. ☎ (509) 865-1911. September and October.
Tumbleweed Music Festival. Richland. ☎ (509) 943-2787. 🖳 http://visittri-cities.com/. Early.
Walla Walla Fair & Frontier Days. Walla Walla. ☎ (509) 527-3247. Early.
Western Art Show. Cashmere. ☎ (509) 782-3230. Early.
Wheatland Communities Fair. Ritzville. ☎ (509) 659-1936. Early.
Wheelin Walla Walla Weekend. Walla Walla. ☎ (509) 529-8755. Early.
Adams County Fair/PRCA Rodeo. Othello. ☎ (509) 488-6130. Mid.
Antique Equipment Show & Threshing Bee. Ellensburg. ☎ (509) 925-1943. Mid.
Civil War Reenactment. Pasco. ☎ (800) 260-5997. 🖳 http://visittri-cities.com/. Mid.
Columbia County Fair. Dayton. ☎ (800) 882-6299. Mid.
Deutschesfest. Odessa. ☎ (509) 982-0049. Mid.
Fall Festival. Waitsburg. ☎ (509) 337-6287. Mid.
Gaited Horse Show. Spokane. ☎ (509) 928-5690. Mid.
Garfield County Fair & Rodeo. Pomeroy. ☎ (509) 843-1211. Mid.
Kidney Car Show. Toppenish. ☎ (509) 452-2024. Mid.
Ponies in the Sun. Yakima. ☎ (509) 697-7891. Mid.
Sunnyside Sunshine Days. Sunnyside. ☎ (800) 457-8089. Mid.
Wenatchee River Salmon Festival. Leavenworth. ☎ (509) 548-5807. Mid.
Almira Country Fair. Almira. ☎ (509) 639-2237. Late.
Antique and Collectibles Show. Pasco. ☎ (509) 924-0588. Late.
Blues Festival. Grand Coulee Dam Area. ☎ (800) 268-5332. Late.
Catch the Crush. Tri-Cities. ☎ (509) 588-6716. Late.
Central Washington State Fair. Yakima. ☎ (509) 248-7160. Late.
Fall Festival. Harrington. ☎ (509) 253-4345. Late.
Fall Harvest & Community Festival. Walla Walla. ☎ (509) 525-7703. Late.
Harvest Festival and Balloon Rally. Prosser. ☎ (800) 408-1517. Late.
Harvest Festival. Sunnyside. ☎ (800) 814-7004. Late.
Hydro Feste. Chelan. ☎ (800) 424-3526. Late.
National Indian Days Pow Wow. Toppenish and White Swan. ☎ (509) 865-5121 or
☎ (800) 569-3982. Late.
Old West Wine Fest. Zillah. ☎ (509) 829-6333. Late.
Pioneer Day. Ephrata. ☎ (509) 754-3334. Late.
Valley Fest. Spokane. ☎ (509) 924-6829. Late.
Washington State Autumn Leaf Festival. Leavenworth. ☎ (509) 548-5807. Late.

October

1900s Harvest Fest. Wilson Creek. ☎ (509) 345-2250. Early.
    Apple Days. Cashmere. ☎ (509) 782-3230. Early.
    Columbus Day Classic/Half Century Bicycle Tour. Chewelah. ☎ (509) 935-8991. Early.
    Fall Antiques and Collectors Sale. Spokane. ☎ (509) 924-0588. Early.
    FDR Days. Grand Coulee Dam area. ☎ (800) 268-5332. Early.
    Great Yakima Duck Race. Yakima. ☎ (509) 453-8280. Early.
    Historical Home Tours. Dayton. ☎ (509) 382-2026. Early.
    Italian Heritage Days Festival and Parade. Walla Walla. ☎ (509) 529-1509. Early.
    Mennonite Country Auction. Moses Lake. ☎ (509) 765-8683. Early.
    Norm Evans Memorial Radio Controlled Hydro Race. Chelan. ☎ (800) 424-3526. Early.
    Oktoberfest. Leavenworth. ☎ (509) 548-5807. Early.
    Pumpkin Festival. Granger. ☎ (509) 854-1413.
    Quilts Cover Washington. Wenatchee. ☎ (509) 664-3340.
    Quilts: Warmth and Wonder. Cashmere. ☎ (509) 782-3230.
    White Swan Indian Summer Celebration. White Swan. ☎ (509) 865-5121. Early.
    Wings Over Walla Walla Air Show. Walla Walla. ☎ (509) 529-8147. Early.
    Apple Feste. Pateros. ☎ (800) 424-3526. Mid.
    Fall Leaf Festival. Spokane. ☎ (509) 624-4832. Mid.
    Harvest Feste. Chelan. ☎ (800) 424-3526. Mid.
    Harvest Feste. Manson. ☎ (800) 424-3526. Mid.
    Central Washington Artists Exhibition. Yakima. ☎ (509) 574-4875. Late.
    Fall Festival of Foliage & Feathers. Walla Walla. ☎ (509) 529-8755. Late.
    Family A'Fair. Kennewick and Pasco. ☎ (509) 736-1939. 🖳 www.visittri-cities.com/. Late.
    Halloween on the Avenue. Wenatchee. ☎ (509) 662-0059. Late.
    Halloween Parade and Carnival. Cle Elum. ☎ (509) 674-5958. Late.
    Hoptoberfest. Yakima. ☎ (509) 865-4677. Late.

November

Blue Mountain Chorus of Sweet Adeline's. Walla Walla. ☎ (509) 525-0709. Early.
    Christmas Arts & Crafts Show. Pasco. ☎ (509) 924-0588. 🖳 http://visittri-cities.com/. Early.
    Christmas Arts and Crafts Show. Spokane. ☎ (509) 924-0588. Early.
    Yakima Nation Veteran's Day Celebration. White Swan. ☎ (509) 865-5121. Early.
    Tri-Cities Northwest Wine Festival. Pasco. ☎ (509) 375-3399. 🖳 http://visittri-cities.com/. Mid.
    Veteran's Day Pow Wow. Toppenish. ☎ (800) 569-3982. Mid.
    Winefest. Spokane. ☎ (509) 926-0164. Mid.
    Christkindlmarkt. Leavenworth. ☎ (509) 548-5807. Late.
    Christmas at the End of the Road. Winthrop. ☎ (888) 463-8469. Late.
    Christmas Kickoff. Dayton. ☎ (800) 882-6299. Late.
    Christmas Lighting. George. ☎ (509) 787-2003. Late November to early December.
    Community Tree Lighting Ceremony. Wenatchee. ☎ (509) 662-0059. Late.
    Holiday Magic Festival of Trees. Wenatchee. ☎ (509) 665-9096. Late.
    Hometown Celebration–Lighting Ceremony. Republic. ☎ (509) 775-2704. Late.
    Kris Kringle Market. Loon Lake. ☎ (509) 233-2829. Late.
    Moments to Remember. Ellensburg. ☎ (888) 925-2204. Late.
    Parade of Lights. East Wenatchee. ☎ (509) 884-2514. Late.
    Quincy Valley Christmas Light Show. Quincy. ☎ (509) 787-2140. Late.
    Soroptimist Holiday Craft Auction. Chelan. ☎ (800) 424-3526. Late.
    Thanksgiving in the Wine Country. Prosser and Yakima. ☎ (800) 258-7270. Late.
    Winterfest. Roslyn. ☎ (509) 674-5958. Late.

December

Agricultural Lighted Holiday Parade. Moses Lake. ☎ (509) 765-0227. Early.

Annual Christmas Tour. Colville. ☎ (509) 684-5968. Early.
Asotin Christmas Parade. Asotin. ☎ (509) 243-4411. Early.
Caroling Cruise. Chelan. ☎ (800) 424-3526. Early.
Centennial Plaza Christmas Celebration. Newport. ☎ (509) 447-5812. Early.
Central Washington Artists Exhibition. Yakima. ☎ (509) 574-4875. Early.
Christmas Bazaar & All-Indian Talent Show. Toppenish. ☎ (509) 865-5121. Early.
Christmas Bazaar. Pomeroy. ☎ (509) 843-3740. Early.
Christmas Craftfest. Chewelah. ☎ (509) 935-8779. Early.
Christmas Fest. Odessa. ☎ (509) 982-0049. Early.
Christmas Juried Arts & Crafts Sale. Spokane. ☎ (509) 625-6677. Early.
Christmas Lighting Festival. Leavenworth. ☎ (509) 548-5807. Early.
Christmas Open House. Pasco. ☎ (509) 547-9755. 🖳 http://visittri-cities.com/.
Christmas Parade of Lights. Walla Walla. ☎ (509) 529-8755. Early.
Christmas Twilight Parade and Christmas Lighting Festival. Clarkston. ☎ (509) 758-7712. Early.
    City of Lights. Grand Coulee Dam area. ☎ (800) 268-5332.
    Country Christmas Lighted Farm Implement Parade. Sunnyside. ☎ (800) 457-8089. Early.
    Deck the Falls Christmas Festival. Metaline Falls. ☎ (509) 446-4108. Early.
    Dickens Comes to Colfax. Colfax. ☎ (509) 397-3712. Early to mid-December.
    Festival of Lights. Chewelah. ☎ (509) 935-8991. Early.
    Festival of Lights. Othello. ☎ (800) 684-2556. Early.
    Festival of Trees. Pasco. ☎ (509) 546-2307. Early.
    Holiday Concerts. Leavenworth. ☎ (509) 548-5234. Early.
    Hometown Christmas. Waitsburg. ☎ (509) 337-6287. Early.
    Kris Kringle Market. Loon Lake. ☎ (509) 233-2829. Early.
    Old-Fashioned Christmas. Pomeroy. ☎ (509) 843-1211. Early.
    Old Time Holidays in Cashmere. Cashmere. ☎ (509) 782-7404. Early.
    Quincy Valley Christmas Bazaar. Quincy. ☎ (509) 787-2140. Early.
    Reflection on the Confluence. Clarkston. ☎ (509) 758-7712. Early.
    Santa's Social. Chewelah. ☎ (509) 935-8991. Early.
Toppenish Western Lighted Christmas Parade. Toppenish. ☎ (800) 569-3982. Early.
Tri-Cities Christmas Light Boat Parade. Tri-Cities. ☎ (509) 582-8709. Early.
Victorian Holidays Craft Sale. Chelan. ☎ (800) 424-3526. Early.
Winter Fest. Soap Lake. ☎ (509) 246-1821. Early.
Winter Fest. Tonasket. ☎ (509) 486-2063. Early.
    Christmas Lights Bus Tour. Pasco. ☎ (509) 547-9755. 🖳 http://visittri-cities.com/. Late.
    Holiday Art in Action. Walla Walla. ☎ (509) 529-8755. Mid-November to late December.
    Ski Rodeo. Mazama. ☎ (509) 996-3287. Late.
Wapato Longhouse Christmas Celebration & Pow Wow. Wapato. ☎ (509) 865-5121. Late.

Chapter 24
Washington Tourism Organizations

City and State Resources

Everett. 🔳 www.everett.net/.
    Seattle. 🔳 www.pan.ci.seattle.wa.us/.
    King County. 🔳 www.metrokc.gov.
    Seattle Net. 🔳 www.seattle.net/.
    Seattle–King County Convention and Visitors Bureau. 🔳 www.seeseattle.org/.
    Snohomish County Visitors Bureau. 🔳 www.snohomish.org/.
    Washington State Department of Transportation. Information on mountain passes and road conditions. ☎ (888) 766-4636 or ☎ (206) 368-4499. 🔳 www.wsdot.wa.gov.
    Washington State Tourism. 🔳 www.tourism.wa.gov/001.htm.

Ferry Services

Coastal

Cathlamet-Wesport, Oregon. Wahkiakum County Piget Island Ferry. ☎ (360) 795-3301.
    Westport–Ocean Shores. Bill Walsh Westport/Ocean Shores Ferry. ☎ (360) 268-0047.

Puget Sound

Seattle–Bainbridge Island, Seattle-Bremerton, Seattle-Vashon, Edmonds.
    Kingston, Keystone–Port Townsend, Tacoma–Vashon Island. Washington State Ferries. ☎ (800) 843-7977 in Washington or ☎ (206) 464-6400. 🔳 www.wsdot.wa.gov/ferries/.
    Port Orchard–Bremerton. Horluck Transportation Co. ☎ (360) 876-2300.
    Steilacoom Dock–Anderson Island. Pierce County Ferries. ☎ (253) 581-6290.

San Juan Islands

Anacortes–Guemes Island. Skagit County Guemes Island Ferry. ☎ (360) 293-6356.
    Anacortes–San Juan Islands. Washington State Ferries. ☎ (800) 843-7977 in Washington or ☎ (206) 464-6400. 🔳 www.wsdot.wa.gov/ferries/.
    Bellingham–Orcas Island. San Juan Island Shuttle Express. ☎ (360) 671-1137. 🔳 www.orcawhales.com.
    Bellingham–San Juan Islands. San Juan Islander. ☎ (888) 734-8180.
    Bellingham–San Juan Islands. Victoria/San Juan Cruises. ☎ (800) 443-4552. 🔳 www.whales.com.
    Gooseberry–Lummi Island. Whatcom County Ferry. ☎ (360) 676-6759.
    Port Townsend–San Juan Island. P.S. Express. ☎ (360) 385-5288.

Alaska

Bellingham-Alaska. Alaska Marine Highway System. ☎ (800) 642-0066.

Canada

Anacortes–Sidney, B.C. Washington State Ferries. ☎ (800) 843-7977 in Washington or ☎ (250) 381-1551. 🖳 www.wsdot.wa.gov/ferries/.

Bellingham–Victoria, B.C. Victoria/San Juan Cruises. ☎ (800) 443-4552. 🖳 www.whales.com.

Port Angeles–Victoria, B.C. Black Ball Transport, Inc. ☎ (360) 457-4491. 🖳 www.north olympic.com/coho.

Port Angeles–Victoria, B.C. Victoria Express. ☎ (800) 633-1589 or ☎ (360) 452-8088. 🖳 www.northolympic.com/ferry.

Seattle–Victoria, B.C. Victoria Clipper. ☎ (800) 888-2535 or ☎ (206) 448-5000. 🖳 www. victoriaclipper.com.

Seattle–Victoria, B.C. Princess Marguerite. ☎ (800) 888-2535 or ☎ (206) 448-5000. 🖳 www.victoriaferry.com.

Visitor Bureaus

Anacortes. Anacortes Chamber of Commerce. 819 Commercial Avenue, Suite G., Anacortes, WA 98221. ☎ (360) 293-3832. 🖳 www.anacortes.org/.

Aberdeen. Grays Harbor Chamber of Commerce. 🖳 www.graysharbor.org/. 506 Duffy Street, Aberdeen, WA 98520. ☎ (360) 532-1924 or ☎ (800) 321-1924.

Aberdeen. Grays Harbor Historical Seaport. Box 2019, Aberdeen, WA 98520. ☎ (360) 532-8611 or ☎ (800) 200-5239. 🖳 www.graysharbor.com/seaport/.

Aberdeen. Port of Grays Harbor. Box 660, Aberdeen, WA 98520. ☎ (360) 533-9528. 🖳 www.pgh.wa.gov/.

Aberdeen. Tourism Grays Harbor. Box 225, Aberdeen, WA 98520. ☎ (360) 533-7895 or ☎ (800) 621-9625. 🖳 www.graysharbor.com/.

Arlington. Greater Arlington Chamber of Commerce. Box 102, Arlington, WA 98223. ☎ (360) 435-3708.

Auburn. Auburn Area Chamber of Commerce. 228 First Street Northeast, Auburn, WA 98002. ☎ (253) 833-0700.

Bainbridge Island. Bainbridge Island Chamber of Commerce. 590 Winslow Way East, Bainbridge Island, WA 98110. ☎ (206) 842-3700. 🖳 http://bicomnet.com/bicham ber/.

Battle Ground. Battle Ground Chamber of Commerce. 912 East Main Street, Battle Ground, WA 98604. ☎ (360) 687-1510.

Bellevue. Bellevue Chamber of Commerce. 10500 Northeast Eighth Street, Suite 212, Bellevue, WA 98004. ☎ (425) 454-2464. 🖳 www.bellevuechamber.org/.

Bellevue. East King County Convention and Visitors Bureau. 520 112th Avenue Northeast, Suite 101, Bellevue, WA 98004. ☎ (425) 455-1926 or ☎ (800) 252-1926. 🖳 www.eastkingcounty.org/.

Bellingham. Bellingham/Whatcom County Chamber of Commerce. Box 958, Bellingham, WA 98227. ☎ (360) 734-1330. 🖳 www.bellingham.org/cvb.html.

Bellingham. Custer Visitor Information Center. 2851 Cornwall Avenue, Bellingham, WA 98225. ☎ (360) 366-5010.

Birch Bay. Birch Bay Chamber of Commerce. 4550 Birch Bay Lynden Road, Birch Bay, WA 98230. ☎ (360) 371-5004. 🖳 www.birchbay.net/.

Blaine. Blaine Visitor Information Center. 215 Marine Drive, Blaine, WA 98230. ☎ (360) 332-4544 or ☎ (800) 624-3555.

Bothell. Northshore Chamber of Commerce. 18414 103rd Avenue Northeast, Suite A, Bothell, WA 98011. ☎ (425) 486-1245. 🖳 www.northshorecc.org/.

Bremerton. Bremerton Area Chamber of Commerce. Box 229, Bremerton, WA 98337. ☎ (360) 479-3579. 🖳 www.bremertonchamber.org/.

Brewster. Brewster Chamber of Commerce. Box 1087, Brewster, WA 98812. ☎ (509) 689-3589. 📖 www.rvcamping.com/wa/brewstrv.html.

Bridgeport. Bridgeport Chamber of Commerce, Box 395, Bridgeport, WA 98813. ☎ (509) 686-4101.

Buckley. Buckley Chamber of Commerce. Box 168, Buckley, WA 98321. ☎ (360) 829-0975.

Burlington. Burlington Chamber of Commerce. 120 East George Hopper Road, Ste. 104, Burlington, WA 98233. ☎ (360) 757-0994.

Camano. Camano Island Chamber of Commerce. Box 1012, Camano Island, WA 98292. ☎ (360) 629-7136. 📖 www.whidbey.net/camano/.

Castle Rock. Castle Rock Chamber of Commerce. Box 721, Castle Rock, WA. 98611. ☎ (360) 274-6603. 📖 www.mtsthelens.net/.

Centralia. Tourism Lewis County. 1301 Lum Road, Centralia, WA 98531. ☎ (800) 525-3323. 📖 www.tourlewiscounty.com/.

Chelan. Lake Chelan Chamber of Commerce. Box 216, Chelan, WA 98816. ☎ (509) 682-3503 or ☎ (800) 424-3526. 📖 www.lakechelan.com/.

Cheney. Cheney Chamber of Commerce. Box 65, Cheney, WA 99004. ☎ (509) 235-8480.

Chewelah. Chewelah Chamber of Commerce. Box 94, Chewelah, WA 99109. ☎ (509) 935-8991. 📖 www.panoramaland.com/chamber/index.html.

Clallam Bay. Sekiu Chamber of Commerce. Box 355, Clallam Bay, WA 98326. ☎ (360) 963-2339. 📖 www.northolympic.com/cbs/.

Clarkston. Clarkston Chamber of Commerce. 502 Bridge Street, Clarkston, WA 99403. ☎ (509) 758-7712 or ☎ (800) 933-2128.

Cle Elum. Cle Elum/Roslyn Chamber of Commerce. Box 43, Cle Elum, WA 98922. ☎ (509) 674-5958.

Clinton. Clinton Chamber of Commerce. Box 317, Clinton, WA 98261. 📖 www.whid bey.com.

Colfax. Colfax Chamber of Commerce. 402 South Main Street, Colfax, WA 99111-1999. ☎ (509) 397-3712.

Columbia Gorge. Lower Columbia Economic Development Council Visitor Information Center. Box 98, Skamokawa, WA 98647. ☎ (360) 795-3996. 📖 www.waedn.org/-edcs/edc0078.

Colville. Colville Chamber of Commerce. Box 267, Colville, WA 99114. ☎ (509) 684-5973. 📖 http://206.96.80.14/.

Coulee City. Coulee City Chamber of Commerce. Box 896, Coulee City, WA 99115. ☎ (509) 632-5043. 📖 www.couleecity.com/.

Crystal Mountain. Silver Creek Visitor Information Center. 33000 Crystal Mountain Blvd., Crystal Mountain, WA 98022. ☎ (360) 663-2265.

Dayton. Dayton Chamber of Commerce. Box 22, Dayton, WA 99328. ☎ (509) 382-4825 or ☎ (800) 882-6299. 📖 www.historicdayton.com/.

Edmonds. Edmonds Chamber of Commerce. Box 146, Edmonds, WA 98020. ☎ (425) 776-6711.

Edmonds. Edmonds Visitors Bureau, Waterfront Visitor Information Center. Box 1133, Edmonds, WA 98020. ☎ (425) 776-6711.

Enumclaw. Enumclaw Area Chamber of Commerce. 1421 Cole Street, Enumclaw, WA 98022. ☎ (360) 825-7666. 📖 http://chamber.enumclaw.wa.us/.

Ephrata. Ephrata Chamber of Commerce. Box 275, Ephrata, WA 98823. ☎ (509) 754-4656.

Ephrata. Grant County Pioneer Village & Museum. Box 1141, Ephrata, WA 98823. ☎ (509) 754-3334.

Everett. Everett Area Chamber of Commerce. 1710 West Marine View Drive, Everett, WA 98201. ☎ (425) 438-1487. 📖 www.snobiz.org/default.cfm.

Federal Way. Federal Way Chamber of Commerce. Box 3440, Federal Way, WA 98003. ☎ (253) 838-2605. 📖 http://federalwaychamber.com/.

Ferndale. Ferndale Chamber of Commerce. 5640 Riverside Drive, Ferndale, WA 98248. ☎ (360) 384-3042.

Fife. Fife Chamber of Commerce. 5303 Pacific Hwy East, Suite 272, Fife, WA 98424. ☎ (253) 922-9320. 🖳 www.mninc.com/fife/.

Forks. Forks Chamber of Commerce. Box 1249, Forks, WA 98331. ☎ (360) 374-2531 or ☎ (800) 443-6757. 🖳 www.forkswa.com/.

Freeland. Freeland Chamber of Commerce. Box 361, Freeland, WA 98249. ☎ (360) 331-1980. 🖳 www.islandweb.org/freeland/.

Gig Harbor. Gig Harbor Peninsula Chamber of Commerce. 3302 Harborview Drive, Gig Harbor, WA 98332. ☎ (253) 851-6865.

Goldendale. Greater Goldendale Area Chamber of Commerce. Box 524, Goldendale, WA 98620. ☎ (509) 773-3400.

Goldendale. Klickitat County Public Economic Development Association. 131 West Court Street, Goldendale, WA 98620. ☎ (509) 773-7060. 🖳 www.gorge.net/cgeda/.

Goldendale. Klickitat County Tourism. 131 West Court Street, Goldendale, WA 98620. ☎ (509) 773-3466. 🖳 www.klickitatcounty.org/.

Grand Coulee. Grand Coulee Dam Area Chamber of Commerce. Box 760, Grand Coulee, WA 99133-0760. ☎ (509) 633-3074 or ☎ (800) 268-5332. 🖳 www.grand couleedam.org/.

Grayland. Cranberry Coast Chamber of Commerce. Box 305, Grayland, WA 98547. ☎ (360) 267-2003 or ☎ (800) 473-6018.

Issaquah. Front Street Issaquah. 17 Northwest Alder Place, Suite 203, Issaquah, WA 98027. ☎ (425) 391-1112. 🖳 www.issaquah.org/.

Issaquah. Greater Issaquah Chamber of Commerce. 155 Northwest Gilman Boulevard, Issaquah, WA 98027. ☎ (425) 392-7024. 🖳 www.issaquahchamber.com/.

Kalama. Kalama Tourist Center. 5055 North Meeker Dr., Kalama, WA 98625. ☎ (360) 673-2456 or ☎ (800) 750-2456.

Kennewick. Tri-City Area Chamber of Commerce. Box 6986, Kennewick, WA 99336. ☎ (509) 736-0510.

Kent. Kent Chamber of Commerce. Box 128, Kent, WA 98035. ☎ (253) 854-1770. 🖳 www.kentchamber.com/.

Kettle Falls. Kettle Falls Chamber of Commerce. Box 119, Kettle Falls, WA 99141. ☎ (509) 738-2300. 🖳 www.kettlefalls.com/.

Kirkland. Greater Kirkland Chamber of Commerce. 401 Parkplace Center, Suite 102, Kirkland, WA 98033. ☎ (425) 822-7066. 🖳 www.kirkland.net/.

Kitsap. Kitsap Peninsula Visitor and Convention Bureau. Box 270, Port Gamble, WA 98364. ☎ (360) 297-8200 or ☎ (800) 416-5615. 🖳 www.kitsapedc.org/.

La Conner. La Conner Chamber of Commerce. Box 1610, La Conner, WA 98257. ☎ (360) 466-4778 or ☎ (888) 642-9284. 🖳 www.laconner-chamber.com/.

Lake Stevens. Lake Stevens Chamber of Commerce. Box 439, Lake Stevens, WA 98258. ☎ (425) 334-0433. 🖳 www.lakestevens.com/.

Leavenworth. Leavenworth Chamber of Commerce. Box 327, Leavenworth, WA 98826. ☎ (509) 548-5807. 🖳 www.leavenworth.org/.

Long Beach. City of Long Beach. Box 310, Long Beach, WA 98631. ☎ (360) 642-4421. 🖳 www.funbeach.com/.

Long Beach. Long Beach Peninsula Visitor's Bureau. Box 562, Long Beach, WA 98631. ☎ (360) 642-2400 or ☎ (800) 451-2542. 🖳 www.funbeach.com/.

Longview. River Cities Chamber of Commerce, Kelso & Longview. 1563 Olympia Way, Longview, WA 98632. ☎ (360) 423-8400. 🖳 www.tdn.com/longview chamber.

Lopez Island. Lopez Island Chamber of Commerce. Box 102, Lopez Island, WA 98261. ☎ (360) 468-3663. 🖳 www.lopezisland.com/.

Maple Valley. Greater Maple Valley/Black Diamond Chamber of Commerce. Box 302, Maple Valley, WA 98038. ☎ (425) 432-0222. 🖳 www.maplevalley.com/.

Marysville. Marysville/Tulalip Visitor Information Center. Box 1086, Marysville, WA 98270. ☎ (360) 653-2634.

Mercer Island. Mercer Island Chamber of Commerce. Box 111, Mercer Island, WA 98040. ☎ (206) 232-3404.

Metaline. Metaline Chamber of Commerce. Box 388, Metaline Falls, WA 99153. ☎ (509) 446-4012.

Montesano. Montesano Chamber of Commerce. Box 688, Montesano, WA 98563. ☎ (360) 249-5522 or ☎ (888) 294-0483.

Moses Lake. Moses Lake Chamber of Commerce. 324 South Pioneer Way, Moses Lake, WA 98837. ☎ (509) 765-7888 or ☎ (800) 992-6234. 🖳 www.moses-lake.com/.

Mount Adams. Mount Adams Chamber of Commerce. Box 449, White Salmon, WA 98672. ☎ (509) 493-3630. 🖳 www.gorge.net/mtadamschamber/.

Mount Vernon. Mount Vernon Chamber of Commerce. Box 1007, Mount Vernon, WA 98273. ☎ (360) 428-8547. 🖳 www.mvcofc.org/.

Mount Adams. USDA FS—Mount Adams Ranger District Visitor Information Center. 2455 Hwy. 141, Trout Lake, WA 98650. ☎ (509) 395-2501.

North Bend. Upper Snoqualmie Valley Chamber of Commerce. Box 357, North Bend, WA 98045. ☎ (425) 888-4440. 🖳 www.snovalley.org/.

North Cascades. North Cascade Chamber of Commerce. Box 175, Marblemount, WA 98267. ☎ (360) 873-2210.🖳 www.marblemount.com/.

Oak Harbor. Greater Oak Harbor Chamber of Commerce. Box 883, Oak Harbor, WA 98277. ☎ (360) 675-3535. 🖳 www.whidbey.net/oakchamber/.

Ocean City. Washington Coast Chamber of Commerce. 2602 SR 109, Ocean City, WA 98569. ☎ (360) 289-4552 or ☎ (800) 286-4552. 🖳 www.techline.com/~wacoast/.

Ocean Park. Ocean Park Area Chamber of Commerce. Box 403, Ocean Park, WA 98640. ☎ (360) 665-4448. 🖳 http://willapabay.org/~opchamber/.

Ocean Shores. Ocean Shores Chamber of Commerce. Box 382, Ocean Shores, WA 98569. ☎ (360) 289-2451 or ☎ (800) 762-3224. 🖳 www.oceanshores.org/.

Ocean Shores. Ocean Shores–Grays Harbor County Visitor and Convention Bureau. Box 1447, Ocean Shores, WA 98569. ☎ (360) 289-4411 or ☎ (800) 874-6737.

Okanogan. Okanogan Chamber of Commerce. Box 1125, Okanogan, WA 98840. ☎ (509) 422-9882.

Olympia. Olympia/Thurston County Chamber of Commerce Visitor Information Center. Box 1427, Olympia, WA 98507. ☎ (360) 357-3362. 🖳 www.olympia chamber.com/.

Olympia. Washington State Capitol Visitor Services. Box 41020, Olympia, WA 98504. ☎ (360) 586-3460. 🖳 www.ga.wa.gov/visitor/visitor.htm.

Omak. Omak Visitor Information Center. 401 Omak Avenue, Omak, WA 98841. ☎ (509) 826-4218 or ☎ (800) 225-6625.

Orcas Island. Orcas Island Chamber of Commerce. Box 252, Eastsound, WA 98245. ☎ (360) 376-2273. 🖳 www.sanjuanweb.com/OrcasIslandChamber/.

Orcas Island. Orcas Island Visitor Information Center. ☎ (360) 468-3663.

Oroville. Oroville Chamber of Commerce Visitor Information Center. Box 2140, Oroville, WA 98844. ☎ (509) 476-2739 or ☎ (877) 478-6639. 🖳 www.okanogannet.com/-Oroville/.

Packwood. Packwood Ranger District Visitor Information Center. 13068 U.S. Hwy. 12, Packwood, WA 98361. ☎ (360) 494-5515.

Pasco. Greater Pasco Area Chamber of Commerce Visitor Information Center. Box 550, Pasco, WA 99301. ☎ (509) 547-9755. 🖳 www.cbvcp.com/pascochamber/.

Point Roberts. Point Roberts Chamber of Commerce Visitor Information Center. Box 128, Point Roberts, WA 98281. ☎ (360) 945-2313.

Port Angeles. North Olympic Peninsula Visitor and Convention Bureau. Box 670, Port Angeles, WA 98362. ☎ (360) 452-8552 or ☎ (800) 942-4042. 🖳 www. olympicpeninsula.org/.

Port Angeles. Port Angeles Chamber of Commerce Visitor Information Center. 121 East Railroad Street, Port Angeles, WA 98362. ☎ (360) 452-2363. 🖳 www.cityofpa.com/.

Port Hadlock. Port Hadlock Chamber of Commerce. Box 1223, Port Hadlock, WA 98339. ☎ (360) 379-5380. 🖳 www.northolympic.com/porthadlock/.

Port Ludlow. Olympic Peninsula Gateway Visitor Center. Box 65478, Port Ludlow, WA 98365. ☎ (360) 437-0120. 💻 www.portludlowconnections.com/PLCpg244.html.

Port Ludlow. Port Ludlow Chamber of Commerce. Box 65305, Port Ludlow, WA 98365. ☎ (360) 437-9798. 💻 www.northolympic.com/portludlow/.

Port Orchard. Port Orchard Chamber of Commerce. 839 Bay Street, Port Orchard, WA 98366. ☎ (360) 876-3505 or ☎ (800) 982-8139. 💻 http://portorchard.com/.

Port Townsend. Port Townsend Chamber of Commerce. 2437 East Sims Way, Port Townsend, WA 98368. ☎ (360) 385-2722 or ☎ (888) 365-6978. 💻 www.olympus. net/ptchamber/.

Poulsbo. Greater Poulsbo Chamber of Commerce. Box 1063, Poulsbo, WA 98370. ☎ (360) 779-4848 or ☎ (877) 768-5726. 💻 www.poulsbo.net/.

Prosser. Prosser Chamber of Commerce. 1230 Bennett Avenue, Prosser, WA 99350. ☎ (509) 786-3177 or ☎ (800) 408-1517.

Pullman. Pullman Chamber of Commerce. 415 North Grand Avenue Pullman, WA 99163. ☎ (509) 334-3565 or ☎ (800) 365-6948. 💻 www.pullman-wa.com/.

Pullman. WSU Visitor Center. 225 North Grand Avenue, Pullman, WA 99164. ☎ (509) 335-8633. 💻 www.wsu.edu/visitor/

Puyallup. Chamber of Eastern Pierce County. Box 1298, Puyallup, WA 98371. ☎ (253) 845-6755. 💻 www.puyallupchamber.com/.

Quincy. Quincy Valley Chamber of Commerce. Box 668, Quincy, WA 98848. ☎ (509) 787-2140.

Raymond. Raymond Chamber of Commerce. 300 Fifth Street, Raymond, WA 98577. ☎ (360) 942-5419.

Redmond. Greater Redmond Chamber of Commerce. Box 628, Redmond, WA 98073. ☎ (425) 885-4014. 💻 www.redmondchamber.org/.

Renton. Greater Renton Chamber of Commerce. 300 Rainier Avenue North, Renton, WA 98055. ☎ (425) 226-4560.

Richland. Richland Chamber of Commerce. Box 637, Richland, WA 99352. ☎ (509) 946-1651.

San Juan Island. San Juan Island Chamber of Commerce. Box 98, Friday Harbor, WA 98250. ☎ (360) 378-5240. 💻 www.sanjuanisland.org/.

San Juan Island. San Juan Islands Visitor Information Services. Box 65, Lopez Island, WA 98261. ☎ (360) 468-3663 or ☎ (888) 468-3701. 💻 www.guidetosanjuans.com/.

Seattle. Greater University Chamber of Commerce Visitor Information Center. 4519½ University Way Northeast, Ste. 203, Seattle, WA 98105. ☎ (206) 547-4417.

Seattle. Lake City Chamber of Commerce. 12345 Thirtieth Avenue Northeast, Ste. F-G, Seattle, WA 98125. ☎ (206) 363-3287.

Seattle. SeaTac International Airport Visitor Information Center. 17801 International, Seattle, WA 98158. ☎ (206) 433-5218.

Seattle. Seattle–King County Convention & Visitors Bureau. 800 Convention Place, Seattle, WA 98101. ☎ (206) 461-5840. 💻 www.seeseattle.org/.

Seattle. Seattle Central Area Chamber of Commerce Visitor Information Center. 2108 East Madison, Seattle, WA 98112. ☎ (206) 325-2864.

Seattle. Shoreline Chamber of Commerce. 18560 First Avenue Northeast, Seattle, WA 98155. ☎ (206) 361-2260.

Seattle. Southwest King County Chamber of Commerce. Box 58591, Seattle, WA 98138. ☎ (206) 575-1633 or ☎ (800) 638-8613. 💻 www.swkcc.org/.

Seattle. University of Washington Visitors Information Center. 4014 University Way Northeast, Seattle, WA 98105. ☎ (206) 543-9198. 💻 http://depts.washing ton.edu/visitors/.

Seattle. West Seattle Chamber of Commerce. Box 16487, Seattle, WA 98116. ☎ (206) 932-5685. 💻 www.wschamber.com/.

Seattle. Westlake Center Visitor Info Center. 1601 Fifth Avenue, Ste. 400, Seattle, WA 98101. ☎ (206) 467-1600.

Seattle. White Center Chamber of Commerce. 1612 Southwest 114th Street #108, Seattle, WA 98146. ☎ (206) 763-4196.

Sedro-Woolley. Sedro-Wooley Chamber of Commerce. 714-B Metcalf Street, Sedro-Woolley, WA 98284. ☎ (360) 855-1841 or ☎ (888) 225-8365. ▦ www.sedro-woolley.com/.

Sequim. Sequim Visitors Information Center. Box 907, Sequim, WA 98382. ☎ (360) 683-6197. ▦ www.cityofsequim.com/.

Silverdale. Silverdale Chamber of Commerce. Box 1218, Silverdale, WA 98383. ☎ (360) 692-6800. ▦ www.silverdalechamber.com/.

Snohomish. Snohomish Chamber of Commerce Visitor Information Center. Box 135, Snohomish, WA 98291. ☎ (360) 568-2526. ▦ www.historicsnohomish.org/default-f.htm.

Snohomish. Snohomish County Tourism Bureau. 909 Southeast Everett Mall Way, Ste. C300, Everett, WA 98208. ☎ (425) 348-5802 or ☎ (888) 338-0976. ▦ www.snohomish.org/.

Snohomish. Snohomish County Visitor Information Center. 101 128th Street Southeast, Ste. 5000, Everett, WA 98208. ☎ (425) 338-4437.

South Bend. Pacific County Historical Society Museum. Box P, South Bend, WA 98586. ☎ (360) 875-5224.

Spokane. Spokane Area Chamber of Commerce. Box 2147, Spokane, WA 99210. ☎ (509) 459-4109. ▦ www.spokane.net/.

Spokane. Spokane Area Convention & Visitor Bureau. 801 West Riverside Avenue, Ste. 301, Spokane, WA 99201. ☎ (509) 624-1341. ▦ www.spokane-areacvb.org/.

Spokane. Spokane Area Visitor Information Center. 201 West Main Street, Spokane, WA 99201. ☎ (509) 747-3230 or ☎ (800) 248-3230. ▦ http://spokane-areacvb.org.

Spokane. Spokane Valley Chamber of Commerce Visitor Information Center. 8817 East Mission Avenue, Ste. B, Spokane, WA 99212. ☎ (509) 924-4994. ▦ www.svcc.org/.

Sultan. Sultan Chamber of Commerce. Box 46, Sultan, WA 98294. ☎ (360) 793-1939.

Sultan. Sultan Merchants Tourism Information Center. Box 369, Sultan, WA 98294. ☎ (360) 793-2215.

Sunnyside. Sunnyside Chamber of Commerce. Box 329, Sunnyside, WA 98944. ☎ (509) 837-5939 or ☎ (800) 457-8089.

Tacoma. Tacoma–Pierce County Visitor and Convention Bureau. 1001 Pacific Avenue, Ste. 400, Tacoma, WA 98402. ☎ (253) 627-2836 or ☎ (800) 272-2662. ▦ www.tpc tourism.org/.

The Dalles. Columbia River Gorge Visitors Association. 404 West Second Street, The Dalles, OR 97058. ☎ (800) 984-6743. ▦ www.gorge.net/crgva/.

Toppenish. Toppenish Chamber of Commerce. Box 28, Toppenish, WA 98948. ☎ (509) 865-3262 or ☎ (800) 569-3982. ▦ www.wolfenet.com/~cowboyup/.

Toutle. Hoffstadt Bluffs Visitor Center. Box 127, Toutle, WA 98649. ☎ (360) 274-7750 or ☎ (800) 752-8439. ▦ www.mt-st-helens.com/.

Tri-Cities. Tri-Cities Visitor and Convention Bureau. Box 2241, Tri-Cities, WA 99302. ☎ (509) 735-8486 or ☎ (800) 254-5824. ▦ www.visittri-cities.com/.

Tumwater. Tumwater Area Chamber of Commerce. 488 Tyee Drive, Tumwater, WA 98512. ☎ (360) 357-5153.

Vancouver. Greater Vancouver Chamber of Commerce, Gateway WA State Visitor Information Center. 404 East 15th Street, Ste. 11, Vancouver, WA 98663. ☎ (360) 694-2588. ▦ www.vancouverusa.com/gvcc/index.html.

Vashon. Vashon–Maury Island Chamber of Commerce. Box 1035, Vashon, WA 98070. ☎ (206) 463-6217. ▦ www.vashonchamber.com/.

Walla Walla. Walla Walla Valley Chamber of Commerce. Box 644, Walla Walla, WA 99362. ☎ (509) 525-0850 or ☎ (877) 998-4748. ▦ www.wwchamber.com/.

Westport. Westport-Grayland Chamber of Commerce. Box 306, Westport, WA 98595. ☎ (360) 268-9422 or ☎ (800) 345-6223.

Whidbey. Central Whidbey Chamber of Commerce. Box 152, Coupeville, WA 98239. ☎ (360) 678-5434. ▦ www.whidbey.net/coup/.

Whidbey. Deception Pass Visitor Center. Box 157, Coupeville, WA 98239. ☎ (360) 675-7277.

Whidbey. South Whidbey Information and Accommodation Referral Service. Box 403, Langley, WA 98260. ☎ (360) 221-6765. ▦ www.whidbey.com/lang ley/.

Woodinville. Woodinville Chamber of Commerce. 13205 Northeast 175th, Wood-inville, WA 98072. ☎ (425) 481-8300. 🖳 www.woodinvillechamber.org/.

Yakima. Greater Yakima Chamber of Commerce Visitor Information Center. Box 1490, Yakima, WA 98907. ☎ (509) 248-2021. 🖳 www.yakima.org/.

Yakima. Yakima Valley Visitors and Convention Bureau. 10 North Eighth Street #51, Yakima, WA 98901. ☎ (509) 575-3010 or ☎ (800) 221-0751.

Attractions

Museum of History and Industry. 🖳 www.historymuse-nw.org/index.html.
   Nordic Heritage Museum. 🖳 www.artguidenw.com/Nordic.html.
   Seafair. 🖳 www.seafair.com/.
   Seattle Art Museum. 🖳 www.seattleartmuseum.org.
   Seattle Mariners. 🖳 www.mariners.org/.
   Seattle Seahawks. 🖳 www.nfl.com/seahawks/.
   Seattle Sounders. 🖳 www.halcyon.com/mcoker/sounders/.
   Seattle SuperSonics. 🖳 www.nba.com/sonics/.
   Wing Luke Museum. 🖳 www.wingluke.org.
   Woodland Park Zoo. 🖳 www.zoo.org/.

Theater and Performing Arts

A Contemporary Theatre. 🖳 www.acttheatre.org/.
   Art Guide Northwest. 🖳 www.artguidenw.com/.
   Early Music Guild of Seattle. 🖳 www.halcyon.com/emg.
   Federal Way Philharmonic. 🖳 www.scn.org/ip/fwp/.
   Fifth Avenue Theater. 🖳 www.speakeasy.org/5thavenue.
   Green Stage. 🖳 www.greenstage.org.
   Hokum Hall—Vaudeville, Theater and Music. 🖳 www.hokumhall.org/.
   Meany Theater. 🖳 www.meany.org.
   Northwest Opera. 🖳 http://weber.u.washington.edu/~dvictor/opera/nwopera.html.
   Northwest Sinfonietta. 🖳 www.nwsinfonietta.com/page1.html.
   On the Boards. 🖳 www.ontheboards.org.
   Open Circle Theater. 🖳 www.opencircletheater.org/.
   Orchestra Seattle and the Seattle Chamber. 🖳 www.scn.org/arts/osscs/.
   Pacific Northwest Ballet. 🖳 www.pnb.org.
   Pilgrim Center for the Performing Arts. 🖳 www.pilgrim.org.
   Seattle Children's Theatre. 🖳 www.sct.org.
   Seattle Choral Company. 🖳 www.wolfenet.com/~scc/.
   Seattle Folk Dancing. 🖳 http://seattledance.org/.
   Seattle Omnidome Theatre. 🖳 www.imaxtheatre.com/seattle.
   Seattle Peace Concerts. 🖳 www.seapeace.org/.
   Seattle Philharmonic Orchestra. 🖳 www.seattlephil.com/.
   Seattle Symphony. 🖳 www.seattlesymphony.org.
   Seattle Youth Symphony Orchestras. 🖳 www.syso.org/.
   Spectrum Dance Theater. 🖳 www.scn.org/ip/spectrum/.
   The Paramount Theater. 🖳 www.theparamount.com/.
   The Repertory Actors Theater. 🖳 www.angelfire.com/wa/reactworkshop/.
   Theater Schmeater. 🖳 www.schmeater.org/.
   Thistle Theatre—Puppet Theatre for Families. 🖳 www.thistletheatre.org/.
   Village Theatre. 🖳 www.vt.org.

Part IV
British Columbia

Chapter 25

Introduction to British Columbia

If British Columbia was a country by itself, it would be celebrated for its spectacular beauty, diverse culture, and, not the least, for its sheer size. British Columbia is seven times the size of New York State, four times as large as Great Britain, and two-and-a-half times as large as Japan. It is equal to the combined size of France, Germany, Austria, and Belgium.

Here you'll find huge mountain peaks, Pacific Ocean beaches, thousands of square miles of pristine wilderness, coastal rainforests, and gigantic frozen glaciers and snowfields. You'll also discover one of the most handsome and cosmopolitan port cities in Vancouver; and across the Strait of Georgia in Victoria, it's a picture-perfect island port that feels like one of the last outposts of the British Empire.

British Columbia is Canada's west coast. To the east is the province of Alberta; to the north is the Yukon Territory and the western portion of the Northwest Territories. On the south are three American states, Washington, Idaho, and Montana. In the extreme northwest corner of B.C. is the 554-mile-long panhandle of Alaska.

More than three-quarters of the province's land area is mountainous. The Rocky Mountains run the length of British Columbia on a diagonal southeast to northwest. On either side of that central spine are the Columbia, Monashee, Cariboo, Selkirk, Purcell, Cassiar, Omineca, and Skeena ranges. More than half of the land is 4,200 feet above sea level or higher.

In the moist coastal areas stand thickets of massive Douglas fir and western red cedar. In the higher and drier interior are vast forests of pine, spruce, and hemlock. All told, almost 60 percent of the province is forest. And more than 90 percent of the land in British Columbia is crown land, meaning it is owned and managed by the provincial government.

And, of course, British Columbia is *large,* at some 366,000 square miles, which leaves a tremendous amount of space for about 3.3 million people. Most of the population is clustered around Vancouver and across the Strait of Georgia around the capital of Victoria.

BRITISH COLUMBIA

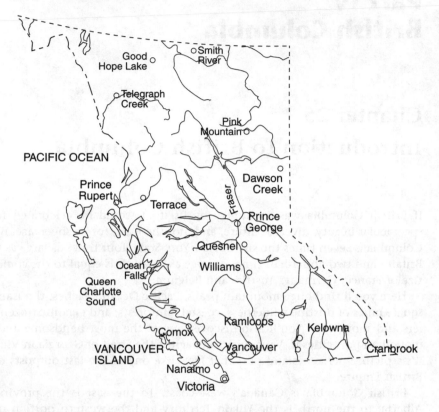

The abundant water of the rivers and streams of British Columbia discharge about 2.2 million gallons of water for every resident of the province each year; the liquid asset is used in hydroelectric dams for electricity, as well as for irrigation and drinking water.

In the Coastal Mountains about ninety miles above Vancouver is the Whistler Blackcomb resort, one of the world's best ski resorts and a major summer recreation draw as well. Across the strait on Vancouver Island are several other significant ski areas that draw prodigious amounts of snow.

The southwest corner includes hundreds of islands and mountainous fjords along a coastline that folds in on itself to meander more than 16,780 miles. Off the coast lies Vancouver Island, which stretches some 280 miles northwest.

Vancouver Island could be an island nation of its own, an area about the size of Holland with a spine of mountains, fishing villages, vast nature preserves, and a deep-water international port. At its southern tip is Victoria, the capital of British Columbia, with a population of more than 300,000 in the metropolitan area. The next largest city is Nanaimo, about sixty miles away, with a population of more than 71,000.

Most of the communities on Vancouver Island are on the east coast, along the sheltered Inland Passage that leads from Vancouver north to another inland waterway on the protected side of the Alaskan islands. The east side is also the home of some magnificent, lush forests and the main industry of the island involves forestry.

The exposed west coast of the island is mostly uninhabited with few roads, and there are some impressive beaches; the Alberni Inlet cuts more than halfway through the island to the community of Port Alberni.

History

Nomadic tribes lived in British Columbia in the south near present-day Vancouver and the Fraser River Valley and in the northern interior.

Many were killed off by diseases imported into the area by the white man, including smallpox and venereal diseases.

Russian explorer Alexei Chirkov sailed along the northwestern coast in 1741; the Russian influence in Alaska was already tenuously established. From the other direction, Juan Perez Hernandez came from Mexico to the Queen Charlotte Islands soon afterward. Other Spanish explorers sailed north from Spanish America in 1774 and 1775. A number of the islands in the Strait of Georgia, including Galiano, Valdes, and Quadra, bear their names.

Then in 1778 and 1779 Great Britain's grand explorer of the Pacific arrived in the area in search of an entrance to the much sought-after Northwest Passage. Among his staff was George Vancouver, who returned in 1792 to chart the coast in detail and in the process give the settlement his name.

It was not until the mid-1800s that the developing coal and lumber industries drew settlers to lower British Columbia. With the coal and lumber came the need to transport the commodities to market, and so the Canadian Pacific Railway was built to Vancouver.

In 1858 a gold rush brought thousands to the inhospitable interior of British Columbia.

Regions of British Columbia

The **Lower Mainland** region faces the Strait of Georgia, the trough (a submerged valley) at the mouth of the inland passage between the Coast Mountains on the mainland and the mountains of the lower end of Vancouver Island. About half the population of British Columbia, nearly two million people, live in the city of Vancouver and its suburbs, including Richmond, Burnaby, Delta, Surrey, North and West Vancouver, New Westminster, and Coquitlam.

South of Vancouver, the **Fraser River** empties into the strait. The Fraser is the longest river in the province, traveling 850 miles from near Mount Robson on the western slopes of the Rockies at the Alberta border, flowing first north and then looping south. It cuts the deep gorges of the Fraser Canyon before emptying into the Pacific Ocean at Vancouver.

The Fraser Canyon runs mostly north-south from the high Central Plateau at Cache Creek through the Coast Mountains to Hope and from

Dial tones. To call Vancouver, use the area code 604 for the city and surrounding areas. For the rest of British Columbia, including Victoria, use the 250 area code.

there west out to the Pacific. A gold strike in the canyon during the 1850s was part of the Cariboo gold rush to the central interior of the province. The main line of the Trans-Canada Highway follows the canyon and railroad tracks run along each side.

The **Okanagan Region** is a rolling highland plateau between the Cascade range to the west and the Monashee mountain range on the east. Okanagan Lake runs the length of the valley, a popular summer recreation area. The dry and relatively warm climate is the center of a large fruit-growing region, as well as a burgeoning wine industry.

The **Kootenay Region**, located in the southeast corner of the province, is carved into slices by the north-south Rockies, the Purcells, the Selkirks, and the Monashees. Long, thin, and deep lakes and rivers fill many of the valleys between the mountain ranges. The Columbia River rises out of a series of small tributaries from the Rocky Mountain Trench in the north at Mount Robson, the highest point in the Canadian Rockies. These tributaries feed into Kinbasket Lake, over the Mica Dam and form the Arrow Lakes system, including Revelstoke and Arrow, before they cross the border into the United States and eventually flow to the Pacific Ocean at the Washington-Oregon border.

There are major ski areas in Fernie and Kimberly, as well as a burgeoning helicopter ski industry in the remote mountains.

The high plateau of the **Central Interior** is home to the largest cattle ranches in the world. Some, like the Douglas Ranch, are hundreds of thousands of acres in size.

The commercial center of the region is Prince George, population about 76,500. The city is transected by the east-west Trans-Canada Highway and the north-south Caribou Highway that runs from Vancouver along the Fraser River.

Nearly half of the province lies in the virtually untouched North, above Prince George. The Alaska Highway starts in Dawson Creek and winds more than 600 miles northwest and into the Yukon Territory; the road was a major wartime project of Canada and the United States, built to help protect Alaska and northwestern Canada from a possible Japanese assault.

High honors. The tallest mountain in British Columbia actually lies mostly across the border in Alaska. Mount Fairweather in the northwestern corner of the province stands 15,298 feet tall; its summit lies in British Columbia. On the other side of the province is Mount Robson, partially in Alberta, at 12,972 feet the highest point in the Canadian Rockies.

Most of the region is mountainous and isolated with no roads other than the Alaska Highway and the Liard Highway, which branches off into the Northwest Territory near Fort Nelson. The Cassiar Highway runs north to the Yukon from Prince Rupert on the Inland Passage to Alaska.

Spectacular wilderness parks here include the sprawling Spatsizi Plateau and Mount Ediza Park.

The **Inside Passage** threads a needle almost 300 miles from the north end of Vancouver Island to Prince Rupert at the northernmost Pacific Ocean coast of the mainland of Canada. From Prince Rupert, an inland waterway continues north to Juneau, Alaska.

The narrow channels pass hundreds of small islands that have untouched wilderness and vistas of the Coast Mountains and the misty Queen Charlotte Islands. A ferry boat system connects Prince Rupert and other isolated communities to Vancouver and Vancouver Island. Other boats sail from Washington state to Alaska and the waters are plied by massive luxury cruise liners in the spring and summer.

The **Queen Charlotte Islands**, north of Vancouver Island, have been shrouded in mist and mystery for centuries. Once almost impossible to visit, the "Misty Islands" are now served by ferry from Prince Rupert.

The traditional home of the Haida Nation, the isolation of the islands has given rise to a number of subspecies of wildlife that exist nowhere else. Shrouded in mist and rain much of the time, the western ocean coast is rocky and rugged, while the east side has some sandy beaches. In the northeast corner of the islands is the wilderness of Naikoon Provincial Park.

Waterfalls in British Columbia

Here's a trivia question: name the highest falls in Canada. If you said Niagara, you're a few thousand miles wrong.

The tallest cataract in Canada is **Della Falls**, in Strathcona Provincial Park on Vancouver Island. The water drops 1,440 feet down a mountain side. Don't expect to see a street lined with tourist traps, though; for that matter, you won't find that many tourists, either. The falls are at the end of a rugged, unimproved hiking trail.

Other notable falls in British Columbia include **Takakkaw Falls** in Yoho National Park, accessible by road off the Trans-Canada Highway. Glacial meltwater drops an unbroken distance of 1,200 feet.

About 300 miles northeast of Vancouver are **Helmcken Falls** in Wells Gray Park. In winter, a massive ice cone builds up almost to the brink, 450 feet above the isolated basin.

Bridal Veil Falls, along the Trans-Canada Highway seventy miles east of Vancouver, are easily reached by car and then an easy stroll.

British Columbia's Wildlife Resources

The sprawling wilderness and mountains of British Columbia are home to a variety of birds and mammals unmatched in Canada and much of the world.

Some 112 species of mammals have been identified in British Columbia, among them 74 species not found in any other Canadian province. The province has large populations of moose, caribou, elk, deer, black bear, and mountain goat, and also serves as the habitat for numerous endangered species such as white pelican, the burrowing owl, the sea otter, and the Vancouver Island marmot. Some populations may number only in the hundreds.

Three-quarters of the world's Stone sheep are located in British Columbia, two-thirds of the mountain goats, half of the trumpeter swans and blue grouse, and a quarter of the planet's bald eagles and grizzly bears.

At Boundary Bay south of Vancouver, the largest populations of waterfowl to winter anywhere in Canada visit the marshlands of the Fraser River delta.

A population of about 2,500 Rocky Mountain bighorns live along the eastern border of British Columbia, on the slopes of the Rockies from the U.S. border to Golden, in scattered bands north of Mount Robson and in the Kamloops area. Another group, California bighorn sheep, prefers the south central area of the province, in the Okanagan, Similkameen, and South Chilcotin regions.

About 12,000 Stone sheep and 500 Dall thinhorn sheep roam the northern reaches of British Columbia.

British Columbia has more mountain goats than anywhere in Canada or the United States. Actually, it's not a true goat but is instead a close relative of the antelope or chamois of the Swiss Alps; a population of more than 50,000 range over most of the province. They usually stick to the roughest possible terrain, above the timberline or within retreating distance of the rocky bluffs of mountain ranges.

Woodland caribou number about 18,000 throughout British Columbia, ranging in the north from the Coast Mountains on the west to the eastern slopes of the Rocky Mountains and in the south in the Columbia, Rocky, Selkirk, and Monashee mountain ranges.

The rare Roosevelt elk, the largest elk to be found in the world, can be found in British Columbia on Vancouver Island and adjacent parts of the mainland.

There are some 180,000 moose in British Columbia, mostly in the north, but they're on the resurgence as far south as the United States border.

Some 400,000 deer in three species are spread over almost all the province. Mule deer range over the largest part of the province, from the northern reaches of the high central plateau to the mountains and highlands of its south central regions. Columbia black-tailed deer are found along coastal British Columbia and its many islands. White-tailed deer range predominantly in the southeast corner of British Columbia, the Kootenays, and the Peace River district.

In addition to browsing and grazing mammals, British Columbia has its share of predators. The cougar, the largest wild cat native to British Columbia, is found in most areas of the province except on the Queen Charlotte Islands. The cougar is known by other names around the world, including puma, mountain lion, deer tiger, Indian devil, and Mexican lion.

While populations number about 3,000, their secretive hunting habits mean that cougars are rarely seen, except where they find themselves accidentally in conflict with human settlement.

During recent years, a few misguided cougars have wandered deep into residential areas of Victoria from the surrounding highlands. One hid in a basement a few blocks from Victoria's Parliament Buildings and another in the basement parking garage of the Empress Hotel.

Black bears in British Columbia number some 140,000, and they range over almost every type of terrain from coastal beaches to forests to dry grassland and subalpine meadows. In the forest, they like open spaces where berries can be found but they also go fishing in streams for spawning salmon.

Bears generally try to avoid human contact and will retreat upon the sight of humans.

Grizzly bears, distinguishable by the large hump of muscle on their shoulders and a slightly flattened face, are even more shy of civilization and less plentiful than black bears. They are, though, more likely to be aggressive if they are confronted by humans. About 12,000 range over most of the province except Vancouver Island, the Queen Charlotte Islands, and the lower mainland.

Nonresidents of Canada are required to be accompanied by a licensed guide while hunting British Columbian big game, including deer, mountain sheep, mountain goat, moose, caribou, elk, cougar, wolf, grizzly bear, and black bear.

Transportation to British Columbia

The major cities of British Columbia are well-served by air, train, and ferry.

Visitors can drive into southern British Columbia from Washington, Idaho, and Montana in the United States, and from Alberta through mountain passes near Jasper, Lake Louise, Banff, and Crowsnest Pass near Fernie. (Be sure to check for road conditions in eastern and southeastern sections during the winter.)

The interior is served by a limited network of major roads. Route 97 runs north-south through the middle of the province all the way to Fort Nelson, where it splits northwest as the Alaska Highway into the Yukon Territory and on to Alaska, or continues north as the very basic Liard Highway into the deep remote of the central Northwest Territories.

Another north-south road is the Cassiar Highway that heads into the mostly untouched western interior, and also links Prince George to Prince Rupert, which sits just below the Alaskan Panhandle on the Pacific coast.

To get to most coastal communities, the best route is often by floatplane or by boat on one of the ferries that ply the inside passage from Vancouver or Vancouver Island as far north as Prince Rupert. (From there it is possible to continue by boat up the mostly roadless Alaskan coast.)

Air Travel

Vancouver International Airport is the gateway to western British Columbia, as well as Canada's hub for service to Asia and the Pacific. Located about twenty minutes from downtown, the airport is served by taxi (about $21), airport bus (about $9), and limousine (about $26).

Carriers to Vancouver include Air Canada, Canadian Airlines, American Airlines (in shared service with Canadian Airlines), and KLM Royal Dutch Airlines.

Domestic carriers to Victoria and other points in B.C., as well as Alberta, Manitoba, Washington, and Oregon, include AirBC (through Air Canada); Baxter Aviation, ☎ (604) 688-5136; Helijet Airways, ☎ (604) 273-1414 or (800) 665-4354; and West Coast Air ☎ (604) 688-3097 or ☎ (800) 347-2222.

There are also seaplane services that depart from downtown near Canada Place, flying to Victoria and elsewhere in the province. One such carrier is Harbour Air Seaplanes, (800) 665-0212 or (604) 688-1277. 🖥 www.harbourair.com.

Long-Distance Rail Service

Vancouver is linked to the rest of Canada by VIA Rail Canada, ☎ (800) 561-3949 from the United States or ☎ (800) 561-8630 from Canada. Pacific Central Station is located at Main and Terminal streets in downtown Vancouver.

B.C. Rail Passenger Services, ☎ (800) 363-3733, operates year-round service on the Cariboo Prospector between Vancouver and Squamish, Whistler, Williams Lake, and Prince George. Summer scenic day trips on the Royal Hudson Steam Train visit Squamish; the Whistler Explorer runs from Whistler to Kelly Lake.

Transportation to Vancouver Island

Visitors coming from the mainland of British Columbia can fly from Vancouver International Airport to Victoria International Airport near Sidney, a thirty-minute drive from downtown Victoria. There are also harbor-to-harbor floatplane flights between downtown Vancouver and Victoria harbor.

To drive from Vancouver, BC Ferries takes passengers and cars from the Tsawwassen ferry terminal south of the city with a ninety-five-minute crossing to Swartz Bay on Vancouver Island, about thirty minutes from Victoria. Total driving and ferry time is about two-and-a-half hours.

From the United States, there are airport-to-airport flights from Seattle and floatplane services from Seattle directly to Victoria harbor. Car and passenger ferry service from Port Angeles in Washington state connects across the Strait of Juan de Fuca, a ninety-five-minute crossing.

Air Service to Vancouver Island

Major airlines, including Air Canada, Canadian Airlines, and American Airlines, have service to Victoria, usually after a change to smaller planes in Vancouver or Seattle.

Kenmore Air, ☎ (800) 543-9595, flies from Seattle to Victoria and other locations in the islands. Helijet Airways, ☎ (250) 382-6222 or ☎ (800) 665-4354, connects from Vancouver International Airport. 🖳 www.helijet.com.

Floatplane service from Vancouver to Victoria is offered by carriers that include West Coast Air, ☎ (250) 388-4521 or ☎ (800) 347-2222 or 🖳 www.westcoastair.com, and Harbour Air, ☎ (800) 665-0212 or 🖳 www.harbourair.com.

Ferry Service from Vancouver

The highways of British Columbia's mountainous coast outside of the southwest corner near Vancouver are on the water.

There are no maintained roads above the Powell River area, just seventy-five miles north of Vancouver. And there is no way—other than boat or float plane—to any of the hundreds of islands in the Strait of Georgia or to the massive Vancouver Island.

Instead, there are the more than forty boats in the BC Ferries fleet. They operate almost entirely in protected waters, insulated from the open ocean by Vancouver Island and the many smaller islands. Large ferries, which can carry nearly 500 cars and more than 2,000 passengers, connect the lower mainland to Vancouver Island. Boats run several times a day and as often as hourly in peak summer periods on some routes.

BC Ferries has two terminals on the mainland for service to Vancouver Island. Tsawwassen, located about twenty-five miles south of the city (just over the border from Washington state) is the terminal for ferries to Swartz Bay near Victoria and to Nainamo and the Southern Gulf Islands. In recent summer seasons, ferries departed in both directions every hour on the hour from 7 A.M. to 10 P.M., with a crossing time of ninety-five minutes; additional boats are available at busiest times. Service is somewhat curtailed in the winter.

Horseshoe Bay, north of Vancouver, connects to Nainamo on Vancouver Island, as well as to Bowen Island, and the Sunshine Coast further north on the mainland. In recent years, boats departed on the ninety-minute crossing at least eight times a day from 7 A.M. to 9 P.M. in summer, with fewer trips in the winter.

The prettier of the two crossings is the one through Tsawwassen, which sends the ferry on a winding path between some of the green, hilly islands of the Strait of Georgia. And several of the boats in the fleet from Tsawwassen are closer to cruise ships than workaday ferries; you'll find restaurants, observation lounges, arcades, and gift shops at sea.

For information on fares and schedules for BC Ferries, call ☎ (888) 223-3779 in British Columbia or ☎ (250) 386-3431. You'll also find details on the ships, itineraries, and fares on a web page at 🖳 www.bcferries.com.

BC Ferries also serves many of the small islands in the strait, either from the mainland ferry terminal at Tsawwassen or the island ferry terminal at Swartz Bay. Boats connect to Galiano, Mayne, Saturna, the Pender islands, Saltspring, Thetis, and Kuper islands. From Nanaimo, ferries serve Gabriola Island, the most northerly of the Gulf Islands.

. The handsome Sechelt Peninsula is part of the mainland of British Columbia north of Vancouver, but it is accessible only by small plane or boat. Known as the Sunshine Coast, it takes its name from a claim to some fourteen more days of sunshine than sunny Victoria on the other side of the Georgia Strait. BC Ferries connects from Horseshoe Bay to Langdale with a forty-minute trip.

Ferry Services from Washington State

International ferry service connects to Victoria and Sidney from Seattle and other ports in Washington.

The *Victoria Clipper,* a high-speed catamaran, carries passengers from downtown Seattle to Victoria. The *Princess Marguerite III* carries passengers and vehicles from Seattle to Victoria, from May to September.

For information on either ship, call ☎ (250) 382-8100 in Victoria, ☎ (206) 448-5000 in Seattle, or (800) 888-2535, or consult 🖳 www.victoriaclipper.com.

Washington State Ferries operates passenger and vehicle ferries from Anacortes to Sidney. For information, call ☎ (250) 381-1551 in Victoria or ☎ (206) 464-6400 in Seattle.

Victoria San Juan Cruises carries passengers from Bellingham to Victoria from May to October. Call ☎ (360) 738-8099 in Bellingham or ☎ (800) 443-4552 for information.

Black Ball Transport runs passenger and vehicle ferries from Port Angeles to Victoria. For information, call ☎ (250) 386-2202 in Victoria or ☎ (360) 457-4491 in Port Angeles.

Ferry Service to Coastal British Columbia

BC Ferries' *Queen of the North* runs from Port Hardy at the north end of Vancouver Island, sailing on an all-day trip through the Inside Passage to Prince Rupert, the last significant town on British Columbia's North Coast.

The *Queen* leaves Vancouver Island to enter a short stretch of open ocean and then picks up the Inland Passage behind Calvert Island into Fitz Hugh Sound. The ferry continues through the protected Finlayson and Grenville channels all the way to Prince Rupert just short of the Alaskan panhandle.

Grenville Channel is a narrow waterway flanked by forested mountains. It's a bit like floating through a long, green tunnel.

At Prince Rupert, you can make connections to the Alaska Marine Highway System ferry, which docks alongside; that system reaches to Skagway, Alaska, and beyond.

You can also pick up ferries in Prince Rupert to the Queen Charlotte Islands. And Prince Rupert is also the terminus of the Trans-Canada Highway, all the way from the East Coast.

Service on the *Queen of the North* daily alternates direction in the summer; and there are weekly sailings in winter. About 150 cars can be carried on the ship to Prince Rupert.

BC Ferries also operates a local service to some isolated communities on the Inside Passage between Port Hardy and Prince Rupert on a route it calls the Discovery Coast Passage. Boats leave Port Hardy on Vancouver Island, making stops at Finn Bay, Namu, McLoughlin Bay/Shearwater, Klemtu, Ocean Falls, and Bella Coola.

Vehicles can be carried to many of the destinations, except for the final stop at Bella Coola. What few roads there are do not penetrate too far into the interior and there are no roads that run along the coast.

The ferry lands first at Finn Bay at the mouth of Rivers Inlet, a well-known sport-fishing mecca. Namu is near a favorite ocean kayaking area and one of the world's richest in-shore salmon fisheries. McLoughlin Bay/Shearwater is near Bella Bella, the largest native community of the mid-coast region. Klemtu, the most isolated port of call and the most northerly point on the route, is the home community of the Kitasoo people, who have preserved their culture and customs. The Kitasoo share with visitors their heritage, including traditional native dance and cuisine.

Not all sailings make stops at the same ports, and some schedules can take as long as twenty-four hours to complete; there are sleeper seats and showers available on board. Contact BC Ferries for schedules and necessary reservations.

The terminus is Bella Coola, a village about seventy-five miles inland from the coast. The ferry follows the Dean Channel to the Labouchere Channel. There you can pick up the very basic Route 20, which winds its way east through South Tweedsmuir Park inland to Williams Lake. From there, you pick up Route 97, which runs south to distant Vancouver or north to Prince George and the Trans-Canada Highway.

The connection to Bella Coola allows travelers to make a round trip by water in one direction and by road in the other.

Chapter 26
Vancouver, B.C.

The impressive glass-and-steel towers of Vancouver are sometimes hard to find when your eyes are distracted by the backdrop of the mountains across the bay and the reflection of the busy cruise and commercial port of Burrard Inlet. No complaint here; Vancouver is quite simply one of the most attractive major cities in the world. In some ways it's a Western version of Hong Kong.

Vancouver has the beautiful green of Stanley Park and the cultural bonuses of several universities, as well as one of the most cosmopolitan mixes of nationalities in the world.

The largest cultural groups of Vancouver are the British, who were among the earliest settlers and developers of the West, and the Chinese, many of whom began to arrive near the end of the nineteenth century, as workers on the construction of the Canadian Pacific Railway, and as miners.

Vancouver's Chinatown is the largest in Canada and third largest in North America after San Francisco and New York. The older Chinese community has been augmented in recent years by an influx of people from Hong Kong (which gives one reason for the city's "Hongcouver" nickname), as well as Vietnam and other Asian countries. Other important immigrant groups are comprised of various European populations including farmers from the Ukraine.

Located on the mainland in the southwest corner of British Columbia, greater Vancouver is made up of eighteen municipalities that occupy about 1,100 square miles in and around the Fraser River delta.

The population of the City of Vancouver itself is just over 520,000, but with the surrounding area, including Richmond, Surrey, Burnaby, Delta, North Vancouver, West Vancouver, New Westminster, Coquitlam, Port Moody, and White Rock, there are more than 1.75 million people in the community.

The metropolitan hub of the City of Vancouver is located on the Burrard peninsula. To the north are the Coast Mountains; to the west the Strait of Georgia; and to the east, the lush green farmlands of the Fraser Valley. South, about twenty-five miles away, is the state of Washington in the United States.

Vancouver's deep port, sheltered from the Pacific Ocean by Vancouver Island, is North America's second busiest port, shipping coal, minerals, grain, and oil.

VANCOUVER AND VANCOUVER ISLAND

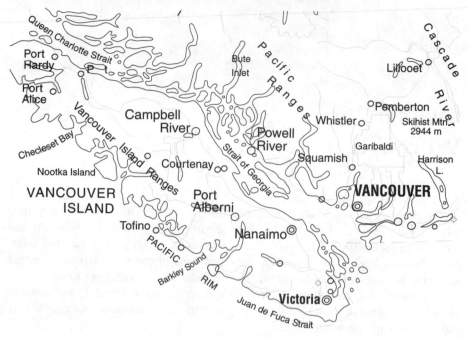

Climate

Moderated by Pacific Ocean currents, Vancouver's weather is the mildest in Canada with daytime temperatures averaging 70 degrees Fahrenheit in summer and 35 degrees in winter.

Spring comes early, with flowers usually in full bloom by early March. Late summer and autumn days, through October, tend to be warm and sunny. Winter is the rainy season; an average rainfall of fifty-seven inches translates into snow on nearby mountains, but relatively little in the waterside Vancouver area.

Stanley Park

A green jewel just minutes west of downtown Vancouver, at 1,000 acres it is larger than New York's Central Park. Trails lead into nearly untouched wilderness and to a wide range of attractions, which include the Vancouver Aquarium, a miniature train, a petting zoo, and a collection of totem poles.

The road that circles the park provides spectacular views across Burrard Inlet; a seven-mile-long seawall promenade for pedestrians offers even better vistas. At the western end of the park is the Lions Gate suspension bridge, leading to the Georgia Strait and English Bay. Entrance to the park is free, but drivers must pay for parking.

Within Stanley Park, the award-winning **Vancouver Aquarium** has an impressive collection of Pacific sea life including killer whales, sea otters, harbor seals, and some incredible species of fish. There's also an indoor rain forest and a collection of some of the largest fresh water fish in the world in the "Giant Fishes of the Amazon" exhibit. The aquarium is open every day. Admission: adult, ❹; youth (13–18), student, senior ❹; child (4–12) ❸. Family (two adults and as many as three youths or children), $45.95. For information, call ☏ (604) 659-3474 or consult 🖳 www.vanaqua.org.

Vancouver's Neighborhoods

The area in the vicinity of Water, Carrall, Cordova, and Powell streets in downtown Vancouver began as the site of the Stamps sawmill. In 1867 "Gassy Jack Deighton" came to town and gave what was then officially known as Hastings the nickname **Gastown**. In 1870, it was officially renamed Granville and sixteen years later incorporated as the City of Vancouver.

Gastown was leveled by fire in 1886 but rose again as a commercial area. Eventually it became, shall we say, the seedy side of town, including a skid row and worse.

Today most of the warehouses and shops have been converted to boutiques and restaurants. A late nineteenth-century atmosphere attracts hordes of visitors by day and cabaret patrons by night. Seediness perseveres in areas to the south and east, although I doubt tourists will be shanghaied out to sea. I'm more worried about being assaulted to purchase tacky souvenirs.

Gastown's most famous object is the steam-powered clock at the corner of Cambie and Water streets; it whistles and whoops on the quarter hour and puts on a gassy show on the hour, surrounded by visitors and video cameras.

The Chinese are the second largest ethnic group in British Columbia, after the British. **Chinatown** is also home to the world's thinnest office building, at the corner of Pender and Carral.

It's a place of won-ton houses, meat stores that have windows festooned with crimson barbecued ducks and coils of Chinese sausage, and displays of exotic roots, meats, and glands. Shops sell finely lacquered pots, jade, carved wood, and embroidered dresses. If you want to cook Chinese food, the grocers here can supply just about anything you can get in the Far East.

Little Tokyo or Japantown lies a few blocks beyond China-

The Steam Clock in Gastown
Photo by Corey Sandler

DOWNTOWN VANCOUVER

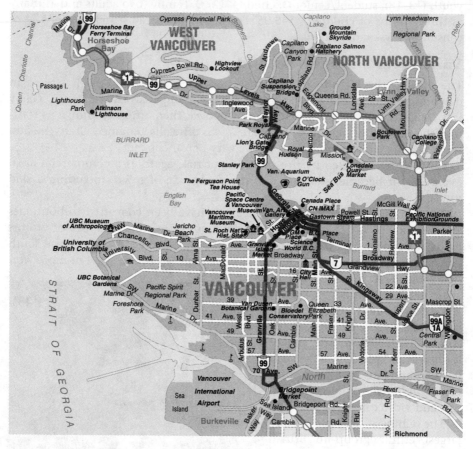

town on Powell Street between Gore and Dunlevy, the historical center of Japanese settlement in Vancouver. Many of the residents were forcibly relocated to interior British Columbia during World War II. **Sunrise Market** at 300 Powell is a popular shopping and informal dining area.

Little India, the cultural center of the thousands of citizens of Indian descent, is on Main Street between East Forty-Ninth and Fifty-First avenues, where some eighteen jewelry stores and twenty-five fabric shops make up the Punjabi Market.

In its rowdy heyday as a warehouse district, **Yaletown** boasted more saloons per acre than most anywhere in the world. Today the area is home to the city's hippest galleries, shops, and loft apartments for architects, designers, and filmmakers—a Vancouver version of Tribeca or Soho.

Nearby are False Creek, North False Creek, and South False Creek, all former waterfront districts reclaimed for homes and shops, especially at the sprawling **Granville Island Public Market** near South False Creek.

The redevelopment of **Granville Island**, under the south end of Granville Street Bridge, started out as an attempt to convert run-down waterfront pack-

ing houses and industrial property to public markets and avant garde retail space.

Today the area is a world of stylish restaurants,
art galleries, artist studios, craft shops, and theaters. Buskers add a carnival atmosphere.

The Granville Island Information Centre houses
historical exhibits and excellent audio-visual presentations that show the development of the area.

About a mile outside downtown, in East Vancouver, is Grandview-Woodland and Commercial
Drive, an area traditionally known as **Little Italy.**
Today the area has expanded to include ethnic
and cultural minorities of many origins. Here
Italian gelaterias are shoulder to shoulder with
reggae record shops and health food restaurants.

Once home to the rich and powerful of the
Edwardian era, the inner city neighborhood of
the **West End** stretches from sea to sea (Coal
Harbour to English Bay), with Stanley Park on

> **Key to Prices**
> **CANADIAN DOLLARS**
> ❶ $5 and under
> ❷ $5 to $10
> ❸ $10 to $20
> ❹ $20 and more
> Prices are listed in
> Canadian dollars.
>   When prices are listed
> as a range, this indicates
> various combination
> options are available.
> Most attractions offer
> reduced-price tickets for
> children and many have
> family rates that include
> two adults and two or
> three children.

one side. The West End is a mix of old homes and new developments. It is the
most densely populated area of Victoria. Denman Street, a favored place to
stroll, is a seven-block-long stretch of some fifty restaurants and coffee shops.

Museums and Attractions in Vancouver

For an impressive view of a great-looking city, you can take a glass-enclosed
elevator for a 500-foot ride to the top of the Harbour Centre Tower, along the
waterfront in downtown. **Lookout! at Harbour Centre**, at 555 West Hastings
Street, offers 360-degree views of the city, mountains, and the ocean. Admission also includes a twelve-minute multimedia show, "Once in a World, Vancouver." Admission ❸. A day pass includes the right to return the same day after
dark. For information, call ☎ (604) 689-0421. 🖳 www.harbourcentretower.com

(And you might also want to cross over Burrard Inlet to North Vancouver and
check out the view from the other side. The tram to the top of **Grouse Mountain** offers even higher views looking back toward the city. And while you're on
that side of the water, you can also visit the venerable Capilano Bridge.)

The star collection of the city is the **Vancouver Museum**, Canada's largest
civic museum, which showcases the history and culture of the city. The museum
is about as disparate as the wonderfully expansive province, ranging from
ancient baskets to totem poles to modern Vancouver through World War I. The
museum, located at 1100 Chestnut Street, is open year-round. Admission ❸. For
information, call ☎ (604) 736-4431.

Attached to the Vancouver Museum is a newer gallery, the **H. R. McMil-
lan Space Centre.** This is an attractive exploration of the solar system and
our attempts to visit our nearest neighbors. There are lots of hands-on exhibits and experiments, and items that include hardware and uniforms that have
been in space; some are related to Canada's active participation in the Amer-

Visitor information.
Tourism Vancouver's
information center is
located on the plaza level
of 200 Burrard Street
near Canada Place. For
information, call (604)
683-2000.
  Tourists can also call a
central number for
information and
reservations, (800) 663-
6000. www.hellobc.com.

ican Space Shuttle Program. A new program in the Planetarium Theatre is Electric Sky, an exploration of the Northern Lights. Joint tickets are available with the Vancouver Museum. For information, call ☎ (604) 738-7827.

A short walk away in Vanier Park is the **Vancouver Maritime Museum**, a rather low-key collection of old photographs of early Vancouver and its port along with some low-energy exhibits of artifacts. The museum is located at 1100 Chestnut Street. Admission: adult, ❸; youth and senior, ❸. For information, call ☎ (604) 736-4431 or consult 📖 www.vmm.bc.ca.

For a real sense of British Columbia's maritime history, step outside the museum and head for the water and the *St. Roch* **National Historic Site** at 1905 Ogden Street in Vanier Park.

In the 1920s the Royal Canadian Mounted Police operated the *St. Roch,* a wooden schooner powered by sails and an auxiliary engine. The *St. Roch* left Vancouver in June 1940 for a crossing of the Northwest Passage; she ended up trapped in ice for two winters, and did not reach Halifax until October 1942. The return trip took only eighty-six days, thus making the *St. Roch* the first known vessel to sail a round-trip through the Northwest Passage.

For information, call ☎ (604) 666-3201. The site is open daily May to September; closed Monday September to May. Admission: adult, ❸; child, student, and senior, ❷; children (6–younger), free; family, ❹.

The impressive **British Columbia Museum of Anthropology** presents a world-class collection of totem poles, ceremonial objects, and artifacts in an attractive, airy structure on the University of British Columbia campus.

Located at 6393 Northwest Marine Drive, the museum is open daily from mid-May to early September, and daily except Monday the remainder of the year. For information, call ☎ (604) 822-5087 or consult 📖 www.moa.ubc.ca. Recorded message: ☎ (604) 822-3825. Admission for adult, ❷; senior and student, ❶; family, ❹.

For a state-of-the-art dose of "gee-whiz," there's **Science World British Columbia,** a wondrous world of hands-on science exhibits, and home to one of the largest Omnimax domed-screen theaters.

The main gallery explains physics; you can light up a plasma ball or try to blow square bubbles. In the music gallery, you make music with your feet on a walk-on synthesizer. Another gallery explores natural history and yet another digs into mining in British Columbia.

The museum, nearby to the Main Street/Science World SkyTrain Station, is located at 1455 Québec Street. For information, call ☎ (604) 443-7443 or consult 📖 www.scienceworld.bc.ca. Admission packages, with one or more films, range from about $7.75 to $10.50.

In downtown Vancouver, the **Vancouver Art Gallery** is a small but imposing structure, home to a collection of about 4,000 paintings, sculptures, photographs, prints, drawing, and objects. There's also a gallery devoted to Emily Carr's haunting post-impressionist paintings. The gallery is located at 750 Hornby Street, at Robson Street. For information, call ☎ (604) 662-4700. Admission: adult, ❹; senior and student, ❸; child (12–younger), free.

The imposing carved granite neo-classical structure was built as the Vancouver Courthouse in 1911. Inside, the walls are constructed of marble from Alaska, Tennessee, and Vermont; a copper-sheathed dome that has a glass oculus tops the central rotunda.

Its use as a courthouse ended in 1979; it was converted to use as the new home of the Vancouver Art Gallery in 1983.

Entry to the lobby is from Hornsby Street, through the original colonnaded link be-

Vancouver Art Gallery
Photo by Corey Sandler

tween the old courthouse and its annex, or through a new colonnade that repeats the five columns of the portico above.

Ground-floor galleries are used as the home for long-term showings of the gallery's collection of historical and contemporary art. Access to the second floor, used for major temporary exhibitions, is gained by a dramatic double staircase flanking the rotunda. The third level is primarily dedicated to the gallery's collection of works by Emily Carr and British Columbia art.

For a decidedly modern multimedia experience, the **CN IMAX Theatre at Canada Place** shows films on a five-story screen. The theater, a legacy of Expo '86, is located at the Canada Place cruise ship terminal, near the SkyTrain Waterfront Station. For information, call ☎ (604) 682-2384 or ☎ (800) 582-4629 or consult 🖳 www.imax.com/vancouver. Admission: adult, ❸; senior (65+), ❸; child (4–12), ❸. Second film, $4 additional for all rates.

In Vancouver's thriving Chinatown, the **Dr. Sun Yat-Sen Classical Chinese Garden** at 578 Carrall Street is a classical garden in the style of the Ming Dynasty, perhaps the first of its kind ever built outside China. This special place was created by artisans brought from the mother country, who used imported natural and man-made items from Suzhou, the garden city of China.

Downtown Vancouver nestles against Burrard Inlet and the Coastal Mountains
Photo courtesy of Tourism Vancouver

Classical gardens were originally designed by Taoist poets, intended to create a place of ordered tranquility for contemplation and inspiration. The four principal elements of the garden—part of the Taoist concept of opposites in balance, yin and yang—are water, rocks, plants, and architecture.

The inscription above the entrance to the garden reads "Garden of Ease."

A gift shop at the gardens offers porcelains, books, and other items from China, elsewhere in Asia, and from local artisans. For information, call ☎ (604) 662-3207 or ☎ (604) 689-7133 or consult 🖳 www.discovervancouver.com/sun.

Another impressive patch of greenery lies under glass at the **Bloedel Floral Conservatory** in Queen Elizabeth Park. Here you'll find a large collection of plants, free-flying tropical birds, and colorful koi fish. The conservatory is located at Thirty-Third at Cambie. For information, call ☎ (604) 257-8584 or ☎ (604) 257-8570.

> **Hollywood north.** Vancouver has a very active filmmaking industry, both for Canadian movies and for Hollywood productions that use the city and surrounding areas as a stand-in for American locales. For information on projects in production, call the B.C. Film Commission's Hot Line at (604) 660-3569.

Shopping on Robson Street

Train tracks were laid along a broad street in Vancouver in 1895 and the road quickly became lined with small shops.

The street was given its name in honor of John Robson, premier of British Columbia from 1889 to 1892. After World War II, it was known for a while as Robsonstrasse, a recognition of the many European shopkeepers in the area.

Today Robson and the surrounding area offers a wide range of high-end retail clothing, accessory shops, and fancy restaurants. But you'll also find many small independent operations, offering an eclectic selection of art and other items.

The Robson Street Business Association maintains a website at 🖳 www.robsonstreet.bc.ca.

North Vancouver

The north side of the harbor is a very green bedroom community to Vancouver, the gateway to the Sunshine Coast, and the winter and summer attractions of Whistler. It also has some interesting attractions of its own.

You can drive across the Lion's Gate Bridge or take a bus tour that crosses the water.

In 1889 Scottish entrepreneur George Grant Mackay built a swinging pedestrian bridge across the rushing waters of Capilano Canyon. Today, more than 100 years later, the bridge—updated ever so slightly—sways 230 feet above the floor of the canyon on a 450-foot crossing.

The **Capilano Suspension Bridge and Park** in North Vancouver was one of the original tourist attractions of the northwest; today it is still one of the more spectacular hikes you'll find anywhere.

The five-foot-wide walkway, hung from steel cables, sways from side to side and ripples up and down when the steps of tourists cross from one side to another. A sturdy handrail is on either side of the crossing; it's fun to watch some overly self-assured visitors attempt to cross without touching the rail.

On the far side of the canyon is a cool nature park that wanders through the forest to a view of a 200-foot waterfall. At the entrance is the Capilano Trading Post, offering native art, apparel, and souvenirs. Nearby is the Bridge House Restaurant, an old-style eatery in the former home of some of the early owners of the bridge.

The bridge, located at 3735 Capilano Road in North Vancouver, is open from 8 A.M. to dusk in the summer, and 9 A.M. to 5 P.M. in the winter. For information, call ☎ (604) 985-7474 or consult 🖳 www.capbridge.com.

Admission: adult, ❹; senior, ❸; student (with ID), ❸; child (6–12 years), ❷. Off-season (November through April) rates slightly lower.

A bit further up the road from the Capilano Suspension Bridge, the **Grouse Mountain Skyride** offers a panoramic view of the city and harbor. The enclosed tramway cabin rises 4,100 feet to the top in an eight-minute climb.

Year-round visitors can explore hiking trails at the summit, and there is an hour-long multimedia show at the Theatre in the Sky. In the winter, there is downhill skiing, with thirteen runs and a respectable 1,200-foot vertical drop. Non-skiers can take a mountaintop sleigh ride. In the summer visitors can also ride some of the ski chairlifts at the summit.

The Skyride, located at 6400 Nancy Greene Way in North Vancouver, operates daily from 9 A.M. to 10 P.M. For information, call ☎ (604) 984-0661 or consult 🖳 www.grousemountain.com. Admission: adult, ❹+; youth (13–18), ❹; child (6–12), ❸; senior (65+), ❹; family (2 adult, 2 child), $45.

Vancouver Transportation

BC Transit covers more than 695 square miles of the lower mainland with bus service, a light rail service known as SkyTrain, and passenger ferry service known as SeaBus. The area is divided into three fare zones; fares are the same for any mode of transportation. 🖳 www.bctransit.com.

Buses run on the busiest routes from 5 A.M. to 2 A.M., and late night "Owl" service on some downtown-to-suburban routes until 4:20 A.M.

In 2000 fares during peak hours were $1.75 for service within one zone, $2.50 for trips that are within two zones, and $3.50 for trips that pass through three zones. Off-peak fares of $1.75 for any trip are in effect after 6:30 P.M. on weekdays and all day on weekends and holidays.

SkyTrain, an automated light rapid transit system, follows an eighteen-mile route between downtown Vancouver and Surrey with twenty stations along the way. SeaBus connects Vancouver with the North Shore via a twelve-minute harbor crossing. For information, call Vancouver Regional Transit System at ☎ (604) 521-0400 or consult 🖳 www.translink.bc.ca/.

Chapter 27
Victoria and Vancouver Island

Vancouver Island lies across the water from the city of Vancouver on the mainland, about thirty miles west across the Strait of Georgia, and north across the Strait of Juan de Fuca from Seattle, in Washington state.

A mountainous spine runs along most of the length of the 280-mile-long island, breaking into long mountain fjords on the west coast that cut deeply into the island. One of them, Alberni Inlet, cuts more than halfway through the island, ending at Port Alberni.

The west coast, which faces the Pacific Ocean, is mostly uninhabited with just a few small and isolated communities. The island's major settlements and roads are clustered on the protected east coast. Lush forests of large Douglas fir and cedar thrive in the moderate, wet ocean climate.

Victoria, on the southern tip of Vancouver Island, is the capital of British Columbia, with more than 300,000 residents in the city and its suburbs. Nanaimo, sixty-two miles north, has a population of about 71,000. The island economy is based primarily on the forest industry, with several mills located up and down the eastern coast.

North of Vancouver Island lie the Queen Charlotte Islands, a scenic, mist-shrouded world little touched by modernity.

Victoria

A walk around the harbor of Victoria is a step back in time to the heyday of the British Empire.

In some ways, Victoria is the most British of any major city in Canada. It's a place where they still serve high tea at the ornate Empress Victoria Hotel, and it's home to more portraits per block of the Queen (both old Victoria and today's Elizabeth II) than anywhere else I have visited in the country.

Located at the southern tip of Vancouver Island, Victoria is the most southerly and most urban of the municipalities that make up Greater Victoria.

The capital region includes Victoria, Oak Bay, Esquimalt, Saanich, Colwood, Langford, View Royal, Metchosin, Central Saanich, North Saanich, and Sidney, with a regional population of more than 330,800.

The MV Coho *pulls into Victoria's Inner Harbour after a trip from Port Angeles*
Photo by Corey Sandler

Victoria draws its modern history back to 1843, when Fort Victoria was established as a Hudson's Bay Company post. About fifteen years later, it became one of the main stopping-off and supply stations for miners seeking their fortunes in the Cariboo goldfields on the mainland. And in 1865, Esquimalt Harbour was designated as a British naval base.

But by the turn of the century, Vancouver had overtaken Victoria as an economic center. Victoria has held onto its past and grown more slowly than the city on the mainland.

Victoria has also held onto its designation as the capital of the province of British Columbia and government is one of the major employers on the island. Other industries include tourism and fishing.

Bastion Square in downtown is the original site of Fort Victoria. The Maritime Museum, prominent on the square, the Courthouse, and several other buildings from the turn of the century have been restored and currently house shops and offices.

The Empress Hotel lords over the inner harbor. The hotel maintains the tradition of railway hotels that were constructed across the West around the turn of the century. Now operated as part of the upscale Canadian Pacific group, the Empress still serves afternoon tea.

A few blocks away is Market Square, a busy packing house and warehouse from gold rush times, now home to a collection of unusual boutiques.

On the intriguingly named Pandora Street, an old feed warehouse has been transformed from an ugly duckling to the quirky but attractive Swans Hotel. The twenty-nine two-story suites combine modern amenities with old beams. On the street level are the bustling Buckerfield's Brewery and the Fowl and Fish Café, with an eclectic menu that on my visit included an ostrich stir fry (tastes like chicken).

A block further inland is Chinatown, once covering several city blocks but now mainly Fisgard Street. The street is capped by the ornate Gate of Harmonious Interest, which stands on the site of wooden gates that once barred entrance to Chinatown. Off to the side is Fan Tan Alley, a narrow passage that has shops and hidden windows and counters that are used in commerce of various sorts.

Victoria's Chinatown outdates most other Chinese settlements in Canada. It was founded in 1858, ahead of the major wave of Asian immigrants who were brought to Canada in the late 1800s to work as laborers in the building of the Canadian Pacific Railway.

Attractions in Victoria

The premier museum of Victoria is the **Royal British Columbia Museum**, located on the inner harbor. It's an impressive collection of British Columbia history and culture. At the museum you can walk through the streets of a pio-

Empress Hotel, Victoria
Photo by Corey Sandler

VICTORIA

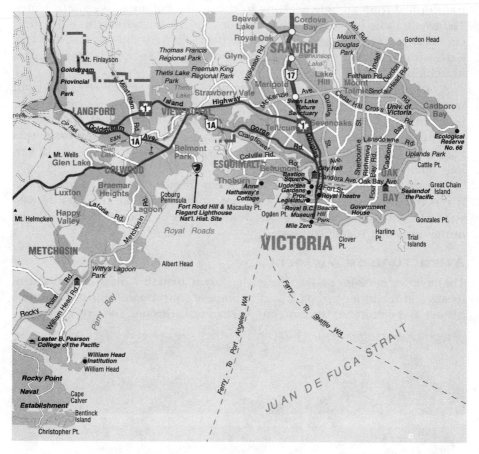

neer town, to an old working Gold Rush waterwheel, aboard Captain Vancouver's ship *Discovery*, into a native Indian longhouse, to the bottom of the ocean, through a coastal rain forest, or along a seashore.

Outside, there is a garden of B.C.'s native wildflowers. In the summer native carvers are at work.

One of my favorite spots in all of British Columbia is a room that's full of totem poles, located on the lower floor of the museum; arboreal lighting and sound effects transport you to the remotest coastal villages of the province.

The museum, founded in 1896, draws close to a million visitors per year and has burst through the seams of several structures during the years.

A recent addition is the National Geographic Theatre, showing IMAX large-format films.

In the attached Fannin Tower, more than 10 million artifacts are housed in anthropological, biological, and historical collections for researchers.

The museum is located at 675 Belleville Street. Admission: adult, ❷; senior, ❶; child (6–18), ❶; child (6–younger), free. For information, call ☎ (250) 387-2944 or ☎ (888) 447-7977 or consult 💻 www.royalbc-museum.bc.ca.

For information about the IMAX theater, consult 💻 www.imaxvictoria.com.

Alongside the Royal British Columbia Museum is **Thunderbird Park**, where you'll find a collection of totem poles, many of which feature the mythical thunderbird. According to legend, thunder emanated from the movements of the bird's wings and lightning radiated from its eyes.

The **Crystal Garden** was built in 1925 by the Canadian Pacific as a saltwater pool and lounge, an adjunct to the Empress Hotel across the road. The grand design echoed some of the great glass halls of Europe, including London's famous Crystal Palace.

At one time it was the largest indoor swimming pool in the British Empire.

The pool closed in 1971, the victim of soaring

Key to Prices
CANADIAN DOLLARS
❶ $5 and under
❷ $5 to $10
❸ $10 to $20
❹ $20 and more
When prices are listed as a range, this indicates various combination options are available. Prices are for adult admission; most attractions offer reduced-price tickets for children and many have family rates that include two adults and two or three children.

maintenance costs that included damage caused by corrosion from the saltwater pool. The community protested the loss and in 1980 the structure reopened with backing from the government of British Columbia. Today it is operated by the British Columbia Provincial Capital Commission.

Within you'll find a lush tropical paradise under glass with flamingos, butterflies, orchids, banana trees, and seasonal flowerbeds. A small collection of animals include lemurs, tiny pygmy marmosets and golden lion tamarins, and birds such as touracos, toucans, kookaburras, lorries, and ibis.

Crystal Garden is located at 713 Douglas Street. ☎ (250) 381-1277. 💻 www. bcpcc.com/crystal/. Admission: adult, ❸; child (5–16), ❷; senior (65+), ❸. A family ticket for two adults and as many as three children is $20.

Helmcken House, also next to the Royal British Columbia Museum, is the oldest home in British Columbia. Dr. John Sebastian Helmcken came to Fort Victoria in 1850, becoming the first Speaker of the Vancouver Island Assembly and one of three delegates sent to Ottawa in 1870 to negotiate British Columbia's union with Canada.

Filled with family relics, Helmcken House also has one of Canada's finest nineteenth-century medical collections, including Helmcken's medical kit. The Helmcken Family Christmas is a holiday highlight in Victoria; tickets are very difficult to obtain.

Admission: adult, ❷; senior (65+), ❶; child (6–12), ❶; child (6–younger), free. For hours and information, call ☎ (250) 356-5137 or consult 💻 www.heritage. gov.bc.ca/helm/helm.htm or 💻 www.tbc.gov.bc.ca/culture/schoolnet/helmcken/.

Vancouver Island has a rich maritime history well celebrated at the **Maritime Museum of British Columbia** in historic Bastion Square in Victoria's Old Town.

The museum features seventy model ships and some 5,000 marine related arti-

Maritime Museum of British Columbia

Photo by Corey Sandler

facts. The passenger travel section tells the stories of the Princess, Empress, and Pioneer lines. Star of the adventure gallery is the tiny vessel *Tilikum*, which circled the globe.

Another gallery tells the story of the island's lifeline, the BC Ferry system. A commerce display shows how the development of Fort Victoria helped build the maritime industries of the west coast.

The maritime museum was established in 1954 as a naval museum on Signal Hill just outside the gates of the HMC Dockyard; it moved to its present location in 1965.

The museum is located in the former Provincial Law Courts, built in 1899. In the paneled courtroom on the top floor, Chief Justice Matthew Ballie Begbie, renowned as the province's "Hanging Judge," handed down his sentences. Up the core of the building is an ornate open grill "bird cage" elevator, the oldest operating lift in Canada, also dating from 1899.

The museum is at 28 Bastion Square. Admission: adult, ❶; senior (65+), ❶; child (6–11), ❶; family rate, ❸. For information, call ☎ (250) 385-4222 or consult http://mmbc.bc.ca.

Scottish immigrant Robert Dunsmuir built himself a castle in the 1880s, paid for with the riches he amassed as a coal baron on Vancouver Island.

The **Craigdarroch Castle** sat atop a hill on a twenty-eight-acre estate. Dunsmuir spared no expense on construction. The walls are paneled with intricately carved walnut, mahogany, cedar, spruce, and other woods. Other features include magnificent stained glass windows and complex designs executed in exotic wood in the parquet floor throughout the castle's thirty-nine rooms. The massive entryway staircase leads through four floors to a glass-walled sitting room in the tower, which offers panoramic views of Victoria and the Olympic Peninsula. Craigdarroch is a Gaelic word meaning "rocky oak place."

Dunsmuir was the son and grandson of English coal masters; he came to

British Columbia in 1851 to pursue coal for the Hudson's Bay Company. In 1869 his company managed to secure the Wellington mine near Nanaimo; Dunsmuir became one of the richest men in the province and also one of the most hated because of his tough labor practices, including his successful breaking of an 1877 strike at the mine with replacement workers from San Francisco. His holdings eventually included railways, shipping, lumber, and iron works.

Dunsmuir died before the castle was finished, but his widow Joan lived there until her own death in 1908; at the time of her death, her net worth was estimated at $20 million. The castle was stripped of its furnishings and sold in a raffle in 1909. For much of the succeeding

Craigdarroch Castle
Photo by Corey Sandler

seven decades it served as a public building, including stints as the Craigdarroch Military Hospital in the aftermath of World War I, the first home of Victoria College (now the University of Victoria), the Greater Victoria School Board, and the Victoria Conservatory of Music.

The surrounding land was subdivided and now consists of a leafy suburb up the hill from the slightly funky University of Victoria district.

Since 1979 the Craigdarroch Castle Historical Museum Society has worked to refurbish the home to its former glory and recover some of the original furnishings. The hand-painted ceiling of the elaborate drawing room on the first floor included pastoral scenes; the artwork was painted over in the 1930s. In 2000 an art conservator was at work removing five layers of paint to restore the original scenes.

Self-guided tours of the castle take about an hour, and involve as many as eighty-seven steps up to the tower; there are no elevators or ramps.

Craigdarroch Castle is located at 1050 Joan Crescent, about a forty-five minute walk from town or a short taxi or bus ride. ☎ (250) 592-5323. ▣ www.craigdarrochcastle.com. Admission: adult, ❷; student, ❷, and child (6–12), ❶. The castle is open daily from 9 A.M. to 7 P.M. in the summer and from 10 A.M. to 4:30 P.M. from September through mid-June.

Several blocks south of the Legislative Buildings is the **Emily Carr House**. The home was built for the family of Victoria merchant Richard Carr in 1863; it was here, in 1871, that artist and author Emily Carr was born.

Emily Carr, considered one of the most important Canadian artists, specialized in paintings and sculptures inspired by the landscape and native tribes of British Columbia. After ill health made it impossible for her to travel, she turned to writing, producing six autobiographical books. Never married, she died in Victoria in 1945.

The dining room, drawing room, and sitting room have been restored to period elegance from the Victorian era. Some of the rooms include possessions of the Carr family, including some of Emily's pottery and sculpture.

One room is now dubbed the "People's Gallery," presenting the work of contemporary Canadian artists.

Open from mid-May to mid-September. Admission: adult, ❷; senior (65+), ❶; child (6–12), ❶; child (6–younger), free. For information, call ☎ (604) 356-5137 or consult 💻 www.emilycarr.com.

The **Art Gallery of Greater Victoria** has a small but eclectic collection. Some of the holdings are housed in a mansion built in 1890 as the residence for Alexander A. Green, a Victoria banker. Perhaps with a glance up the hill toward the neighboring Craigdarroch Castle, he named his residence Gyppeswyk. Green was only able to occupy his house for a year before his bank failed and he was dispossessed.

After a fire destroyed nearby Cary Castle, the mansion served as Government House, the seat of power in British Columbia for three years. During that time, in 1901, the Duke and Duchess of Cornwall and York, the future Queen Mary and King George V, visited Victoria and were entertained at a state dinner at the elegant home.

The museum's collection includes works by local favorite Emily Carr, as well as works by Canadian contemporary artists, North American and European historical artists, and a large collection of Asian artifacts. On permanent exhibition outside in the interior courtyard is a fourteenth-century Buddha head and a wooden Shinto shrine, perhaps the only one of its kind outside Japan.

The Art Gallery of Greater Victoria is located at 1040 Moss Street. ☎ (250) 384-4101. 💻 http://aggv.bc.ca/. Admission: adult, ❷; senior and student, ❶. Open Monday to Saturday from 10 A.M. to 5 P.M. and until 9 P.M. on Thursday. On Sunday the gallery is open from 1 to 5 P.M.

Point Ellice House was built in 1862, an Italianate villa on the shores of Victoria's Selkirk Water. The house contains British Columbia's most complete collection of Victoriana in its original setting. The well-documented nineteenth-century garden is one of the best examples of a Victorian domestic garden. Costumed staff members greet visitors; events include high tea and croquet and badminton on the lawns.

The house is located on Pleasant Street, off the Bay Street Bridge, five minutes from downtown Victoria. The site can also be reached by taking a fifteen-minute ferry ride from the Inner Harbour. Open from mid-May to mid-September. Admission: adult, ❷; senior (65+), ❶; child (6–12), ❶; child

(6–younger), free. For information, call ☎ (250) 380-6506 or consult 🖳 www.heritage.gov.bc.ca/point/point.htm.

The **Craigflower Manor and School House** is a recollection of life in Victoria in the mid-nineteenth century. Only the farmhouse is left from the former 900-acre Craigflower Farm, established by a Hudson's Bay Company subsidiary in 1853. Built in the 1850s, the Georgian-style house has been restored to reflect that era; exhibits include farming and home life.

The restored School House, also built in the 1850s, served the children of the farm and nearby settlements. It became a museum in 1931 and is the oldest standing school building in western Canada.

The complex is located at Craigflower and Admirals Road, ten minutes from downtown Victoria. Open from June to September. Admission: adult, ❷; senior (65+), ❶; child (6–12), ❶; child (6–younger), free. For information, call ☎ (250) 383-4627 or consult 🖳 www.heritage.gov.bc.ca/craig/craig.htm.

In Esquimalt, west of Victoria, the **Fort Rodd Hill National Historic Site** commemorates the Victoria-Esquimalt Coast Defenses that served from 1878 to 1956. Sites include three battery structures, defensive walls, gun mountings, observation posts, a World War II hut, an underground plotting room, and prehistoric archeological features.

The site is located at the entrance to Esquimalt Harbour, about eight miles from downtown Victoria. Open from March to the end of October; call ☎ (250) 478-5849 for hours, openings at other times, and for admission charges, or consult 🖳 www.harbour.com/parkscan/frh. Admission to Fort Rodd Hill and Fisgard Lighthouse: adult, ❷; youth (6–16), ❶; senior (65+), ❶; family, ❷.

Alongside Fort Rodd Hill is the **Fisgard Lighthouse National Historic Site**, the first permanent lighthouse on Canada's west coast. Completed in 1860, it was a sentinel for mariners entering Esquimalt Harbour. Automated in 1928, it is still in operation.

Fisgard Island is also an excellent vantage point for viewing Esquimalt Harbour and marine wildlife.

Entry to the site is through Fort Rodd Hill. Open year-round with limited services in winter. Call ☎ (250) 478-5849 for hours and admission charges.

Their royal highnesses, along with some of the lowest humans of history, are on display at the **Royal London Wax Museum**, on the inner harbor of Victoria.

A walk-through of the exhibit includes encounters with wax models that include the city's namesake Queen Victoria, as well as royalty of the past and present, and a recreation of the British Crown Jewels. Other sections include a Galaxy of Stars for actors of stage and screen; the Between Friends section that celebrates the friendship between Canada and the United States; some especially horrific images if you choose to enter a detour to the Chamber of Horrors; and for children, Storybook Land with characters from favorites that include *Anne of Green Gables*, the *Wizard of Oz*, and several Disney classics.

The exhibition claims a link to a branch of the Tussaud family of England and France, although the museum is not affiliated with the famed Madame Tussaud's collection in London.

Royal Row at the Royal London Wax Museum
Photo by Corey Sandler

Located in the former Canadian Pacific Marine Terminal, built in 1924, it was used for decades as a ferry and steamship terminal; soldiers departed from there for World War II. It was last used for passenger service in 1963.

The museum is located at 470 Belleville Street. ☎ (250) 388-4461. 🖳 www.waxworld.com. Admission: adult, ❷; young adult and student, ❷; child (6–12), ❶; senior (55+), ❷.

Attractions on Vancouver Island

Outside Victoria, Vancouver Island's best-known attraction is **Butchart Gardens**, a world-class collection of formal and theme gardens, spread over fifty-five acres.

Robert Pim Butchart, son of a Scottish emigrant, was born in Ontario in 1856. In 1884, at the age of 28, he married Jennie Foster Kennedy, an accomplished artist whose interests included ballooning, flying, and chemistry; on their honeymoon in England, Butchart learned the process for the manufacture of Portland cement. In 1888 he founded the Owen Sound Portland Cement Company in Ontario, pioneering the industry in Canada.

In 1902 Butchart came to Tod Inlet on Vancouver Island and then started a cement plant there two years later. The factory tapped into the growing market for the construction of permanent buildings, roads, and sidewalks on the island and the mainland of British Columbia.

Jennie Butchart took to decorating around her home with plants and flowers, and her husband supplied men from the cement plant to help her. When the limestone supply from the quarry was exhausted in 1908, she began work on what was to become the sunken garden there. She also planted Lombardy and white poplars and Person plums to block the view of the cement plant.

Workers brought in massive amounts of topsoil by horse cart and wheel-barrow to create garden beds on the floor of the quarry. The project was completed in 1921.

By the 1930s the gardens were drawing thousands of visitors and had become a major tourist attraction. Today, more than 1.25 million visitors a year come through the gates.

The gardens have always been a family operation, moving first to a grandson, R. Ian Ross, who remained in charge from 1939 through his death in 1997. Today Butchart's great-grandson, Christopher Ross, runs the company and personally supervises the pyrotechnics for the summertime fireworks show.

The fireworks show, presented Saturday nights from early July to early September, are considered among the world's best. Crowds of as many as 5,000 pack the gardens for the show, and entrance roads often close by 5 P.M.

Theme areas include the English Rose Garden, Japanese and Italian Gardens, and the Sunken Garden, with its dancing fountain. More than 135,000 bulbs are imported from Holland each year to add to the spring displays.

Butchart Gardens
Photo by Corey Sandler

The gardens open every day at 9 A.M., closing as late as 10:30 P.M. in the summer and during the Christmas holiday season. In the spring, closing time is as early as 4 P.M., advancing to 7 P.M. by mid-June. Be sure to call ahead to check on the schedule.

Butchart Gardens is located on Tod Inlet near Brentwood, about twelve miles north of Victoria. Admission prices vary by season, with highest rates from mid-June to the end of September and lowest rates from mid-January to mid-March. In 2001 admission rates are adult, ❷–❹; youth, ❶–❷; child (5–12), ❶ at all times. For information, call ☎ (250) 652-4422 or consult 🖥 www.butch artgardens.com.

Tour buses travel regularly from Victoria to the gardens, and you can also take municipal buses to a stop near the entrance. Gray Line runs a shuttle service to Butchart Gardens from the Victoria Bus Depot behind the Empress Hotel at 700 Douglas Street for about $4 each way. You can also take a Gray Line double-decker tour bus from the front of the Empress Hotel to Butchart Gardens, with scheduled drop-off and pickup and admission to the gardens included for $24.50 for adults and $7 for children. For information on Gray Line service, call ☎ (250) 388-6539 or consult 🖥 www.victoriatours.com.

The indoor tropical world of **Victoria Butterfly Gardens** was built specifically for housing and breeding butterflies and moths from all over the world. The rainforest environment is computer regulated to create the proper temperature and humidity (approximately 80 degrees Fahrenheit and 85 percent humidity) for the butterflies to carry out their life cycle and breed naturally in the garden.

Butterfly pupae are imported from butterfly farms every week to ensure a minimum of 700 to 1,000 butterflies from thirty-five varieties are in the garden at any given time.

Pupae are displayed in the "nursery" until metamorphosis is complete and they naturally emerge from their chrysalis and eventually are released into the garden for their first flight.

Typical imported members of the butterfly zoo include Blue Morpho, White Tree Nymph, Monarch, Caroni Flambeau, the Blue Clipper, the Brown Clipper, and the Giant Swallowtail. In addition, the facility has bred a number of species on site, including the Giant Owl, the Palm Fly, the Red Periot, the Tailed Jay, the Postman, the Zebra Butterfly, the Pink Rose, the Pink Cattleheart, the Great Mormon, and the Atlas Moth, the largest moth in the world.

Most of the plants in the garden are used as "host plants" that are necessary for the butterfly's life cycle or as food sources for the butterflies. Tropical plants in the garden include bougainvillea, banana plant, coconut and papaya trees, the African shield, the hibiscus, bird of paradise, passion vines, antherium, lantana, chenille, and angel's trumpet.

The gardens are located at the intersection of West Saanich Road and Keating Cross Road, at the base of the access road to Butchart Gardens. The gardens are included in some packaged bus tours. You can also reach the gardens on BC Transit bus 75 from Victoria. ☎ (250) 652-3822 or ☎ (877) 722-0272. 🖥

www.butterflygardens.com. Admission: adult, ❸; student, ❸; senior, ❸; child (5–12), ❷. Family admission is a 10 percent discount from the total.

The **Cowichan Native Heritage Centre** in Duncan, north of Victoria midway to Nanaimo, preserves the culture of the First Nations people. On the banks of the Cowichan River you'll find a traditional Big House, a gallery of west coast art, and a modern-day multimedia presentation. Activities include storytelling, a carving shed, weaving, Cowichan sweater knitting, moccasin beading, and craftmaking. In the summer the center presents a four-hour evening feast and storytelling program.

Located at 200 Cowichan Way in Duncan. Admission: adult, ❹; senior and student, ❸; child, ❸. For information, call ☎ (250) 746-8119 or consult 📖 www.cowichannativevillage.com.

Nearby is the **British Columbia Forest Museum**, where 100 years of logging history in British Columbia are commemorated with exhibits and seven steam locomotives.

The park covers more than 100 acres with indoor and outdoor exhibits and walking trails that detail the history of forestry in British Columbia. An original steam locomotive takes you from the entrance to the main exhibits of logging and milling equipment, passing over an old wooden trestle bridge.

The museum is just north of Duncan on the Trans-Canada Highway at 2892 Drinkwater Road, about forty-three miles north of Victoria. Open from May to September. Admission: adult, ❹; senior and student, ❸; child, ❸; child (5–younger), free. For information, call ☎ (250) 715-1113 or consult 📖 www. bcforest museum.com.

An old logging locomotive at the British Columbia Forest Museum

Photo by Corey Sandler

In the former Duncan train station on Canada Avenue is a hidden treasure, the **Cowichan Valley Museum**. Displays trace the railroad history of the area as well as two extraordinary collections; one room holds the contents of a general store, frozen in time from about 1920, and the other, a hospital emergency room from not long after. The museum is open daily except Sunday. For information, call ☎ (250) 746-6612.

Northwest of Port Alberni at the end of a fjord that nearly transects the island is the **McLean Mill National Historic Site.** Here is the last surviving steam sawmill in Western Canada. You'll find a complete logging village, a millpond, dam, rainforest, and a small railway. The site on Smith Road is open from May to August. Admission: free. For information, call ☎ (250) 723-8284.

At Long Beach on the west coast of Vancouver Island, some 200 miles northwest of Victoria on Highway 4, the **Pacific Rim National Park Reserve** includes Long Beach, the West Coast Trail, and the Broken Group Islands.

Long Beach is the easiest to reach; it is a spectacular seven-mile-long stretch of sand on the Pacific Ocean. Considered one of the most beautiful stretches of ocean coast in British Columbia, huge rolling waves carry in a wealth of fascinating sealife and spread it on a broad expanse of fine golden sand.

Wickaninnish Centre, next to Long Beach, provides informative displays on the Pacific Ocean and guided nature tours of the beach and adjacent forests.

The general store at the Cowichan Valley Museum
Photo by Corey Sandler

The forty-eight-mile-long West Coast Trail travels through a dense coastal rain forest of cedar, hemlock, spruce, and fir trees. Call the park for trail reservations.

An annual Whale Festival in March and April celebrates the migration of 20,000 gray whales along the park's shoreline.

Long Beach is open year round; the West Coast Trail is open April to October, and the Broken Group Islands from May through September. The preserve is located on the west coast of Vancouver Island between Ucluelet and Tofin, about 200 miles from Victoria. Highway 4 is the only road to the area.

Hourly, daily, and annual parking permits are available at Long Beach. Contact the park at ☎ (250) 726-7721 for more details.

West of Parksville on Highway 3 toward Port Alberni on the road to Long Beach is **Cathedral Grove**. This stand of giant Douglas fir and western red cedar is one of the few remaining on the west coast, one of the best examples of the virgin forests that greeted the first Europeans to visit the west coast. Natives regarded Cathedral Grove as a sacred place.

The tops of the tall trees form a cathedral-like ceiling high above your head while the thick tree trunks, some as old as 800 years, rise as pillars from a forest floor of delicate fern.

Strathcona Provincial Park is a mountain wilderness near the center of Vancouver Island. Its 520,000 acres feature mountains, valleys, lakes, alpine meadows, fast-flowing streams, and small glaciers. The trees in this area were already old when Captain James Cook of the Royal Navy landed at Nootka Sound on the west coast in 1778.

At 7,150 feet, the Golden Hinde is the island's highest point. And Della Falls is the highest in all of Canada, with a total drop of 1,400 feet in three cascades.

Strathcona Provincial Park is located off Highway 28, thirty miles west of Campbell River. Admission: Ralph River ❹ per party; Buttle Lake ❹ per party.

The **Mount Washington** ski area straddles the provincial park. The mountain is a prodigious snow magnet, although the surrounding areas have a relatively temperate climate. In a typical year, some or all of the six golf courses in the Comox Valley stay open all year, permitting a combination of skiing and golfing on the same day.

The Mount Washington Resort is accessible via the Strathcona Parkway out of Courtenay. Skiers will find forty-two runs and five chairlifts, with a 1,657-foot vertical drop. Cross-country skiers can enjoy twenty-five miles of marked trails along high alpine lakes and forests. For information on the resort, call ☎ (250) 334-3234.

Another smaller ski area, Forbidden Plateau, nineteen miles from Courtenay, shut down in 2000 with uncertain prospects for reopening.

Other Communities on Vancouver Island

Nanaimo. On the east coast of the island, about forty miles north of Victoria, Nanaimo is the second-largest city on the island, with a population of more than 71,000.

Nanaimo's economy is based on forestry, with a large pulp mill nearby and a commercial herring and salmon fishing fleet.

For tourists, Nanaimo is a jumping off point for Long Beach across the island on the west coast, for saltwater fishing in the Strait of Georgia, and for skiing at Mount Washington and Mount Arrowsmith in winter.

North Cowichan. The local economy is based around forestry. The area includes the small communities of Chemainus, Crofton, and Maple Bay, and is adjacent to the City of Duncan.

Wall-sized murals all over the Village of Chemainus draw half a million people each year. Near Duncan, the BC Forest Museum attracts several hundred thousand visitors as well.

Campbell River. The small city of about 30,000 residents sits at about the midway point of the island, on the east coast, about eighty-seven miles from Nanaimo.

Campbell River claims to be the salmon capital of the world, a label also claimed by Port Alberni nearby. Campbell River is the gateway into the oldest provincial park in British Columbia, Strathcona Park, and close to skiing opportunities at Mount Washington.

A bit closer to Nanaimo are the twin communities of **Comox** and **Courtenay**, both drawing economic sustenance from the Canadian Forces Base in Comox and the forest industry. Rich agricultural land of the Comox Valley is used for dairy farming and hog, sheep, and cattle operations, as well as for numerous horse farms.

The Southern Gulf and Coastal Islands

The many islands between mainland British Columbia and Vancouver Island are a delight to explore. You're very likely, though, to have to share the scenery with whales, and bald eagles hunting salmon, and tourists in search of all three.

The Southern Gulf Islands sit in the channel between Vancouver Island and the mainland of British Columbia, just above the border between Canada and the United States. They are served by the passenger and car ships of BC Ferries. The principal islands, from north to south, include Gabriola, just offshore of Nanaimo; Salt Spring; Galiano; Mayne; Pender; and Saturna.

Gabriola is an artist and writer's colony, well off the beaten path for most tourists.

Salt Spring Island is very green, home to many sheep and goat farms. The population of about 10,000 is based around Ganges Village, where a weekly agricultural and handicrafts market is held, as well as larger spring and fall fairs. There are more than a hundred bed and breakfasts on the island, seventy shops, and several dozen studios and galleries; road signs are keyed to a map that delivers visitors to the studios. For information about the studio tour, call ☎ (250) 537-9865 or consult 🖳 www.saltspring.com/studiotour.

Just west of Ganges Village, a winding gravel road leads to the top of Mount Maxwell, a park with spectacular views of the region.

Salt Spring is served by ferry from Vancouver Island with large vessels from Swartz Bay to Fulford and smaller ferries from Crofton to Vesuvius. There is also service from Tsawassen on the mainland to Long Harbour.

The ferry from the mainland to Vesuvius on Salt Spring Island arrives
Photo by Corey Sandler

Galiano Island was named after Spanish explorer Dionisio Alcala Galiano, who sailed the local waters more than two centuries ago. Local tribes of the Coast Salish Nation visited the island to harvest grapes, salal, and salmon berries and hunt elk, deer, and grouse.

Today the island's bluffs and beaches offer places to view eagles riding the updrafts and otters, seals, and orca whales swimming just off shore; some 130 species of birds live there or visit. Jewels includes Montague Provincial Park, with three white shell beaches. Dionisio Provincial Park, at the far west tip and reachable only by boat, offers spectacular views of the North Shore mountains.

BC Ferries pull into Sturdies Bay on the island from the Swartz Bay terminal on Vancouver Island or from Tsawassen on the mainland.

For information, call ☎ (250) 539-2233 or consult 💻 www.galianoisland. com.

Mayne Island was visited by Captain George Vancouver in 1794; members of his crew camped at Georgina Point, leaving behind a coin and knife that were found more than a century later by early settlers. In the 1850s, Captain George Richards of the Royal Navy surveyed the area aboard HMS *Plumper*; he named the island after his lieutenant, Richard Charles Mayne.

Early homesteaders settled in the areas around Miners Bay, named after the hopeful visitors to the area who used the island as a midway stopping point en route to the Cariboo Gold Rush of 1858.

The temperate climate of the island lead to an industry of hothouse tomatoes, including some greenhouses large enough to drive horsedrawn cultivators through the plants. Much of that industry ended when Japanese gardeners who had lived on the island were forcibly relocated to inland Canada during World War II.

Today the island's year-round population is less than one thousand. Ferries from the mainland and Swartz Bay put in at Village Bay.

For information, consult 💻 www.gulfislands.com/mayne_chamber.

Pender Island, actually two nearby islands connected by a small bridge, is reachable by BC Ferries from Swartz Bay or Tsawassen, or by an inter-island connection to the terminal at Otter Bay on North Pender Island.

You'll find information at a web page run by a bed and breakfast on the island, 💻 www.penderislands.com.

Saturna Island is the southernmost of the Canadian islands in the Gulf. It includes about a dozen small bed and breakfast and cottage resorts and a few stores. BC Ferries serves the island from Swartz Bay and Tsawassen to a terminal at Government Wharf at the western tip. Winter Cove Park to the west includes trails through mixed forest and marsh and sanctuary to ducks, eagles, shore birds, seals, and otters. At East Point Regional Park, a lighthouse marks the end of the island and the swirling currents of Boundary Pass; orca whales regularly summer just off shore.

For information, consult 💻 www.saturnatourism.bc.ca.

Scattered among the islands are hundreds of overnight anchorages and a system of thirty-four marine parks that offer safe anchorage and moorings. Some provide fresh water supplies and sanitary facilities while others are undeveloped.

The largest marine provincial park, Desolation Sound on the mainland north of Powell River, includes thirty-seven miles of shoreline set against the snow-peaked Coast Mountains, a marine park of stunning beauty that is virtually unmatched in the world.

Sail and motor boats can be chartered at marinas up and down the B.C. coast. If you are qualified to operate a vessel, you can charter on a bare-boat basis, or you can hire a boat and captain for several days or more. Some of the charter boat companies offer luxurious vessels with gourmet chefs and amenities.

Other waterborne adventures cruise from Campbell River (served by air from Vancouver) to the Johnstone Strait to the north, and among the Queen Charlotte Islands as well. Stops may include abandoned Haida villages such as Skedans, Tanu, and Ninstints. The strait is populated with large numbers of killer whales, humpback whales, Dall's porpoises, harbor porpoises, and Stellars sea lions; its shores and tidal shelves are home to sea stars, sea cucumbers, barnacles, mussels, scallops, red rock crabs, moon snails, and more.

To reach cruises further north among the Queen Charlotte Islands, visitors usually fly to Sandspit on Moresby Island.

The Queen Charlotte Islands

The 138 islands in the Queen Charlotte group cover some 1,100 square miles, featuring a diverse range of vegetation zones, from rain forest to alpine tundra. Thousands of years of isolation have resulted in the evolution of several distinctive island species. More than a million seabirds nest along the shoreline, and even more migratory birds pass through in the spring and fall.

QUEEN CHARLOTTE ISLANDS

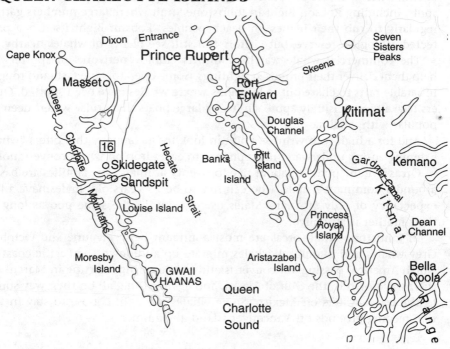

Ferry service runs from Prince Rupert on the far north coast of the mainland of British Columbia. You can also fly to the islands from Prince Rupert or by floatplane from Vancouver and other points.

The **Queen Charlotte Islands Museum** in Skidegate displays Haida totem poles, ethnological and archaeological collections, as well as historical and paleontological materials. The museum at Second Beach is open daily in summer, and daily except Tuesday and Sunday the remainder of the year. Admission: adult, **❶**; child (13–younger), free. For information, call ☎ (604) 559-4643.

The **Gwaii Haanas National Park Reserve and Haida Heritage Site** in south Moresby Island in the Queen Charlotte Islands is open to a select few visitors under a program of Parks Canada and the Council of the Haida Nation.

Call ☎ (604) 559-8818 for information and reservations, or write to the Gwaii Haanas National Park Reserve, Box 37, Queen Charlotte, B.C. V0T 1S0.

Whale Watching

The Queen Charlotte Strait off the northeast coast of Vancouver Island and narrow Johnstone Strait on the Inside Passage have the largest concentration of killer whales (Orcina orcas) anywhere on the planet. And the waters on the exposed west coast of the island are popular vacation spots for gray whales and humpbacks.

Whale watching companies leave from a number of ports on Vancouver Island, including the west coast ports of Tofino and Ucluelet, at the south end near Victoria and Sooke, and on the northeast coast of Vancouver Island near Port McNeill and Telegraph Cove.

And when it comes to vacationing, orcas have some very particular favorite spots, including Robson Bight in Johnstone Strait where large numbers gather regularly to rub their bellies on beach pebbles. Robson Bight itself is a protected ecological reserve, but visitors can still see plenty of whales nearby.

The commercial whale watching outfits employ networks of spotters to help them deliver their promised sightings. Some operators use fast (and rough) inflatable rafts to chase out to locations where whales have been spotted. Others take a more leisurely approach, using large boats that cruise waters deemed popular with whales.

And for a high-tech wrinkle, you can look for a company that offers "whale listening" using underwater microphones to eavesdrop on whale conversations.

Orcas live in "pods" of about five to twenty animals. The families are based around a dominant female, who can live to be 75 years old; males have a life expectancy of only 50 years. Males usually stay in the same pod as long as their mother is still alive.

In Johnstone Strait, orcas are most abundant between June and October. Grey whales and humpback whales migrate up and down the Pacific coast of North America, passing Vancouver Island in the spring (starting in March) on their way north to the Gulf of Alaska, and again in the fall on their way south to the warm waters off Mexico. Some whales, though, choose to stay in the rich feeding grounds off Vancouver Island all summer.

Chapter 28
Coastal Mountains and Interior British Columbia

From Vancouver, Route 99 heads due north to Whistler; on the way up, the Strait of Georgia is on your left to just beyond Britannia Bay and the Coastal Mountains loom off the right shoulder.

The Britannia Beach mine, thirty-two miles north of Vancouver, was once a major source of copper in North America. Today mining operations have ended, but the **B.C. Museum of Mining** offers a rare glimpse into the underground world.

The mineral wealth of the area was first discovered in 1888, when a prospector shot at a deer; the animal's thrashing hooves exposed mineralized rock below the moss, which lead to a determination that Britannia Mountain held copper.

In 1899 mining engineer George Robinson sought capital to exploit the riches; eventually the site came under control of the Britannia Mining and Smelting Company, a branch of the Howe Sound Company, which was to operate the mine for the next sixty years. The first ore was shipped to the Crofton Smelter on Vancouver Island in 1904. The mine reached a peak of copper production during World War I.

On March 21, 1915, an avalanche descended on the Jane Camp at the base of the mountain, killing sixty men, women, and children. The town was rebuilt at a higher level on the mountain. Tragedy struck again, twice, in 1921 when Mill No. 2 burnt to the ground, and then a massive flood destroyed the small community on the banks of Britannia creek, killing thirty-seven people.

The company towns at Britannia included theaters, libraries, billiard rooms, swimming pools, and more.

By 1929 the Britannia mines were the largest copper producer in the British Commonwealth; during the next decade, the mine also began to produce zinc and pyrite. And once again, military demands for copper—this time during World War II—drove up the prices.

In 1956 a rail line was completed from Squamish to North Vancouver, and two years later the Squamish highway was completed, ending Britannia's reliance on boats for access. During the next two decades, the price of copper declined while expenses rose, and by 1974 the mine was finally closed.

Today the mine lives again as a tourist attraction. Visitors board a mine train at the West Portal for a view of workings 1,200 feet under the ground, demonstrating many of the old methods of hard rock mining.

Other parts of the tour include a visit to the base of the massive Mill No. 3, built in 1922; it is one of the last remaining gravity-fed concentrators in North America. Here you will also find the restored Assay Lab, which contains the museum's geology collection.

Impossible to miss is a modern-era 235-ton super mine truck in the industrial yard; nearby are older and smaller pieces of mining equipment.

The museum is open from May to October, plus selected periods during the school year, including spring break in late March, and by appointment during off-season.

The museum is an industrial site; wear proper footgear and warm clothing for the ninety-minute tour. Admission: adult, ❷; student, ❷; senior, ❷; family (2 adults, 3 students), ❹.

For information, call ☎ (604) 688-8735, or consult 🖳 www.bcmuseumofmining.org.

Garibaldi Provincial Park is a high mountain wilderness that surrounds one of Canada's deepest lakes about an hour's drive north of Vancouver. Lake Garibaldi, formed from a natural dam of shale known as The Barrier, descends nearly 10,000 feet below the surface. Dominated by Mount Garibaldi, the rugged, glacier-worn mountains were formed during a relatively recent period of volcanic activity.

Other distinctive mountains throughout the park's 480,000 acres are the Black Tusk, Guard Mountain, and the Table. The park features a pristine forest of red cedar, hemlock, and the majestic Douglas fir.

In the summer, the park is open for camping and hiking; in the winter, there are cross-country and ski touring trails.

The park is located east off Highway 99 (north of Squamish), forty miles north of Vancouver. For information, call ☎ (604) 898-3678.

Northwestern British Columbia

One of the more remote significant museums in Canada, the **Museum of Northern British Columbia** in Prince Rupert traces 10,000 years of human habitation on British Columbia's north coast. Included is a collection of Tsimshian, Tlingit, and Haida ethnographic and archaeological artifacts dating from prehistory to recent times, and the history and artifacts from the fur

COASTAL AND INTERIOR BRITISH COLUMBIA

trade with Europeans, rail construction, and the establishment of the Port of Prince Rupert.

In addition to guided museum tours, the museum offers a three-hour Archaeology Harbor tour.

For more information, call ☎ (250) 624-3207. Located at First Avenue and McBride Street in Prince Rupert, the museum is open daily in the summer and daily except Sunday for the remainder of the year. General admission is free. Guided tours: ❷ per person. Harbor tours offered in summer, Monday to Saturday 9 A.M. to 5 P.M., ❶.

In Port Edward, a small community just below Prince Rupert—near the end of the British Columbia coastline where it meets the Alaskan panhandle, the **North Pacific Cannery Village Museum** is the oldest and most complete restoration of its kind in British Columbia, with exhibits on fishing and the fish processing industry, life in an 1889 cannery village, and the role of Chinese and First Nations people in the fishing industry.

Each day during July and August, and on weekends in May, June, and September, there is a live, one-half hour play, *The Skeena River Story*, on the history of the fishery.

The museum is located at 1889 Skeena Drive in Port Edward. For information, call ☎ (250) 628-3538. Open daily May to September; closed Monday and Tuesday remainder of the year. Admission: adult, ❷; youth (6–12), ❶; student and senior ❷.

Way up north, above Prince Rupert on the British Columbia border with Alaska's Misty Fjords National Monument, the **Kitwanga Fort National Historic Site** commemorates the culture of the Tsimshian people and their history. The site consists of *Ta'awdzep* or Battle Hill, a natural feature. On top are archaeological remains of fortified houses occupied during the historic period. Situated near an important trade route between the Skeena and Nass Rivers, the site was fortified with a palisade and enclosed five houses and food storage pits at the beginning of the nineteenth century.

From the fort, Gitwangak people under their powerful chieftain, Nekt, waged battles to control fishing sites, protect trade routes, and enhance their prestige. The fort was abandoned after Nekt's death. Although not part of the site, totem poles located at nearby village Gitwangak tell the story of Nekt.

Visitors must climb a long flight of stairs to reach the site. For information, call ☎ (250) 996-7191. The site is located seventy-five miles northeast of Terrace, near the village of Kitwanga on Highway 16. Call for hours and admission prices.

The largest park in British Columbia is **Tweedsmuir Provincial Park**, with more than 2.4 million acres of wilderness scenery, located east of Bella Bella on the coast and Bella Coola inland. There is a canoe route with six portages from Turner Lake to Kidney Lake; canoes may be rented at Turner Lake.

For information, call Tweedsmuir North in Smithers at ☎ (250) 847-7320 or Tweedsmuir South in Williams Lake at ☎ (250) 398-4414.

East of Prince Rupert in Hazleton is the **'Ksan Indian Village**, a reconstructed Gitksan Native Village such as the one that stood on the same site when the first European explorers came to the Hazelton area. Tribal houses are decorated with paintings, carved interior poles, and screens painted in traditional Northwest Coast Indian style.

'Ksan dancers perform traditional dances and you can take a guided tour of several historic structures in the area. This is one of the few places that really provides insights into aboriginal life before the advent of Europeans.

The 'Ksan village is located in Hazelton, 762 miles north of Vancouver by road, in the interior roughly between Prince Rupert on the coast and Prince George in the interior.

Interior British Columbia

About 100 miles west of Prince George is the **Fort St. James National Historic Site**, a commemoration of the role of the redoubt in the Pacific Slope fur trade. The fort, founded by Simon Fraser in 1806 during his exploration of a route to the west coast via the Fraser River, includes five original and two reconstructed log buildings.

This site is also part of a research program with the Nak'azdli Elders Society that records their oral history and transcribes it into written documents to be utilized by the elders. The site is open from May through September. For information, call ☎ (250) 996-7191.

The highest point in the Canadian Rockies is 12,900-foot-high **Mount Robson**, southeast of Prince George. Unlike many other great mountains, it is easily seen from a major highway, visible from the Yellowhead Highway near the Alberta border.

Hiking trails lead from the highway through the Valley of the Thousand Falls to the mountain's north face, visible only from the vicinity of Berg Lake, where chunks of Berg Glacier break off and dot its surface.

From the decaying remnants of a once-bustling gold rush town, **Barkerville**, east of Quesnel, has been brought back to life as it was at the height of the gold rush days. In the 1860s, when gold was valued at $15 an ounce, more than $50 million worth was taken out of the area and Barkerville seemed headed to becoming the biggest community north of San Francisco and west of Chicago. But it all stopped as quickly as it began when the gold rush ended.

There are more than fifty buildings that predate 1900 in today's Barkerville. There are 100 displays and more than 40,000 artifacts in the site's collection. Interpreters offer demonstrations of mining, blacksmithing, and domestic skills and explain Victorian etiquette and British justice. Sermons are delivered in St. Saviours Church. In the summer season, live theater productions are offered at the Theater Royal.

Barkerville has also been the set for several western movies. For information and seasonal hours, call ☎ (250) 994-3332.

Eastern British Columbia to the Alberta Border

In southeastern B.C., on the border with Idaho, the **Rossland Historical Museum and Gold Mine Tour** tells the mining and social history of the area through artifacts, displays, and an underground mine tour.

Located at the junction of highways 22 and 3B in Rossland, the museum is open from mid-May to mid-September. For information, call ☎ (250) 362-7722; off-season, ☎ (250) 362-5820. Admission to museum and mine tour: adult ❷; senior and student, ❷; child, ❶; child (6–younger), free with adult.

Kokanee Glacier Provincial Park is a virtually undeveloped park of rugged, untouched mountains, glaciers, lakes, rivers, and forests. Most of the park is higher than 5,500 feet in the Sloan range of the Selkirk Mountains in southeastern B.C.

Kokanee is a Kootenay First Nation word meaning *red fish,* a reference to the land-locked salmon of Kootenay Lake.

From Highway 3A, Kokanee is about twelve miles northeast of Nelson, and from Highway 31A, just north of Kaslo. Open year-round.

One of the region's most important waterfowl habitats is the **Creston Valley Wildlife Management Area** in the southeast corner of the province on the Idaho border. During migration in the spring and fall, thousands of birds rest and feed at the fifteen managed ponds in the center's 17,000 acres. The area has more than 250 species of birds, 50 species of mammals, and 30 species of reptiles and amphibians.

Open year-round for hiking, biking, birdwatching, canoeing, fishing, or camping; the Interpretation Centre is open from mid-April to mid-October. The peak season for migration is the fall and spring. Admission: entrance fee to Intrepretation Centre, ❸ per person; family, ❹. For more information, call ☎ (250) 428-3259.

Fort Steele Heritage Town is a lovingly restored East Kootenay town of about 1890 to 1905, including more than sixty restored, reconstructed, and original buildings. You can visit an operating bakery, general store, newspaper office, confectionery, and restaurant. The Wasa Hotel has a museum with exhibits on the history of Fort Steele and the area. There's also a working steam railroad and horse-drawn wagons.

Living history street dramas bring to life the rise and fall of Fort Steele; interpreters portray characters such as homemakers, gardeners, and blacksmiths who lived and worked in the town at the turn of the century.

Fort Steele is located ten miles northeast of Cranbrook on Highway 93–95. Open year-round. Admission: adult, ❸; family, ❹. For information, call ☎ (250) 417-6000 or consult 📖 www.fortsteele.bc.ca.

Kootenay National Park, on the west side of the border with Alberta, is traversed by the Kootenay Parkway (Highway 93). You'll find a variety of plant life, from alpine tundra in the upper reaches to stands of Douglas fir and prickly pear cactus at lower altitudes in the south. You may see Rocky Mountain bighorn sheep, mountain goats, elk mule deer, and whitetail deer.

A nature trail leads across the Vermilion River, past iron-rich clay banks, up along Ochre Creek and on to the cold mineral springs known as the Paint Pots. The iron in the water has seeped into the clays, giving them a vivid orange color. Aboriginal people from both sides of the Great Divide gathered clay for decoration and trade, and considered the area to be sacred.

There are more than 125 miles of hiking trails branching off the parkway.

The park is in the southeast corner of B.C. The north entrance of the park borders Banff National Park on Highway 93 South; the park is about twenty miles from Banff, Alberta. Open year-round; some facilities and services are seasonal. For information and fees, contact the park in Radium Hot Springs at ☎ (250) 347-9615 or the West Gate Information Centre (summer only) at ☎ (250) 347-9505.

The Radium Hot Springs Pools at the southern end of Kootenay National park are built around hot mineral springs in a beautiful mountain setting. You can soak in 40 degree Celsius (about 102 degrees Fahrenheit) water or swim in a cooler Olympic-sized pool. The pools are located near the town of Radium Hot Springs. Open daily with reduced hours in winter; for information and rates, call ☎ (250) 347-9331.

From the warmth of a hot spring to the near-permanent frost of the icefields is a short distance in southeastern B.C.

More than 400 glaciers are still at work sculpting the mountains of **Glacier National Park** above Cranbrook. As much as seventy-five feet of snowfall each year and steep slopes make it one of the world's most active avalanche zones. Snow sheds protect sections of the Trans-Canada Highway #1 and the railway from avalanches.

Half of its area is tundra, where alpine meadows burst into flower for a few weeks each summer. At lower altitudes, the high precipitation yields a lush rain forest of spruce and fir. Services include guided hikes, strolls, and workshops. In the winter there is back-country skiing.

The park is located between Golden and Revelstoke on the Trans-Canada Highway 1, about 200 miles west of Calgary. Open year-round.

For information, call the Revelstoke office at ☎ (250) 837-7500 or the Glacier Park visitor center at ☎ (250) 837-6274.

A century ago the region was an awesome challenge for the builders of the Canadian Pacific Railway. At the **Rogers Pass Centre** in Revelstoke, you can learn how the builders of the Canadian Pacific Railway blazed a path through the rugged Selkirk Mountains. The interpretive center is built to resemble part of the four miles of snow sheds constructed to protect the rail line and the highway.

The center is located on the Trans-Canada Highway 1, fifty miles west of Golden and forty miles east of Revelstoke. Open daily in summer, from Thursday to Monday in the winter. For information and rates, call ☎ (250) 837-6274 or ☎ (250) 837-7500.

A sixteen-mile drive in Mount Revelstoke National Park on the Summit Parkway passes through dense, old-growth rain forests of giant cedar and pine, sub-alpine forest, and alpine meadows and tundra. The Giant Cedars hiking trails take visitors through a stand of 1,000-year-old red cedars.

Mount Revelstoke offers a view of the ice-clad peaks of the Monashee Range and, on the eastern horizon, the Selkirk Mountains. Running through the park are the Columbia and Illecillawaet rivers. Location: Near Revelstoke on the Trans-Canada Highway 1, 400 miles northeast of Vancouver and 245 miles west of Calgary. Summit Road is open late May to September. A paved parkway to the summit of Mount Revelstoke is open during the snow-free season.

East of Vancouver, from Burnaby to Kamloops

At the **Burnaby Heritage Village** just east of Vancouver, costumed interpreters guide visitors through an historical village museum that has more than thirty buildings, recreating British Columbia from the 1890s through 1925.

Exhibits include an old Chinese herbalist shop stocked with potions, snakeskins, toads, and exotic herbs. The latest news of 1925 is available at the town printer. And children can join a class in a one-room schoolhouse, complete with a school marm.

Heritage Village is located within Deer Lake Park, off Highway 1. For information, hours, and rates, call ☎ (604) 293-6500 or consult 🖳 www.burnabyparksrec.org.

One of the best thrill rides you can take without approval from your insurance agent may be the **Hell's Gate Airtram**, located in the Fraser Canyon on the Trans-Canada Highway 1, about thirty miles north of Hope.

The cable car makes a 500-foot descent into the Fraser River Canyon to Hell's Gate, where at peak springtime runoff as much as 200 million gallons of water per minute flows through the 110-foot-wide gorge. At the bottom are spectacular overlooks and walking trails and the Salmon House Restaurant, famed for its salmon chowder and grilled salmon steaks.

Hell's Gate was a barrier to all but the strongest salmon as they journeyed inland to spawn. A fish ladder built in 1945 gave them a way around the most treacherous part.

The airtram is located about 125 miles east of Vancouver on the Trans Canada Highway 1 at the Hope exit. Open mid-April through mid-October; admission ❸; family tickets available. For information, call ☎ (604) 867-9277 or consult 🖳 www.hellsgateairtram.com.

The Salmon Run on the **Adams River**, about forty miles east of Kamloops, is one of the biggest sockeye salmon runs in the world, a river of writhing red fish.

The river is protected in its seven-mile run between Adams and Shuswap lakes.

Salmon that have fought their way up the Fraser and Thompson rivers start arriving in Adams River in October. In a dominant run on the Adams River, which occurs about once every four years, as many as two million salmon jam into the creek to spawn, viewed by up to 200,000 human visitors.

Near Harrison Hot Springs, about seventy-five miles east of Vancouver, Minter Gardens offers ten tiered gardens with three aviaries, a petting zoo, and other entertainment. This is a place of topiary Victorian ladies, waterfalls, a living maze, and a rare collection of Penjung Rock Bonsai.

The gardens are on Trans Canada Highway 1 at 52892 Bunker Road, Rosedale. Open from April to October; for rates and information, call ☎ (604) 794-7191 or ☎ (800) 661-3919. 🖳 www.mintergardens.com. Admission: adult, ❹; youth (6–18), ❷; family rate, ❹.

South of Vancouver

The **Fort Langley National Historic Site** is a restored Hudson's Bay Company trading post of 1827. Besides trading with the local aboriginal community, the fort traded sea otter pelts to the Russians, and its salmon packing operation sold products to Hawaii and Australia. A farm included a dairy and livestock operation.

In the 1850s Fort Langley became the principal staging point in the Fraser River gold rush.

Located in the village of Fort Langley, on the Fraser River, about twenty-five miles southeast of Vancouver via the Trans-Canada Highway 1. Open daily year-round. For information and rates, call ☎ (604) 513-4777.

In Steveston, the **Gulf of George Cannery National Historic Site** tells the tale of fish canneries in a factory that first opened in 1894 at the mouth of the Fraser River. The cannery was used until 1979. Exhibits include a canning line, demonstrations, and a film. The nearby waterfront is home to Canada's largest commercial fishing fleet.

The cannery is located thirty minutes south of Vancouver. Open daily in July and August, daily except Tuesday and Wednesday in the spring and fall, and closed in the winter. Call ☎ (604) 664-9009 for hours and rates.

Chapter 29
British Columbia Ski Resorts

They grow them high and pile them deep in British Columbia, with more than three dozen ski areas that anywhere else in North America would be among the biggest and best. But they all have to compete with the two-headed monster of Whistler and Blackcomb Mountains, in the town of Whistler about two hours northeast of Vancouver.

The next time someone tells you something is "mile-high," think of Blackcomb, 5,280 feet of vertical drop. The top is a set of awesome bowls with views of the spectacular Spearhead Range of Garibaldi Provincial Park. The bottom funnels down to a lively base ski town . . . and a short traverse across the base area you'll find the lifts that lead up to the summit of Whistler Mountain, a mere 5,020 feet high.

Operated for years as separate but cooperative neighbors, Whistler and Blackcomb came together through the merger of Intrawest and Whistler. Together, they are now operated and marketed as the Whister Resort.

Whistler and Blackcomb stand shoulder-to-shoulder in the Coastal Mountain Range, twin peaks of fabulous skiing sharing a single, bustling village at the base. Both mountains are consistently at the top of annual survey lists of all of the skiing and snowboarding magazines.

One other point: though both mountains are huge, they start at a relatively low base of about 2,000 feet, with lifts topping out at 7,494 feet. This means you'll be about a mile lower than the highest mountains in Colorado and Utah, greatly reducing the effects of high altitude on visitors from lower places.

With seven Alpine bowls, Whistler is the larger of these two mammoths, but Blackcomb's upper steeps are more awe-inspiring, if awe is what you're after.

Taken together, you have a megaresort with nearly 7,000 acres of skiable terrain (20 percent novice, 55 percent intermediate, and 25 percent expert) and more than 200 marked trails, three glaciers, and twelve bowls, with thirty lifts.

Average annual snowfall is thirty feet at the summit. Both mountains hold the snow deep into the spring.

The Canadian Olympic Association chose Whistler as the bid city for the 2010 Winter Olympics; a final decision is expected in 2003.

Besides the outstanding ski facilities, there is Whistler itself—not officially a town, but the Resort Municipality of Whistler. The entire valley, with more than 3,500 rooms, is made up of dozens of condominium complexes, small luxury hotels, and a resort village with shopping, restaurants, and entertainment.

For information on the Whistler resort, call ☎ (604) 932-3141 or ☎ (800) 766-0449 or consult 🖳 www. whistler-resort.com.

★★★★ Whistler Mountain

Whistler, B.C., Canada V0N 1B0. Information: ☎ (604) 932-3141, ☎ (800) 766-0449. 🖳 www.whistler-resort.com. Ski conditions: ☎ (604) 932-4221. Central lodging: ☎ (888) 284-9999. Typical season: Late November to late April.

Peak: 7,160. Base: 2,140. Vertical: 5,020.

Trails: 100. Skiable acres: 3,657. Average natural snowfall: 360 inches. Snowmaking: 3%. Longest trail: 7 miles. Trail rating: 25% Novice, 55% Intermediate, 20% Expert. Features: 30 km cross-country trails.

Lifts: 14 (1 ten-person gondola, 1 six-person gondola, 3 high-speed quads, 3 triples, 1 double, 5 surface).

Recent prices: (Can $) Whistler and Blackcomb adult, $61–$63; junior/senior, $52–$54; child, $31–$32. Prices vary by time of year.

★★★★ Blackcomb Mountain

4545 Blackcomb Way, Whistler, B.C., Canada V0N 1B4. Information: ☎ (604) 932-3141, ☎ (800) 766-0449. 🖳 www.whistler-resort.com. Ski conditions: ☎ (604) 932-4211. Central lodging: ☎ (888) 284-9999. Typical season: Late November to late May. Summer ski season mid-June to early August.

Peak: 7,494. Base: 2,231. Vertical: 5,280.

Trails: 100. Skiable acres: 3,444. Average natural snowfall: 400 inches. Snowmaking: 11%. Longest trail: 7 miles. Trail rating: 15% Novice, 55% Intermediate, 30% Expert. Features: 30 km cross-country trails.

Lifts: 20 (1 eight-person gondola, 6 high-speed quads, 3 triples, 10 surface).

Recent prices: (Can $) Whistler and Blackcomb adult, $61–$63; junior/senior, $52–$54; child, $31–$32. Prices vary by time of year.

★★★ Apex Mountain Resort

1000 Strayhorse Road, Penticton, B.C., Canada V2A 7N7. Information: ☎ (250) 292-8222. 🖳 www.apexresort.com. Ski conditions: ☎ (250) 492-2929, ext. 2000. Central lodging: ☎ (800) 387-2739. Typical season: Mid-November to mid-April.

Peak: 7,187. Base: 5,187. Vertical: 2,000.

Trails: 60. Skiable acres: 505. Average natural snowfall: 175 inches. Snowmaking: 25%. Longest trail: 3 miles. Trail rating: 16% Novice, 48% Intermediate, 36% Expert. Features: 52 km cross-country trails.

Lifts: 4 (1 high-speed quad, 1 triple, 2 surface).
Recent prices: (Can $) all-day adult, $42; teen, $35; child/senior $27

★★★ Big White Ski Resort

Highway 33, Kelowna, B.C., Canada V1X 4K5. Information: ☎ (250) 765-3101. 🖳 www.bigwhite.com. Ski conditions: ☎ (250) 765-7669. Central lodging: ☎ (800) 663-2772. Typical season: Mid-November to mid-April.

Peak: 7,606. Base: 4,950. Vertical: 2,656.

Trails: 100. Skiable acres: 2,075. Average natural snowfall: 294 inches. Snow-making: 0%. Longest trail: 4.5 miles. Trail rating: 18% Novice, 56% Interme-diate, 26% Expert. Features: 25 km cross-country trails.

Lifts: 8 (4 high-speed quads, 1 quad, 1 triple, 1 double, 1 surface tow).

Recent prices: (Can $) adult, $48; youth, $40; senior, $33; junior, $25

★★ Cypress Bowl

West Vancouver, B.C., Canada V7V 3N9. Information: ☎ (604) 926-5612. 🖳 www.cypressbowl.com. Ski conditions: ☎ (604) 419-7669. Typical season: Early December to late April.

Peak: 4,750. Base: 3,000. Vertical: 1,750.

Trails: 25. Skiable acres: 173. Average natural snowfall: 150 inches. Snow-making: 0%. Longest trail: 2.5 miles. Trail rating: 21% Novice, 38% Interme-diate, 41% Expert. Features: 16 km cross-country trails.

Lifts: 5 (1 quad, 3 doubles, 1 surface tow).

Recent prices: (Can $) all-day adult, $36; youth, $30; child, $17; senior, $15

★★★ Fernie Alpine Resort

Fernie, B.C., Canada V0B 1M1. Information: ☎ (250) 423-4655. 🖳 www.skifer nie.com. Ski conditions: ☎ (250) 423-3555. Central lodging: ☎ (888) 754-7325. Typical season: Mid-November to late April.

Peak: 6,316. Base: 3,500. Vertical: 2,811.

Trails: 92. Skiable acres: 2,500. Average natural snowfall: 350 inches. Snow-making: 1%. Longest trail: 3 miles. Trail rating: 30% Novice, 40% Intermedi-ate, 30% Expert. Features: 15 km cross-country trails.

Lifts: 9 (1 high-speed quad, 2 quads, 2 triples, 4 surface).

Recent prices: (Can $) all-day adult, $54; student/senior, $43; youth, $36; child, $15

★★ Grouse Mountain Resort

6400 Nancy Greene Way, North Vancouver, B.C., Canada V7R 4K9. Informa-tion: ☎ (604) 984-0661. 🖳 www.grousemountain.com. Typical season: Mid-November to late April.

Peak: 4,016. Base: 2,500. Vertical: 1,210.

Trails: 78. Skiable acres: 163. Average natural snowfall: 250 inches. Longest trail: 1 mile. Trail rating: 20% Novice, 65% Intermediate, 15% Expert. Fea-tures: 5 km cross-country trails.

Lifts: 9 (1 44-passenger tramway, 1 double, 7 surface).
Recent prices: (Can $) all-day adult, $32; youth, $24; child/senior, $17

★★★ Mount Washington Resort

Courtenay, (Vancouver Island) B.C., Canada V9N 5N3. Information: ☎ (250) 338-1386. 🖳 www.mtwashington.bc.ca. Typical season: Mid-November to late April.

Peak: 5,215. Base: 3,558. Vertical: 1,657.
Trails: 42. Skiable acres: 1,000. Average natural snowfall: 300 inches. Snowmaking: 0%. Longest trail: 1 mile. Trail rating: 20% Novice, 45% Intermediate, 35% Expert. Features: 32 km cross-country trails.
Lifts: 8 (1 high-speed quad, 2 triples, 2 doubles, 3 surface).
Recent prices: (Can $) all-day adult, $44; junior/senior, $36; child, $23

★★★ Panorama Ski Resort

Invermere, B.C., Canada V0A 1K0. Information: ☎ (250) 342-6941. 🖳 www.panoramaresort.com. Ski conditions: ☎ (250) 342-6941. Central lodging: ☎ (800) 663-2929. Typical season: Mid-December to mid-April.

Peak: 7,800. Base: 3,800. Vertical: 4,000.
Trails: 82. Skiable acres: 2,400. Average natural snowfall: 145 inches. Snowmaking: 50%. Longest trail: 3 miles. Trail rating: 20% Novice, 55% Intermediate, 25% Expert. Features: 12 km cross-country trails.
Lifts: 9 (1 high-speed quad, 1 triple, 2 doubles, 5 surface).
Recent prices: (Can $) adult, $49; teen/senior, $39; junior, $27; child, $9

★★★ Red Mountain

Rossland, B.C., Canada V0G 1Y0. Information: ☎ (250) 362-7384. 🖳 www.ski-red.com. Ski conditions: ☎ (250) 362-5500. Central lodging: ☎ (800) 663-0105. Typical season: Early December to early April.

Peak: 6,699. Base: 3,888. Vertical: 2,800.
Trails: 79. Skiable acres: 1,100. Average natural snowfall: 300 inches. Snowmaking: 0%. Longest trail: 5 miles. Trail rating: 10% Novice, 40% Intermediate, 50% Expert. Features: 50 km cross-country trails.
Lifts: 5 (3 triples, 1 double, 1 surface tow).
Recent prices: (Can $) all-day adult, $42; student, $34; senior, $27; junior, $22

★★★ Sun Peaks Resort

Sun Peaks, B.C., Canada V0E 1Z1. Information: ☎ (250) 578-7222. 🖳 www.sunpeaksresort.com. Ski conditions: ☎ (250) 578-7232. Central lodging: ☎ (800) 807-3257. Typical season: Mid-November to mid-April.

Peak: 6,824. Base: 3,790. Vertical: 2,894.
Trails: 64. Skiable acres: 10,227. Average natural snowfall: 208 inches. Snowmaking: 3%. Longest trail: 5 miles. Trail rating: 24% Novice, 54% Intermediate, 22% Expert. Features: 40 km cross-country trails.
Lifts: 6 (2 high-speed quads, 1 quad, 1 triple, 2 surface).
Recent prices: (Can $) full-day adult, $46; child, $26; youth, $41; senior, $32

Chapter 30
British Columbia Events and Festivals

The arts are alive and well in British Columbia, especially in and around Vancouver and Whistler on the mainland and Victoria on Vancouver Island. Following is a list of some of the best festivals and annual events. For a more complete list and specific dates, call ☎ (800) 663-6000 for a copy of the B.C. calendar of events.

February

Chinese New Year Fair and Parade. Vancouver. Commercial displays, cultural performances, and a food festival at the Pacific National Exhibition Grounds; parade in Chinatown. Admission to fair: adult, ❷; child and senior, free. Exact date varies from year to year.

April

Terri Vic Dixieland Jazz Festival. Victoria. The five-day Jazz Festival is one of the largest events of its kind, with more than 25,000 attendees, showcasing some twenty leading jazz bands from all over the world. Held in April at eight venues at various locations in Victoria. Festival and daily passes sold.

May

Canadian Northern Children's Festival. Prince George. ☎ (250) 562-4882. Puppetry, mime theater, and music at Fort George Park in Prince George. An associated show features science education and activities for children. Free admission to the festival, charges vary for main stage performances. Early.

Chilliwack Dixieland Jazz Festival. Chilliwack. ☎ (604) 795-3600. National and international musicians at a three-day festival at the Ag-Rec Centre and Exhibition grounds in Chilliwack. Festival passes and daily tickets sold. Mid.

Music West. Vancouver. ☎ (604) 684-9338. Spread over twenty-five venues throughout Vancouver, with some 200 bands and a conference that attracts some 2,500 songwriters, musicians, and recording industry representatives. Admission varies by event. Mid.

Vancouver International Children's Festival. Vancouver. ☎ (604) 687-7697. Children's theater, puppetry, music, and dance in open-air and tent performances at Vanier Park. Mid.

June

Jazzfest International. Victoria. ☎ (604) 388-4423. Jazz, blues, and world music. Held at various venues in Victoria, indoors and outdoors. Early.

Canadian International Dragon Boat Festival. Vancouver. ☎ (604) 688-2382. Local and international dragon boat races, performing and visual arts, a culinary festival, and children's activities at the Plaza of Nations at Pacific Place. Mid.

Sam Steele Days. Cranbrook. ☎ (250) 426-4161. Four days of old-time celebration that includes a parade, sports tournaments, loggers' competitions, and barbecues. Admission varies with events; many events are free. Mid.

Vancouver International Jazz Festival/DuMaurier Ltd. International Jazz Festival. Vancouver. ☎ (604) 872-5200. Indoor and outdoor concerts and street performers at two dozen venues in downtown Vancouver. Mid.

July

Gold Fever Follies Summer Theatre. Rossland. ☎ (250) 362-5666. Performers tell Rossland's history through song and dance at historic Miners Hall. Held Tuesday through Saturday during July and August. Admission: adult, ❷; child, ❶.

Kaslo Summer Music Festival. Kaslo. ☎ (250) 353-7538. Jazz, classical, rhythm and blues, and New Age performances in Kaslo Bay Park. Prices vary for festival passes and daily tickets. Mid.

Vancouver Folk Music Festival. Vancouver. ☎ (604) 602-9798. 🖳 www.thefestival.bc.ca. Local, national, and international performers take the stage at Jericho Beach Park. Admission prices vary by performance. Mid.

Vancouver International Comedy Festival. Vancouver. ☎ (604) 683-0883. A public celebration of comedy, with performers from British Columbia, elsewhere in Canada, and around the world. Held in late July and early August on Granville Island. Some events are free.

August

Hornby Island Festival. Hornby. ☎ (250) 335-2734. For eleven days in August each year, a festival of music, dance, theater, film, and exhibits, held in Hornby's hand-crafted community hall and other venues. Prices vary for festival passes and daily tickets. Mid.

Kamloops Pow-Wow. Kamloops. ☎ (250) 828-9700. Celebration of First Nations culture, with competitions in dancing, singing, and drumming held at the Kamloops Reserve Special Events Centre. Admission: ❸ per day; ❹ weekend pass. Mid.

Merritt Mountain Music Festival. Merritt. ☎ (604) 739-7077. A four-day event that draws the celebrities of country and western music to the Ewalt Ranch. Visitors can take part in line dancing, amusement rides, family activities, street entertainers, and clowns. Festival passes and daily tickets sold. Mid.

September

Fringe Theatre Festival. Vancouver. ☎ (604) 257-0350. 🖳 www.vancouverfringe.com. An eleven-day celebration of drama, music, comedy, and dance in the Mount Pleasant area. Early.

Vancouver International Film Festival. Vancouver. (604) 685-0260. Canadian and international feature films, short films, a trade forum, seminars, and workshops. Held at movie theaters in downtown Vancouver from late September to mid-October.

October

The Vancouver International Writers Festival. Vancouver. ☎ (604) 681-6330. Readings and debates by Canadian and international writers, a Literary Cabaret, Poetry Bash, and authors' brunch held at various venues on Granville Island. Early.

Part V
Alberta

Chapter 31
A Bit of Alberta

Alberta is the Canada of most people's imagination, a place of awesome mountains, high alpine lakes, impossibly blue glaciers, and vast oceans of snow. And somewhat incongruously, Alberta is also the home of two of Canada's most modern cities, the beefy brawn of Edmonton and the energy capital of Calgary.

Alberta is in some ways the Texas of Canada. A big, sprawling place that has mountains and prairies, cowboys and oil men, small towns and prosperous cities. Although Alberta is not strictly a part of the Pacific Northwest, many travelers to British Columbia or Washington include a jaunt across the border to Calgary or the winter and summer wonderlands of Banff and Lake Louise. In this chapter you'll find some of the highlights of Alberta; for more full coverage, you may want to see another book in this series, *Econoguide Canada*.

Calgary

Calgary is a glittering, modern city of chrome-and-glass skyscrapers. It rises out of the prairies to the east and runs head-first into the Canadian Rockies to the west.

The entire city has sprung up in just over a century, with much of its growth occurring in the last few decades. The oil industry soared in the 1970s during the energy crisis, then fell back to earth in the 1980s. The energy business has had a slow but steady resurgence in recent years. Today something like three out of four jobs in Calgary are in some way related to the energy industry.

Calgary welcomed the world to the XV Olympic Winter Games in 1988, with facilities at the Canmore Nordic Centre, Nakiska ski resort, and the Canada Olympic Park just outside of town. The Calgary Winter Festival celebrates winter activities and commemorates the Olympics every February.

Calgary Stampede

The biggest hoopla in this brash city is the famed **Calgary Stampede**, which draws about 250,000 excited spectators and participants for two weeks in July. (In 2001, the party runs July 6–15.)

The Stampede is one of the world's biggest rodeos, as well as a huge agricultural fair, but it's also a lot more than that. To some observers, it's a spectacle on the Roman scale, without the Christians and lions but including gladiator races in the form of chuckwagon sprints.

It all starts with a grand parade, the streets of Calgary overflowing with observers; the front curb positions are usually gone well before dawn. A typical two-hour parade features something like 700 horses, a few thousand marchers, and more than 150 floats and bands.

Downtown, Olympic Plaza offers a free pancake breakfast along with Western entertainment from concerts to square dancing to mock gunfights. Each night most of the city goes gaga, with music, dancing, gambling, fireworks, and a general party atmosphere at every turn.

Park admission: ❷; extra charges are levied to enter the stadium for races and special events.

Each afternoon spectators watch a rough-and-ready rodeo where events include saddlebronc and bareback riding, calf roping, steer wrestling, wild cow milking, and perhaps the most dangerous event, bull riding. The chuckwagon races pit four teams of four horses in an all-out sprint for the finish line of a track that is five-eighths of a mile long.

Stampede grandstand event admission: ❹, including admission to the park itself. Two-day tickets are also available. Tickets for the best seats sell out well in advance of the Stampede, and some events may be completely booked ahead of time. You can order tickets in advance through the Calgary Exhibition and Stampede office; for information, call ☎ (800) 661-1260, ☎ (800) 661-1767, or ☎ (403) 261-0500 in Calgary or consult 🖳 www.calgary-stampede.com. Tickets are also sold through Ticketmaster at ☎ (403) 270-6700.

Attractions in Calgary

The **Glenbow Museum** in the heart of downtown is a must-see in Calgary. Western Canada's largest museum, it is renowned for its display of artifacts depicting the cultural history of the settlement of western Canada, a mineralogy gallery, and a display of military history of many stripes, from knights in armor to Japanese samurai outfits to equipment of the two world wars.

The museum in the Convention Centre complex across from the Calgary Tower at 130 Ninth Avenue Southeast, is open daily from 9 A.M. to 5 P.M., and until 9 P.M. on Thursday and Friday nights. The summer is the busiest season. Admission: adult, ❷; student and senior, ❷; children, (4–12), ❶. For information, call ☎ (403) 268-4100 or ☎ (403) 268-4209 or consult 🖳 www.glenbow.org.

On a clear day or night, the view from way above at the **Calgary Tower** covers the modern buildings of downtown, the ski jump towers of the 1988 Winter Olympics, and the snow-covered Rockies in the distance.

There's a one-minute elevator ride, or 762 steps for the ambitious, to the top of the 620-foot-tall tower. You can stop to ogle from the Observation Terrace, or sit down at the Panorama Dining Room, which makes a one-hour revolution as you dine on fine fare.

An elevator ticket costs ❷ for adults; the observation gallery is open from 7:30 A.M. until 11 P.M. year-round. The tower is at 101 Ninth Avenue Southwest. For information, call ☎ (403) 266-7171 or consult 🖳 www.calgary tower.com.

The **Calgary Zoo, Botanical Gardens and Prehistoric Park** is just outside downtown on St. George's Island. Canada's largest zoo, and one of the best in North America, the world-renowned institution is home to more than 1,400 animals, thousands of species of plants, and an unusual Prehistoric Park populated with life-sized models of dinosaurs.

One of the stars of the show is Kamala, an African elephant who wields a paintbrush. The paintings are sold to support the zoo. I don't know much about art, but there is a certain unschooled exuberance to her abstracts.

Admission: adult, ❷. The zoo is open year-round, from 9 A.M.; closing times vary from 4 to 6 P.M. The Prehistoric Park is open June through September. For information, call ☎ (403) 232-9300 or consult 🖳 www.calgary zoo.ab.ca.

At the **Calgary Science Centre**, you can travel through space, or through a DNA molecule. This lively hands-on museum is also home of the Pleiades Mystery Theatre and the Science Theatre.

The museum is located at 701 Eleventh Street Southwest. The center is open daily from 10 A.M.; closing hours vary by season. In the winter, the museum is closed on Monday. For information, call ☎ (403) 221-3700 or consult 🖳 www.calgaryscience.ca.

The **Aero Space Museum of Calgary** offers one of the largest collections of aircraft, engines, and artifacts in North America, tracing the history of Canadian aviation. The museum has extensive research materials, including technical manuals, drawings, and photographs.

The museum is located at #10, 64 McTavish Place Northeast, near Calgary International Airport. Open daily from 10 A.M. to 5 P.M. Admission: adult, ❷; student and senior tickets available; child (6–younger), free; family, ❸. For information, call ☎ (403) 250-3752 or consult 🖳 www.asmac.ab.ca.

Fort Calgary Historic Park, an historic forty-acre riverside park and reconstructed 1875 fort, tells some of the colorful stories of Calgary's past.

The fort was built by the North West Mounted Police as home base for a command that stretched from Edmonton in the north to Fort Macleod in the south, a distance of some 350 miles. The present-day city of Calgary grew up around the fort, which remained in operation until 1914 when it was knocked down and the site covered over by railroad tracks and buildings.

The park in the crook of the Bow and Elbow rivers is about eight blocks east of downtown, at 750 Ninth Avenue Southeast. Open daily from May 1 to early October; hours vary. Admission: adult, ❶; student, ❷; child (6–younger), free. For information call ☎ (403) 290-1875 or consult 🖳 www.fortcalgary.ab.ca.

One of Canada's largest living historical villages is at **Heritage Park Historical Village**, about ten miles southwest of downtown Calgary.

The sixty-acre village includes more than 150 exhibits and thousands of artifacts depicting area life prior to 1915. You can ride on a steam train, a horsedrawn wagon, or sail across a reservoir on the restored paddlewheeler SS *Moyie*. Hundreds of costumed volunteers and staff bring the park to life with shops and crafts demonstrations, and the Wainwright Hotel offers old-style meals.

Admission: adult, ❸; senior ❷; child (3–17), ❷. A free pancake breakfast is served between 9 A.M. and 10 A.M. in the summer. The village is open daily from May through September and during holiday periods until the end of the year; hours vary by season.

The park is located at 1900 Heritage Drive SW. For information, call ☎ (403) 259-1900 or consult 🖳 www.heritagepark.ab.ca.

Sports and Recreation

The ski jump towers from the 1988 Olympic Winter Games are visible from many parts of the city of Calgary. Today they are the centerpiece of the **Canada Olympic Park**, which includes a small skiing hill, bobsled and luge tracks, a museum, ice skating, miniature golf, and summer activities.

Skiing at the hill runs from October to February, with 90 percent of the snow produced by machine. The slopes are open during the week from 10 A.M. to 10 P.M. and on the weekends until 5 P.M. The chilling plant runs most of the year, which permits use of the luge track for training in the summer, even when temperatures soar up to 85 degrees.

The bobsled run includes the famed Kreisel Turn, a 270-degree turn where riders are subjected to as much as 5 gs of force. If the turn looks familiar, you may be replaying in your mind the famous crash there of the Jamaican bobsled team—the longest outside shot of the Olympics. The film about the team, *Cool Runnings*, was partially filmed at the Canadian Olympic Park, and the sled used in the movie is on display at a museum in the park.

Above the ski lodge is a small Olympic museum that has some interesting exhibits and interactive demonstrations. You can try out your timing on a bobsled start, utilize your logic on a ski racing gate layout, and test endurance and strength as demonstrations of the skills required of skiers and ice skaters.

The park is located at 88 Canada Olympic Road Southwest. For information and rates, call ☎ (403) 247-5452 or consult 🖳 www.coda.ab.ca.

Dinosaur Country

Drumheller is a strange outpost of time in the "dinosaur country" of the Red Deer River Valley, about ninety-five miles northeast of Calgary.

Alberta's badlands, gouged out of the prairie by ancient rivers and ice, were once the domain of the dinosaur. The exposed rock of the Badlands reveals more than seventy million years of geological history in a mysterious moonscape.

The badlands, named by earlier settlers who found the soil "bad" for farming, were later found to be quite rich in fossil beds and coal.

In Drumheller the **Royal Tyrrell Museum of Palaeontology** is home of one of the world's foremost collections of dinosaur specimens, including a rare complete reconstruction of the fearsome tyrannosaurus rex and a 100 million-year-old skeleton of a giant sea creature that was uncovered in the oil sands of northern Alberta. In fact, the museum claims the world's largest gathering of complete dinosaur skeletons with some 50 in the collection and nearly 100,000 specimens of various types.

Tourist information.
Travel Alberta. ☎ (800) 661-8888.
 Alberta Visitor Information. ☎ (800) 661-8888.

The Tyrrell is about four miles northwest of downtown Drumheller on North Dinosaur Trail in Midland Provincial Park, about ninety minutes northeast of Calgary. Open daily from May to September; daily except Mondays for the remainder of year, except holidays. Admission: adult, ❷; student, ❷; child (6–younger), free; family, ❸. For information, call ☎ (403) 823-7707 or ☎ (888) 440-4240.

About twelve miles east of Drumheller is the **Historic Atlas Coal Mine**, the last of 139 coal mines in the Drumheller Valley. All of the above-ground workings—tipple, washhouse, mine office, and mine residences—have been restored. The tipple (where coal was sorted into sizes, stored, and then shipped) is the last of its kind in Canada. Interpretive programs concentrate on the history of mining and the valley's social history. Tipple tour requires a moderate climb to the top of a six-story-high structure. The mine is off Highway 10. For information, call ☎ (403) 822-2220. Open mid-May to mid-October. Admission: adult, ❶; extra fee for tipple tour.

Heading further south from Drumheller, southwest of Calgary, you'll come to **Dinosaur Provincial Park** in the Alberta Badlands. The park in the Red Deer River Valley is one of the world's richest fossil fields; dinosaur skeletons have been discovered dating back 75 million years. To protect the fossils, much of the park is now accessible only through interpretive tours and hikes.

The park is thirty miles northeast of Brooks on Trans-Canada Highway 1; a three-hour drive from Drumheller. Open May to late October. Museum admission: adult, ❶; student ❶; child (6–younger), free. Park admission: free. For information, call ☎ (403) 378-4342.

Edmonton

Edmonton is less of a tourist draw than Calgary or Banff, although not for lack of effort. The capital of the Province of Alberta has

- a world-class museum of culture and anthropology,
- an out-of-this-world science and space center,
- a step back into the past at a restored frontier trading post and fort,
- a huge indoor water park,
- an indoor NHL-sized skating rink,
- an outrageous roller coaster, indoors of course,
- a reproduction of Columbus's *Santa Maria,*
- four working submarines on an indoor lake,
- more than 800 trendy shops within a few square blocks, and
- at least 100 varied places to eat within twenty minutes' walk of each other.

That's the good news. The strange news: the last seven out of the ten are in one place, the almost indescribable West Edmonton Mall.

Located on the banks of the North Saskatchewan River, near the geographic center of Alberta, greater Edmonton encompasses more than three-quarters of a million people. From a small trading post in the late 1700s, it is now Canada's fifth-largest city and the hub of Alberta's extensive oil, gas, coal, forestry, and agricultural industries.

Attractions and Museums in Edmonton

Fort Edmonton brings back the original 1846 Hudson's Bay Trading Post, using many of the old construction materials and techniques. The most important building is the Big House, the home of the Chief Factor of what was known as the Saskatchewan District.

You'll also find a remembrance of Edmonton in its early days in 1885, a reconstructed Jasper Avenue as the capital city in 1905, and the city as it was during the 1920s. Visitors can ride on a 1919 steam train, street cars, wagons, ponies, and a stagecoach.

Located southwest of the city on the North Saskatchewan River, the park is open from mid-May to September. City buses let off passengers about ten minutes' walk from the fort. Admission: adult, ❷. For information, call ☎ (780) 496-8787 or consult 🕮 www.gov.edmonton.ab.ca/fort/.

The culture and history of the entire area is gathered at the **Provincial Museum of Alberta**, a very traditional but very well presented collection from ancient fossils and tools to the First Nations to today's people and animals.

The Habitat Gallery recreates locations in four natural regions: grassland prairie, parkland, mountain, and boreal forest. The Natural History Gallery tells the geological history from dinosaurs to the Ice Age. The Native Peoples Gallery traces the history of aboriginal people in the province. And the Ninteenth- and Twentieth-Century Gallery portrays the settlement of the west.

The museum is located about three miles west of downtown, at 12845 102nd Avenue in Edmonton's western suburbs. Admission: ❶–❷. For information, call ☎ (780) 453-9100 or consult 🕮 www.pma.edmonton.ab.ca.

The **Edmonton Space and Science Centre** in Coronation Park offers insights into the heavens with educational displays, films in the Devonian IMAX Theatre, and planetarium shows in the Margaret Zeidler Star Theatre.

At the Challenger Centre, visitors can take part in a simulated Space Shuttle mission. A computer lab offers explorations of the latest and greatest in high-tech machines. And there is also an observatory for young astronomers.

The museum, located at 11211 142nd Street, is open daily except non-holiday Mondays. Admission: ❷. For information, call ☎ (780) 451-3344 or ☎ (780) 451-9100.

The glass pyramids of the **Muttart Conservatory** hold the sometimes frigid outside at bay, keeping alive indoor tropical and temperate worlds. The conservatories include plants, trees, and a small number of birds from places very different from Edmonton. The museum, located at 9626 96A Street, is open Monday to Saturday, 9 A.M. to 6 P.M. Admission: ❶. For information, call ☎ (780) 496-8755.

A City Under Glass

Edmonton's biggest tourist draw is not your ordinary Kmart and a food court.

This is the big kahuna of shopping malls, not just the biggest one in Alberta, or in Canada for that matter; some 20 million people pass through its doors each year. The **West Edmonton Mall** is the world's largest cathedral to commerce, enclosing some 5.2 million square feet with more than 800 stores, including 8 major department stores, 19 movie theaters, and 110 eating establishments.

That might be enough to earn the mall more than its share of superlatives. But wait, there's more: the mall has an amusement park with twenty-five rides and attractions, a water park with the world's largest indoor wave pool, an ice skating rink, a dolphin lagoon, a submarine voyage on the world's largest indoor lake, and, for some reason, an exact replica of Christopher Columbus's flagship, the *Santa Maria*. Oh, and an indoor bungee jumping tower, a miniature golf course, a bingo hall, a dinner theater, and a gambling casino.

For information, call ☎ (800) 661-8890, ☎ (780) 444-5200, or consult information at 🖳 www.westedmontonmall.com.

The Klondike Days

The rivalry between Edmonton and slightly smaller and much brasher Calgary includes the **Klondike Days Exposition**, Edmonton's smaller and less rowdy answer to the wildly successful Calgary Stampede.

Klondike Days is held in the second half of July each year in Northlands Park. The event includes a parade with floats, marching bands, and drum corps. The exposition features the Klondike Chuckwagon Derby, with four days of competition; events in the King of the Klondike frontier competition include log sawing and chopping, axe throwing, and rope climbing; and there's Sunday Promenade, entertainments all around town that are attended by many dressed in 1890s-era finery. There's also a midway with more than fifty rides.

For information, call ☎ (888) 800-7275 or consult 🖳 www.northlands.com.

Banff and Lake Louise

Picture a landscape of craggy snow-covered peaks at every turn. Up the valleys, electric blue glaciers hang like prize ribbons; below, waterfalls of 100-year-old melted ice cascade into deep, pristine lakes. Elk and caribou are on patrol at lower levels; way above, mountain goats cling to impossible crevices.

Down below, there are only minimal invasions of human civilization in the ancient hills. A castle-like chateau sits at one end of a small town hemmed in on all sides by mountains. In another place, a chateau lords over a lake fed by a glacier. The picture in your mind is the Canadian Rockies northwest of Calgary: Banff, Lake Louise, and Jasper.

The town of Banff, about seventy-five miles from Calgary, lies within the protected bounds of the Banff National Park. Established in 1885, Banff is Canada's oldest and most-visited national park, spreading over more than 2,500 square miles. Included within the park are Lake Louise, nestled below the Victoria Glacier; Moraine Lake, in the valley of the Ten Peaks; and the unreal turquoise waters of Peyto Lake.

The town of Banff is the gateway to the activities of the park; there are very few areas within the huge region where development is permitted and scarcely a spadeful of earth can be turned in Banff without permission from authorities. The busiest time of the year in Banff is June to September, but the town comes back to life in the winter as a base for skiers heading for spectacular resorts that include Banff Mount Norquay, Sunshine Village, and Lake Louise.

At the same west end of town, the **Sulphur Mountain Gondola** offers rides to the top at 7,500 feet in four-passenger gondolas year-round; views cover all of Banff and surrounding peaks. Open year-round except for mid-December to late January, the gondola is about two miles from the town on Mountain Avenue. Admission: ❸. For information, call ☎ (403) 762-2523.

Sunshine Village, about fifteen miles outside of Banff, is a jaw-dropping Shangri-la of a ski resort. You park your car way down the valley and clamber into a six-passenger gondola that wends its way three miles through untouched wilderness to the base of the spectacular Goat's Eye Mountain and further along to the automobile-less base village.

It starts snowing in the valley in October and sometimes ends by summer, with an average of thirty feet of the stuff each year. Most of the land lies in Alberta, although parts of the resort meander across the line to neighboring British Columbia. For information, call ☎ (403) 762-2523 or consult 💻 www.skibanff.com.

Johnston Canyon, sixteen miles west of Banff toward Lake Louise, is a narrow passageway along Johnston Creek. There are two waterfalls in the canyon; the upper falls are more than 100 feet high. Both are mostly frozen in the winter. It's a relatively easy hike of less than a mile to the lower falls and then another three miles to the upper cascade and the Ink Pots, six springs that bubble out of the ground year-round.

In the winter, you can make an icewalk to the same spot, but you'd do well to invest in a pair of ice grips for your shoes to help you keep your balance on the frozen pathways. Several sightseeing companies offer guided tours through the canyon, offering the ice grips as part of the package.

Lake Louise

Named for Queen Victoria's daughter, Princess Louise Caroline Alberta, Lake Louise is more than a mile above sea level. At the east end of the lake is **Chateau Lake Louise**, an imposing formal hotel; at the other end are Mount Victoria and the Victoria Glacier, which ends in a waterfall into the lake.

In the winter, the chateau clears a skating rink on the lake, the most handsome setting for sliding or a game of pickup hockey I have ever experienced. You can also bundle into a horsedrawn sleigh for a tour of the lake on a pathway that leads to the frozen waterfalls. We rode to the end of the lake at sunset and looked back in awe at the alpenglow on the mountain as the sun set.

The **Lake Louise Ski Area** is Canada's largest ski area, and one of the biggest in North America. For information, call ☎ (403) 522-3555 or consult 💻 www. skilouise.com. The view of Pyramid Peak from the top of the ski resort is beyond compare. Non-skiers can enjoy some of the same thrill by taking a trip on the Lake Louise gondola in the summer; the lift operates from June 1 to the end of September. Admission: ❷.

The resort's extraordinary Lodge of the Ten Peaks, a huge alpine post-and-beam log cabin, is open for breakfast and lunch for riders.

Four Points®
Sheraton

Save 50% off the following Four Points by Sheraton hotels:

Four Points by Sheraton Portland Downtown
Located at Waterfront Park, overlooking Willamette River; Near Convention Center, Portland Zoo, Oregon Museum of Sciences & Industry; Guests enjoy FREE use of Gold's Gym (directly across from hotel).
503-221-0711

Four Points by Sheraton Portland East
Located at the mouth of the Columbia Gorge, 10 miles from downtown; 37 rooms equipped with PC & T1 high speed Internet connection; 24-hr fitness center, indoor pool & spa; All rooms have microwave oven and refrigerator.
503-491-1818

Save $50 CDN off the following Four Points by Sheraton hotels:

ALBERTA

Four Points by Sheraton Hotel & Suites Calgary West
Opp. Canada Olympic Park; minutes from downtown; indoor heated pool w/ waterslide
403-288-4441

Four Points by Sheraton Canmore
Outdoor whirlpool; near Banff National Park & Canmore Nordic Center
403-609-4422

BRITISH COLUMBIA

Four Points by Sheraton Nanaimo
Heated indoor pool; 9-hole par 3 golf course on site.
250-758-3000

Four Points by Sheraton Vancouver Airport
Indoor pool, Jacuzzi. In the heart of the shopping, entertainment & business district.
604-214-0888

Reservations may be booked by calling **800-325-3535** or by contacting the participating hotel directly and requesting rate plan **ECONO.**

Offer is valid at participating properties only 1/1/01–12/30/01. Offer is subject to availability and change. ECONO rate plan must be requested at time of reservation. Advance reservations are required. Offer is not applicable to groups. Additional service charge and tax may apply. Discount is available on rack (non-discounted) rates only. Discount is reflected in the rate quoted. Offer can not be combined with other promotional offers. Blackout dates and additional restrictions may apply.

STARWOOD PREFERRED GUEST
www.preferredguest.com | 1-888-625-4988

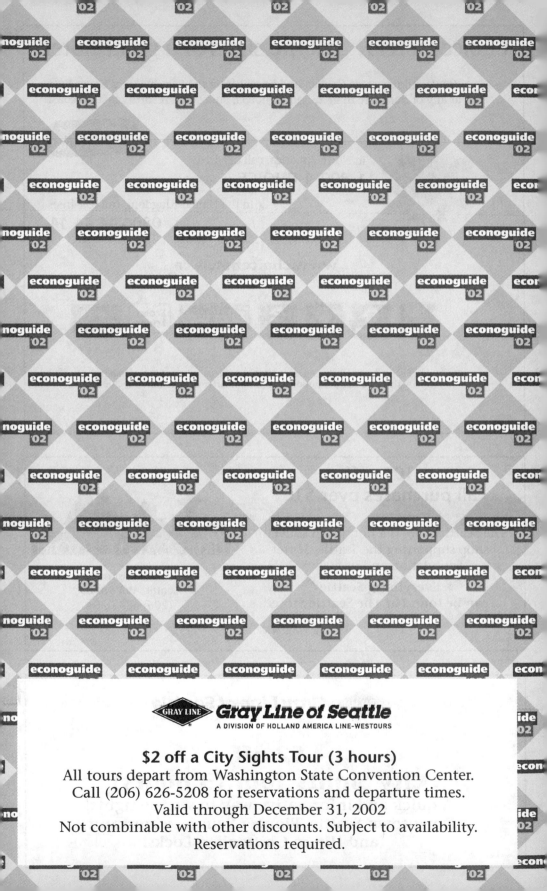

Save 10%

Off our regular low rack rate

- FREE Continental breakfast
- FREE 24-hour airport shuttle
- Jacuzzi and family suites
- Guest laundry facilities
- FREE local calls
- Kitchenette rooms
- Exercise room
- Cable TV with free HBO

3 blocks from airport, just minutes from downtown and major mall

Mention VIP Code #0099. Present coupon at check-in. Subject to availability, with advance reservations. Not valid with any other discount or package rate. Not available July 9 through July 13, 2001. Valid through December 31, 2002

PNW02-23

DAYS INN®

Seattle/Tacoma International Airport
19015 International Blvd. South
Seattle, WA 98188
(206) 244-3600

Save 10%

Off our regular low rack rate. Our NEW hotel offers:

- FREE 24-hour airport shuttle
- FREE Continental breakfast
- Meeting facility
- Guest laundry
- FREE HBO
- In-room coffee
- Pay per view movies
- Exercise room

Only minutes from Seattle/Tacoma International Airport

Present coupon at check-in. Subject to availability, with advance reservations. Not valid with any other discount or package rate. Not available July 9 through July 13, 2001. Valid through December 31, 2002

PNW02-22

Sleep

SeaTac Airport
20406 International Blvd. South
SeaTac, WA 98188
(206) 878-3600

Save 10%

Off our regular low rack rate

- FREE Continental breakfast
- Kitchenette rooms
- Guest laundry facilities
- FREE local calls
- Jacuzzi rooms
- Cable TV

Minutes from U of W downtown, Edmonds waterfront, and ferry

Mention VIP Code #0099 Present coupon at check-in. Subject to availability, with advance reservations. Not valid with any other discount or package rate. Not available July 9 through July 13, 2001. Valid through December 31, 2002

PNW02-21

DAYS INN®

North Seattle
19527 Aurora Ave. North
Seattle, WA 98133
(206) 542-6300

$79 Promotional Rate

Included are the following complimentary services:
- FREE Continental breakfast
- FREE 24-hour airport transportation
- FREE Local phone calls
- FREE Parking
- Kids 12 and under eat free

Must mention coupon at time of reservation and present coupon upon check-in. Subject to availability. Not valid July–September.
Expires 12/31/2002

1-800-HOLIDAY

PNW02-02

Holiday Inn®

HOTEL & SUITES

22318 84th Ave. South
Kent, WA 98032
(253) 395-4300

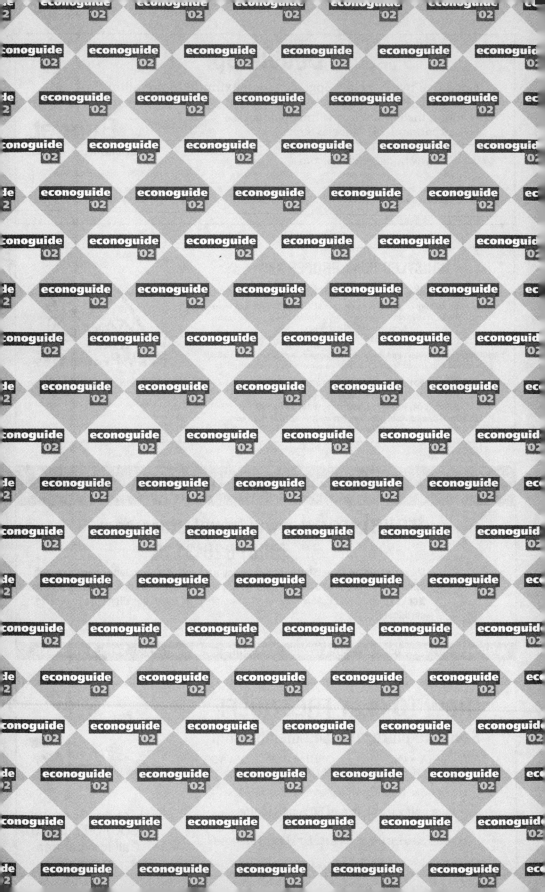

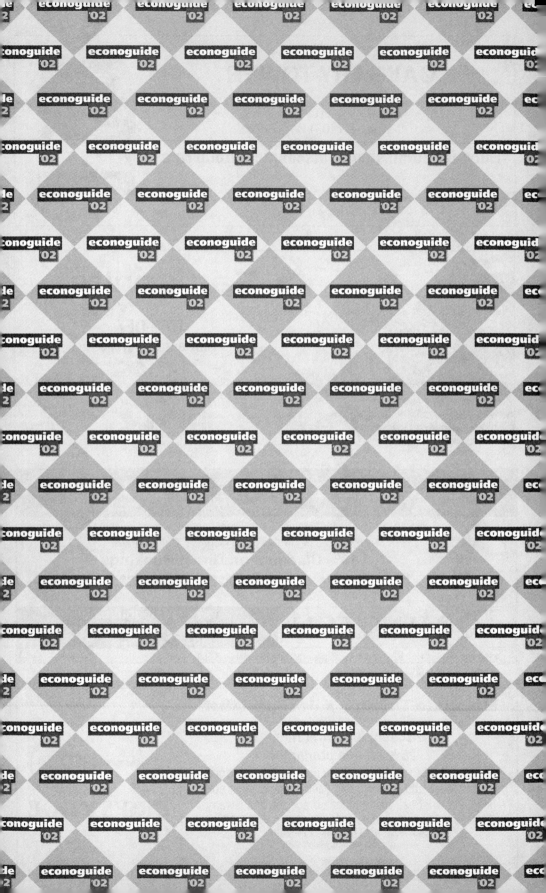

Quick-Find Index to Pacific Northwest